# THE LONDON MOB

# The London Mob

## Violence and Disorder
## in Eighteenth-Century England

Robert B. Shoemaker

Hambledon and London

London and New York

Hambledon and London

102 Gloucester Avenue
London, NW1 8HX

175 Fifth Avenue
New York, NY 10010
USA

First Published 2004

ISBN 1 85285 389 1

A description of this book is available from the
British Library and from the Library of Congress.

Typeset by Carnegie Publishing, Lancaster,
And printed in Great Britain by Cambridge University Press.

Distributed in the United States and Canada
exclusively by Palgrave Macmillan,
A division of St Martin's Press.

# Contents

# Illustrations

## Charts

# Abbreviations

| | |
|---|---|
| BL | British Library |
| CLRO | Corporation of London Record Office |
| GL | Guildhall Library |
| LMA | London Metropolitan Archives |
| DL/C ... | Consistory Court Records |
| MJ/OC ... | Middlesex Orders of the Court |
| MJ/SBB ... | Middlesex Sessions Books |
| MJ/SPB ... | Middlesex Sessions Process Books |
| MJ/SP ... | Middlesex Sessions Papers |
| MJ/SR ... R ... | Middlesex Sessions Rolls Recognizance number |
| OB/SP | Old Bailey Sessions Papers |
| WJ/SP | Westminster Sessions Papers |
| *OBP* | *Old Bailey Proceedings Online* (www.oldbaileyonline.org) |
| TNA | The National Archives (formerly Public Record Office) |

# *Preface*

In the eyes of its more fearful residents, eighteenth-century London teetered on the brink of being ruled by 'the mob'. This was how they referred both to the huge crowds of mostly lower-class people found on its streets and to the disorderly activities they engaged in, from fights and insults to tumults and riots. According to the novelist and magistrate Henry Fielding, by 1752 the mob was so 'very large and powerful [a] body' that it had become the fourth estate in the constitution. Encroaching on the powers of the king, lords and commons, he claimed that it had acquired the power of determining which laws would be enforced. According to him, it claimed 'exclusive rights' to, among other things,

> those parts of the streets, that are set aside for the foot-passengers. In asserting this privilege, they are extremely rigorous; insomuch, that none of the other orders can walk through the streets by day without being insulted, nor by night without being knocked down.

For Fielding, the mob was composed of not just those who rioted, it comprised everyone in London's lower classes who was present on its streets, and it referred to every aspect of their unruly behaviour: insults, knocking people down and 'mobbing'. And his worry was that this disorderly throng had become so powerful that it 'threaten[ed] to shake the balance of our constitution'.[1]

The mob was, in fact, a new phenomenon: the word itself, shortened from the Latin phrase *mobile vulgus* (the movable or excitable crowd), was only introduced into the English vocabulary in the late seventeenth century, primarily as a replacement for the more passive term 'rabble'. One of the first uses of the word in print was in Thomas Shadwell's play *The Squire of Alsatia* (1688). Sir William Bedford encounters Lolpoop, a servant, with a prostitute on a street in Whitefriars and beats him up. This causes a 'rabble' to gather, and William encourages them to punish the woman for her misbehaviour:

> *Sir William*: Here honest mob, course this whore to some purpose. A whore, a whore, a whore.
> *She runs out, the rabble ran after, and tear her, crying a whore, a whore.*
> *Sir Edward Belfond*: This is wisely done! If they murder her, you'll be hanged.[2]

Looking back from the early eighteenth century, Roger North observed that it was in 1680 that 'the rabble first changed their title, and were called *the mob*'.[3] North was making a political point when he identified the Exclusion Crisis (1678–81) as the historical moment for the emergence of the word. In fact, the change was not quite as dramatic as North suggests, but the unabbreviated form of the term, 'mobile', followed shortly by 'mob', gradually entered the English vocabulary in the 1680s and 1690s. In addition to Shadwell's plays, the words can be found in the works of Aphra Behn, John Dryden, John Dunton and Daniel Defoe. Both words were used to describe crowds, disorder and the lower classes ('the rabble') more generally. By the early eighteenth century the word was beginning to be used frequently in newspaper reports of riots in London, in the complaints of disorderly behaviour brought before justices of the peace, and in a variety of published works, including fiction, historical accounts and political tracts.[4] Both the widespread use of this new word and the belief that the disorder it described was increasing reflect growing unease in the early eighteenth century over the ungovernability of the throngs of people who crowded London's streets. For contemporary observers the mob was a characteristic and unsettling feature of metropolitan life in the eighteenth century.

'The mob' was variously conceived of as those who rioted on almost a daily basis on the city's streets; the totality of the people who frequented those streets; and all lower-class Londoners. This imprecision was of course a result of the fact that it was assumed that the composition of all three groups was fundamentally the same. Clearly it wasn't – many middle- and upper-class men and women could be found walking the streets, and sometimes even rioting – but the loose definition given to the term reflects contemporary beliefs about who was responsible for the disorder which characterised public life in the metropolis.

Taking the most inclusive definition of the mob, *The London Mob* is about all its public disorderly activities, whether committed individually or collectively, and whether with or without official sanction. In addition to insults, fighting, boxing and rioting, attention is paid to popular participation in the apprehending and punishment of criminals (as was the case in *The Squire of Alsatia*). Because the patterns of behaviour found in elite duelling are very similar to some of these other activities, duels are also included. The book explains how the mob became a dominant feature of public life, giving rise to exaggerated fears of social upheaval, and considers how disorderly it actually was. It also demonstrates how over the course of century London's streets became more orderly. By the end of the century the number of riots, insults and murders had declined, and foreign observers were commenting on the fundamental orderliness of the city. This book is therefore about the rise and fall of the London mob.

I would like to thank the British Academy, the Arts and Humanities Research Board (AHRB), and the Department of History, University of Sheffield, for providing the funding and the research leave necessary to conduct the research for this book and to write it. I would also like to acknowledge the generous funding provided by the New Opportunities Fund and the AHRB to the Old Bailey Proceedings Online project, since the digitisation of the *Proceedings* has contributed significantly to this book; indeed some of the research carried out would not have been completed without it. For their help in getting the project completed, I am grateful to the project staff: Tim Hitchcock, co-director; Louise Henson, the senior data developer; John Black, Edwina Newman, Kay O'Flaherty and Gwen Smithson, data developers; Jamie McLaughlin and Christiane Meckseper, technical officers; and Simon Tanner and Geoff Laycock, of the Higher Education Digitisation Service; Mark Greengrass and David Shepherd, directors of the Humanities Research Institute at the University of Sheffield.

As explained in the Appendix, the research for this book also benefitted enormously from several other digitisation projects carried out in recent years, notably the creation of electronic catalogues of the holdings of the British Library and the National Archives (formerly the Public Record Office), and I am grateful to the people who have brought these huge endeavours to completion. Nonetheless, I was not deprived of the joy of getting my hands dirty conducting proper archival research, and I am grateful to the staff of the British Library, Corporation of London Record Office, Guildhall Library, Lincoln's Inn Library, London Metropolitan Archives, The National Archives, the Special Collections Department of the University of Sheffield Library and the Westminster Abbey Library Muniment Room for their help responding to my enquiries and in supplying books and documents. I am also grateful to the Harrowby Manuscripts Trust for permission to quote from the transcript of Dudley Ryder's law notes kept in the Lincoln's Inn Library.

Parts of some chapters have appeared previously in different forms, and I would like to thank the editors and publishers for permission to reproduce material from 'The Decline of Public Insult in London, 1660–1800', *Past and Present* 169 (Nov. 2000), pp. 97–131; 'Male Honour and the Decline of Public Violence in Eighteenth-Century London', *Social History* 26 (May 2001), pp. 190–208 [www. tandf. co. uk]; 'The Taming of the Duel: Masculinity, Honour and Ritual Violence in London, 1660–1800', *Historical Journal* 45 (2002), pp. 525–45; and 'Streets of Shame? The Crowd and Public Punishments in London, 1700–1820', in S. Devereaux and P. Griffiths, eds, *Penal Practice and Culture, 1500–1900* (Palgrave, 2004).

I am fortunate that this field of historical research is inhabited by a very affable and generous bunch of scholars, and over the past several years I have benefitted from numerous suggestions given to me by colleagues. At the risk of unintentionally omitting some names, I would like to thank Donna Andrew, Fay Bound, Penelope Corfield, Louise Falcini, Harriet Jones, Michael MacDonald, John Styles and Susan Whyman. John Beattie, Christopher Brooks, Lawrence Klein and Vanessa Toulmin read individual chapters and offered helpful feedback. Most heroic of all were the three people who read the whole manuscript, offering a judicious mixture of criticism and encouragement: Wendy Bracewell, Tim Hitchcock and Martin Sheppard. As the publisher, Martin Sheppard had little choice but to read it, but I am grateful for his careful attention to detail and constant support. As a spouse, it might be said that Wendy Bracewell also had little choice, but the enthusiasm and critical distance she brought to this project has helped me every step of the way. When the book was nearing completion our son Roland helped with some research, and I am pleased to acknowledge his assistance.

My greatest debt, however, is without a doubt to Tim Hitchcock, who has by turn inspired, encouraged and criticised this work from the start. I could not have been more fortunate to have had as a friend and colleague someone with such a fertile imagination, who has researched this field so extensively, and who suggested new ideas and potential sources in virtually every communication. Tim does not agree with some of the interpretations offered in this book, and he is not to blame for any mistakes which remain. But this book would unquestionably be the poorer were it not for his limitless enthusiasm and generosity. It is a real pleasure to have the opportunity now to acknowledge his help.

## Illustration Acknowledgements

The author and publishers are grateful to the following for permission to reproduce images: British Library, figures 24 (from *The Malefactor's Register; or the Newgate and Tyburn Calendar* [London, 1779], frontispiece to volume 3, 1485. p.8), 31 (from Sarah Sophia Banks, Collection of Broadsides, L. R. 301. h. 3, fol. 57aa); British Museum, figures 3 (frontispiece to [Edward Ward], *The Fourth Part of Vulgus Britannicus* [London, 1710]), 5, 13, 27; Corporation of London Record Office, figure 25 (Sessions Papers, August 1695); Guildhall Library, Corporation of London, figures 4, 7, 9 (from John Seller, *A Booke of the Punishments of the Common Laws of England* [London, c. 1678]), 14, 15, 16, 17, 18, 19, 20, 22, 23, 28, 30; Tim Hitchcock, figures 1, 2, 6, 11; London Metropolitan Archives, figure 29 (ref. SC/PD/XX/45/13A); Nottingham City Museums and Galleries, Nottingham Castle, figure 12; Tate Galleries, figure 26; University of Sheffield, figure 8 (from Walter Besant, *London in the Eighteenth Century* [London, 1902], p. 520), 10 (from ibid., p. 350), 21 (Egerton Castle, *Schools and Masters of Fence* [London, 1893], p. 290).

# Street Life

In 1770 a German visitor, Georg Christoph Lichtenberg, wrote a letter to a professor in Göttingen which included 'a hasty sketch of an evening in the streets of London', giving the example of Cheapside and Fleet Street around 8 p.m. First, he set the scene:

> Imagine a street about as wide as the Weender in Göttingen, but, taking it altogether, about six times as long. On both sides tall houses with plate-glass windows. The lower floors consist of shops and seem to be made entirely of glass; many thousand candles light up silverware, engravings, books, clocks, glass, pewter, paintings, women's finery, modish and otherwise, gold, precious stones, steel-work, and endless coffee-rooms and lottery offices. The street looks as though it were illuminated for some festivity ...

Then, in contrast to the beauty of the shop fronts, he turned his attention to the street, starting with a warning of what was likely to happen if one stopped and lingered to admire the magnificence:

> Crash! a porter runs you down, crying 'By your leave', when you are lying on the ground. In the middle of the street roll chaises, carriages and drays in an unending stream. Above this din and the hum and clatter of thousands of tongues and feet one hears the chimes from church towers, the bells of the postmen, the organs, fiddles, hurdy-gurdies, and tambourines of English mountebanks, and the cries of those who sell hot and cold viands in the open at the street corners. Then you will see a bonfire of shavings flaring up as high as the upper floors of the houses in a circle of merrily shouting beggar-boys, sailors, and rogues. Suddenly a man whose handkerchief has been stolen will cry: 'Stop thief', and everyone will begin running and pushing and shoving – many of them not with any desire of catching the thief, but of prigging for themselves, perhaps, a watch or purse. Before you know where you are, a pretty, nicely dressed miss will take you by the hand ... Then there is an accident forty paces from you ... Suddenly you will, perhaps, hear a shout from a hundred throats, as if a fire had broken out, a house fallen

down, or a patriot were looking out of the window … I have said nothing about the ballad singers who, forming circles at every corner, dam the stream of humanity which stops to listen and steal.[1]

Commentators on London life in the eighteenth century invariably noted that the streets were crowded and chaotic. One of William Hutton's first observations, following his arrival in the capital on a trip from Birmingham in 1785, was that 'there seems nothing in London so much wanted as room'. Daniel Defoe commented that on the 'public streets … nothing is more remarkable than the hurries of the people'.[2] The constant traffic of pedestrians, carts and coaches gave rise to frequent accidents and quarrels, as travellers struggled to make their way past each other and fought for the advantage of 'the wall', the part of the street furthest from the mud- and excrement-filled gutter. But as Lichtenberg suggests, it was not so much the traffic that caused the chaos as the fact that it had to compete for road space with people (and their vehicles) who sauntered and loitered for a variety of purposes: shoppers, casual strollers, street sellers, beggars, prostitutes, ballad singers, coachmen waiting for fares, and the spectators and pickpockets who gathered around the inevitable incidents and accidents arising from all these activities and obstructions.

At 7 o'clock on a typical Sunday morning, for example, 'beggars, apple-women, and shoe-blacks repair[ed] to their respective stands':

> Beggars, who have put on their woeful countenances, and also managed their sores and ulcers so as to move compassion, are carrying whads of straw to the corners of the most publick streets, that they may take their seats, and beg the charity of all well-disposed Christians the remaining part of the day.

Fruit sellers and shoeshine boys, who although they provided services can also be interpreted as beggars, took up similar positions, as did the drivers of hackney coaches.[3] An increasingly popular method of travel for wealthier Londoners who wished to avoid encountering at first hand the dirt and congestion of the streets, this eighteenth-century version of the modern taxi blocked thoroughfares while coachmen waited for fares, despite the best efforts of the authorities to regulate the practice.[4] Later in the day, prostitutes took up their positions and accosted passing men. Defoe complained that, while walking 'upon important business' from Charing Cross to Ludgate,

I have every now and then been put to the halt; sometimes by the full encounter of an audacious harlot, whose impudent leer shew'd she only stopped my passage in order to draw my observation on her; at other times, by twitches on the sleeve, lewd and ogling salutations; and not infrequently by the more profligate impudence of some jades, who boldly dare to seize a man by the elbow, and make insolent demands of wine and treats before they let him go.

According to the French visitor Pierre-Jean Grosley, 'women of the town ... are more numerous than at Paris, and have more liberty and effrontery than at Rome itself ... they range themselves in a file in the foot-paths of all the great streets ... whole rows of them accost passengers in the broad day-light'.[5]

The streets were not just used for travel and making a living, but also for recreation. The Swiss visitor Béat-Louis de Muralt observed the 'common people' throwing at cocks, watching men and beasts fight, and playing football, 'where they take a great deal of pleasure in breaking windows, and coach glasses if they meet any'. Between 5 and 6 p.m. on a Sunday one could observe 'great numbers of footmen near the gate at the entrance to Hyde Park, wrestling, cudgel playing and jumping' while they waited for their mistresses to return from the park.[6] The open spaces surrounding the built-up area were frequently used for a variety of sports, which were often the subject of wagers. The grand jury for the City complained in January 1740 of 'the frequent concourse of disorderly persons and idle vagrants in Moorfields' who gathered together for 'cudgelling, dice, lotteries and other games, and particularly for cock-throwing during several weeks at this season of the year'. But the most common outdoor recreation was probably simply walking: on Sunday evening 'the principal streets [are] filled with whores, shoemakers, butchers, joiners, and all sorts of handicraft tradesmen passing and repassing one another'. While some walked for exercise or to converse with their friends, showing off seems to have been the principal motivation: according to the Swiss visitor César de Saussure, 'English women walk fast and well, but in reality I think they do it more in order to show their clothes than for the pleasure of the exercise'. Depending on the time of day, the parks could provide a more socially selective company for this activity. According to an anonymous description of St James's Park, people went there 'to see and be seen, to censure and be censured;

the ladies to show their fine clothes and the product of the toilet; the men to observe all the beauties, and fix on some favourite to toast that evening in the tavern'.[7] But since entry to the parks was not controlled, the elite had to share the space with their social inferiors, at least during non-working hours. On Sunday evening the 'well-dressed gentlewomen and ladies [were] drove out of St James Park, Lincoln's Inn Gardens, and Gray's Inn Walks, by milliners, mantua-makers, sempstresses, stay-makers, clear-starchers, French barbers, dancing masters, gentlemen's footmen, tailor's wives, conceited old maids, and butchers' daughters'. Similarly, the pleasure gardens built on the edge of the metropolis, including the fashionable Ranelagh Gardens in Chelsea (opened in 1742), attracted a mixed clientele: Horace Walpole noted that the opening day crowds included 'the Prince, Princess, Duke, much nobility, and much mob besides ... everybody that loves eating, drinking, staring, or crowding is admitted for twelve pence'.[8]

The streets were also an important ceremonial space, used to stage official processions on occasions such as coronations and Lord Mayor's Day, when crowds not only watched pageants but also created their own fun. Muralt noted that 'when there's any publick rejoicings, [the common people] make a lane, and toss people, passing by, to and again. Many of these diversions are proof of their happy condition, since even some of the grandees partake of them.' Ned Ward's descrip-tion of the Lord Mayor's Procession in 1699 was more graphic: once the pageant had passed, 'the industrious rabble, who hate idleness, had procur'd a dead cat, whose reeking puddings hung dangling from her torn belly ... she was handed about ... as an innocent diversion, every now and then being toss'd into the face of some gaping booby or other'.[9] Bonfires lit to celebrate military victories and royal anniversaries provided other occasions for crowds to gather. From the late seven-teenth century these traditional festivities were all adapted (and subverted) for party political purposes.[10] Crowds had even more licence during the processions of the condemned criminals from Newgate to their place of execution, which occurred several times a year, since the mob on those occasions was almost entirely plebeian. The procession ended at Tyburn, where the disorder continued amongst the vast crowds which watched the executions.[11] There were thus numerous officially-sanctioned occasions when the mob was expected to participate: not only in official processions and at public punishments, but also in apprehending criminals.[12]

Londoners, however, did not need official licence in order to form crowds, which gathered whenever and wherever a recreational opportunity arose or a grievance needed to be expressed. Plate 6 of William Hogarth's 'Industry and Idleness' series (Figure 1), shows a crowd gathered in front of the house of the industrious apprentice, Francis Goodchild, following his marriage to his master's daughter. Butchers, with marrowbones and cleavers, and musicians are shown making 'rough music' in order to protest at the unequal marriage and extract some money in return for their silence.[13] Also in the print are other well-known features of the London street scene, including a legless beggar and ballad seller.

Of course, not all London's public spaces shared the same characteristics, nor were they all used in the same ways. The contrast between the broad boulevards of Cheapside and the Strand and the numerous narrow dead-end lanes, alleys and courts was dramatic. While the former were sometimes labelled 'public streets', the latter were often considered private spaces, accessible only to those who lived there. In an account of the placing of candles in windows to celebrate the birthday of war hero Admiral Vernon in 1741, the *Daily Post* noted that it was 'remarkable that at night not only the high streets, but the private ones, nay even the courts and alleys, were illuminated'. Because they were effectively controlled by their inhabitants, these spaces could seem threatening to outsiders: Henry Fielding worried that criminals hid in them in order to avoid arrest. John Gay, on the other hand, noted that the absence of crowds and slower pace allowed pedestrians a greater chance of interacting with each other:

> But sometimes let me leave the noisie roads,
> And silent wander in the close abodes
> Where wheels ne'er shake the ground; there pensive stray,
> In studious thought, the long uncrouded way.
> Here I remark each walker's different face,
> And in their look their various bus'ness trace.[14]

Whereas some outdoor spaces thus had a private character, many indoor spaces served a public or semi-public function, notably shops

1. William Hogarth, 'Industry and Idleness', plate 6: 'The Industrious 'Prentice out of his Time and Married to his Master's Daughter' (1747). (*Tim Hitchcock*)

and places of refreshment. While traditional methods of selling on the streets by hawkers and in markets continued, many consumer goods, particularly luxury items, were now sold in shops, with large window displays as witnessed by Lichtenberg.[15] While such displays were designed to invite customers to come inside, not everyone was equally welcome. Worried about shoplifting, shopkeepers tried to keep a watchful eye on those they did not know, or who appeared unable to afford the goods on sale. This must have proved difficult, however, when up to sixty people at a time were squeezed into a single shop.[16] Indoor spaces like these thus shared some of the chaos of the streets.

The eighteenth century also witnessed a remarkable expansion of public indoor sociability in London. Providing food, drink and warmth to people whose living quarters were often very cramped, these places allowed street life to spill over into more hospitable surroundings. Some establishments, well supplied with the latest newspapers, aspired to provide a home for more refined social conduct than was possible on the streets, thereby promoting rational discourse.[17] But this was probably only realised in a minority of the 207 inns, 447 taverns (which sold wine), 531 coffee houses, 5955 alehouses, and 8659 spirits shops recorded in London in 1737, altogether about one for every forty inhabitants. According to Saussure, 'all men, even churchmen, have a particular club or tavern, where they meet at least twice in the week to drink together in company'. The traditional alehouse, often divided into separate rooms, was a site for an extraordinary mixture of public and private activities: reading, conviviality, arguments, fights and duels, meetings of clubs and societies, and even illicit sex. Alehouses were also used for political celebrations and to plan strikes, demonstrations and riots.[18]

A cheaper and potentially more disorderly alternative emerged early in the century with the growing popularity of spirits, particularly gin, which were inexpensive and sold in stalls and wheelbarrows on the streets as well as in shops and houses; it was estimated that they could be purchased at one in every eleven houses in the city.[19] Drunkenness was widespread ('drunk for a penny, dead drunk for two pence, straw for nothing' was the sales pitch), but it is impossible to determine how much public disorder gin drinking actually caused. It is certain, however, that contemporaries exaggerated the problem, because the drink was most popular among women and the poor and thus, like the mob in general, gin drinking threatened to subvert traditional relations of hierarchy and deference. As Lord Hervey complained, gin put 'an end to subordination', and raised 'every man to an equality with his master, or his governor'. Lord Lonsdale's description of the public consequences of gin drinking provides a written equivalent to William Hogarth's graphic portrayal in 'Gin Lane' (Figure 2).

> whoever shall pass among the streets, will find wretches stretched upon the pavement, insensible and motionless … others … think themselves in the elevation of drunkenness intitled to treat all those with contempt whom their dress distinguishes from them, and to resent every injury which in the heat of their imagination they suppose themselves to suffer, with the utmost rage of resentment, violence of rudeness, and scurrility of tongue.[20]

Unlike alehouses, most of the trouble allegedly caused by gin took place on the streets and was therefore more visible.

Coffee houses, introduced in the late seventeenth century, sold a more sobering drink and provided theoretically a more polite venue for sociability, where tradesmen and gentlemen could meet to discuss business, politics, and the latest news. For all who could afford the relatively low price of admission, they offered the possibility of conversation with anyone, regardless of status, who happened to be seated nearby at one of the long tables. Thomas Brown described how a gentleman sat down next to him, 'and perceiving us to be strangers, under pretext of civility accosted us with discourses related to the town'. Yet the discourse was not always so respectable, and was sometimes little more than gossip or slander. Another observer complained about 'coffee-house orators' who 'daily strain their throats for the interest of Christendom, and judiciously distribute their deep ignorance and conjectures, to such as sit round them'. Although women (except keepers and bar ladies) and the lower classes were generally excluded, this did not guarantee respectable behaviour, as is evident in the title and coffee-throwing behaviour found in 'The Coffee House Mob' (Figure 3). Gin was frequently sold, and sword-fights and duels often occurred, or were arranged, there. Different coffee houses served a diverse range of clienteles, including political parties, businessmen and various professional groups, as well as rakes and prostitutes. Saussure reported that 'some coffee houses are a resort for learned scholars and for wits; others are the

2. William Hogarth, 'Gin Lane' (1751). (*Tim Hitchcock*)

resort of dandies or of politicians, or again of professional newsmongers; and many others are temples of Venus'.[21]

Not only was public life in the city conducted in a diverse collection of often disorderly spaces, but experiences of these places varied considerably depending on the time of day. Eighteenth-century London was truly a twenty-four hour city, where the overlapping lifestyles of its socially disparate inhabitants meant that as night-time revellers returned home at dawn others were getting up to work or beg (Figure 4). According to one account the streets were only really quiet between the hours of three and four in the morning, after the drunks, prostitutes and thieves had finally gone to bed and before the fish-women got up to go to Billingsgate to await the arrival of the boats, shortly followed by the beggars, shoe-blacks and hackney coachmen who went to claim their usual prominent places on the streets, and the labourers, porters and craftsmen who started work.[22]

How had London's streets and public houses become so vibrant and chaotic? To understand why this disorderly 'mob' became such a dominant feature of public life in the eighteenth century, it is necessary to consider how a relatively compact, closely-governed medieval town became in the eighteenth century the largest and most prosperous city in Europe, surpassed in the rest of the world only by the cities now known as Tokyo and Beijing. From a population of around 200,000 in 1600, the metropolis grew to 575,000 in 1700 and 900,000 in 1800.[23] This dramatic growth was fuelled by social, political, and above all economic changes in the country.[24] The growing presence of the aristocracy and gentry in the metropolis for at least part of the year (the London 'season' ran from October to June) dates from the early seventeenth century and, although encouraged by the increasing importance of Parliament, was cemented by their desire to partake in urban culture and pursue their business interests. This provided work for skilled craftsmen including, in addition to those found by Lichtenberg on Cheapside, watchmakers, jewellers, peruke makers, tailors, furniture makers, and coach builders, not to mention providers of services such as barbers and the keepers of inns and coffee houses. But luxury craftsmen were only the top end of a vast manufacturing sector, comprising perhaps a third of London's workforce, which catered to the demands of both national and international

3. 'The Coffeehouse Mob' (1710). (© *The British Museum*)

trade. By the early eighteenth century the city had become the largest industrial centre in Europe, with a particular concentration in textiles, notably silk weaving which was stimulated by the arrival of the French Huguenot refugees who settled in Spitalfields in the 1680s. Nonetheless, London manufacturing went into relative decline during the century with the expansion of manufacturing in northern cities where costs were lower.

Trade and finance were most responsible for London's dramatic economic growth in the eighteenth century, as its port was not only the nodal point of British coastal trade but also became the centre of an overseas commercial empire. New colonial consumer products such as sugar, tobacco and rice were imported (and in many cases re-exported to other European countries), while manufactured goods were exported to both Europe and the colonies. One quarter of the city's workforce earned their living directly from the port, as sailors, lightermen, wharfingers, porters, coopers, sugar refiners, ship builders, ship owners and financiers, not to mention associated occupations such as alehouse keepers and prostitutes. Observers frequently commented on the forest of ships' masts which filled up riverside views. Already in the 1720s Daniel Defoe counted from Limehouse Reach to the Customs House 'above two thousand sail of all sorts, not reckoning barges, lighters, or pleasure boats, and yachts; but vessels that really go to sea'.[25] The managing, financing and insuring of this trade (long voyages sometimes took a year for a return trip) promoted the growth of joint-stock companies (notably the East India Company), the stock exchange, banks and insurance companies, turning London into an international financial centre. Both feeding on and protecting this wealth and commerce were the professions: law, medicine (several hospitals were built during the century), and the armed forces and government service (both of which increased as a result of Britain's participation in numerous foreign wars). Luxury crafts, manufacturing, trade, finance, the professions: so diverse was the range of economic activity in London that a directory of the 'merchants, manufacturers and principal traders in the metropolis' published in 1791 listed 492 occupations, and these were only those respectable enough to be included![26]

Rapid demographic and economic growth had profound consequences for social life in the metropolis, disrupting or complicating traditional patterns of social relations and increasing the potential for disorder on

4. Louis Phillipe Boitard, 'The Covent Garden Morning Frolic' (1747). (*Guildhall Library, Corporation of London*)

its streets. Owing to poor sanitary conditions and high infant and child mortality, there was a surplus of deaths over births in London for most years of the eighteenth century. The city only grew through a vast influx of migrants, a net immigration of some 8000 per year by one estimate, and these people had to be integrated into London life. The majority of immigrants were young (typically between the ages of fifteen and twenty-five), full of energy and keen to take advantage of metropolitan street life and its pleasures. But many were also poor, having been driven to migrate at least partly by economic hardship. Well over half were women, often attracted by the prospect of finding a job as a domestic servant, which created a sex imbalance in the urban population that no doubt encouraged the growth of prostitution.[27] Most young women who migrated to London were unmarried, which allowed them to lead independent lifestyles unusual for the time. As John Fielding noted of London women in 1776, 'the greatest latitude of freedom and behaviour is indulged to them. They frequent all public places of entertainment'. But the independence of urban women also made them vulnerable to both economic and sexual exploitation; the combination of opportunity and desperation thus created is reflected in the fact that in the early eighteenth century women accounted for more than half of all the defendants prosecuted for property crime at the Old Bailey, a rare statistic in the history of crime.[28] Another notable characteristic of London's immigrants is that they came not only from England but from the rest of the British Isles and much of the rest of the world: continental Europe, the West Indies, North America and India. Prejudices arising out of national, religious and racial differences fuelled violence and disorder on several occasions in the metropolis.[29]

Urban life was disrupted not only by the consequences of geographical mobility (with large numbers of people also choosing to leave London for the countryside or the colonies every year), but also by high levels of social mobility. With the guilds no longer in control of many sections of the economy, especially those which were expanding the fastest, the possibility of rapidly acquiring large sums of money in a profitable job or enterprise was matched by the very real possibility of losing them just as quickly. As Defoe was at pains to point out, tradesmen could easily be ruined by loss of trade, bankrupt creditors or their own extravagance: while 'one steady motion carries him up ... many things assist to pull him down; there are many ways open to his ruin, but few to his rising'. Ordinary craftsmen and labourers, most of whom did not enjoy the charity and protection offered by the guilds, could easily be ruined by illness or lack of work and often found themselves dependent on parochial poor relief, charity, or begging for support.[30]

Consequently, traditional social status labels did not always match the fluctuating economic positions of Londoners, especially as new forms of wealth emerged which derived from financial investments rather than land. Definitions of status became more fluid. Gentlemen, for example, were no longer defined solely by their family background and the label was increasingly ascribed on the less precise criteria of current wealth and behaviour. Guy Miège observed in 1703 that 'use has so far stretched the signification of this word [that] anyone that, without a coat of arms, has either a liberal or genteel education, that looks gentleman-like (whether he be so or not) and has wherewithal to live freely and handsomely, is by the courtesy of England usually called a gentleman'. More cynically, Nathaniel Bailey wrote in 1730 that 'in our days all are accounted gentlemen that have money, and if he has no coat of arms, the King of Arms can sell him one'.[31] Contemporaries worried about the social instability caused by this elastic definition. François Misson complained in 1719 that 'a thousand worthless fellows call themselves gentlemen and esquire' (though he noted that nobody was so bold as to falsely adopt the title of knight). Another commentator complained about vain 'fops', who maintained 'a splendid appearance, the title of esquire, and its attendant dignities for a few months' until their debts caught up with them and they had to be 'sneaked from the bailiffs' clutches'. 'Of all the follies and fallacies which reign in London', this author opined, 'none is more glaring than affectation, [of] endeavouring to impose ourselves on the world, for what we are not.'[32] This social fluidity continued all the way down the social scale, and the use of clothes for social advancement fuelled the consumer revolution of the eighteenth century.[33] In a city populated with so many newcomers and at a time when appearances had become such an unreliable measure of status, it became difficult to determine the social position of one's fellow inhabitants: were they superiors, inferiors, or equals? In response to this uncertainty, salutations to respectable passers-by on the street became attenuated and less deferential: the female curtsy was reduced to a bob, and instead of doffing their hats men simply touched or raised them slightly.[34] But this remained a hierarchical society, and judgements of status still had to be made, and as they were frequently based on superficial appearances, they were often wrong. While such misunderstandings could be a source of enjoyment (the masquerade was a popular form of entertainment at the time),[35] they could also have damaging consequences.

At stake were not just questions of social respect, but trust, which was crucial to the conduct of economic and social relations in the city. Credit was often given on the basis of how 'substantial' a tradesman appeared, but as we have seen appearances could be deceptive. According to *The Cheats of London Exposed: or The Tricks of the Town Laid Open* 'such is the prevalence of power and parade, that merit of character is with great difficulty ascertained, especially in a place where disguise and artifice are daily practiced'. One bankrupt banker allegedly fraudulently regained the faith of his creditors by repainting his house and making a big purchase of coal, to make it look like he had re-established his finances on a solid footing. While new mechanisms for regulating credit, not to mention the threat of debtors' prison, mitigated some of these problems, the difficulty of not knowing whom to trust remained.[36] Consequently, newcomers were advised to be extremely wary of anyone who tried to befriend or assist them:

> if you have no acquaintance in town, be very cautious in keeping company. If anyone behaves with extraordinary civility to you, or affects to desire your friendship, beware of him, listen not to his enticements, for as you are a stranger to him, his desire of cultivating an acquaintance with you must arise from base or selfish views. If you are accosted in the street, park or any place of public resort, in the ordinary way of converse … affect either not to hear, or turn aside.
>
> In short, take nothing on trust, nor make any acquaintance, till assured of their way of life and moral character.[37]

Clearly, personal knowledge of the people one dealt with was desirable, but where this was not possible one had to rely on reputations. One guidebook advised, 'if we would really enquire into a man's character, we should repair to the place of his abode, and there procure information … from his neighbours of equal rank, with whom he has lived in his own natural manner'.[38] Maintaining a good reputation was essential if one was to prosper in London, and to reach a wide enough audience that reputation had to be established publicly. Paradoxically, we shall see that this contributed to the disorder on London's streets, as frequently men used violence and both sexes used insults to defend their reputations and attack those of others.[39]

Traditional hierarchical social relations were further disrupted by the changing nature of employment practices. Historically most London workmen had been trained as apprentices while living with their masters, and had then eventually became masters and freemen themselves, and the guilds regulated their working practices. The development of new forms of economic activity, the expansion of London beyond the City, and the law courts' growing reluctance to enforce guild regulations all undermined this paternalist form of employment in the eighteenth century. Masters increasingly took on more apprentices and journeymen than they were allowed, or employed men who had not served an apprenticeship, and these young men often did not live with them. Owing to their large number and the increasing amount of capital needed to set up a business, these workers stood little or no chance of becoming masters themselves. Moreover, while small workshops remained the norm, some businesses became very large, with dozens if not hundreds of workers employed by individual employers in trades as diverse as glass manufacturing, sail-cloth manufacture, the needlework trades, silk weaving, silk throwing and shoemaking. As relations between employers and employees were depersonalised, and increasingly centred solely around an exchange of labour for wages, masters and the guilds no longer looked out for the interests of their workers. Consequently, journeymen began to set up their own clubs and associations to defend their working practices and to press for improved conditions; these fought over a hundred labour disputes in London over the course of the century.[40] It was feared that even domestic servants were becoming uppity, as the huge increase in demand for servants altered the balance of power so that masters could no longer exercise tight control over their servants' lives as they had done previously. One author complained of the 'devilish pride' of servant maids, who had become 'their own law-givers, nay, I think they are ours too ... they hire themselves to you by their own rule'.[41]

In fact commentators frequently berated the independence and insolence of London's workers. Commenting on the behaviour of mechanics and journeymen, Grosley noted that 'nothing, but want of money, can compel them to work. If they are obliged to do business, they, as it were, fight with their task: they go to it like madmen, and like people enraged at being confined to labour.' When they want their wages increased, 'they enter into associations, they refuse to work, they revolt'. He found a similar uncooperativeness among workmen on the streets:

> the porters, sailors, chairmen, and the day-laborers who work in the streets ... are as insolent a rabble as can be met with in countries without law or police ... Inquire of them your way to a street: if it be upon the right, they direct you to the left, or they send you from one of their vulgar comrades to another. The most shocking abuse and ill language make a part of their pleasantry on these occasions.

Another commentator complained that coachmen and carters deliberately drove their vehicles close to 'richly dressed' gentlemen and ladies so that they could splatter them with mud and ruin their apparel.[42]

Concurrently, lower-class Londoners were finding a political voice. Facilitated by growing literacy and the expiration of press licensing in 1695, there was an explosion of cheap printed material in the eighteenth century in the form of ballads, broadsides, newspapers and pamphlets, and their widespread availability (hawked by ballad singers in the streets, pasted up on outside walls and read in alehouses and coffee houses) meant that the news was constantly being discussed. Saussure reported that 'all Englishmen are great newsmongers. Workmen habitually begin the day by going to coffee-rooms in order to read the latest news. I have often seen shoeblacks and other persons of that class club together to purchase a farthing paper'.[43] Interest in politics was fuelled by the frequently contested parliamentary elections in Westminster (where all householders could vote) and by the broad participation of the inhabitants of the City in running their wards, which meant that, unusually in eighteenth-century England, a high proportion of adult men in London had a formal political role. Moreover, the intense party conflict of the late seventeenth and early eighteenth centuries led politicians to appeal to the wider public for support, encouraging them to participate in demonstrations and even riots. Although it was thought that the 'public' in the newly legitimated 'public opinion' should be confined to respectable middle-class householders, and that others should only be responsive and not active in initiating protests, politicians frequently appealed to the mob, according legitimacy to their point of view. A German visitor, Charles Moritz, witnessed the speeches in Covent Garden following a parliamentary election in 1782: 'In the area before the hustings, immense multitudes of people were assembled, of whom the greatest part seemed to be of the lowest order. To this tumultuous crowd, however, the speakers often bowed very low, and always addressed them by the title of gentlemen.' Key political crises throughout the century, including the opposition to the Hanoverian accession in 1714–15 and the defeat of the Excise Bill in 1733, were accompanied by street protests, and by the 1790s working-class Londoners had formed their own radical political association, the London Corresponding Society.[44]

London's local government was unable to cope with the growing economic, social and political independence of the large numbers of men and women who made up the mob. While in many respects the medieval City continued to be closely governed, the practice of systematic searching for deviance by wardmote officers declined.[45] The rest of the metropolis was governed by justices of the peace and parish vestries, institutions intended to regulate rural communities, not densely packed urban parishes with populations of 10,000 or more. By 1800 only a fraction of London's population lived in the City. The rest lived in Westminster, in the rapidly growing suburbs north of the river, and, particularly following the opening of Westminster Bridge in 1750 and Blackfriars Bridge in 1769, south of the river in Southwark. Overall responsibility for governing these suburbs lay with the county JPs of Middlesex and Surrey, and as the growing burdens of office dissuaded gentlemen from undertaking this unpaid task, those who filled this office were often accused of corruption, by acting as 'trading justices' who turned the office into a profitable enterprise. The responsibilities for policing and poor relief lay primarily with officials appointed by parish vestries, many of which were narrow oligarchies, and these were also accused of inefficiency and corruption. While these charges of corrupt practices were exaggerated for political reasons, they reflect widespread unease about the ability of London's local governors to cope with problems of disorder on its streets.[46]

Although Parliament attempted to address these issues with the creation of numerous statutory improvement commissions and by passing the Middlesex Justices Act in 1792, there was no attempt to coordinate

local government across the metropolis. Earlier efforts by the crown and
Parliament to control the growth of London had been notoriously
unsuccessful and were abandoned.[47] Contemporaries lamented the dis-
orderliness of the city's growth and the resulting fragmentation of the
urban fabric. Asking 'how much farther it may spread, who knows?'
Defoe commented,

> it is the disaster of London, as to the beauty of its figure, that it is thus
> stretched out in buildings, just at the pleasure of every builder, or undertaker
> of buildings, and as the convenience of the people directs, whether for trade
> or otherwise; and this has spread the face of it in a most straggling, confused
> manner, out of all shape, uncompact, and unequal.[48]

As the metropolis grew, it was feared that it was breaking up into separate
fragments, anticipating nineteenth-century concerns about the existence
of no-go areas, such as the 'rookeries' supposedly controlled by the
criminal underworld.[49] But this fragmentation was already evident in 1700
when Thomas Brown wrote 'We daily discover in [London] more new
countries, and surprising singularities, than in all the universe besides. There
are among the Londoners so many nations differing in manners, customs
and religion, that the inhabitants themselves don't know a quarter of
them.' The most obvious contrast was between the wealth and splendour
of aristocratic west end streets and squares and the dirt and poverty of
working-class riverside parishes east of the City (even if many paupers
and working people could also be found living in the alleys and court-
yards of the west end). According to the magistrate John Fielding,

> when one goes into Rotherhithe and Wapping, which places are chiefly
> inhabited by sailors, but that somewhat of the same language is spoken, a man
> would be apt to suspect himself in another country. Their manner of living,
> speaking, acting, dressing, and behaving, are so very peculiar to ourselves.

Incomprehension could lead to hostility. The Prussian visitor von
Archenholz commented that these differences between the eastern and
western suburbs gave rise to 'a kind of hatred between the inhabitants
of each'.[50]

These were the circumstances which gave rise to the crowded conditions
and disorder of London's streets, and to the considerable fears of social
anarchy which they generated. Ordinary Londoners were increasingly

cut off from traditional hierarchical paternalist relationships and sought to establish their reputations and improve their living conditions in new ways. Their actions, governed as they were by informal rules and expectations, were not necessarily very disorderly. As was the case with elite duelling, the practices of public insults, fights and riotous protests were regulated by shared cultural understandings of honour and fairness which severely limited the amount of interpersonal violence actually committed. Nonetheless, the apparent independence of those involved made such behaviour appear threatening. As the term 'mob' implies, it was feared that London's street population would form a coherent collective body and overturn existing structures of authority. In practice, of course, the mob was potentially composed of hundreds of thousands of individuals from different social classes and with varying ambitions and strategies, and, with the exception of the Gordon Riots of 1780, it never threatened to take over the city. Nonetheless, crowds, accidents, insults, violence and protests *were* ever present on the streets. In response, new strategies were developed during the century to reform public life in London. Improvements to policing, the physical fabric of the streets and the guidance available to pedestrians were all designed to create some order out of the disorder. Whether these reforms actually achieved their intended results is of course another question; in fact, they led to some significant unintended consequences.

Early efforts at improving policing came from voluntary societies, which sought to effect a 'reformation of manners' in the decades following the revolution of 1688, primarily by encouraging private citizens to report the activities of prostitutes, drunkards, profane swearers and cursers, gin sellers, shoe blacks and wheelbarrow boys (the last two were accused of encouraging gambling) to justices of the peace. In addition, the societies tried to suppress vice and disorder at fairs such as Bartholomew Fair and May Fair. By suppressing all these 'nuisances', the reformers thought they would clear the streets of thieves, vagrants and other disorderly people. Unsurprisingly they failed, and indeed their aggressive tactics arguably increased rather than diminished disorder, as their informers were frequently attacked by mobs. Nonetheless, this campaign demonstrates how much concern there was at the start of the eighteenth century to remove disorder from London's streets. The reformers also distributed admonitory pamphlets as a means of encouraging more virtuous behaviour. Later reformation of manners societies followed this approach and used persuasion rather than persecution as their principal tactic.[51]

From the 1690s, official efforts to fight crime and disorder centred on increasing the punishments for the most serious offenders and offering rewards for their arrest and conviction. The latter led to the growth of 'thief-takers', men who turned this activity into a way of making a living, and consequently encouraged an increase in malicious prosecutions. Although the creation of the 'Bow Street Runners' by Henry and John Fielding in the 1750s helped make thief-taking respectable, we shall see that the growing reliance on third parties to identify and arrest suspected criminals had the effect of discouraging ordinary Londoners from carrying out their traditional responsibility of apprehending anyone they witnessed committing a felony. In contrast to thief-takers, the purpose of the nightly watch, which was reformed by the growing use of salaried watchmen in place of householders serving by rotation, was to prevent crimes. But the reformed watch was still the subject of trenchant criticism, especially by foreigners. Grosley reported that 'London has neither troops, patroll, nor any sort of regular watch; and it is guarded during the night only by old men chosen from the dregs of the people; who have no other arms but a lanthorn and a pole'. While the watch may have done little to prevent crime and disorder, the withdrawal of ordinary Londoners from active participation in law enforcement (both serving on the watch and apprehending felons) did paradoxically make the streets less chaotic, because passers-by became reluctant to get involved in disputes whenever they arose.[52]

The same institutional arrangement which facilitated the hiring of salaried watchmen, the local improvement commission created by statute, also facilitated improvements to the lighting and physical fabric of the streets. Traditionally, householders had been responsible for putting lamps outside their doors on dark evenings, sweeping refuse on the streets in front of their houses into piles, and repairing the pavements between their houses and the gutter in the middle of the streets. New statutes, notably the City Lighting Act of 1736 and the Westminster Paving Act of 1762, both of which were subsequently adapted for other parts of the metropolis, not only replaced this individual obligation with contractors paid for by rates, but they improved the standard of provision by extending coverage, introducing more effective lamps, providing a uniform street surface, and creating separate raised pavements for pedestrians, sometimes separated by bollards.[53]

These improvements complemented the clean, symmetrical lines of the new Georgian architectural style (Figure 5), itself encouraged in part by statutes, passed in the aftermath of the Great Fire, which regulated the construction of buildings in order to prevent the spread of fire.[54] These new ordered streetscapes were meant to be experienced differently from their medieval predecessors. With straighter thoroughfares and pedestrians separated from wheeled traffic, streets were conceived of as arteries of movement, not as places for crowds to gather. Moreover, as emblems of taste and regularity they were intended to improve the morals of those who passed through them. As John Gwynn argued, 'publick magnificence' encouraged 'a love of elegance ... among all ranks and degrees of people ... in a mechanic [it will] produce at least cleanliness and decorum'. Despite these optimistic aspirations, riots unsurprisingly continued to occur in beautifully symmetrical Georgian streetscapes (Figure 14), and rioters even used the new paving stones to break windows.[55] Nonetheless, this new urban planning had the potential to undermine the communal life of London's streets and make them less welcoming to those who wished to loiter (unless, of course, they were window shopping). The more efficient removal of mud, excrement and other waste, for example, deprived crowds of the materials they used to throw at their enemies, or at those punished on the pillory. Similarly, despite the vast areas covered by the elegant squares which sprang up in the west end, pedestrians were discouraged from congregating by chains, rails and enclosed gardens. It is remarkable how many visitors commented on how empty these squares seemed. According to Muralt, 'there are a great many places in London called squares, where people may walk and few do'.[56]

Further depersonalising public spaces was the introduction of street signs and street numbering in the 1760s, which, together with published maps and guidebooks, allowed travellers to find their way without having to ask fellow pedestrians. When the creation of street signs was proposed a decade earlier, one of the advantages listed was that a stranger

> might, with the assistance of a small pocket map, find his way into any part of these contiguous cities and their extended liberties, without being at the

pain and trouble of enquiring his way of a populace, not the most remarkable for their politeness to strangers, or such as do not speak their language in the native accent.[57]

A spate of published literature, much of it influenced by the reigning ideal of politeness, also helped both visitors and Londoners move about the metropolis, and advised them on how to conduct themselves during their journey. John Gay's *Trivia: or The Art of Walking the Streets of London* (1716), for example, advised pedestrians

> How to walk clean by day, and safe by night,
> How jostling crouds, with prudence, to decline,
> When to assert the wall, and when resign ...

A set of 'rules of behaviour, of general use, though much disregarded in this populous city' published in 1780 contained the same advice about the wall, as well as the following:

> Not to walk arm in arm, as if the street was made for us only.

> Not to use the sauntering gait of a lazy Spaniard in this busy town of trade and hurry.

> To be cautious of staring in the faces of those that pass by us, like an inquisitor general; for an overbearing look has the air of a bully, and a prying one that of a bailiff.[58]

The streets, if this advice was followed, had become unsuitable places for interpersonal contact – pedestrians should just keep moving. When they needed information, both visitors and Londoners could rely on published maps, street lists, trade directories, lists of coaches and carriers, and guidebooks to help them find their way and avoid conflicts while moving around the metropolis.[59]

As London emerged as the first modern city, filled with a large and diverse population unfettered by traditional social ties, its streets and public houses offered apparently limitless opportunities for work, recreation and social advancement, but these contributed to the growth of public conflict. Violence, insult and riot were frequently used in order to defend and enhance Londoners' reputations and advance their interests. Although most such disorder was limited by cultural norms, it

5. Thomas Sandby, 'View of Beaufort Buildings Looking Towards the Strand' (1765). (© *The British Museum*)

generated real fears of mob rule among those with power and property. In response to this perceived threat, a series of policing, administrative, architectural and literary initiatives attempted to discipline the mob and create some order on the streets. As we shall see, however, most of these top-down initiatives had only a limited impact, and some had surprising unintended consequences. Street life *did* become more orderly over the course of the eighteenth century, but the mob changed itself as much as it was changed by others, as ordinary Londoners adapted to their changing urban environment. Owing to the altered relationship between the individual and the community found in a modern city, the way people established their reputations changed fundamentally. Consequently, the ways Londoners used the streets for expressing their grievances and conducting disputes were transformed.

Before considering patterns of unofficial disorder, however, it is necessary to consider the mob's officially-sanctioned role in apprehending criminals, an activity which itself created no small amount of disorder.

# Stop Thief!

In John Gay's *Trivia: or The Art of Walking the Streets of London* (1716), a pickpocket working a crowd is detected and apprehended:

> But lo! His bolder theft some tradesman spies,
> Swift from his prey the scudding lurcher flies;
> Dext'rous he scapes the coach, with nimble bounds,
> Whilst ev'ry honest tongue *Stop Thief* resounds.
> So speeds the wily fox, alarm'd with fear,
> Who lately filch'd the turkey's callow care;
> Hounds following hounds, grow louder as he flies,
> And injur'd tenants joyn the hunter's cries.

He stumbles, falls, and is seized by a mob, which proceeds to punish him.[1]

Much of the work of apprehending suspected criminals in the eighteenth century fell to the ordinary Londoners who were victims and witnesses of crime. A case from the *Old Bailey Proceedings*, published accounts of trials held at London's central criminal court, illustrates just how much effort this could involve. When Henry Styles was collecting casks of butter from a cheesemonger in Whitechapel in 1761, a cask went missing. A little child nearby said 'she saw a man take one of the tubs up' and go towards Newcastle Street. Styles then looked all up and down the neighbouring streets and alleys, leaving word at shops that if anyone offered a cask of butter to sell they should inform his master. In the end, he was informed that the butter had been offered for sale at a shop in Winsford Street. Styles went there, and a man said 'I'll shew you the man, he is at a barber's shop'. Styles later testified in court that 'we went into the barber's shop, and there I saw the cask standing, and the barber was shaving' the suspect, whose name was Thomas Pearce. A constable was sent for, and Pearce eventually admitted taking the cask, saying that he was drunk and thought it was a cask of brandy.

He was put in the watch house, and the next day Styles took him to Justice John Fielding.[2] As this case suggests, upon experiencing a theft victims immediately set about locating the stolen goods and finding the culprit, and they successfully enlisted the participation of anyone nearby who might be able to help. Victims, aided by passers-by, engaged in substantial detective work themselves, and usually found the goods, and the thief, *before* a constable was sent for or a justice of the peace became involved.

A significant feature of London street life in the eighteenth century was that ordinary residents played a much greater role in policing the streets and apprehending suspected criminals than they do today. Since the activities of constables and watchmen rarely extended to performing detective work, they had no other choice. Indeed, English men and women were legally obliged to arrest anyone who they witnessed committing a felony or inflicting a dangerous wound, and to join the official 'hue and cry' in pursuing any escaping felon or suppressing an affray.[3] In addition to acting as detectives and assisting neighbours and constables, male householders were also expected to serve without pay as neighbourhood watchmen and constables on a regular basis. Detecting and apprehending suspected criminals was thus an officially sanctioned aspect of public participation in street life. Paradoxically, it also contributed to the disorder on the streets, since crowds making arrests did not always stay within the law. Over the course of the century, however, practices of apprehending criminals changed considerably, in ways which reduced the participation of the mob.

Many thefts were committed by people known to the victim, as their servants, apprentices, lodgers, or visitors, and in such cases the victim usually knew where to find the thief, or where he or she might have pawned the goods; the typical response was to go and find the culprit, or the goods, without the assistance of officials or neighbours. When Henry Coombe lost several perukes and bunches of hair from his shop in February 1761, he immediately suspected John Cuthbertson, a journeyman he had just hired. Coombe testified at the Old Bailey that 'I went to the person that had recommended him to me, and he gave me information where the prisoner lodged. Then I went to Justice [John] Fielding, and got a warrant, and took him, about nine at night, and in about three quarters of an hour he confessed he had three perukes, and the hair.' Cuthbertson further confessed that he had sold some of them in Middle Row, Holborn. The next day Coombe, accompanied by Cuthbertson and a constable, went to Middle Row and found two of the perukes in a shop.[4] Coombe, the victim, was clearly the central player in this criminal investigation. This case can serve as a proxy for the tens of thousands of cases in the *Old Bailey Proceedings* where victims did their own detective work in solving the crime.[5]

Victims were frequently assisted, however, by neighbours and passers-by who had witnessed the crime. In May 1735 William Power was walking in Lamb's Conduit Fields when four men came up to him, struck him on the breast, and robbed him of his watch. The noise of the robbery alerted at least five men walking or working nearby, who all came to Power's assistance. As Mr Elkins, a carpenter, testified in court, 'a man and a woman came by and said, there's a man has been robb'd, and will be murdered. I ran towards them with my trowel in my hand.' When he arrived on the scene, Elkins reportedly said, 'Ye dogs, do you rob at this time o' day? I'll run my trowel in your guts.' Two of the robbers were apprehended and taken to St Giles Roundhouse.[6] Sometimes witnesses even alerted victims who did not realise they were being robbed. When William Manwaring was going down Ludgate Hill in February 1761, according to his testimony in court, he observed two men walking along, and followed them 'a good while'.

> Just as they got beyond the place where Ludgate stood ... I saw the prisoner at the bar put his hand to the prosecutor's pocket, and in an instant turned about, and gave something to the other man ... They immediately retreated ... I went and overtook the prosecutor, and told him what I had seen; and said, if he would step back with me, I would shew him the fellows.[7]

Victims often actively recruited passers-by to help apprehend suspects. Occasionally, particularly in the case of highway robberies committed outside the metropolis, the formal 'hue and cry', initiated by a constable, obliged bystanders to participate, but this formal institution was rarely invoked in the eighteenth century.[8] Londoners, however, frequently engaged in a variant of this practice by calling out for help, with shouts such as 'stop thief!' or 'murder!' Although without the authority of a constable, this practice was nonetheless sometimes described by witnesses as the 'hue and cry', and it was an effective means of taking advantage of the willingness of passers-by to assist in apprehending criminals. When in 1731 Alexander Russel knocked down a fourteen-year-old boy, Thomas Godbut, and stole a shoulder of mutton and a bundle of goods from him, Godbut got up, followed him, and 'cry'd out, stop Thief, upon which some persons stopped him'. Four men testified in court that they had heard the cry and responded. One, John Harris, 'deposed that hearing an outcry of murther and stop thief, he look'd out, and saw the prisoner running with a bundle, and he ran to him, and collar'd him'.[9] When William Sidwell assaulted Elizabeth Woodnot outside her house one night in May 1733 and stole her cloak, she successfully cried out 'stop thief!' As one witness testified, 'As I stood at my own door, in Angel Court, I heard a cry of stop thief, and going to the end of the court, I saw two chairmen who had stopt a man. They said he had robb'd Mrs Woodnot; they had not hold of the prisoner, but they (and others) surrounded him.'[10] In 1755 John Hayman grabbed eleven pairs of women's stockings out of a shop in Westminster and ran away. After the shopkeeper called out 'stop thief!' he was taken by nearby residents and passers-by who went to considerable trouble to secure him. As Thomas Griffith testified,

> I live opposite the prosecutor. The gentlewoman call'd, stop thief. I ran and enquired of several people, if they saw a man running. I was told they had. I went on to Dean's Place, and a gentleman laid hold of him, and left him with me, till he went and got assistance. In the mean time he ran away, and I after him, and in Queen Street, Westminster, he was laid hold on and secured.[11]

The phrase 'stop thief!' occurs with increasing frequency in the *Old Bailey Proceedings* in the first half of the eighteenth century, demonstrating just how often Londoners were recruited to apprehend criminals. Victims of crime increasingly sought assistance from the crowds of pedestrians who thronged the streets, and their pleas were successful. One of the most common activities of the London mob was to assist in law enforcement, rather than breaking the law, and as the streets became more crowded and the forces of formal law enforcement were overwhelmed, ordinary Londoners played a growing role in apprehending criminals.

The cry of 'murder!' was also often used. It appears in some 600 Old Bailey trial accounts between 1714 and 1799, many of which did not involve actual murder. Those under threat of robbery, rape, or other physical attack used this cry to summon help, often (as we have already seen) in conjunction with the cry of 'stop thief!' Responding to a plea for help, Thomas Smith stopped a robber one night in April 1733. As he told the court, 'As I was walking over Moorfields, between 8 and 9 at night, I heard the cry of Murder! Thieves! It was a little darkish, and running towards the noise, I met the prisoner coming full speed from the woman ... I stopp'd him.'[12] Sometimes there really was a murder, though the call for help was not always in time to prevent the killing. Around 3 or 4 o'clock one afternoon in July 1747, Susannah Hill heard the cry of 'murder!': 'I heard murder cry'd out several times. I ran into the court ... and I saw Mrs Powel, and she cry'd out murder. She had a shoemaker's knife in her hand all over bloody. I ask'd her what was the matter? She said, Mrs Williams had killed her husband.' Hill went upstairs and found Mrs Williams standing next to the corpse.[13] In other cases, the murderer had to be apprehended: Hogarth's fictional murderer Tom Nero was captured by a crowd in a country churchyard (Figure 6).

Soliciting assistance in this manner was not always successful: sometimes the summons was ignored, and other times it summoned the wrong sort of help. Because the cry of murder was used so often, and in contexts where no one was in danger of being killed, it was often ignored. Edmund Brewer heard the same cries as Hill, but failed to respond. When asked why, he replied, 'because it was a common thing, she often cry'd out murder'. Those involved in domestic quarrels and drunks used the cry frequently. When Richard Horseford and James Furnell were walking along Ropemaker's Fields early one morning in December 1732, they 'heard several blows, and coming nearer, a woman's voice cry'd, for God's sake, Robin, spare my life! – Murder! – For God's sake spare my life this time.' Horseford, alarmed, said 'this fellow will kill his wife', but Furnell replied, 'no ... 'tis only a family-quarrel, and we shall get no thanks for meddling betwixt a man and his wife'.[14] A quarrel between two watchmen led to a murder in 1781, despite the fact the deceased's cries for help were heard by several witnesses, including fellow watchmen. As Sarah Taylor testified, 'I did not take any notice.

I did not think there was any murder done. I never went to look at them, but went away about my business.' 15

When help *was* successfully summoned by cries of stop thief! and murder!, those who arrived on the scene took control of the situation, but they did not always support the victim. While many of the suspects seized were taken to watchmen or constables, in other cases the crowd acted on the spot as both judge and jury. In many cases the crowd arrested the suspect or punished him or her directly, but in others the crowd did not believe the victim's story and discharged the prisoner. In July 1739, the *Weekly Journal: or British Gazetteer* reported:

> Thursday night about eleven o'clock a Gentleman very well dressed, was apprehended near the Royal Exchange, by a woman who charged him with taking her handkerchief from her neck, assaulting her, but it being believed she was a person of ill fame, the mob discharged their prisoner.16

It was easy to mislead those who responded to a cry for help. When some bailiffs encountered difficulty in trying to arrest a man for debt in 1751 they decided to facilitate the process by calling out 'stop thief!' Consequently, 'he was surrounded and knocked down by the mob to prevent his flight'. The bailiffs' 'dubious strategem', however, was condemned by the *London Evening Post* as 'a striking instance of cruelty'.17

Anyone could call out 'stop thief!', and indeed anyone could respond, as those with criminal motives could take advantage of Londoners' propensity to respond to such cries for help. Shouting 'stop thief!' could sometimes be counter-productive, summoning assistance for the thief rather than the victim. When John Richard saw Elizabeth Coventry take a bottle of wine and some money from a grocer's shop in Thames Street in 1731, he followed her, crying out 'stop thief!' As he testified in court, 'there were two fellows that before stood by her, who ran, and under pretence of assisting him, stopp'd *him*, and threw him down', allowing her to get as far away as Tower Street before she was apprehended.18 Thieves, too, called out for help when they were detected. In 1771 the *General Evening Post* reported that 'the pickpockets have a new method of rescuing each other. When one is detected, an accomplice, of genteel appearance, charges him with having picked his pocket, and, under pretence of taking him before a magistrate, procures his escape'.19 Equally, those sympathetic to, or scared of, thieves might fail to respond

6. William Hogarth, 'Cruelty in Perfection' (1751). (*Tim Hitchcock*)

to cries for help. When James Bramstead was robbed of his watch in a lodging house by Anne Sullivan in 1766, he cried out murder. Although two other residents of the house testified in court that they had heard the cry, they failed to respond and no one came to his rescue. One of them was on bad terms with Sullivan and may have feared retribution from her fellow lodger.[20]

Perhaps because witnesses and passers-by came to be perceived as unreliable, victims began to resort to other strategies for getting suspects arrested. In the Old Bailey trials of the 1740s there is a noticeable increase in the number of victims whose first response to a crime was to summon official, rather than unofficial, assistance. Rather than simply calling out 'stop thief!' when pursuing a criminal, they called out 'watch!' or 'thieves and watch!' Whereas only four trial accounts between 1715 and 1739 include phrases such as 'cried watch' and 'called out watch', there were thirty-two in the 1740s and 1750s. This increasing willingness to summon the watch when in trouble, or, if this had previously been the case, a growing tendency to mention the fact during trials, may reflect the growing professionalisation of the watch in the 1730s. Although many householders had been hiring substitutes in lieu of serving on the watch by rotation since at least the late seventeenth century, the passage of Watch Acts for seven Westminster parishes in 1735–36, and for the City of London in 1737, formally established the practice of using salaried watchmen, paid for by rates, and established rules for their patrols or 'beats'.[21]

Consequently, watchmen became more actively involved in the pursuit of thieves in the second quarter of the century. Londoners may have become conscious that they were now paying for a service which they had a right to call upon as soon as they experienced trouble; they also seem to have trusted it more, despite the contemporary stereotype of watchmen as old and inactive. With regular, relatively short 'beats', watchmen *were* often nearby when Londoners needed them. In 1761 William Hastings was walking with Mary Smith, a prostitute, after midnight, when she picked his pocket of two silver buckles. When he noticed the theft he failed to charge her with the crime immediately because, he said, 'I was afraid of mischief, so I staid till [the watchman] came up'.[22] Thomas Milward was walking near Well Close Square around twelve o'clock one summer night in 1748 when he was approached by William Clarenbolt, who said 'D—n you, sir, your money'. As Milward told the court, 'I struck him on the hand, run after him, and called out watch; and at the end of Neptune Street there were two watchmen'; Clarenbolt was soon seized and taken to the watch house. Significantly, when the prisoner's counsel asked Milward 'when you called out stop thief, did not he run backwards towards you?', Milward corrected him: 'I did not call out stop thief, I called out watch.' [23]

The first response of some Londoners when they were victims of crime became to call the watch. In December 1743, for example, the shop of William Young, a silversmith, was broken into about 2 or 3 o'clock in the morning, and a 'show glass' containing some of his work was stolen. He immediately summoned the watch, which was amazingly effective in retrieving his stolen goods. As Young testified,

> about 2 or 3 I was alarmed by my boy, who lives in the shop; he came up stairs, and knocked at my chamber door, says he, for God's sake come down, for I am afraid your show-glass is gone; and the street door is wide open. I jumped out of bed, called out watch, went down stairs, found the shop door open, and the show-glass taken away ... upon my calling out, three or four watchmen came, and in about an hour and a quarter a watchman brought my show-glass back again, with about nine or ten pounds worth of goods in it.[24]

Summoning the watch, however, was not always an effective strategy. In an incident reported in the *General Evening Post* in 1771, a watchman failed to respond to an appeal for help. When a neighbour of Sir Robert Ladbroke on St Peter's Hill (off Thames Street) was awakened at three o'clock in the morning 'by a noise which he thought resembled the breaking open of a house', he

> jumped out of bed, and snatching a blunderbuss which he kept in his chamber, threw up the sash, and seeing a watchman stand on the opposite side of the way, called to him, and asked him if he had not heard a disturbance, on which the fellow answered, he heard no noise, but what was occasioned by the violence of the wind, and said everything was very safe in that quarter.

Of course, the house was robbed, but nothing was done about it until another watchman happened to arrive.[25] At other times the wrong sort of person responded, or the act of summoning the watch was a decoy used by criminals. In December 1742 Thomas Osbourne called out after two women had grabbed him in order, he thought, to steal from him. Osbourne cried out 'watch!', but, as he reported

> Instead of the watch, one Richard Lucas (who I have a warrant against) came up; one of the three hit me a knock on the face, that stunned me, and laid me on my back; they robbed me of three guineas, and 26s. my hat and wig, buckles out of my shoes, and neck cloth off my neck.[26]

Like 'stop thief!', the cry of 'watch!' could be used to undermine law enforcement as well as support it. When Ann Wade stole a watch from John Lemonere in a public house late one night in 1764, he chased her out of the house and into an alley, upon which *she* called out for the watch.[27] Similarly, when John Piercy accused Cicily Hicky of stealing his watch out of his pocket near Fleet Street in 1761, both Piercy *and* Hicky summoned the watch (Hicky alleged Piercy had tried to be 'rude' with her), and both were confined overnight.[28]

For those unable or unwilling to cry out 'stop thief!' or 'watch!', new strategies for responding to crime were developing, allowing victims to offer rewards to people who solved the crime for them. Dating from the late seventeenth century, and facilitated by the rapid growth of the press in London in the early eighteenth century, advertisements and handbills were often used by victims to procure the return of stolen goods and by relatives of the deceased to locate murderers.[29] The fact that rewards were offered suggests a significant transfer of responsibility from those on the streets being expected to help out of a sense of duty to giving those with information an *incentive* to come forward. At nine o'clock one evening in 1736 James Smith was attacked as he was walking along Great Russell Street by two men, who struck him on the breast, seized his sword, and 'bid him deliver': he was robbed of the sword, a silver watch and 10 guineas. Smith testified in court that it all happened so fast that he had no idea who his attackers were or what they looked like, so he advertised the crime. As he testified in court,

> they were very expeditious, in their work, and I had not time, while they were robbing me, to take particular notice of them. I went to the printer of the *Daily Advertiser*, and described the watch, promising a reward of five guineas for it again; and notice was brought me from Mr Goddard, who

keeps the Crown at St Giles's, that the prisoners were taken that night. I went to Mr Goddard, and he inform'd me that he had found the goods upon the prisoners. The next day we carry'd them before Justice De Veil.[30]

As this example suggests, advertisements often achieved quick results. When Richard Pitt, an auctioneer, lost a silk and damask window curtain in 1781, he first made some enquiries on a Friday, presumably to pawnbrokers, but when these were unsuccessful he sent an advertisement to a paper, hoping it could be inserted on Saturday. In fact, it appeared on Monday, with the offer of a reward of five guineas on conviction of the party. Almost immediately Pitt received information, and was able to apprehend the culprit on Wednesday.[31] This method of seeking the return of stolen goods became increasingly popular over the century; while there were just fifty-one Old Bailey trials in which it was mentioned in the 1720s, this increased to 285 in the 1750s, and such advertisements are mentioned in virtually every edition of the *Proceedings* for the rest of the century. Another option, though relatively rarely used, was to have the theft 'cried' by a bellman. In a place like London, where there were several newspapers competing for readers' attention, this could be both a cheaper and a more effective method of reaching those who might have useful information. When Thomas Hern lost several items of clothing on the evening of 9 April 1781, he 'had the things cried; in consequence of which the things were found, in possession of Mr Litchfield [an alehouse keeper] on the 11th'.[32]

One group which paid particular attention to announcements of recently stolen goods was pawnbrokers, who, concerned to avoid the accusation of being receivers of stolen goods, immediately became suspicious when they were offered goods for an unrealistically low price, or by people who they did not know or trust. One, Walter Rotchford, even kept a book listing all the watches that had been advertised. When John Howland brought in a watch in 1757 and demanded three and a half guineas for it, Rotchford told the court, 'I said to the boy bring the book, that is, a book in which we set all the watches down we find advertised to be stolen. There I saw, lost a gold watch, a shagreen case, name William Wright.' He grabbed Howland and took him to Justice Fielding's office.[33] Sometimes, cautious pawnbrokers actually advertised suspicious goods themselves. When Margaret Allcock brought a wig to

James Young on 4 March 1721, she asked 7s. 6d. for it. Young, however, 'judging it to be worth £7, suspecting she had stole it had her committed to New Prison, and advertised it in the *Daily Courant*, upon which the prosecutor came and owned it'.[34]

Advertisements also facilitated the growing practice of thief-taking, of men and women (but mostly men) turning the practice of returning stolen goods in order to obtain rewards into a way of making a living. Thief-takers date back to the early seventeenth century but became increasingly common from the late seventeenth century owing to the increased availability of a second type of income: rewards offered by the state for the conviction of felons. Official concern about increasing crime and the difficulty of obtaining convictions in the 1690s led to increased use of statutory rewards for the conviction of those found guilty of specified felonies. The 1692 statute establishing rewards for apprehending and convicting highwaymen justified the need for such rewards as owing to the lack of 'due and sufficient encouragement given, and means used, for the discovery and apprehension of such offenders' – without rewards, witnesses were not coming forward.[35] Depending on whether they chose to arrange the return of stolen goods to their owner or turn the thief over to the authorities, thief-takers profited from the rewards offered by either the victim or the state. The process of returning stolen goods gave thief-takers an intimate know-ledge of the criminal underworld, and they were able to use that knowledge both to control thieves and occasionally to orchestrate their arrest and conviction.[36]

By the early eighteenth century, resorting to a thief-taker became the first response of some victims upon discovering that they had been robbed. In 1720 Elizabeth Cole had her silk purse containing 11 guineas stolen by passengers sitting next to her when she was crossing the Thames in a boat. She did not discover the theft until after she had left the boat, but upon the discovery her response was not to try and find the culprits herself, or go to a constable or justice of the peace, but to find a thief-taker. She went immediately back to Pepper Alley Stairs, informed the waterman of the theft, and asked if 'he knew any thief-taker'.[37] But thief-takers did not always wait for business to come to them. In search of business, they scanned the newspapers looking for advertisements placed by victims of theft and they listened carefully for news of crimes which had occurred. When William Hanks was robbed in a court at midnight of his watch, buckles and money, he was too drunk to do much about it. But a witness 'happen'd to speak of this robbery [the] next morning, and the thief-takers got hold of it, and it run like a hue and cry through a town'; this explains how Joseph Casey came to be arrested.[38]

Thief-takers served an obviously useful function, but when they acted as informers they had to overcome popular resistance to the idea that otherwise disinterested parties could legitimately profit from the conviction of others. Moreover, owing to the activities of Jonathan Wild in the late 1710s and early 1720s, and the McDaniel gang in the late 1740s and early 1750s, thief-takers acquired an unsavoury reputation as thief-*makers*, unscrupulous individuals who encouraged people to steal and then profited from collecting the rewards for their conviction, or from blackmailing them with the threat of prosecution.[39] The fact that thief-takers acted out of mercenary motives was often used to try and undermine their courtroom testimony. George Anderson, on trial for burglary in 1742, pleaded to the judge, 'my Lord, here are a parcel of thief-takers here, they would swear our lives away'.[40]

Despite their bad reputation, victims continued to resort to thief-takers because they served a useful function; victims of crime who did not wish to or could not rely on the assistance of passers-by, and did not have the time, inclination or knowledge to search for the culprit themselves, chose to pay someone else to do it. The authorities, too, depended on thief-takers for the arrest of criminals, particularly members of large gangs; without the thief-takers' knowledge of criminal networks, far fewer major criminals would have been apprehended. With the advent of thief-takers, for the first time policing involved a significant element of *detection*, and this was much needed in a huge metropolis where it was very easy for criminals to hide. Stimulated by the growing number of parliamentary rewards offered from the 1720s, the number of thief-takers increased considerably in the second quarter of the century, and it came to be recognised that they played a vital role in apprehending criminals.[41] Nonetheless, the fact that the thief-takers worked out ways of obtaining these (and other) rewards that were widely recognised as corrupt may have further alienated ordinary Londoners, who were already reluctant to serve as watchmen and constables, from participation in policing. According to Henry Fielding, one of the reasons people failed to apprehend felons was their 'fear of shame' of being labelled an informer or thief-taker; he worried that the odium attached to thief-taking was undermining the whole criminal justice system.[42]

Confronted with a perceived crime wave following end of the War of Austrian Succession in 1748, Henry Fielding, as 'court justice' in Westminster (succeeded, following his death in 1754, by his half-brother John), responded by trying to clean up the reputation of thief-takers by giving them quasi-official status under the direction of a magistrate. By keeping experienced constables in his service after the completion of their year in office by paying them a retainer (and supporting their claims for rewards), he built up a force of thief-takers who operated under his supervision.[43] By the early 1770s, they had also been given a more respectable name: 'runners'.[44]

A public office had existed on Bow Street since 1739 where a justice was available at regular times to receive reports of crimes. Advertisements placed by Henry Fielding in the *Covent Garden Journal* in 1752 urged the victims of crimes to report the fact at once:

To the Public

All persons who shall for the future, suffer by robbers, burglars, etc. are desired immediately to bring, or send, the best description they can of such robbers, etc. with the time, and place, and circumstances of the fact, to Henry Fielding, Esq., at his house in Bow Street.[45]

Later notices in the *Public Advertiser* promised that the stolen goods would be advertised, thereby bringing them to the attention of pawnbrokers, who would 'stop' them if anyone tried to pawn or sell them. The addition of the 'runners' meant that, upon hearing of a crime, the justice could dispatch a thief-taker in pursuit of the culprit, as was promised in front page advertisements placed by John Fielding from December 1754:

Whereas many thieves and robbers daily escape justice for want of immediate pursuit; it is therefore recommended to all persons who shall henceforth be robbed on the highway or in the streets, or whose shops or houses shall be broke open, that they give immediate notice thereof, together with as accurate a description of the offenders as possible, to *John Fielding*, esq.; at his House in Bow Street, Covent Garden ...

> And if they would send a special messenger on these occasions, Mr Fielding would not only pay that messenger for his trouble, but would immediately despatch a set of brave fellows in pursuit.[46]

The Fieldings sought to transform Londoners' *immediate* response to crime from one of self-help to one of relying on the police. As John Fielding wrote in a 1753 pamphlet, 'in frauds and felonies, which are attacks on our lives and properties, not a moment's time should be lost in giving notice to the magistrate'.[47]

Evidence from the *Old Bailey Proceedings* suggests that Londoners responded accordingly. Over the course of the 1750s, the availability of the Bow Street Runners made a big difference to how victims responded to crime, as is evident in a decline in the number of trials in which the victim reported having summoned help from passers-by by crying out 'stop thief!' or 'murder!' Shortly after John Fielding began promising to 'immediately despatch a set of brave fellows in pursuit' of the culprits in 1754, the number of trials which include a mention of 'stop thief!' and a variant of crying out 'murder!' declined dramatically. This suggests that for many people the responsibility for detection and arrest of criminals was transferred in the 1750s from the general public to magistrates and their quasi-official employees, thief-takers. Analysis of the trials in which the phrase 'Justice Fielding' appears leads to a similar conclusion. Whereas for the first few years following their appointment as JPs, victims went to Henry and then John Fielding only after they had secured the culprit, or at least after they had identified him or her and only needed a warrant in order to make an arrest, from around 1756 they increasingly reported that they went to Fielding *first* to ask for assistance. When twenty pairs of worsted stockings were stolen from a window in Clare Reeve's haberdashers shop one evening in February 1756, 'about an hour after [she] went to justice Fielding, and told him the affair'. Similarly, according to her testimony in court, when Jane Dalton was robbed by her servant Ann Hunt in 1781, she 'ran directly to Bow Street, and told Justice Fielding's men that I had been robbed'.[48]

When confronted with such cases, John Fielding did not always assume total responsibility for solving the crime; victims were still expected to participate. Sometimes, Fielding simply advised the victim about the best way of finding the thief. On other occasions, he gave victims the name of a suspect and told them to look for him or her: Reeve was told to go find Charles Cane and 'enquire in Chick Lane of people that bought stolen goods', while Dalton was told to go to Kensington, where Hunt had formerly been employed, to enquire as to her whereabouts. In other cases, however, Bow Street took over the case, and the only thing the victim had to do was advertise the theft in the papers, with readers being invited to report any information directly to Bow Street. When James Wright reported he had been robbed in 1757 Fielding told him to advertise it, after which the next thing Wright knew about the case was that the prisoners had been arrested and Wright was 'ordered to Justice Fielding's' to attend their examination. Although victims still had a role to play it was much diminished. When William Saunders was robbed of a silver watch in the same year, he reported the crime to Fielding the next morning and gave him a description of the robbers, upon which Fielding sent out some men; by night time two men had been arrested.[49]

Concerns about corruption nonetheless persisted, with those who sought to discredit the runners continuing to describe them as 'thief-takers'. A defence argument from 1765 sought to discount the prosecution evidence: 'the two last evidences are bad men, one goes to bawdy houses to take up girls; and the other is one of Sir John's thief-takers, that does this for the reward'.[50] It is not difficult, however, to see why Londoners found thief-takers attractive. Making an arrest without assistance from experienced practitioners was often dangerous, and victims and witnesses were increasingly reluctant to get involved. After George Thorne was robbed by two women in George Alley in 1745, a witness, Matthias Keys called out 'watch!' Thorne told Keys 'the women were run away', but when Thorne proposed to go after them, Keys said 'I will not go after them now, for they have knives, and we shall be in danger of our lives'. Instead he gave Thorne his name and address, so he could be contacted later in the event of a prosecution. A few days later, Thorne went to see John Berry, a thief-taker, who helped him locate the culprits. As John Fielding commented in his plan for preventing highway robberies, 'honest men will always be found ready enough, on being paid for their trouble, without any other reward' to take a message reporting a crime to Bow Street and to warn alehouse keepers and innkeepers, 'though, perhaps, they would not choose to run any hazard of their persons by attacking a rogue in desperate circum-stances'. Thomas Emms, who was robbed while visiting a prostitute in King Street, near Drury Lane, in 1781, reported that when he 'went downstairs to fetch a constable, no body would come; there were some decent people lived over the way, they said *they were afraid they should be knocked on the head if they gave me any assistance.* I went to the rotation office and got John Godfrey [a headborough] to assist me and we took the prisoner.'[51]

Growing concern about crime following the end of the Seven Years War in 1763 prompted the number of trials where victims cried out 'stop thief!' to increase once again, suggesting that Londoners continued to rely on the immediate assistance provided by passers-by. But there were problems with this method of detection, with those accused frequently (and often plausibly) complaining that the crowd had arrested the wrong man (and sometimes that he had actually been involved in the pursuit of the culprit). In his Old Bailey trial in 1760, Saunders Solomon, a Jewish second-hand clothes dealer accused of stealing a trunk full of clothes, testified:

> As I got to the Mansion House I heard the cry of stop thief. Several people ran, and I ran after them ... there might be near fifty people. I was running up again ... and was not got a yard out of the alley when a gentleman laid hold of me and said I must stop you, there is a cry of stop thief. I said, you are mistaken in the person, when up came several butchers and said, here is a Jew thief. They pulled me this way and that way, and when the man that had lost the box came up they said to him, that is the man; said he, I believe he is, and they would not let me say one word more.[52]

In fact, in many cases a cry of 'stop thief!' secured assistance from watchmen or runners. From the 1770s references to 'runners' become more frequent in the Old Bailey trials, and, unlike comments about thief-takers, the references are usually positive. After Mary Wilds was raped and robbed in Bethnal Green Field in 1772, she described her attackers to a 'runner of the night' in the watch house. That was on Sunday evening, and the following Tuesday evening she was taken to the Red Lion public house, where her attackers were present along with 'two of Justice Wilmot's runners' who had apparently apprehended them.[53] The reputation of the runners benefited from the frequent favourable reports of their activities in the newspapers, such as the following one from 1780:

> Yesterday three of the daring villains who robbed the house of Dr Miller, near Epping, and cut and hacked him in so brutal a manner that his life is now in danger, were apprehended by some of Sir John Fielding's people in a house at Westbourn Green, near Paddington, and brought to Bow Street.[54]

The increasing professionalisation of thief-taking in the second half of the century accelerated the process by which the routine response of victims of crime became to seek official assistance, rather than first trying to apprehend the culprits themselves. At the end of the century, the practice of going immediately to a rotation office when a burglary or robbery of property of 'considerable value' took place was described by Patrick Colquhoun as 'the usual method at present'.[55]

Another innovative law enforcement technique of the second half of the eighteenth century was the formation of associations for the prosecution of felons, groups of householders who banded together to share the costs of apprehending and prosecuting criminals. An example of the associational culture of the age,[56] these societies of gentlemen, merchants and tradesmen were formed in response to anxieties about increasing levels of particular types of crime, such as highway robbery or theft from warehouses, and in order to encourage the increasingly lethargic victims of crime to take action. The purpose of one of London's earliest prosecution societies, the Society for the Prevention of Frauds and Felonies Committed on Tradesmen and Shopkeepers, founded in 1767, was described as 'to pursue the most vigorous and effectual methods to bring such offenders to justice; as they frequently escape the punishment their crimes deserve, through the inability, timidity, avarice, or indolence of those they injure'.[57] Although these societies could be interpreted as an example of private citizens continuing to take the initiative in responding to crime, in fact their primary method of operation was to pay others to apprehend criminals, utilising all the new strategies of the day. Upon being notified of a crime, a solicitor or other officer of the association would usually arrange for the publication of handbills or newspaper advertisements offering a reward and the payment of costs for the return of the stolen goods and arrest of the suspect, thereby encouraging thief-takers and enthusiastic or mercenary constables to respond. They also paid any expenses incurred by the victim in pursuing the suspect and the cost of prosecuting the case in court (including lawyers' fees). In fact, one of the primary purposes of the associations was to provide insurance against the often high cost of conducting a trial.[58]

Compared to other parts of the country, there is actually relatively little evidence of such associations in London, and their impact was limited. The earliest societies were formed by merchants to encourage the prosecution of thieves who stole from boats and docks along the Thames and the receivers of those stolen goods. A subscription was established in 1749 to hire a body of 'merchant's constables' to police the riverside, and another merchants' committee was formed to encourage prosecutions in January 1751, but these initiatives led to very few prosecutions at the Old Bailey.[59] The Society for Prosecuting Felons, Forgers, Etc., founded in 1767 with the support and encouragement of John Fielding, continued to meet until the end of the century, but its committee appears to have spent as much time organising the annual dinner as in prosecuting felons: its records show that an average of only 4.2 prosecutions were initiated each year.[60] There is no evidence in the *Old Bailey Proceedings* to suggest that these societies played any direct role in apprehending offenders; rather, their role appears to have been behind the scenes, paying costs. The only other prosecution associations active in the London area in the eighteenth century were to be found on the urban periphery where highway robbers were a constant threat and thief-takers were thin on the ground: in Barnet, Enfield, Hammersmith and Rotherhithe.[61]

Innovations in policing in the eighteenth century, such as the use of rewards and thief-takers, as well as arguments demanding further reforms, were frequently justified by statements that ordinary Londoners could no longer be relied upon to fulfil their traditional obligations of locating and apprehending criminals. One of the reasons adduced by Henry Fielding to explain 'the late increase in robbers' in 1751 was the reluctance of ordinary people to arrest felons. Complaining that the common view was that 'what is the business of every man is the business of no man', he argued that in no other country was 'less honour ...

gained by serving the public. He therefore who commits no crime against
the public, is very well satisfied with his own virtue; far from thinking
himself obliged to undergo any labour, expend any money, or encounter
any danger on such account.' This complaint was echoed in the *London
Evening Post* in December of that year, when it proposed as a solution
to this problem that the best method of 'suppressing street robberies'
would be 'to distribute small rewards, of five or ten pounds, to such as
should assist in apprehending, upon an outcry in the streets, any person
charged upon oath with a capital offence'. What previously had been
done out of a sense of obligation now had to be achieved by offering a
reward. At the end of the century Patrick Colquhoun, in seeking improvements to the detection and arrest of criminals, made a similar
argument. Centring his proposals around the role of the 'police', he
argued that no one could be expected to contribute to law enforcement
without proper remuneration. Information was still needed from the
public, but such people needed to be paid: it could not be expected that
'men, capable of giving [the police] useful information, will return a
second time, if they have not some adequate reward bestowed on them
for their labour, risk, and trouble'.[62]

Although these commentators arguably overstated their case in pursuit
of their reforming agendas, there *does* appear to have been a significant
decline in the propensity of Londoners to help locate and arrest felons.
In the second half of the century it became more difficult to obtain
assistance from passers-by on the streets, both in stopping crimes as they
occurred and in subsequently identifying and arresting suspects.
Saunders Welch, high constable of Holborn division in Middlesex,
complained already in 1754 that summoning people to assist in making
arrests 'has of late years been treated with contempt by the community'.[63]
Some people refused to get involved because they appear to have thought
that it was none of their business. In a chase after a burglar in Bell Yard
near Temple Bar in 1763 the response of those present on the street was
decidedly mixed, with some choosing not to take part and simply getting
in the way. According to one witness, 'I heard the cry of stop thief, the
prisoner came running (by a parcel of chairmen, who never attempted
to stop him) up Bell Yard, he forced by some people, and knocked one
down; I knocked him down with my hand, there was assistance, and we
secured him'.[64] After Mary Wilds was raped and left naked around

midnight one night in December 1771 (a case discussed earlier), she went to the house of John Thorn and reported that she was in distress and wanted to come in. He refused to help, and 'bid her go down to the watch house'. She said she was unable to, and just stood there until a watchman appeared.[65] In 1781 Joseph Lewis, an apprentice, observed three people removing things from a cart as it was going up Fish Street Hill. He told the court: 'I asked a man to assist me to take them, but he would not have any thing to do with it.' Lewis then told the boy who was driving the cart, and they both ran down Houndsditch after the culprits, but they escaped. Ultimately, as Lewis told the court, it was thief-takers who made the arrest.'[66]

Cases where bystanders *failed* to help make arrests were obviously less likely to be reported in the trial proceedings, but they sometimes provoked comment in the newspapers. In 1741 the *London Evening Post* reported a story about the inhabitants of Stoke Newington, who 'for some time ... have been pestered with a set of rogues who have robbed all their outhouses'. The report continued: 'One of the inhabitants heard them at work as he lay in bed, but believing it was only next door, he thought every man was to take care only of his property, and went to sleep.' Of course, in the morning he discovered that it was his house that had been robbed.[67] On 28 July in the same year the paper reported that a man had been robbed and stabbed in Stepney Fields, but 'the culprits got clear off, notwithstanding there were many people walking in sight'. There were many other reports of robberies committed in the presence of witnesses who did nothing about them,[68] thereby lending support to John Fielding's claim in 1755 that 'not one in a hundred of [highway] robbers are taken in the fact', despite the fact that 'within this distance from London there is scarce a mile without a town or village, and ... there are always numbers of people passing and repassing on these public roads'. Fielding gave an example of the victim of a robbery on Hounslow Heath who chased the culprit 'through a public town at noon-day, crying out highwayman! highwayman! both being in full view of the populace, yet no one joined the pursuit'.[69] During the 1751 panic over the increase in street robbers the *General Evening Post* complained that, whereas such crimes were 'formerly impracticable', they now flourished due to a decline in 'the old honest alacrity to assist [magistrates] in the populace'. Reports in the newspapers of incidents in which crowds apprehended suspected offenders decreased over the century. Instead, there were complaints that when people cried for help, others did not respond: there were stories of a man who fell in the mud and suffocated because no one responded to his groans; a man who drowned in the Thames because no one responded to his cries for help; a woman knocked down by a coach who was unaided by the 'crowd of people' who 'immediately gathered around her'; and a man who was accidentally locked up in St Paul's Church and, although a mob gathered about the church door, 'not a soul offered to stir himself to relieve him from his confinement' until a young gentleman came along and secured his release.[70]

Of course, many trial accounts continued to include evidence of witnesses coming to the aid of victims and playing a key role in apprehending suspects. The cry of 'stop thief' can be found in the accounts of about fifty trials a year at the Old Bailey in the 1780s and 1790s. But, perhaps owing to increasing suspicions that those who assisted had mercenary motives (in seeking rewards), some now felt obliged to justify those actions. In 1771 David Levi, keeper of a shoe and hat warehouse, became suspicious when Lyon Backeruc entered his shop and tried to sell him sixty new hats; Backeruc eventually admitted 'they were not honestly come by'. Telling him to come back later, Levi then set about laying a trap. As he told the court, 'I thought it my duty as a member of society to apprehend him'. Similarly, when innkeeper William Parry was told that Joseph Bowman had been robbed outside his inn in 1780, he asked the barmaid if she knew the woman who had done it. She did, and Parry told the court that he went 'immediately in search of her, thinking it a duty incumbent upon me'. What is significant in both these cases is that apparently disinterested witnesses felt they needed to explain why they had worked so hard to pursue a thief; this may be because such voluntary actions were becoming increasingly rare.[71] At the same time, those apprehended by crowds responding to cries of 'stop thief' began to question more assertively the legitimacy of such actions, claiming they had been victims of false arrests.[72]

The role of ordinary Londoners in identifying and apprehending criminals was a key feature of London street life in the eighteenth century, and we shall see that it was complemented by popular participation in both official and unofficial public shaming punishments.[73] Paradoxically, the law enforcement activities of the mob also caused disorder, thereby contributing to the chaotic image of metropolitan street life. Over the course of the century, however, a significant alteration took place in the attitudes of individual Londoners towards their responsibilities for detecting and arresting suspected criminals. The abandonment of this public duty was not as great as reformers like the Fieldings and Colquhoun complained, nor did it apply to all aspects of crime and public life. In the case of fights and duels Londoners became *increasingly* likely over the course of the century to interfere and stop the violence; the need to prevent injury and maintain standards of civilised conduct took precedence over Londoners' growing unwillingness to get involved in disputes.[74] But there appears to have been increasing reluctance to get involved in cases after crimes had been committed. One cause of this shift was the growing fear of being attacked while attempting to make arrests, but this reluctance is evident even where there was little danger.

As we shall see, this change was part of a more general withdrawal of Londoners from participation in street conflict, particularly in the second half of the century. Directly encouraging this withdrawal was the declining practice of householders serving periodically in rotation as watchmen and constables, and the increased reliance on a small group of men for the performance of these duties who saw law enforcement as a form of employment. By the end of the century virtually the entire metropolis was served by salaried watchmen paid for by the rates, and almost two-thirds of all constables were hired deputies. Rather than a civic duty expected of all male householders, law enforcement became a job for a small number of professionals.[75] Many fewer Londoners had experience of, or any desire to participate in, law enforcement, and this created a strong temptation to leave all responses to crime to more experienced men, especially since new methods were available to encourage such people to act through financial incentives. Consequently, by the end of the century ordinary Londoners played a much reduced role in apprehending criminals. They were no longer as willing to police the streets as they once were – they expected the streets to be policed for them.

# 3

# *Public Insults*

Just as preindustrial Londoners were accustomed to apprehending criminals, they also frequently used public spaces to censure the antisocial activities of their neighbours. In Cock Alley, East Smithfield in August 1690, Mary Whitfield kicked Anne Smith, spat in her face and called her a 'rotten, lowsy, nasty whore and drop as you go'; the last phrase probably referred to the fact Smith was pregnant. This insult caused several people to gather in the alley.[1] Scenes like this were repeated endlessly. Women, and to a lesser extent men, who were accused of sexual or other misdeeds were frequently publicly defamed by both words and actions. Those who heard such insults, whether they took place in streets and alleys or inside houses, immediately rushed to the scene. The power of defamation can be seen in the fact Smith subsequently miscarried, allegedly as a result of the distress caused by the insult. Londoners valued their honour and reputations highly. 'To rob [a man] of that', one commentator noted, 'is the highest injury that can be done to him.'[2] Both men and women needed a good reputation in order to engage in trade and business, conduct courtships and marry, and generally be considered a respectable member of the community. Reputations were established and destroyed publicly, by what was said on the streets and in the alehouses and coffee houses of the metropolis. Consequently, to have one's honour undermined by a public insult was a very cruel blow.

During the seventeenth and early eighteenth centuries public insults and other defamatory acts were a common feature of London street life. Londoners of both sexes enforced social norms by discussing the misbehaviour committed by their neighbours in their gossip, and by making public these accusations.[3] Not just sexual immorality, but a wide range of deviance was censured in this way. The power of these insults was such that many of those who were defamed felt the need to attempt to vindicate their reputations by filing lawsuits for defamation in the church courts, at sessions, or, less frequently, in the Westminster common law courts. These prosecutions were a staple item of court business, and involved litigants from the middle and lower classes (but few gentry), and both sexes. During the eighteenth century, however, such cases declined, and by the end of the century they had become rare. While Londoners no doubt continued to insult each other, they did so less often in public, and insults were no longer seen as sufficiently important to merit a court case. The cultural significance of defamation diminished.

In his 1709 diatribe against the sins of the tongue, Henry Hooton emphasised the importance of reputation, and therefore the damage caused by public insults:

> For since all persons (such especially as have any true notion of honesty or honour) so set a higher value upon their good name, than upon any of their goods or possessions, yea upon their very lives ... all the comforts and conveniences of this life depend upon it: so that being deprived of his good name, he is robb'd of all; except a good conscience ... [4]

A good name was established, and destroyed, by what was said in public. After Peter Chevalier was defamed by comments made by Peter Gallowsly, his father-in-law, in 1729 (telling tradesmen Chevalier was 'determined to cheat all he could and then run away' and 'for certain [he] was raving mad'), Chevalier wrote to Gallowsly asking him to 'contradict by word of mouth', what he had previously said.[5] It is remarkable how often those who made insults in the late seventeenth and early eighteenth centuries sought a public audience, to ensure that the reputation of the victim was effectively called into question. In 1700 an argument erupted in Barbara Dyke's house over accusations that Dyke had committed adultery, leading to William Parker calling Dyke's husband, a doctor, a cuckold. Although there were already several witnesses to these insults, Parker sought to gain greater publicity for his accusation by taking the dispute outdoors; later in the day and several times afterwards he cried out 'cuckoo' in the streets below Dyke's window. One evening, 'as he was standing in the said street [he cried] aloud several times, where is the doctor, what is become of the cuckoo doctor?'[6] When Frances Brockett quarrelled with Jane Seyrie about the selling of some asparagus in St James's Market in 1715 and the quarrel led to an exchange of insults, Seyrie called attention to the incident by following Brockett out of the market, 'clapping her hands towards and directing her words to' Brockett, and saying 'go you whore and louse your father'. This caused about forty people, who were strangers to the deponent who reported this information, to gather together.[7] Upon hearing an insult, Londoners were prone to gather around the disputants, find out who was being defamed and why, and police the dispute. Most sought to prevent any violence from taking place and some tried to defuse the conflict.

Given the audiences such insults attracted, it is not surprising that defamers often succeeded in damaging the reputations of their victims. Insults were discussed and repeated by witnesses and neighbours. After Brockett called Seyrie 'a whore and a strumpet', one witness in the consistory court testified, Seyrie's 'good name hath thereby been much prejudiced by reason that since then she hath heard severall of the neighbours of the said Jane speak very disrespectfully of her'.[8] After Martha Branch and Christopher Backhouse were seen kissing each other, 'feeling nudityes' and engaging in 'indecent postures' in Backhouse's kitchen while Martha was smoking a pipe, Mary Palmer went into a public coffee house, asked the customers 'if they did not hear the news', and gave an account of what she had seen. Prosecuted for defamation, Palmer's defence was that the story 'was publicly talked of in the marketplace before [she] spoke of it to any person'.[9] Those with damaged reputations suffered serious consequences: courtships were broken off; husbands threatened to leave their wives; and servants were dismissed from their posts. Following accusations that Ann Tamett, a servant maid, had had a bastard child, her mistress Frances Fletcher dismissed her, 'knowing how much the entertaining of such a person would reflect on her credit'. Tamett's courtship with the seal keeper of the Chancellor of England was also ended.[10]

Deviants were defamed by actions as well as words. Certain actions symbolically but effectively expressed public contempt for those who misbehaved. Men and women were spat at, drenched with water or urine, had dirt or excrement thrown at them, or were thrown into the mud, bodies of water, or the kennel (gutter). These actions, as violations of the peace, frequently led to the perpetrators being bound over to appear before the Middlesex justices of the peace at their sessions. In a typical case from 1723, Ann Callieau, the wife of a weaver, was accused of assaulting Mary Agar, spitting in her face, and 'giving her very abusive and opprobrious language'. Pelting with urine and excrement (often readily to hand in the age of the chamber pot) was clearly meant symbolically to place the victim beyond the pale of acceptable society.[11] In 1733 a woman was accused of assaulting and 'grossly abusing' another woman by 'throwing kennel dirt upon her'; ten years later a cabinet maker assaulted a man by 'throwing a pisspot of nastiness upon his head'.[12] Dirt and mud, which were often also thrown (along with excrement) at convicts placed in the pillory, served a similar function.[13] In 1693, Martha Rosailund and Peter Split were bound over at the request of John Snipe for 'abusing and disturbing him daily in his own house and ... throwing dirt in his face'.[14]

Whereas women were more likely to spit or throw dirt and mud, men used their physical strength to achieve a similar effect by throwing their victims into the dirt or rolling them in the kennel in the middle of the street, a particularly nasty experience as the kennel was often full of urine, faeces, mud and dirty water. In 1743 Joseph Beesley, a firkinman (beer seller) living in Drury Lane, was bound over for assaulting, beating and bruising Mrs Jane Green, 'rolling her in the kennel and grossly abusing her'. Ditches served a similar function: in 1690 William and Ann Savage accused James Rust, a labourer from Shoreditch, of assaulting William 'and struggling to throw him into a deep ditch and swearing to stiffle [sic] him in the mud and further abusing him and his said wife in filthy language'. John Savage was also bound over on the same day for calling his father an 'old rogue son of an old bitch' and Ann an 'old bitch nasty old whore and giving both of them other vile and filthy names too odious to be repeated'. Rolling in the mud thus had the same significance as 'filthy language'. Less obviously, plain water also appears to have served a shaming function, possibly as a proxy for urine. Water was readily to hand, and, together with spitting, was the most common type of defamatory act prosecuted at sessions. Richard Collett complained to a justice of the peace in 1745 when Isabella Knight threw water on him and called him a 'sodomite'. The bedraggled appearance of someone who had had a pail of water dumped over their head, or had their head shoved under a water pump, effectively called public

attention to their misdeeds. Elizabeth Thompson complained when
Joseph Owen, a clog maker from Soho, shoved her, knocked the cap
off her head (another disrespectful act), 'threatened to have her pump'd,
and grossly abused her'.[15]

The frequent combination of insulting words with demeaning acts
makes it clear that the act of spitting or throwing dirt was meant to
stain symbolically the character and reputation of the victim as effectively as defamatory words. Indeed, contemporaries often used the
metaphor of 'besmirching' or 'bespattering' to describe the damage
inflicted on reputations by words. In 1709 Henry Hooton described
insulting words as a defamatory *act* when he wrote that 'slander is a
fruitful vice, and can easily find matter, there being dirt enough to be
found on every street for those who have a mind to throw it at their
neighbours'. Similarly, he demonstrated the power of such words when
he compared 'calumny to London dirt, with which tho' a man may
be bespattered in an instant, yet it requires much time and pains to
scour it out again'.[16]

A wide range of deviant behaviour was punished by defamatory words
and acts. Sexual immorality appears to have been the most common
misdeed, but this was a consequence of the fact that one of the most
accessible courts for filing complaints about defamation was the consistory court, and the court's jurisdiction only extended to insults
concerning forms of deviance that were actually punishable by that
court. Although in practice defamers sought to punish a much wider
range of misbehaviour, over 98 per cent of the defamation cases prosecuted at the consistory court of London involved sexual insults, and
almost all involved women being called a 'whore'.[17] By including this
word in their formal allegation, victims could be certain that their case
would be heard by the court. The accusation of whoredom was of course
a powerful weapon against women, since their honour depended so
fundamentally on the maintenance of a reputation for chastity. According to one commentator, women's honour was so fragile that even
the slightest imputation of misbehaviour could be fatal: 'only one drop
of ink falling into a bottle of fair water is enough to discolour it all'.
And without sexual honour, women found it difficult to maintain a
reputation in any other part of their lives, including work and business.[18]

In practice, the word 'whore' had a variety of meanings, and the range of alleged offensive behaviour was much wider than simple prostitution, which itself encompassed a wide range of activity.[19] Some insults did accuse of women of being a 'common whore', of suffering from venereal disease (a 'pocky whore'), of acting as a bawd, or of committing a specific act of prostitution (she 'did lie with one Ward for a shoulder of mutton').[20] But it is likely that those who made their living out of prostitution relatively rarely prosecuted cases of defamation, because it would have been difficult to prove that their reputation had been damaged by the slur.[21] More typical were cases of alleged adultery. Rachel Heard was defamed by David Wilkinson when he said 'Robin Heard's wife kept company with Mr Bowes the butcher's brother night and day and she was a lewd incontinent person and the common stallion of St James's Market'. While the second half of this insult implied Heard was driven by a masculine degree of lust and that Bowes hadn't been Heard's only partner, other insults called attention to a single liaison, claiming, for example, that Barbara Merchant had had a bastard when her husband was at sea, or telling Elizabeth Walsh that she was 'a whore and John Harding's whore, who fuck'd her the new fashion way'.[22] Almost three-quarters of the women who initiated cases were married, and sometimes husbands also complained, when they were called 'cuckolds' owing to their failure to prevent their wives' infidelity. Single women accounted for a further 17 per cent, many of whom were accused of having given birth to bastard children.[23] In some cases men who exploited the double standard, which tolerated male sexual incontinency while condemning it in women,[24] actually called attention to their exploits. Edward Hilson told Anne Fletcher she was a whore 'and he had lain with her a hundred times', while Thomas Lever told Mary Ann Gasken, a widow, 'you are a common whore and a jilt as any as walk the streets and damn you I will prove you as such, and I have lain with you several times myself'.[25]

The power of sexual insult to undermine a woman's character meant that such outbursts were often provoked by quarrels over other issues. Neighbours were no doubt often aware of each other's delinquencies, but chose not to call attention to them until they needed a weapon of attack. The insult to Barbara Merchant, for example, arose when she quarrelled with Ann Ingram over some dirt swept in front of Merchant's door. Ingram, no doubt irritated by Merchant's claim to respectability, took advantage of the fact 'there were many persons present' on their street (Hopkins Street, St James) to make her insult. In some cases, the lack of detail in the insult and the presence of significant other grievances suggests that 'whore' was used as a general non-sexual (but, given its connotations, still very effective) term of abuse. In such cases, the victim could take advantage of the relative ease of prosecuting cases at the consistory court in order to seek revenge. When John Bruce, a constable, called Anna Marlow an 'old whore', she sued him for defamation. But this was only the latest in a series of conflicts between the two, which had also involved the conviction of Marlow's son in a court leet for being a common disturber and an accusation against him for stealing two pounds of butter from a widow.[26] While some prosecutions for defamation were no doubt used as weapons in bigger legal battles, their efficacy arose from the recognised power of accusations of sexual immorality to undermine a woman's reputation.

Defamatory acts also sometimes had an explicitly sexual content. The significant number of women who complained that their pregnant bellies had been pinched or kicked, 'knowing [them] to be with child', suggests that mothers of illegitimate children were vulnerable to such attacks.[27] In other cases, men and women had their private parts exposed or attacked, perhaps as a punishment for their sexual immorality. A woman complained in 1721 when a man threw her down and turned up her clothes, 'exposing her nakedness', while twenty years later Francis Blake prosecuted four tripe men for assaulting him as he lay sick in bed, pulling him onto the floor and 'exposing his privy members to the view of the maid servant'.[28] Attacks specifically directed at the nose, an emblem of sexual dishonour both because it was taken to represent the bottom and because syphilitic infections were visible there, may also have had a sexual meaning. When a glass seller from Shoreditch assaulted a woman in 1761, 'pushing and pulling her by the nose and otherwise ill treating her', the man may have intended to defame as well as wound his victim.[29]

Despite the double standard (a distinction not embodied in law), men, as Blake's experience suggests, were also defamed for their sexual misbehaviour, and they complained about such insults in court. Male victims account for only 2.4 per cent of the defamation prosecutions at the consistory court, but somewhat more, 16 per cent, of the victims of sexually scandalous words prosecuted by recognizance at sessions. The substance of these insults suggests that, despite the fact that some men bragged about their sexual exploits, others were sensitive to accusations that they had committed adultery. In 1684 Robert Nicols bound over Ann Cope

> for maliciously and scandalously reporting that he begot on one's Stanley's wife a bastard child in a wood. And that the said bastard was crooked and bandy leg'd like him the said Robert, with other such lying stories tending so much to his disgrace that he is ashamed to be seen abroad about his father's business.[30]

While the insult in this case may have been as much about Nicols's disability as the allegation of having fathered a bastard child, this was not the only case where men were defamed for illicit sexual activity. According to witnesses, Thomas Winterbottom was much defamed when Thomas Burton told him, speaking 'in anger', 'Winterbottom, you keep three cunts, Mrs Pierce, dirty Doll [his wife], and tother sits by you [a Mrs Joles]'. This comment was interpreted to mean 'that the said producent [Winterbottom, the plaintiff] kept and lay with so many whores'.[31] Men were particularly sensitive to accusations of sodomy, a capital offence regardless of whether committed with a man or a woman, and also a target of visceral popular hatred. In 1727, at a time when several men were prosecuted at the Old Bailey for sodomy, one man was accused of raising a mob and a tumult about another man, and of abusing him 'in a very gross manner ... charging him in the open street with having committed the detestable sin of sodomy with his wife'.[32]

Too much time reading the church court records can give one the misleading impression that reputations, both male and female, in this period were shaped exclusively by sexual conduct. In fact, if men and women were to be able to function in the community as workers, consumers and neighbours, they needed to maintain a reputation as being honest and dependable in other walks of life as well. Londoners were expected to demonstrate many different types of honesty, all of which were seen to be connected. When a quarrel erupted in a shop in the City over whether Abraham Alendon, a coal dealer, should pay some money to Leah Hiam, who had found him a customer, Alendon refused, 'saying if it was an honest demand she should have it'. Hiam replied:

'Honesty. Don't talk to me about honesty, talk to your whore of a wife and your bastard children, you was never married either in church or synagogue.'[33] Alendon's alleged sexual dishonesty meant that his conduct as a coal dealer was also called into question. The most common insults levelled at men in this period were 'rogue' and 'knave'. While these terms could be used to criticise sexual misconduct, they were also used more generally to describe those who were perceived to be dishonest, unprincipled and untrustworthy, as in the term 'perjured rogue'. When Mary Ireland, the wife of a labourer from Ratcliff Highway in Stepney, called Thomas Oatlie 'pocky rogue, lowzie rogue, bastard breecht rogue and such like evil names tending to the breach of the peace' in 1663, the fact that the victim was her former landlord suggests that she may have been criticising more than just his sexual conduct. In the same year Anne Edminston, the wife of a mariner from Shadwell, let loose a torrent of insults against John Guttery, a master mariner who she felt had cheated her husband of his wages. She called him 'a base rogue ... saying he kept none but rogues about him. And like a rogue as he was [he] had sent her husband ... from the pay table without a farthing.'[34]

In a city populated by small businessmen, maintaining a reputation as an honest tradesman was essential. Those who felt cheated frequently complained publicly, accusing butchers of selling unwholesome meat, victuallers of selling short measures, and surgeons and doctors of failing to cure their patients. It was vital to have the reputation that one would fulfil one's financial obligations and had the resources to do so, particularly since the scarcity of currency meant that economic transactions frequently depended on the use of credit. According to Daniel Defoe, 'the credit of a tradesman ... is the same thing in its nature as the virtue of a lady'. In practice, of course, 'credit' and sexual 'virtue' were interrelated and important to both men *and* women.[35] A tradesman's reputation was established publicly, and those who were perceived to be untrustworthy were the subject of public gossip and insult. The victims of such insults hoped that the courts could help restore their reputations. In 1684 William Dyer bound over Thomas Harris, his former apprentice, after Harris endeavoured 'to take away his reputation and credit thereby indangering the loss and ruin of his employment by reporting that he had pawned his silver candlesticks and other plate and was ready to crack break and run away, and [saying] other malitious untruths to the same end and purpose'. Harris had no doubt suffered from Dyer's alleged financial insolvency and spread this gossip both as an act of revenge and in order to warn others not to trade with him.[36]

Public insults also attacked people for other types of untrustworthy and anti-social behaviour. In the late seventeenth century women were still defamed by being called a witch: Mary Archer complained in 1672 when Mary Langley abused her 'in evil language calling her witch and saying she had murdered her child'. Suspected thieves were similarly publicly denounced: Elizabeth Ellyson was 'defamed' by being labelled 'a common thief and shoplifter'. Informers received considerable abuse as a result of their efforts to enforce unpopular laws, from which they received a portion of the fines of those convicted. Until the Act of Toleration in 1689, the most hated informers were those who reported Protestant dissenters; in the 1730s and 1740s it was those who enforced the Gin Acts. In 1684 William Best complained when John Fox, an armourer from Clerkenwell, abused him in the street, 'calling him informing dog and other bad names to the hurt of his reputation, by which he gets his livelihood'. It is easy to see why Best complained; in the 1730s many informers (often women) were attacked by angry crowds and some were even murdered.[37]

While most of these insults were targeted at both men and women, one type of insult was targeted at men only, undermining their masculinity by calling into question their courage and willingness to fight. Owen Lewis, a yeoman from St Pancras, was bound over by Richard Gower, a gentleman from nearby Highgate, 'for reviling and abusing him and calling him knave and challenging him to fight in the field'.[38] In 1692 a political argument erupted in the Young Devil Tavern near Temple Bar, leading to an exchange of insults between John Hoyle and a Mr Pitt, in which the former called the latter a 'pultroon coward' and 'taxing the said Mr Pitt to put the quarrel to an end saying why don't you strike the pipe down my throat'. Despite attempts by on-lookers to prevent it, a sword fight ensued and Hoyle was killed. According to a witness, Pitt said to Hoyle 'that he had given him such an affront as he could not bear, and he would see what the deceased was made on'. Although the role that fighting played in upholding male honour declined significantly over the course of the eighteenth century, calling into question men's courage continued to be sufficiently damaging to their reputations to provoke a response, which often took the form of a challenge to a duel.[39]

The decline of male violence in this period may have actually led to the growing use of public insults by men, as words replaced deeds as men's preferred weapon of attack against their antagonists. What had once been considered a quintessentially feminine activity was now engaged in by both sexes. Richard Allestree wrote in 1674,

> I know we used to call this talkativeness a feminine vice; [but now] 'tis possible to go into masculine company where 'twill be as hard to edge in a word, as at a female gossiping. However as to this particular art of defaming, both the sexes seem to be at a vye ... and I think he were a very critical judge, that could determine between them.[40]

Despite the prevailing stereotype that women were the sex particularly prone to making insults, the authors of pamphlets condemning defamation published in the early eighteenth century, such as Henry Hooton, author of *A Bridle for the Tongue* (1709), assumed that the perpetrators of the 'grievous mischiefs' of the tongue were men, especially men of fashion. Slander, Hooton wrote, 'is become as common as any other [sin] among all persons of whatsoever rank, quality or condition. The bespattering others with foul imputations, is the common entertainment in most companies; the defaming and abusing their neighbours, the most fashionable passing away of time.' Even coffee houses were rife with insults: the Swiss visitor Béat-Louis de Muralt wrote that they 'furnish the inhabitants of this great city with slander, for there one hears exact accounts of everything done in town, as if it were but a village'.[41]

The court records, both ecclesiastical and criminal, confirm that men as well as women made substantial numbers of insults, though up to 1780 women outnumbered men 65 per cent to 35 per cent at sessions and by 62 per cent to 38 per cent at the consistory court. At the latter, however, the proportion of male defamers increased over time, though absolute numbers declined as the practice of public defamation fell into steep decline. Whereas in the late seventeenth and early eighteenth centuries men accounted for about a third of the defamers, by the final quarter of the eighteenth century they made half of the insults prosecuted at the consistory court.[42] If one examines insults which led to public apologies, where sexual defamation was outnumbered by other types of insults, men predominated, accounting for almost three quarters of the defamers between 1745 and 1795.[43]

The growing concern about male rather than female defamation in the eighteenth century was reflected in the declining use of the stereotype of women as particularly prone to the traditional feminine activity of scolding. In 1653 *A Brief Anatomie of Women* had identified a woman's tongue, 'that stirring and active member', as one of her greatest liabilities, both when used offensively and defensively: 'defensive in vindicating and upholding their own supposed credit and good name, though ever so bad; [and] offensive in scolding, abusing and detracting from their neighbours, though ever so good'. However, complaints in conduct books (manuals of advice for both men and women) that women were particularly loose with their tongues virtually disappear after the middle of the century. By the 1740s, women were more likely to appear in texts as *victims* of defamation, or as engaging in 'private defamation' at their tea tables, and after mid century even comments like these are rare, as conduct book writers ceased to see this activity as a typically female fault.[44]

There was also a change in the way scolding was portrayed in popular ballads. In the seventeenth century the female scold was a stock character, and some scolding stories were given a metropolitan setting. *An Account of a Great and Famous Scolding Match* (1699) reports a contest between 'four remarkable fish-women of Rosemary Lane and the like number of basket women of Golden Lane, near Cripplegate upon a wager for five guineas', which was staged remarkably like a duel. The women met at three o'clock in the morning and, in front an audience of 'neighbours and friends', engaged 'in that ancient and famous mystery of scolding'. They proceeded to exchange allegations of sexual misbehaviour: one woman was accused of having been found 'on a heap of dung on Tower Hill, with a pocky Tom Turd-man, playing on [her] dulcimer; and for [her] reward to have a damnable kick on the britch for being sluggish and unactive ...' Ironically, the contest ends when one of the women admits that one of the insults is true and has to quit in order to protect her reputation.[45] Ballads like this were published less frequently in the eighteenth century, and those which were were mostly published outside London. One of the most popular, *An Exmoor Scolding; In the Propriety and Decency of the Exmoor Language, between Two Sisters ... as They Were Spinning* (3rd edition, 1746, and frequently reprinted), seems to have acquired its popularity from the fact that scolding was now seen as a quaint, archaic and predominantly rural activity; it even occurred in a separate dialect. Indeed, the reference in *An Account of a Great and Famous Scolding Match* to scolding as an 'ancient and famous mystery' suggests that these attitudes were already present in the late seventeenth century.

In eighteenth-century London scolding was transformed into gossip, which was perceived as less harmful. An account of a typical Sunday published in 1750 suggests that between four and ten o'clock in the evening 'poor women who live in courts, yards and alleys in the suburbs of London [bring] their chairs into the streets, where they sit with their constant gossips, and pass verdicts on people going into, and coming out of the fields'.[46] By this point gossip was frequently depicted as exchanged primarily over the tea table (rather than on the streets), and the material was less sexually charged. This can be seen in the 1760 London pamphlet, *The New Art and Mystery of Gossiping*, which purported to offer 'a genuine account of all the women's clubs in and about the City and Suburbs', where women exchanged insults and gossip as a recreational activity. Similarly, the gossip portrayed in elite drama at the end of the eighteenth century was much more innocuous and pointless than it was in Restoration plays.[47] This literary evidence suggests that by the mid eighteenth century women were much less likely to engage in public defamation and that their 'gossip' had lost much of its power to damage reputations.

While the tendency to censure others in public appears to have transformed over time from a predominantly female to a predominantly male activity, a far more significant trend was the declining practice by both sexes of making insults in public, and, when such insults occurred, of taking notice of and responding to them. Evidence of the long-term decline of the public insult on London's streets can be found both in court records and in social commentary. The number of defamation prosecutions per year initiated in the consistory court, both in absolute numbers and calculated per capita, peaked in the late seventeenth century and declined over the eighteenth century (Chart 1).[48] From around 1725, rates of prosecution fell dramatically. By the late eighteenth century only one or two cases a year per hundred thousand inhabitants were prosecuted, and numbers fell even further in the ensuing decades until there was only one case a year between 1827 and 1829, when a Royal Commission recommended that the church courts' jurisdiction over the offence be abolished (this finally occurred in 1855).[49]

This long-term decrease in prosecutions could, of course, be explained by the declining authority of the church courts. These courts were weakened by having been abolished during the Interregnum and reinstated at the Restoration, and they were further undermined by the abolition of the controversial 'ex officio' oath (which compelled the accused to testify). Their powers were undermined still further by the Act of Toleration in 1689, which granted limited toleration of religious nonconformity, and by frequent royal pardons issued in subsequent years. However, these legal changes adversely affected the *disciplinary* powers of the courts (so called 'office' cases, prosecuted by church officials), and not private, 'instance' prosecutions such as defamation or matrimonial causes. Through its power of imposing the penalties associated with excommunication, the court retained sufficient legal powers to ensure that the defendants prosecuted by private plaintiffs continued to appear in court. Even after 1689 defamation cases continued to be initiated in significant numbers into the early eighteenth century, and matrimonial business actually increased significantly from the 1770s.[50] The courts were still available for those who wished to use them, and the decline of defamation cases cannot be attributed to institutional decline.[51]

Evidence from the other courts where defamation was prosecuted suggests that they did not pick up the slack left by the decline in church court cases. Prosecutions at common law in the Westminster courts of Common Pleas and King's Bench amounted to only about ten London cases per year during the eighteenth century and there is no sign that business was increasing.[52] At sessions defamation prosecutions in the seventeenth century were much more frequent, owing to the relatively low cost of prosecution by recognizance and indictment. As the Middlesex grand jury complained in 1683, many of the indictments which they

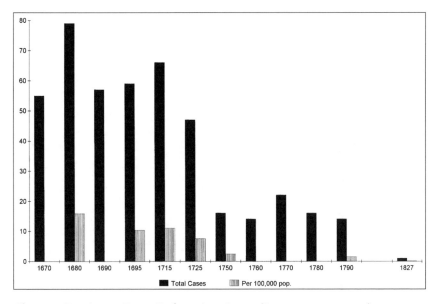

Chart 1. Consistory Court Defamation Cases. (Source: see note 48.)

were asked to approve came from 'poor people, and their offences ... arise from scolding, backbiting, and reproaching one another'.[53] Yet, despite the fact that the authority (and business) of sessions increased over the course of the next century, cases involving defamation declined significantly. Indictments for being a common scold or a barrator (a common disturber, instigator of malicious lawsuits or quarreller) declined from over twenty per year in Middlesex in the 1660s to around four per year in the 1720s.

Recognizances for words also declined dramatically, though defamatory acts did not. Chart 2 shows the changing pattern of recognizances involving defamation, reflecting shifting public concerns about anti-social behaviour between the Restoration and the late eighteenth century. The four types of defamation (common disturbers, specific and general insulting words, and insulting words accompanied by riot) follow different chronological trajectories. 'Common disturbers' were legally defined as people who repeatedly disrupted the peace by instigating malicious lawsuits, causing fights, interfering in the affairs of others, and scolding. In effect, many such people were accused of being habitual defamers; indeed, slanderers were sometimes labelled 'common

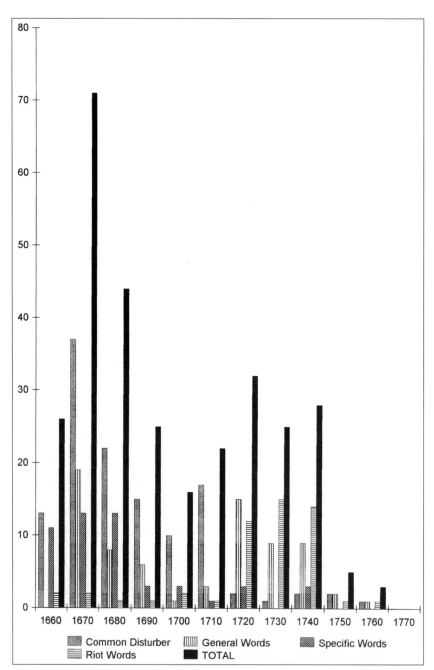

Chart 2. Defamation-Related Recognizances. (Source: Recognizance sample. See Appendix.)

disturbers'.[54] Many men and women were bound over (as well as indicted) for this offence in the Restoration decades and into the early eighteenth century, but, as with indictments, there were few prosecutions after 1730. Similarly, recognizances for voicing specific insulting words (calling someone a 'whore', 'thief', 'sodomite' or 'informer') were common in the Restoration decades, but were relatively rare after 1700. Instead, after a lull, complaints shifted to more general complaints (which had also been common from the 1670s to the 1690s), such as that the defendant had used 'scurrilous', 'opprobrious', or just 'insulting' words: these peaked in the 1720s, 1730s and 1740s, before entering a period of rapid decline. Words accompanying rioting also peaked, like other forms of riot, in the same decades.[55] Recognizances for defamatory acts (spitting and throwing water, mud or excrement; these are not included in Chart 2) follow a still different trend, increasing dramatically in the 1720s and 1730s and remaining frequent into the 1770s.

Essentially, prosecutions shifted from concerns about a general pattern of socially disruptive behaviour to specific incidents of defamation, then from specific insults to general abusive words and from words to riots and acts. The decline in specific insults is consistent with the general pattern in the church courts, while the increasing focus on generally abusive language and acts (including rioting) appears to have resulted from more demanding expectations concerning how Londoners were expected to behave towards one another in public; higher standards of behaviour led to more prosecutions. As the habitual common disturber and the individual defamer disappeared from view in the late seventeenth and early eighteenth centuries, concern shifted to those people who used 'scurrilous' and 'opprobrious' language more generally to attack their opponents. Where these terms were used in depositions for murder cases, the examples given were mostly general terms of abuse, including 'son of a bitch', 'coward', 'rogue', 'scoundrel', 'rascal' and 'villain'.

Sexual insults, which predominated in the late seventeenth century, became less common, with few if any women complaining to justices about having been called a 'whore' after the 1720s. One of the reasons for this remarkable shift is that changing attitudes towards feminine sexuality in the eighteenth century led women to become less willing to contest allegations of sexual immorality in the public forums of the law courts. Respectable women were increasingly seen as too pure and delicate to think about sex, let alone talk about it in the street or in the courtroom. Since women were no longer viewed as the more lustful sex, women were also probably less likely to be insulted in this way.[56] This change in attitudes no doubt contributed even more to the decline in defamation cases in the consistory court, since cases in which women were called whores were virtually the only type of insult prosecuted in that court. But the shifting language of complaints at sessions also reflects the fact that by the 1720s there was far less public concern about the effect that slander had on victim's reputations. Wording on recognizances which suggests that the insults actually attempted to shame the victim and damage his or her reputation, words which describe the defendant as 'reviling', 'upbraiding', 'slandering' and even 'defaming' the plaintiff, disappear from eighteenth-century recognizances. The word 'scandalous', earlier used in expressions such as 'scandalous abuse', also becomes uncommon. Instead, defendants were accused of 'grossly insulting' or 'grossly abusing' their victims, terms which say more about the offensive behaviour of the defendant than they do about damage to the victim's reputation.

In the 1730s and 1740s, defamation cases at sessions were more likely to involve defamatory acts (particularly spitting and throwing water), real or threatened violence, and riots. One woman was accused of assaulting another 'in the streets, afterwards pursuing her home to her house and insulting and very grossly abusing her and threatening her', and another of 'assaulting, beating and bruising [another woman] and dragging her by the hair of the head and grossly insulting her'.[57] It seems likely that such actions had always accompanied public insults, but as the insult itself became less significant (and its content was not specified) concern shifted to physical attack.[58] Although prosecutions for defamatory acts continued into the late eighteenth century, their character suggests that it was the assaults rather than the damage to their reputations that motivated victims to prosecute. When Rebecca Spencer, a widow, filed a complaint in 1772 against two lodgers, Francis Wace and his wife, for repeatedly insulting her, calling her 'double headed bitch', 'whore' and 'bawd', and using other 'scurrilous and abusive language', she gave greater emphasis to the physical danger she lay under. Because they 'often threatened to be revenged of her' (Mrs Mace 'declare[d] she would tear [her] heart and liver out'), she was 'obliged to get a man to

lay in the house to protect her from the insults of Mr and Mrs Wace'.[59]
A new intolerance of physical molestation is also evident in the increasing number of recognizances which state that the defendant had raised
a mob or a tumult of people 'about' their victims. It is likely that it was
the fact that defamation might involve groups of people acting in a
threatening and disorderly manner which was increasingly objectionable.
Thus, when Elianor Cromarty was indicted and bound over in 1719 'for
uttering threatening and scandalous words against William Buchanan
and Mary his wife', they complained that it was 'with an intent to raise
a mob and a tumult about them'.[60]

Changes in the character of defamation prosecutions in the consistory
court also suggest that the nature and significance of insults changed
over the course of the eighteenth century. Most significantly, insults
became less public. Whereas insults in the Restoration and the early
eighteenth century typically occurred during arguments which erupted
in streets and markets, or between men and women standing or sitting
on their doorsteps, later in the century many exchanges of insults had
moved indoors, to shops, taprooms, kitchens, hallways and other rooms.
Although many houses, especially alehouses, lodging houses and households comprising large numbers of servants, were quasi-public places,
fewer people heard these insults than those that took place in the streets.
In many late eighteenth-century cases there was no mention of a wider
audience for the insult beyond the small number of witnesses who
testified at the trial. In 1750 a dispute erupted in the kitchen of a surgeon's
house in the City parish of St Lawrence Jewry, between Mary Callthrup,
a servant, and Ann Bowman, who 'dry nursed' the children of the house.
Bowman told Callthrup that she had caught her in bed with Richard
Blinch and that 'she loved tumbling on the bed with fellows'. Callthrup
answered that 'then it was a wonder she was not with child'. Bowman
replied, accusing Callthrup of using abortifacients, 'no you will not have
anything to come to light for you can gape and swallow pills, and
whenever I have a mind to have a bit, I'll learn to gape and swallow
pills too'. These insults were only witnessed by a select group (the cook
maid, a gentleman's servant and Callthrup's sister, and they were over-
heard by the mistress of the house), yet they led to a prosecution. An
insult made in 1789 in the hallway of a lodging house during a dispute
over whose turn it was to clean the stairs was heard by even fewer

people. Margaret Sanders allegedly called Ann Jarman, the landlady, a 'common whore' in the presence of two other residents. Unsurprisingly, given the limited audience, one of the witnesses was unsure about the impact the words had on Jarman's reputation, testifying first that she believed 'her reputation is much injured among her neighbours and customers', but later stating, in response to cross-examination, that Jarman 'has not to her knowledge suffered by the words, neither does she know whether she has received any injury thereby'.[61]

As fewer people witnessed insults, their power to destroy reputations declined. In the late seventeenth and early eighteenth centuries almost every witness who testified at the consistory court responded affirmatively to the routine question about whether the victim's reputation had been damaged by the insults. Some even provided evidence, saying, for example, that 'by reason of the said defamatory words [the victim] has been often affronted by her neighbours', or that a female teacher 'hath been much prejudiced and has lost all her scholars'.[62] As we have seen, accusations of sexual immorality prevented marriages from taking place, disrupted existing marriages, and caused servants to be dismissed or prevented from finding employment. By the second half of the eighteenth century, however, there was much less certainty about the impact of defamatory words. While some witnesses still testified to their power of destroying reputations, others either reported that they did not know what their impact was, or explicitly stated that the victim's reputation had *not* been harmed. This was not simply because fewer people heard the insults, but also because there was a new scepticism about their validity and power. In 1789, for example, Robert Bower stood in the street at Ann White's window and, in front of 'several neighbours', said 'there lives a redhead whore, a whore in Newcastle Street', and later said to her face 'you are [a] whore in a bagnio and a whore in my house by God'. Despite the serious allegations, the three witnesses who testified on her behalf (all neighbours) were uncertain about the effect of these words. Mary Roberts, who confessed she had 'no particular acquaintance with but knows [White] as a neighbour', reported definitively that White's 'good name, fame and reputation is hurt, injured and aggrieved'. Cornish Badcock said that 'he *thinks* the neighbours *may* entertain an unfavourable opinion of her on account' of the insults. Elizabeth Enon was even less sure: she reported that 'she thinks the neighbours may think slightly of [White] on account of such words but has heard no opinion thereon'.[63] Deponents were uncertain about the impact defamatory words now had on people's reputations, and there even appears to have been a lack of interest in the issue, given the apparent failure of White's neighbours to talk about the insults they had all witnessed.

There is no doubt that reputation still mattered in the late eighteenth century, but in contrast to the Tudor and Stuart period when insults were perceived as harmful regardless of whether or not they were true,[64] there was a new scepticism of the power of defamatory words to damage reputations, especially in cases where the insult occurred spontaneously during a passionate argument. This is evident in the case notes kept by Sir Dudley Ryder, Lord Chief Justice, concerning slander litigation heard at the Middlesex Assizes between 1754 and 1756. Many of these cases appeared to be vexatious, waged as part of wider disputes, and defendants often argued, plausibly to Ryder, that the plaintiff's reputation had not been damaged by the alleged insult. A case involving two jewel sellers in 1756, where the defendant was accused of saying, in the Royal Exchange, 'you are a thief and robber and robbed me of £150', turned out to be a dispute over an unpaid debt. The defendant admitted he had spoken the words, but said that he had done so 'in heat', and argued that 'he did not say this with a view to rob the plaintiff of his character'. The jury and Ryder agreed, giving the verdict to the plaintiff but awarding derisory damages of only one shilling, a common practice in common law cases where the jury thought the prosecution was frivolous.[65] In 1795 an attorney at the Surrey Assizes claimed that 'actions for words had generally fallen into disrepute', in part because such actions were largely 'for words which have been spoken in the moment of passion' and thus did not represent an intentional effort to slander.[66] Similarly, witnesses failed to accord much significance to an insult in a consistory court case brought in 1792 by Hannah Barmore against Ann Morris. Morris allegedly said, in a 'violent passion' during a quarrel in Morris's house over a debt, that Barmore 'was a common whore and had lived with three hackney coachmen before she was married'. William Barmore, Hannah's brother-in-law, testified he 'knows not that the good name fame and reputation of the said Mrs Barmore is in the least injur'd thereby', and Hannah Turner, a neighbour, said 'Mrs Barmore is a person of good character ... and the deponent does not think that her good name fame or reputation is at all injured by such defamatory words, for the deponent does not think that any person believes the same'.[67] By the end of the century, 'good character' was shaped by factors other than what a person said in a 'violent passion' during a quarrel.

Not only did neighbours stop believing the insulting words they heard, they ceased even to pay attention. People became less likely to rush to observe quarrels and listen to the insults used. Some witnesses (despite the fact they had been chosen by the victim to provide eyewitness accounts) testified in court that upon hearing the first insult they had left the scene. In 1749, while John Pratt, a coachman, and fellow servant Mary Branham were having dinner in the servants' hall of the Earl of Effingham's house in the parish of St George, Hanover Square, Pratt accused Branham of having had a bastard child. Three of the four witnesses to this insult, which was subsequently repeated in the kitchen, tried to avoid getting involved by immediately leaving the room. Mary Meachlin, for example, a twenty-year-old spinster, testified that 'she had several times heard the said John Pratt abuse the said Mary Branham which when this deponent so heard she generally left the place where they were'.[68] Similarly, witnesses paid little interest to the insults made during a quarrel which erupted late one night in 1768 in a lodging house in the same parish over whether a door should be kept open or shut. Elizabeth Littlejohn initiated a prosecution in the consistory court, alleging that Mary Forshaw called her 'an hooknose whore', but her witnesses, both also residents in the house, showed very little interest in the case. John Holles said Littlejohn's character was not injured by the insult, and, while testifying that that Forshaw did call Littlejohn a whore 'and many other opprobrious names', he could not remember what any of the other insults were. Mary Brooks agreed Littlejohn's character was not injured, and also demonstrated complete lack of interest, testifying that 'she never troubles herself with the character or concerns of her neighbours'. Evident in this and many other cases is the apparently modern urban habit of having very little acquaintance with immediate neighbours: Brooks testified she was 'an entire stranger to her fellow witnesses', all of whom lived in the same house. When witnesses testified that they knew someone 'as a neighbour' in the eighteenth century, they often meant that they knew them hardly at all, often only by sight. In another case, Mary Roberts testified that, although the prosecutor was her neighbour, 'she has no particular acquaintance with but knows [her] as a neighbour'.[69] The power of insult to shape reputations could no longer function in a world where insults typically took place indoors and even then those who heard them often hardly knew each other and cared little about each other's activities. As Londoners became more selective about whom they formed their acquaintances with, the opinions of their neighbours became an increasingly unreliable basis on which to establish and defend reputations.

Evidence that the power and significance of the spoken insult declined in the eighteenth century can also be found in contemporary comment on defamation. We have seen that the belief that women were particularly prone to insult and scolding waned and this was reflected in judicial attitudes. Justice Whitelock Bulstrode told the Middlesex grand jury in 1718 that scolding only involved a 'silly woman' making 'a noise amongst her neighbours'; while this practice may grate on 'the tender and distinguishing ears of a wise person, [it] sinks no deeper'.[70] Although several works by social commentators decrying the prevalence of slander and the damage it caused were published in the seventeenth and early eighteenth centuries, these were published less often after 1715, and the emphasis of the texts changed. In 1663 William Gearing's *A Bridle for the Tongue: or A Treatise of Ten Sins of the Tongue* identified slander as one of several 'vices of the tongue' alongside swearing, cursing, lying, boasting, and similar sins. Gearing alleged that 'if ever men's tongues were set on fire with hell, it is in this age, and if profaneness, slanders, [etc.] were taken out of men's words, how few would remain!' In other texts, slanderers were branded 'incendiaries of all division in the neighbourhood, as also in Church and State', and their words were said to cause 'much deeper wounds ... than can be [given] by the sword: it being more pardonable manfully to seek to take away another's life, than basely to murder his good name.'[71] In contrast, later tracts described slander as more a failure of etiquette than a sin, and characterised it as damaging the reputation of the slanderer more than the person defamed. George Berkeley advised his female readers in *The Ladies' Library* (1714) that ''tis one of the worst characters a man or woman can have, to be maliciously curious in examining the actions of others,

only to censure them ... slander is quite opposite to politeness'. 'Without the consent of the world', Berkeley wrote, 'a scandal does not go
deep; it is only a slight stroke on the injur'd party, and returns with the
greater force upon those that gave it.' In 1737 women were told to avoid
'being the first in fixing a hard censure; let it be confirmed by the general
voice before you give into it; ... a virtue stuck with bristles is too rough
for this age'.[72] In eighteenth-century comment on defamation a new
concern emerges: slander motivated by religious or political motives.
Berkeley complained that, when it came to religious differences, 'all
parties seem to be agreed, that they do God a great service, in blasting
the reputation of their adversaries'. In 1706 Josiah Woodward argued
that 'a great cause' of slander 'is, that people of a party in any matter
appertaining to church or state, esteem it as a commendable piece of
service to their cause, to bespatter their opposites right or wrong'.[73]
Encouraged by the divisive party conflict of the early eighteenth century,
slander acquired a new type of public significance: in contrast to the
earlier concentration on personal behaviour, slander entered the largely
male realm of politics, where it undermined the reputations of those
who were already in the public eye.

For most people, however, the perceived power of slanderous words
was waning, as both men and women were reminded of the traditional
Christian principle that real merit was determined by internal character,
not the comments of others. Literature intended for gentlemen advised
them to worry less about their reputation, which could be easily damaged
by 'a junto of bad neighbours', and to pay attention instead to their
'real character ... intrinsic to himself, known to God, and approved by
his own conscience'. In 1745, in answer to the question, 'suppose a man
should give me the lie, or call me names, or abuse me with reproachful
language', *The New Whole Duty of Man* advised readers to refrain from
physical retribution or going to law, 'for such trifling offences as do
me no harm'. Forty years later, William Hutton, commenting on the
'ill usage' he had received during a visit to London, advised his readers
'to retreat with the insult'. When John Daws encountered David Davis
calling a 'little man' names on Ludgate Hill in 1793, he told the man
'not to regard him ... and advised him to go to the other side of the way'.
In the late eighteenth century, partly as a consequence of the Evangelical
emphasis on internal character rather than external reputation, many

people came to see honour as a private matter, unsuitable for public discussion.[74]

Londoners still valued their reputations at the end of the eighteenth century, but the ways in which they established and defended their reputations, and attacked those of others, had changed significantly, in ways which depended much less than before on what happened on the streets. To the extent that reputation was still determined externally, as opposed to the increasing role accorded to conscience, the opinions which shaped it were less often those of neighbours, who were often known only 'by sight', and more likely to be those of narrower reference groups, such as voluntary associations, religious congregations, or workplace and business contacts. In this context attacking the reputations of others came to be a more private affair, but in any case defamation had come to be seen as an impolite and indeed disreputable activity which called into question the character of the defamer rather than the defamed. People simply chose not to listen. For those in the public light where publicly established reputations still mattered, such as politicians, the spoken insult was still powerful, but printed libel became the most effective means of spreading political slander.[75] For some lower-class Londoners, the immediate local neighbourhood of the yard, alley and court continued to be the scene of gossip and insult,[76] but such activity no longer occurred London's 'public' streets. An early nineteenth-century print of Billingsgate fishwives engaging in a scolding match (Figure 7), portrays it as a quaint and ridiculous plebeian custom.

By the end of the century, Londoners had largely ceased publicly censuring their neighours' delinquencies with insults. It is not surprising that it was in England's largest city that the public insult declined first. Studies of other consistory courts show that defamation cases lasted somewhat longer in the provinces. In 1832 a Royal Commission noted that, though defamation cases were by then infrequent in London, 'they still prevail to a considerable extent in many of the jurisdictions in the country'.[77] Urban growth did not make city life 'anonymous', but it did change the relationship between the individual and the community by undermining the power of neighbourhoods to police individual behaviour. The declining role played by the community in policing London street life is nicely illustrated in the changing character of defamation

7. C. Williams, 'Scandal Refuted, or Billingsgate Virtue' (1818). (*Guildhall Library, Corporation of London*)

cases initiated by Londoners at sessions. Whereas during the Restoration there were numerous prosecutions of people who were thought to be damaging the community (*common* disturbers), and there were frequent complaints that insults had ruined the plaintiff's reputation in the community, in the eighteenth century repeated use of the terms 'mob', 'tumult' and 'rabble' to describe riotous defamers reveals concerns that the community, or at least part of it, was harming individuals. As the focus of prosecutions shifted to individual suffering, the community ceased to be identified as the victim of public misbehaviour and became instead perceived as its cause.

# 4

## *Shaming Punishments*

Public defamation was effective in early eighteenth-century London because insults attracted crowds, who publicly shamed those who were defamed. Similarly, official punishments frequently depended upon popular participation, with the public expected to act as witnesses and even to join in the punishment. Londoners watched while those convicted in the church courts were required to stand in a white sheet in the parish church during Sunday service, they witnessed many people convicted of petty theft whipped 'at the cart's tail' through the busy streets, and they went to Tyburn to see condemned felons executed. At the pillory, used for people convicted of 'unnatural' sexual offences and other notorious crimes such as seditious words, extortion, fraud and perjury, Londoners pelted the convict with a range of unsavoury objects. An important dimension of all these punishments was the damage to the convict's reputation which resulted from these humiliations. The public labelling of the recipient as deviant, an official version of the public insult, was intended to identify him or her as someone who could not be trusted, to place him or her outside respectable society. But these rituals could also restore reputations: with penance, the aim of the punishment was also to reestablish the reputation of the sinner, through his or her act of repentance. In defamation cases the reputation of the person defamed was also restored, through the retraction of and apology for the insult. This is even true of public executions, since the spectacle on the scaffold served both firmly to identify the culprit for posterity as a convicted felon, and, if he or she behaved appropriately, to rehabilitate him or her as a repentant sinner. In a world where reputations were established by what happened and what was said on the streets, the use of shame was perceived as a very powerful penal tool, not just for punishing offenders, but also for deterring future crime. In 1683 the Middlesex grand jury, confronted with a large number of indictments for assault initiated by the poor, recommended that those convicted should be punished by 'the old legal way of the ducking stool', since 'shame may do that which we find other punishment will not'.[1]

Public punishments, a characteristic feature of metropolitan life, contributed to the disorder on London's streets. Not only did they cause crowds to gather and participate in the destruction of the convict's reputation, but in the case of the pillory those present were actually encouraged to engage in violence. Moreover, as will become evident in the next chapter, these punishments were frequently imitated. Crowds which had arrested suspected criminals often did not hand them over to the authorities but directly punished them instead, often adopting the practices and symbolic vocabulary of official punishments. But just as over the course of the century crowds played a diminishing role in policing deviance, their role in public punishments also attenuated. For different reasons, both the authorities and the mob came to believe that for most criminals such punishments were no longer appropriate.

The judicial authorities ensured that public punishments achieved maximum impact by paying considerable attention to where and when they were staged. Penance, for example, was supposed to take place in the convict's (or victim's, in the case of defamation) parish church, in front of a large audience: the community gathered for Sunday worship. The sinner was expected to stand 'in a white sheet with a white wand in her hand and open faced with a paper of her accusation on her breast', first at the church door 'where most of the people enter the said church', and then in front of the congregation immediately after the service ended, where he or she was expected to confess and acknowledge the offence.[2] The pillory was usually set up in places such as Cheapside or Charing Cross, with markets and considerable traffic, and timed at midday when the streets were busiest.[3] In some cases it was set up near the scene of the crime, where victims or acquaintances of the convict were likely to be present. Jasper Arnold and William Goddard, for example, convicted in 1717 of tearing two pages out of the St Andrew Holborn register of marriages to eliminate evidence of Goddard's bigamous marriage, were sentenced to stand in the pillory in front of the church.[4] When Thomas Lyell and Lawrence Sydney were pilloried for defrauding several gentlemen with false and loaded dice at a masquerade, they stood in the Haymarket, 'facing the Opera House, the scene of their depredations'.[5] When the attorney Edward Aylett stood for perjury (he falsely claimed a legal privilege in order to escape arrest), the punishment took place in New Palace Yard, and the doors to Westminster Hall were thrown open so all the attorneys and barristers in the Hall could see him humiliated. The pillory turned so that 'he was exposed to view in different situations according to the direction of the sheriffs; but the greater part of his time was allotted to afford the gentlemen in the hall a complete view of his person'.[6] Those pilloried were expected not to wear hats, 'so that [they] may be known by the people'. When Christopher Atkinson, a contractor convicted of fraudulent dealing with the Navy Victualling Board, walked around in the pillory in front of the Corn Exchange in 1783 (Figure 8), his hat was removed and placed on top of the central pole around which the pillory turned. The nature of the offence was to be written on a paper and either stuck on the pillory or worn like a cravat,[7] though this requirement appears to have been implemented only erratically.

The pillory was reserved for the crimes which most threatened to disrupt public life, and thus required a public punishment. According to the jurist William Hawkins, it was for 'crimes of an infamous nature', such as those which offended 'against the first principles of natural justice, and common honesty'.[8] At the Old Bailey those so punished were typically found guilty of crimes involving deceit, undermining the judicial process, or flagrant violations of official norms (such as speaking seditious words, or engaging in sodomy). Most commonly they were convicted of violations of trust such as fraud, forgery, perjury and perverting the course of justice, and the punishment announced to the city that such people could not be trusted. Three men convicted of conspiring falsely to charge John Drinkwater with highway robbery (a capital offence) in 1737 were sentenced to stand twice in the pillory, once at the Royal Exchange and once at the end of Fetter Lane in Fleet Street, while Thomas Jones, alias James Derrick, convicted twice of obtaining goods from shops without payment by pretending to be a tailor's servant, was sentenced to stand in the pillory on Cheapside, as well as to be whipped and imprisoned in Newgate Prison for six months.[9]

Public whipping sentences 'until her [or his] back be bloody' were individually prescribed for each offender, along routes (typically one

hundred yards) that were often main thoroughfares in order to gain
maximum publicity. The convict was stripped to the waist, had his or
her hands tied to the back of a cart, and was dragged along the street
while being whipped from behind (Figure 9). In the seventeenth century
many of those punished in this way had been convicted of adultery or
prostitution,[10] but by the eighteenth century most were convicted of
petty larceny, usually on a partial verdict (by which the jury spared
those charged with capital offences the possibility of a death sentence
or transportation). The punishment was clearly meant to deter both the
culprit and others from committing further offences. In December 1741
the justices at the Middlesex sessions sentenced a man and two women
convicted of petty larceny to be whipped, respectively, as follows: from
the 'New Church' in the Strand through Drury Lane to St Giles High
Street; from one end of Monmouth Street in St Giles in the Fields to
the other end of the same street; and from Whitechapel Bars to Whitechapel Church.[11] These routes often began or ended at or near the scene
of the crime. Elizabeth Bond, found guilty of stealing three pewter pint
mugs from an alehouse in Leadenhall Street, was whipped for one
hundred yards in the same street.[12] Towards the end of the period those
convicted of theft from ships and warehouses were frequently whipped
on the docks and quays alongside the Thames; these locations were
clearly chosen in order to combat what was thought to be the growing
problem of dockside theft.[13]

The destruction of reputations through public punishments was further promoted by the active involvement of spectators. The crowd was
actively involved at the pillory; according to César de Saussure, 'the low
populace ... pelts the prisoner with mud, rotten apples, dead cats and
dogs, and that with such gusto and enjoyment that sufferers in some
cases have been removed in a very exhausted condition'. Also thrown
were excrement, rotten eggs, blood and guts from slaughterhouses, and
even bricks and stones (though this was illegal). Of course the response
of the crowd depended very much on its opinion of the nature of the
crime: as François Misson commented, 'if the people think there is
nothing very odious in the action that raised him to this honour, they
stand quietly by ... but if he has been guilty of some exploit disliked
by the tribe of 'prentices, he must expect to be regaled with a hundred
thousand handfuls of mud, and as many rotten eggs as can be got for

8. Christopher Atkinson in the Pillory (1783). (*University of Sheffield*)

the money'.[14] Unlike the pillory, the role of whipping audiences was largely limited to serving as observers. Through this public lesson about the consequences of crime, the publicity of whipping was clearly meant to influence the crowd as much as it did the convict. It is likely, however, that the severity with which the executioner wielded his whip depended on how loud the observers shouted. That the punishment was not always fully implemented is suggested by the fact that one whipping sentence from the Middlesex court, of an incorrigible rogue, particularly specified that 'the person who whips him is required to do his duty'. Sollom Emlyn complained in 1730 that it was 'in the power of the common hangman to make ... whipping as severe or as favourable as he pleases'. It seems likely therefore that the courts depended on the spectators to egg the executioner on.[15]

But perhaps the biggest role of the crowd in these punishments was for it to alter its opinion of the convict and spread the word that he or she could not be trusted. The damage to reputations from these punishments could be more serious than the physical injuries sustained. In 1691 two men managed to get their sentence to the pillory remitted because, they told the justices, if so punished 'they would be exposed to the mercy of the rabble and the scandal of their friends'. Isaac Broderick, pilloried for attempted sodomy in 1730, complained of having to stand 'in so ignominious a manner, exposed to the eyes and censures of thousands'.[16] This infamy could last long after the cuts and bruises healed. In petitioning the Middlesex justices in 1725 to keep Mary O'Bryan bound over by recognizance for suspected theft, Margaret Fox described O'Bryan as 'an old offender [who] was pilloried at Charing Cross in the late Queen's reign for forgery' – the punishment was still remembered, despite the fact it had occurred at least ten years earlier.[17] The existence of underworld slang for those who had been pilloried also indicates that popular memory of who had been punished lasted a long time: those who had stood were called 'stoop nappers' or, perhaps in an ironic comment on the contrast between this barbaric punishment and London's improving streets, 'overseers of the new pavement'.[18] Dr Johnson commented that even if one had been well treated on the pillory one's reputation could still be in tatters: 'people are not very willing to ask a man to their tables who has stood in the pillory'.[19] Whipping could also destroy reputations. In 1768 William Cranmer

The manner of Whipping at the Carts Tayle
For petty Larceny and other Offences

9. 'The Manner of Whipping at the Carts Tayle for Petty Larceny and Other Offences' (c. 1678). (*Guildhall Library, Corporation of London*)

petitioned the Middlesex court for remission of his sentence 'not only with regard to himself (who is of a very weakly constitution) but also for the great scandal that will [be inflicted] on his honest and creditable relations and friends that reside thereabout'.[20]

The most public punishments in eighteenth-century London, which attracted the largest crowds, were of course executions. Most hangings were staged outside the built-up area at Tyburn (where Marble Arch now stands), but some notorious criminals were executed near the scene of their crimes. James Hall, convicted of petty treason for murdering his master in 1741, was executed in the Strand, 'where the fact was committed', and the gibbet was raised 'to an extraordinary height [35 feet], the better to expose so notorious a fellow to the view of the spectators'. As the *London Journal* reported, 'the streets were lined with an innumerable crowd of spectators, curious to behold so execrable a wretch ... Opposite to the gallows in the Strand a scaffold was so loaded with spectators, that it broke down.'[21] Hangings were typically preceded by a long procession from Newgate Prison through London's crowded streets, to which Londoners were summoned by the muffled ringing of church bells and the cries of hawkers selling the convicts' 'last dying speeches'. Huge crowds gathered at Tyburn, and those who could afford to sat on raised stands. Before the execution, the condemned were allowed to speak to the crowd in the expectation that they would confess their crimes and repent their sins. Together, the condemned and the crowd sang the fifty-first psalm.[22] Public participation in this punishment was more circumscribed than in the case of the pillory, since the primary purpose of the publicity was to teach the *crowd* a lesson, in order to prevent further crime. But the death penalty was also perceived as shameful, and carrying it out in public contributed to the disgrace of the convict and his or her family. Around 1708 Barbara Mawgridge petitioned for a pardon for her husband, who had been sentenced to death for murder. She hoped he might be transported, 'rather than [he] should suffer that most ignominious death ... to the utter ruin, shame, and disgrace of your petitioner and her family'.[23] Despite the lessons taught by this carefully constructed ritual, crime continued to be perceived as a serious problem, and in 1752 the 'Murder Act', in order to add 'some further terror and peculiar mark of infamy ... to the punishment of death', mandated that the bodies of murderers should be dissected by the surgeons following the hanging.[24] Not only were such dissections carried out in public, but many people believed that the dismembering of the bodies would prevent them from reappearing at the Resurrection.

Although whippings and hangings continued, the significance of public punishments began to decline in eighteenth-century London. Some shaming punishments had already fallen out of use: no one was sentenced to sit in the stocks or on a ducking stool.[25] Over the course of the century the ways in which the main public punishments were conducted changed, in the sense that their use was constricted and their public impact diminished, as damaging reputations lost its power as a form of punishment. Although the specific chronologies vary, this transformation affected penance, the pillory, whipping and even hanging.

The practice of public penance largely disappeared. In cases of fornication and bastard-bearing the guilty party did continue to stand in a white sheet, first outside the church and then in front of the congregation, but only a small number of people were convicted of these offences in the church courts in the eighteenth century. Already at the start of our period most penances for defamation (the most common offence punished in these courts) were conducted in parish vestries, not the church itself, in the presence not of the entire congregation but of only the minister, churchwardens and the victim, as well as five or six of his or her friends, 'if they be there otherwise in their absence'.[26] By the early eighteenth-century the public dimension of this punishment had thus been largely removed.[27] This may explain why it was sometimes treated with contempt by those expected to perform it: several times they repeated the insults which had led to their convictions for defamation just before or after they conducted the penance.[28] The publicity of the punishment was further eroded in the 1790s by the tendency of the Consistory Court to forego penance in cases of defamation if, after conviction, the parties reached a private agreement resolving their dispute. In 1831 the Royal Commission investigating the church courts found that they had 'very rarely required the performance of public penance'.[29] Private settlements had superseded public humiliation and repentance.

The pillory, on the other hand, by definition could only be used in public, and it continued to be used sporadically throughout the eighteenth and early nineteenth centuries, punishing an average of about five people per year in the metropolis, with a temporary surge to more than ten per year in the 1750s and 1760s.[30] Nonetheless, the range of offences punished was increasingly restricted. Deeming the punishment insufficient for the crime of forgery (seen as a serious crime which posed a growing threat to commerce), a 1729 statute mandated the death penalty rather than the pillory.[31] Doubts about the punishment are evident in the sentencing patterns for those convicted of other crimes which had historically been punished with a stint on the pillory. From the 1730s only one or two people a year were sentenced to the pillory at the Old Bailey, and by the 1760s this had been reduced around five a decade; most of those pilloried were convicted of lesser offences at quarter sessions. No one convicted at the Old Bailey was pilloried for seditious words after 1725, and it was rarely used for sodomy after 1749; the punishment was reserved primarily for fraud, perjury and perverting the course of justice. From the 1730s almost everyone sentenced to the pillory at the Old Bailey was also sentenced to one or more other punishments, typically a fine or imprisonment, or both, indicating that the courts felt that by itself the pillory was an insufficient punishment. Doubts about its efficacy contributed to the passage of a statute in 1816, which restricted the use of the pillory to perjury only, and to the abolition of the punishment in 1837.[32]

Whipping was the next punishment to lose some of its public impact. In the first three decades of the century the vast majority of whippings sentenced by the justices at sessions and the judges at the Old Bailey (excluding those administered as part of the separate punishment of incarceration in a house of correction) were intended to be carried out in the traditional manner at 'a cart's tail' along a length of street. But from the 1720s sentences began to differentiate between what was some-times referred to as 'private whipping' on the one hand, and 'open' or 'public' whipping on the other.[33] A range of sentences evolved with varying degrees of publicity, including sentences carried out in prison or a house of correction, those performed at a public whipping post outside a prison or courthouse, and the traditional whipping at 'a cart's tail' through a street. Given the large number of visitors found in prisons in this period, whippings there were by no means entirely private,[34] but the audiences were clearly much more restricted than those which witnessed outdoor whippings (Figure 10). Indeed, when the Middlesex justices sentenced several offenders to the house of correction to be whipped before discharge in 1724 and 1725, they sought greater publicity for the sentence by ordering it 'to be published in a public newspaper for the terror of evil-disposed persons'.[35]

The abandonment of whipping through the streets for many offenders is evident in the differential fees claimed by sheriffs for carrying out the punishment, first evident in 1757. Whereas the sheriff claimed £3 for arranging the whipping of offenders through a specified length of street, he claimed only £1 for those for whom no place was specified; the latter were either whipped at an outdoor whipping post (there was one on Clerkenwell Green, next to the Sessions House, and another outside the Old Bailey), or they were whipped in prison (this was sometimes referred to as 'private whipping'). No doubt the extra expense of whipping through the streets reflected the need for policing the spectators, as well as the cost of hiring a horse and cart. In 1788, when the level of fees had increased, a ruling on sheriff's expenses specified that £3 was to be allowed 'for all common whipping, whether public (as at Clerkenwell Green, etc) or private, and £6 for whipping at a cart's tail or for distance'.[36]

The shift towards private whipping took a dramatic turn around 1780. In the sheriff's cravings (expense claims submitted to the Exchequer), about half the whippings were recorded as taking place on the streets or at a public whipping post between 1730 and 1779, but in the 1780s and 1790s the proportion whipped in public declined to about a quarter, and then to only 18 per cent in the first decade of the nineteenth century.[37] By 1780 slang had adapted to the new repertoire of punishments: whippings in the Sessions House Yard were termed 'the scrobey' (derived perhaps from 'scrub'), while receiving the punishment privately was referred to as 'to hap the teize'; 'teize' was an obscure form of 'flog', while 'hap' meant by chance or fortune, suggesting the convict's good fortune at avoiding public whipping.[38] By this point, however, private whipping had become the default choice. In the 1783 trial of William Jenkins, for stealing twenty-nine live rabbits, the jury which convicted him suggested he 'should be whipped through Knightsbridge'. Justice Willes replied, however, 'I have a great objection to a public whipping ... unless a man is quite abandoned I never give him a public whipping;

let him be privately whipped twice with severity and discharged'. In the sheriff's cravings for 1790 whipping at a cart's tail was now described as 'extraordinary whipping'.[39]

Those explicitly sentenced to a public whipping were those whose offences were deemed particularly egregious (such as a man who spat at the Princess of Wales in 1719), involved breaches of trust (such as thefts by servants from their employers), were of particular concern (such as thefts from docks and warehouses), or involved open defiance of the law. When Mary Cowen was convicted at the Old Bailey of stealing a pocket book and tobacco pouch worth seven pence in 1761, 'she used very impudent indecent language; on which account she received sentence immediately, to be publicly whipped on the Thursday following' in the busy streets 'from the corner of St Paul's Church to the place where Ludgate stood'.[40] Initially, private whippings were used when the court wished to show mercy to the convict, because it was a first offence, done out of necessity, the convict was ill, or he or she had shown previous good character. When John Aberall was convicted of the theft of two shirts to the value of ten pence in 1727, 'he had several to appear for him, who gave him an extraordinary character'. Consequently, 'the court was so merciful as to order that he should only have some private correction'. Circumstances like these, however, do not explain why the basic sentencing strategy of the courts shifted from public to private whippings over the course of the century. Even stationary whippings outside the Old Bailey or Sessions House became in a sense less visible, as the whipping posts were removed when not in use. In the plans for the new Middlesex Sessions House built next to Clerkenwell Green in 1785, the justices called for a post which could 'be removed occasionally'; by 1790 the sheriff's charges for carrying out whippings there included a charge for setting it up.[41]

Similar changes took place in the method of conducting public executions. In 1759 the permanent gallows at Tyburn were removed and temporary scaffolds were erected before each execution day. In 1783 executions were moved from Tyburn to outside Newgate Prison, thereby eliminating the traditional turbulent two mile long procession from Newgate to Tyburn. Just as some whippings were administered outside the Sessions House or the Old Bailey, after 1783 executions were carried out on a scaffold erected immediately outside Newgate Prison. Although

10. 'Flogging at the Old Bailey' (1809). (*University of Sheffield*)

these could still attract large crowds, only 5000 observers could be accommodated, and crowds were discouraged from gathering by the fact that executions now took place early in the day. Moreover, new arrangements separated the crowd from those punished and expedited the process. Convicts were only exposed to the crowd shortly before their execution, their 'last dying speeches' were discouraged, and a new form of the 'drop' killed them more quickly. The tolling of a 'funeral bell' in Newgate threatened to drown out the sounds of the crowd. The routine sale of the 'last dying speeches' of those executed had ceased in the 1760s, part of a more general decline in published literature about the lives of common criminals, thereby further diminishing the public impact of executions.[42] Although hangings continued to take place outdoors until they were moved inside Newgate Prison in 1868, these eighteenth-century changes served to reduce the involvement of the public.[43]

By 1800 most public punishments were still in use, but the range of offences punished was in many cases reduced, and the role of the public was severely constrained. Overall penal strategies shifted considerably in the eighteenth century as ideas about the possibility of reforming convicts became influential, but these were not fully implemented in penal practice until the next century.[44] The new penal philosophy, first evident to a minor extent in transportation but more extensively implemented with the growing use of imprisonment from the 1770s, operated on very different principles from traditional shaming punishments. Instead of injuring their bodies and damaging their reputations, the new punishments sought to reform convicts from the inside out by changing their frame of mind.[45] Although stimulated by enlightenment and evangelical thought, the new punishments would not have been so widely adopted if considerable dissatisfaction with the existing repertoire of public punishments had not already existed. There were a number of causes of this dissatisfaction, including growing hostility to the use of physical violence, concerns about public order, and worries about crowds undermining the moral messages of these punishments; but it is also necessary to consider the attitudes of those who were expected to form the audience for these rituals: the mob.

Along with the increasing intolerance of physical violence in other contexts (such as wife beating and dueling),[46] there is evidence among late eighteenth-century enlightened opinion of 'a fundamental rejection of punishments that were violent in themselves or that encouraged public violence', an aspect of an increasing cultural intolerance of violence which emerged at this time.[47] Patrick Colquhoun was keen to limit the suffering incurred by those who were whipped when he advised constables in 1803 that the punishment was solely meant 'as an example to others to abstain from criminal offences' and was 'not an act of resentment to the delinquent who suffers. This unpleasant duty should therefore be executed so as to make a proper impression on those who witness the punishment, without exercising a greater degree of severity than is necessary to obtain that object.' Similarly, echoing a parliamentary speech made by Edmund Burke in 1780, Colquhoun argued that the pillory was 'not intended for personal suffering, according to the will or unrestrained licence of a turbulent populace'.[48] The idea that pillory crowds should not inflict personal suffering, or that those whipped should only suffer minimally, would have seemed preposterous to most eighteenth-century Londoners, but attitudes were changing. The few occasions on which people were killed on the pillory encouraged further concerns about crowd violence. Following the brutal treatment of two of the thief-takers from the McDaniel gang in 1756, an observer complained that the 'mob' had acted like animals: 'it is not so truly the greatness of the crime which inflames them, as the scent of the carnage; and now, by one murder, they have got a taste for blood, it is high time that they should be considered as dogs ... and that no more victims should be exposed to their resentment'.[49]

The increasing sensitivity to the use of violence in public punishments was especially marked when the victims were women, for whom such public punishments effectively ended long before the public whipping of women was abolished by statute in 1817. From the 1770s the number of women whipped in public or pilloried declined dramatically, and no women were sentenced to either punishment in London after 1798.[50] The authorities were clearly worried about administering corporal punishments on women in public, particularly in the presence of men. In 1783 Mary Siddon alias Field, convicted of the theft of a pork ham, was sentenced to be 'severely and privately whipped, in the presence of females only'.[51] In 1790 the practice of burning women convicted of petty treason at the stake was abolished by statute. It had been described in 1777 as 'a violation of that natural decency and delicacy inherent, and at all times to be cherished in the [female] sex'. In practice, this punishment had already been mitigated by the fact that, after 1726, such women had been killed first by strangulation. In the 1780s the woman's corpse was totally covered in faggots before the fire was lit. It was no longer acceptable to expose women's bodies publicly in this way. Women, even convicts, were increasingly seen as victims of their weaker natures and therefore as deserving of sympathy, while male judges sought to display their power and chivalry by exercising mercy.[52]

Support for whipping as a punishment for men continued well into the nineteenth century. Public whipping of men apparently ended in the 1830s, though it was not formally abolished until 1861.[53] Nonetheless, most whippings occurred indoors and were apparently only targeted at the lower classes, notably the rank and file of the army.[54] As has been argued with respect to capital punishment, it was elite squeamishness about witnessing violence, rather than disapproval of violence against men *per se*, which explains elite discomfort with corporal punishment.[55] As one contemporary commentator wrote in 1813 following the violent pillorying of the Vere Street gang for sodomy, the offence merited death, but it should be carried out without permitting such 'disgusting spectacles', which offend 'female delicacy and manly feeling'.[56]

There were also of course serious concerns about the maintenance of order during public punishments, particularly at the pillory. From the start of the eighteenth century sheriff's officers, constables and their assistants were routinely summoned to attend, and they formed a ring of protection around the pillory. The number of officers deployed seems to have fluctuated depending on the sheriff's judgement of the extent of disorder expected. In some cases, even early in the period, large numbers of extra officers were summoned. When William Fuller stood three times in the pillory in 1703 for political libel, 'a great many constables and watchmen' were present on the first day, and on the second 'sheriff's officers and others [were] laid tightly about [the pillory] for [his] defence'. When John Middleton stood in the pillory in 1723 for attempting to earn rewards by making false accusations of treasonable practices, such was the popular hostility against him that the high constable summoned twenty constables and 104 assistants to protect him, though even this number could not prevent the crowd from smothering him to death with dirt. As this suggests, the officers occasionally misjudged the number of guards required: when Henry Groves stood for defrauding tradesmen of thousands of pounds in 1755, 'the constables were obliged, in order to save themselves, to leave him to the resentment of the populace'.[57] In some cases where the officers were content to see the offender attacked by the crowd, their efforts at protection appear to have been minimal. After a sheriff's officer, Mr Watson, placed Middleton in the pillory (incorrectly, as it turned out), he went to a tavern to drink a pint of wine, leaving him under the protection of the constables with no one in charge. Watson later confessed 'he was acquainted with the persons against whom Middleton had sworn falsely ... and that he had said to Middleton now he had got him he hoped he should have his true, meaning his due'.[58] In contrast, when they wanted to, the authorities could sometimes maintain perfect order. The reason why two of the thief-takers pilloried in 1756, Stephen McDaniel and John Berry, were well protected, while the other two were violently attacked, was that the former possessed damaging information which the authorities did not want released.[59]

The authorities remained in control of the crowd. Sollom Emlyn claimed in 1730 that officers could 'effectually' protect men on the pillory when they 'find an advantage in it'.[60] When Aylett stood in the pillory outside Westminster Hall in 1786 for perjury, the sheriff took 'uncommon pains ... to preserve the peace, there being every reason to believe that but for the precaution used the prisoner's life would have been taken by the mob'. This included the hiring of thirty-four sheriff's officers and about 550 petty constables, as well as paying the scavenger to clean Palace Yard in advance to prevent the crowd from having anything to throw. Why Aylett was afforded such intense protection, which meant that no one was allowed even to attempt to throw anything at him, is unclear. (The *Times* described Aylett as 'respectable', and suggested that his wealth protected him.)[61] But the sheriff clearly tried to turn the occasion to his financial advantage, claiming a total of £105 expenses, including coffee for the officers and dinner and drinks at a local tavern. The Treasury allowed only £51 4s., less than half the sum claimed.[62]

Although it is sometimes claimed that the problem of maintaining order during public punishments increased during the eighteenth century,[63] there is little evidence that disorder was a *growing* problem. Although the crowds which gathered at Tyburn may have become larger, there were few riots, especially after 1749 when the sheriffs began to oversee the cutting down of bodies following executions, thereby preventing squabbles between the convicts' families and friends and the surgeons' assistants who wished to seize the bodies for dissection.[64] The main reason why hangings were shifted to Newgate in 1783 was not concern about disorder but the fact that London was growing north and west towards Tyburn, and developers sought to increase property values. Another reason advanced was concern about the economic cost of the lost labour of all the spectators.[65]

It is of course difficult to measure crowd disorder over time, for the evidence is limited and perceptions of violence are subjective. Accounts differ of William Holdbrook's experience of standing in the pillory in Bloomsbury Market in 1719 for attempted sodomy. The *Original Weekly Journal* reported that 'the mob had certainly murdered him could they have got him in their power, for a hackney coach was tore to pieces that took him up to carry him to Newgate'. The fact that he was only pelted with rotten eggs and cucumbers, however, suggests that the crowd did not intend to harm him seriously.[66] The number of reported deaths and near-deaths on the pillory in London did not increase over the century.[67] The lack of greater disorder at the end of our period was partly the result of more systematic policing, but it is important to note that the pillory was policed, and crowds were capable of inflicting brutal violence, *throughout* the century. When Middleton stood in 1723 several constables claimed they attempted to prevent the crowd from throwing *any* dirt at him. That he died in the pillory was due both to the vigorous efforts of an angry crowd and the neglect or complicity of the sheriff's officers. The accounts of his death, as well as those of the crowd's treatment of William Fuller in 1703 and John Waller in 1732, are every bit as gruesome as accounts of the pelting of the Vere Street gang in 1810, when the six men convicted of sodomy were attacked by upwards of fifty women 'who assailed them incessantly with mud, dead cats, rotten eggs, potatoes, and buckets filled with blood, offal, and dung'. They were also pelted on their way back to prison: 'the wretches were so thickly covered with filth, that a vestige of the human figure was scarcely discernible ... some of them were cut in the head with brickbats, and bled profusely'. Almost eighty years earlier, Waller was similarly pelted with 'large quantities of cabbage, collyflowers, and artichoak-stalks'. After eight minutes, the crowd managed to pull down the pillory, and the fall fractured his skull. As he lay on the ground the crowd 'stamped so hard on his body, that they broke his ribs'.[68]

What seems clear is that *sensitivity* to disorder on the pillory and at hangings increased over time. When William Smith died on the pillory in Southwark in 1780, the *Gentleman's Magazine* ascribed this to 'the severity of the mob', and Edmund Burke raised the case in the House of Commons. He complained that the pillory had become 'an instrument of death', blamed the death on the 'mob', and asked that the punishment be abolished. But it appears that the true cause of Smith's death was the fact that, as was possibly the case with Middleton, the pillory was improperly set up, with 'the hole for his neck too high, and only his toes touched the stand'. As his widow complained, he 'was absolutely hung in the pillory'.[69] Evidence of a lowering tolerance of disorder also comes from manuals for constables, which, after failing to mention anything about officers' duties to maintain order at the pillory for most of the eighteenth century, instruct the constable attending the pillory in 1790 and 1803 'to do his utmost to preserve the peace, and to prevent all outrage or violence towards the offender from taking place'.[70] Judicial concerns about pillory violence in cases where the offender was a likely target of popular hostility may have contributed to a decline in the number of felons who received this sentence. This is why Jonathan Mann, convicted in 1780 of perjury in his testimony against some of the Gordon rioters (which led to their convictions and death sentences), was spared this punishment. According to the judge, Baron Eyre, 'one part of the punishment for perjury ought to be making you stand in the pillory; but if I were to execute that part of the law, I know the consequence of it would be – I should deliver you over to the fury of a justly incensed multitude, who would take your punishment into their own hands ... I dare not do that'.[71]

Another official concern regarding crowd behaviour at the pillory was the fear that, instead of reviling and attacking the convict, the crowd would subvert judicial intentions and applaud him or her and donate refreshments and money. In 1703 Daniel Defoe was famously pelted with flowers, and when Robert Harrison was placed in the pillory for speaking seditious words in 1718 a vast mob gathered, 'which did generally seem to countenance the prisoner giving him small money and huzzaing him' so that the officers present were afraid he would be rescued. One of the most active among the mob, Catherine Priest, allegedly 'damn[ed] the court and the jury who condemned the said Harrison'. Similarly, John Williams, pilloried for republishing the seditious forty-fifth issue of John Wilkes's *North Briton* in 1765, was given two hundred guineas which had been collected from the crowd.[72] Such subversions of the judicial process naturally caused concern. In 1756 a correspondent in the *Gentleman's Magazine* called attention to the inconsistency that 'butchers' drovers' and the like should determine the extent of punishment for those standing in the pillory, 'when the most substantial master butcher in England is by our laws deemed incapable of serving as a juror in matters of life and death'.[73] In fact, incidents in which crowds praised, rather than pelted, those on the pillory did not occur at all in the last quarter of the century, largely because judges ceased to sentence those found guilty of sedition to the pillory.[74] In 1793 the radical John Frost, convicted of seditious words, was sentenced to imprisonment and to stand on the pillory, but concerns about how the crowd would behave led the judges to remit the pillory portion of his sentence. This was a wise judgement, for according to Francis Place when Frost was released from prison 'the crowd pulled his coach through the streets' in his honour.[75] Owing to judicial caution, by the end of the century the pillory could no longer be turned into a vehicle for popular protest.

Like the pillory, popular responses to whippings and executions varied, depending on the nature of the crime and the identity of the convict. Audiences for the whipping of petty thieves could be sympathetic to the offender and some 'hooted at or jostled' the executioner. In one case, a man about to be whipped 'threw some money against the mob, who thereupon pressed so close on the executioner, that he had not power to strike ten times during the whole length of the way'. Perhaps expecting lenient treatment, those sentenced to be whipped viewed it lightly: when tried for the theft of a hay-fork and a pair of stockings in 1735, John Brown told the court 'this is my first fact, and I hope you'll get me off to shove the tumbler's arse'.[76] At executions, crowds were hostile towards those who were 'least like themselves', owing to the egregious nature of the crimes they committed or because of their high social standing. When Barbara Spencer was saying her prayers before being burned at the stake in 1721 for counterfeiting coins, she was attacked by clods of dirt and stones thrown by the crowd. Those who failed to exhibit the expected penitence were also attacked: Samuel Gregory, convicted on six charges of burglary, robbery and rape in 1735, had dirt thrown at him after he 'behaved in a bold, impudent, senseless manner, talking during the prayers to the people in the cart' (who were also going to be executed). But the execution of Jonathan Wild, the thief-taker whose perjured evidence led to numerous hangings, occasioned the biggest crowd hostility:

> so outrageous were the mob in their joy to behold him on the road to the gallows ... that they huzza'd him to the Triple Tree, and showed a temper very uncommon on such a melancholy occasion, for they threw stones at him ... with some of which his head was broke ... nay, even in his last moments they did not cease their insults.[77]

But such behaviour was clearly unusual. Also rare were crowd protests in favour of those about to be executed, though when participants in riots were hanged the authorities took extra care to ensure an adequate guard was present. The executions of those convicted for their participation in the Gordon Riots were staged in a variety of locations throughout London, not only in order to maximise publicity but also to prevent large crowds from forming.[78] In 1751 Henry Fielding complained that crowd support for the executed was near-universal: 'the day appointed by law for the thief's shame is the day of glory in his own opinion. His procession to Tyburn, and his last moments there, are all triumphant; attended with the compassion of the meek and tender-hearted, and with the applause, admiration, and envy of all the bold and hardened.' More commonly, however, commentators noted that crowds appeared to treat executions as if they provided the opportunity for a holiday. Hangings were the subject of jokes, while some convicts dressed as if they were going to a wedding. The Swiss visitor César de Saussure commented in 1726 that 'one often sees criminals going to their death perfectly unconcerned, others so impenitent that they fill themselves full of liquor and mock at those who are repentant', and the crowd appears to have often adopted similar attitudes. Bernard

Mandeville described the procession to Tyburn as 'one continued fair, for whores and rogues of the meaner sort', and the place of execution as 'the most remarkable scene ... a vast multitude ... that are either abusing one another, or else staring at the prisoners'. Similarly, Fielding described execution day as 'a holyday to the greatest part of the mob about town ... all the avenues to Tyburn appear like those to a wake or festival, where idleness, wantonness, drunkenness, and every other species of debauchery are gratified'.[79]

Certainly images of eighteenth-century hangings at Tyburn, most of which are based on plate 11 of William Hogarth's 'Industry and Idleness' (1747) (Figure 11), show raucous crowds apparently enjoying numerous opportunities for fun and deviance. But we shouldn't take the carnival-esque appearance of these scenes too literally. Popular beliefs in the magical powers of the corpse, the convict's clothing and the hangman's noose testify to popular recognition of the powerful significance of executions. Faced with the terrifying sight of men and women writhing and dying slowly on the gallows, Londoners could not help but take these events seriously, and they coped with the horror by 'staring' (in Mandeville's words) or through various strategies of denial, diversion or pity.[80] As Fielding admitted, crowd sympathy for those executed was almost inevitable: 'to unite the ideas of death and shame is not so easy as may be imagined'. As the *General Evening Post* reported referring to the execution of some of the Gordon rioters, 'the behaviour of the ... unhappy wretches was such as excited pity from the gaping multitude ... The decent behaviour [of two of them] ... drew tears from many.'[81] Such sympathy, however, did not extend to active hostility towards the authorities; crowd disorder at executions was not a serious problem.

Changing attitudes towards violence, new expectations concerning public order, and crowd sympathy for those punished certainly help explain the decline of public punishments in eighteenth-century London. But these issues should not be overemphasized, given the continued use of violence in punishments carried out in private, and the apparent lack of increase in either disorder or vocal crowd support for those punished. Moreover, these factors cannot explain the changes which occurred in the administration of penance, where issues of violence and crowd

disorder did not arise. It is possible that in this case the crucial factor
was the declining interest of the potential audience (the congregation)
in observing this ritual, and this highlights the point that we need to
pay more attention to the views of the crowd itself concerning the merits
and significance of these types of punishment. While there may have
been increasing sympathy for the punished in some circles, other Londoners were losing interest in watching convicts suffer. Although they
may have continued to join the audiences for public punishments, they
became less willing to become subsumed into the crowd, and actively
to engage in heaping abuse on the convict, unless they had specific views
about the particular case.

There is some evidence, for example, that whippings failed to make
the expected impact on their audience. The paucity of surviving eyewitness accounts of public whippings (compared to the larger number
of accounts of the pillory and executions) suggests that audiences were
either small or unimpressed by what they saw. In 1786 the *Times*
complained that as a punishment whipping was 'so trifling, as to be
only a matter of merriment, even to the persons on whom it is inflicted'.
Although the paper goes on to comment that 'the ceremony generally
collects four or five hundred blackguards, and journeymen mechanics,
who wait for hours in the Sessions House Yard, thereby losing the best
part of their day in idleness', the implication is that these spectators
viewed the occasion primarily as a means of avoiding work.[82] Rather
than reinforcing a moral community by reasserting collective disapproval of deviance, public whippings came to be ignored or treated as a
form of merriment.

With the pillory, whose impact as a punishment depended fundamentally on the crowd playing its allotted role in shaming the convict, there
were legal doubts about its popular impact from early in the century.
During the tenure of Chief Justice John Holt there was much discussion
about whether standing in the pillory (and, in theory, the consequent
destruction of one's reputation) automatically disqualified someone
from testifying as a witness in court, and in 1700 it was ruled that it did
not: 'it is not the nature of the punishment, but the nature of the crime
and conviction, that creates the infamy'.[83] In a forgery case involving
counterfeit notes for thousands of pounds tried in 1729, the prosecuting
attorney complained that the damage to one's reputation incurred by

11. William Hogarth, 'Industry and Idleness', plate 11: 'The Idle 'Prentice Executed at Tyburn' (1747). (*Tim Hitchcock*)

standing in the pillory was an insufficient punishment for so notorious an offence: Sergeant Whitaker told the judge 'the pillory, my lord, is nothing'. Later that year Parliament passed the statute making forgery punishable by death.[84] The fact that the judges at the Old Bailey rarely sentenced convicted felons to the pillory after 1760 further supports the view that audience-imposed shame was no longer seen as effective as it once was.

During the second half of the century audiences lost interest in the pillory. Some Londoners ignored the punishment when they encountered it as they were going about the streets. When the McDaniel gang of thief-takers stood in 1756, newspaper reports document a porter attempting to carry some wire *through* the crowd (he lost the wire) and some drovers chasing a bullock nearby (they 'overdrove' it and it charged into the crowd). When John Stephens, a tailor, was 'going through Russell Street' one morning thirty years later, he encountered a crowd watching someone standing in the pillory. Rather than join the crowd, he described it as an obstruction that prevented him from continuing on his way. While trying to make it through the crowd, he had his pocket picked. In 1790 John Turnage experienced the same misfortune as he was walking at two in the afternoon, just as two men were completing their stint on the pillory; as he told the court, 'I was going down Berkley [sic] Square, just facing Berkley Street; I did not want to see the sight, but it was when the men were in the pillory ... there was a vast crowd ... I did not know the men were to stand in the pillory that day'.[85] Although the pillory continued to attract crowds, the principal actors in all these cases showed no interest in the punishment and simply sought to carry on with their business.

Observers also noted changes in the character of the crowds surrounding the pillory. In 1829 Francis Place claimed that, over the previous several decades, a change had occurred in their behaviour, as crowds largely ceased to throw things: while 'formerly there were always on these occasions a sufficiently large number to keep one another in countenance and encourage the more debased "to keep up the game" ... latterly the pelting was confined to what were considered the most atrocious offences only'. Those who tried to attack 'men whose crimes were almost venial, or those whose imputed offences were political, were restrained by the better portion of the spectators, and the constables, and pelting at length was almost wholly limited to men convicted of attempts to commit unnatural crimes'.[86] At least some members of the crowd had adopted more restrained patterns of behaviour. In any case, since by this time very few sodomites were actually sentenced to the pillory, attacks on those who stood became rare. An anonymous tract published around 1820 commented with respect to the pillory, 'how little real disgrace attaches to this exposure', and noted that even when 'the surrounding populace' sought to condemn the offender, they know 'that even in that case, *the law permits not a hand to be raised against him*, [and] will be satisfied with confirming the justice of his sentence with hisses and groans'.[87] A man whose pocket was picked when viewing a man in the pillory in 1780 told the court 'there was a great crowd *observing* the man in the pillory'.[88] Late eighteenth-century illustrations of the pillory do not depict the crowd throwing things and the spectators generally appear passive. In Paul Sandby's image of a 'sock vendor', composed around 1759 (Figure 12), a man in the background stands in the pillory surrounded by a small number of people who pay scant attention to his plight (though it appears that a dead cat has been thrown past his left ear). In contrast, a depiction of Defoe in the pillory in 1703 presents a much more chaotic scene.[89] Whether this change in crowd behaviour was due to higher standards of public conduct or decreasing crowd interest is unclear, but in the second half of the century the pillory was apparently no longer the instrument of shame that it once was.[90]

With the increased policing of the pillory, also depicted in the prints, the role of the crowd was in any case downgraded; we have seen how limited a role was accorded to the spectators when Aylett stood in 1783. With the pillory surrounded by a large cordon of officers there was little left for the spectators to do. Francis Place describes how at Charing Cross the constables 'permitted a number of women to pass between them, into the open space around the pillory'. Only these women, as moral agents of the community, were able to pelt the offender, supplied with materials handed to them by other spectators.[91] Moreover, with improved cleansing of the streets over the course of the century, there was less material immediately available to throw – in sharp contrast to 1723, when the crowd found so much dirt and mire on the streets to throw at Middleton that they left him in a pile two feet deep.[92] Later in the century if the crowd was to have ammunition, it had to be sufficiently organised to bring its own, or purchase rotten refuse from hucksters who had identified a marketing opportunity.

Reports in the *Times* in the 1790s of people standing in the pillory include no mention of crowd hostility, despite potentially provocative behaviour by those supposedly being punished. A man standing in 1796 for the attempted rapes of two children, a crime which normally attracted considerable crowd violence, laughed at and scorned the spectators, while in 1797 an attorney (also unlikely to be popular with the crowd) treated the punishment lightly, wearing a black suit and his 'natural-curled wig'.[93] Either these men relied on crowd apathy or they were confident the constables would protect them from crowd hostility; in either case they do not appear to have been ashamed of their presence on the pillory. There is also some evidence that the intended communal nature of pillory punishments was disrupted by particular groups of people dominating the crowd. Supporters of the prosecutor or the convict (or thugs hired by them) could attempt to direct the crowd's response. When Tousant Urvoy stood in the pillory at the Old Bailey for perjury in 1761, 'some of the mob began to pelt him, according to their usual custom, but were soon prevented by a party of butchers, who drove them off'. In contrast, when Isaac Broderick stood for attempted sodomy in 1730, he alleged that the prosecutor and a justice who had been responsible for initiating the case 'hired a great number of the populace to assault and wound me, insomuch that I was almost cut to the skull'.[94] For many reasons, the role of the ordinary Londoner at the pillory was marginalised. This is not to deny that there continued to be times when crowds inflicted considerable harm on those who stood. But such occasions were far from typical and, indeed, could only occur when the offence both attracted particular opprobrium *and* the authorities lost control of the crowd. At other times there was little left for the crowd to do. In 1786 a large crowd gathered in the expectation that Aylett would be pilloried a second time, but when they discovered that someone else was being punished instead, they lost interest: 'as soon as it was understood who the unfortunate man was, and that the lawyers in general deemed it rather a hard case, the congregation thinned rapidly, and departed in peace'.[95]

Crowds continued to attend hangings, but they too were increasingly

12. Paul Sandby, 'Sock Vendor' (*c.* 1759). (*Nottingham City Museums and Galleries: Nottingham Castle*)

separated from the punishment, both by guards and (after 1783) by the raised gallows at Newgate. Precisely why they continued to attend is unclear, though the neutral word 'curious' was often used to describe onlookers. At the execution of James Hall, who murdered his master, it was reported that 'the streets were lined with an innumerable crowd of spectators, curious to behold so execrable a wretch'. According to the sheriffs of London and Middlesex, those attending executions frequently went 'with the strange expectation of satisfying an unaccountable curiosity'. John Hamilton's 'View of an execution at Tyburn' (Figure 13), which depicts the execution of a banker's clerk in 1767, shows the crowd going to great lengths to get a good view. Onlookers wanted to see and make sense of those condemned for particularly outrageous crimes (those hanged for mundane offences attracted much smaller crowds), and there may have been a kind of primitive fascination with witnessing the process of dying.[96] Others, as commentators complained, treated executions lightly. A letter to the *Gentleman's Magazine* in 1784 complained that the crowds which attended hangings 'go with the same ease and indifference they would go to a race'. Early in the century François Misson commented that the 'extraordinary courage' of the English meant that they viewed hangings 'as a trifle, and they also make it a jest of the pretended dishonour that, in the opinion of others, falls upon their kindred'.[97]

Increasingly there was concern that onlookers experienced a rather different form of apathy from that which affected the pillory: spectators not only became indifferent to the moral lessons they were supposed to be imbibing, but became corrupted by the process. As with whippings, commentators argued that repeated exposure to such brutality hardened onlookers and made it more, rather than less, likely that they would commit crimes. Describing a hypothetical labourer attracted to witness a hanging out of curiosity, the sheriffs suggested in 1784 that the experience of repeated exposure and mixing with bad company would eventually cause him to 'become indifferent to the spectacle', leading to the likelihood that he would commit a crime and end up on the gallows himself. John Scott complained in 1773 that the 'spectacles' of frequent executions 'certainly harden the heart: those who see life taken in so careless a manner, will not have a proper value for their own lives or the lives of others'. At the same time a feeling of shame among elites

13. John Hamilton, 'View of an Execution at Tyburn' (1767) (detail). (© *The British Museum*)

at the possibility that they might enjoy the sight of such suffering led them to stop attending executions.[98] Having lost part of their audience and potentially corrupting the rest, public punishments were no longer shaming the right people.

In a rapidly changing metropolis where most of the people encountered in public were strangers, and where acquaintances between neighbours became increasingly superficial, judgements concerning character and reputation based on public events, or on hearsay from neighbours or others who may have witnessed such events, became increasingly untenable. Consequently, attempts to shame people, whether through public insults, official punishments, or popular imitations of such punishments (discussed in the next chapter), lost their effectiveness. Reputations were instead established and defended in narrower social contexts. By the end of the century, London's streets, their functions now dominated by traffic and architectural display, had become inappropriate places to establish and destroy reputations. The decline of so many forms of public punishment, which had been such an essential feature of the early modern penal regime, cannot therefore be explained solely by changing elite sensibilities and their growing concerns about violence and the maintenance of public order. The mob lost interest in these rituals, not simply because their participation was circumscribed by official policing, but also because their understandings of how reputations were shaped in the city had changed: what happened on the streets had lost its significance. Shame works differently in the modern city.

# 5

# *Crowds and Riots*

Efforts to shame deviants publicly worked so well in early eighteenth-century London because Londoners were accustomed to using the streets for conducting disputes and policing each other's behaviour. It was accepted and even expected that those present on the city's crowded streets would witness and even participate in any disputes which erupted. Even minor disputes thus had the potential to become riots; the seamless transition from a crowd to riot occurred easily, quickly and regularly. As we have seen with public punishments, crowds quickly gathered to witness public spectacles, and this was true not only for officially organised events. Eighteenth-century Londoners were accustomed to taking to the streets to express a wide variety of grievances. This was quintessentially the century of the mob, when, more than before or since, groups of Londoners used the streets on a daily basis to make their views known and to carry out disputes. Indeed, this was the most riotous century in London's history. This chapter charts the history of popular protest in London from its rise in the late seventeenth century to its peak between the Sacheverell riots of 1710 and the Gordon Riots of 1780. It also demonstrates how Londoners' changing attitudes towards the use of public spaces for conducting disputes contributed to the decline of this pattern of street protest in the second half of the century.[1]

Reflecting the introduction and increased use of the new word for rioters, the 'mob', there was a significant increase in rioting in London in the late seventeenth and early eighteenth centuries, and significant changes in its nature. Edward Chamberlayne's book on the state of the English nation, *Angliae Notitia*, went through at least twenty editions after 1669, but it was only in the 1694 and subsequent editions that he included a statement in his description of the people that 'the common sort are rude and even barbarous, as the effects of popular tumults (which

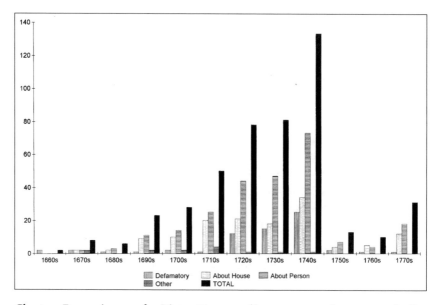

Chart 3. Recognizances for Riot, 1660–1779. (Source: recognizance sample. See Appendix.)

are called the mobile) shows ...' The epidemic of rioting protesting against the Hanoverian accession in 1714–15 prompted Robert Ferguson to write that in the first year of the reign of George I there had been 'more mobs and insurrections in Great Britain than have happened in all the reigns since the Conquest'.[2] This contemporary comment is backed up in more measured form in the court records. The number of defendants bound over for riot at the Middlesex sessions increased dramatically between the Restoration and the middle of the eighteenth century (Chart 3). In addition to recording increasing prosecutions for riot, court records suggest that there were significant changes in the character of street protest: there were big increases in the participation of women, and in the use of insulting words and defamatory actions (such as spitting and pelting with mud), as well as the use of threatened as well as actual violence.

It is not difficult to see why London became a hotbed of street protest in the late seventeenth century. As London's population spilled into the county of Middlesex, where the sophisticated communal controls and conflict resolution mechanisms of the City of London were absent, Londoners acquired a new freedom to express their grievances. At the same time, the emergence of party politics during the Exclusion Crisis led to appeals for popular support from politicians. Not only did crowds provide politicians with a weapon for intimidating opponents, they were a means of claiming widespread public support for their programmes, a useful political strategy despite the deeply hierarchical structure of political power in Westminster. By manipulating existing traditions of public celebrations on official anniversaries, politicians were able to mobilise crowds to demonstrate support for partisan causes. One of the earliest examples of this practice was the Whig-inspired pope-burning processions of 1678–81 on 5 and 17 November (Gunpowder Plot day and Queen Elizabeth's accession day), and as party conflict continued to rage up to the early 1720s, appeals for support from London crowds multiplied.

Although ordinary Londoners were largely spectators, or followers, at such political demonstrations, they had their own reasons for protest, and they developed the capacity both to manipulate organised political demonstrations for their own purposes and to riot on their own. During the protests against the Hanoverian accession, they took advantage of demonstrations organised by political elites to express their own grievances, in this case against Whig support for the reformation of manners campaign, and to complain about economic hardships caused by war, unregulated trade and bad weather.[3] On other occasions, groups of workers, including weavers, tailors and sailors, protested on their own in attempts to raise wages or protect jobs against threats posed by labour-saving machinery and cheap imports. These were just a few of the many grievances which caused London crowds to protest in the eighteenth century.

The elision in contemporary usages of the term 'mob' in the early eighteenth century between descriptions of all those present on London's streets, the lower classes generally, and specifically rioters is revealing of just how easy it was for the vast number of people on the streets to form a riotous crowd. Accounts of street life are replete with evidence of how easily crowds formed. People naturally gravitated towards any loud noise or the sight of a crowd gathering. During the attacks on dissenting meeting houses in 1710 (the Sacheverell riots), Joseph Burges, a journeyman, 'hearing of a tumult at Dr Burgess's meeting house ...

went thither out of curiosity and to see if there were among the rioters any that he knew'. Daniel Damare testified that 'seeing the multitude running and being a little in drink he went thither'.[4] When Margaret Smith accused Joanna Sayer of being a whore and of having had two bastards while she had lodged in her garret, when she encountered her in a doorway in a cheesemonger's shop in 1740, a crowd immediately gathered. The words, spoken in 'an angry reproachful and invidious manner', 'did thereby raise a great mob or tumult of people passing and repassing along the street, who stop'd on account of the noise made by the said' Smith.[5]

Raising one's voice to make an insult or to request help was by itself often sufficient for attracting a crowd. We have seen that victims of crime shouted 'stop thief!' or 'murder!' to secure the assistance of passers-by.[6] The cry of 'informer' was equally effective in rousing community hatred of those who profited from the misery of others: in 1736, when opposition to those who informed on their neighbours for selling gin was at fever pitch, Sarah Miller stood outside Anne Adams's house and screamed 'damn you, informing bitch!', which caused 'great numbers of persons ... to the number of twenty' to assemble in front of the house.[7] In 1719, opposition by weavers to the wearing of calico clothing (the imported cotton was thought to be putting the weavers out of work) led to a series of attacks on women wearing dresses made out of the cloth. Elizabeth Price complained that as she was walking up to a house, 'some people sitting at their doors took up her riding hood, and seeing her gown, cry'd out callicoe, callicoe, weavers, weavers, whereupon a great number came down and tore her gown off all but the sleeve, her pocket, the head of her riding hood, and abus'd her very much'.[8] Slogans shouted repeatedly were frequently used to recruit passers-by and rally support. In 1715 James Harbottle was talking to a friend at eleven o'clock in the morning near the Rose Inn at Holborn Bridge when 'about a dozen men [ran] past him with sticks, hollowing ... he followed them, and ask'd what was the meaning of it'.[9] Almost every major disturbance in the century had its slogan, shouted by the crowds while processing through the streets or at bonfires: in 1710 the cry was 'High Church and Sacheverell!'; in 1715, depending on one's point of view, it was 'No Hanoverian, No Presbyterian!' and 'High Church and Ormond, and the Race of Stuarts for Ever!', or (from the

Whigs) 'King George Forever!'; in 1719 'Down with the Calicos!'; in the 1736 riots against low wage Irish labour 'Down with the Irish!'; in the 1768 riots in support of the radical politician John Wilkes 'Wilkes and Liberty!' and 'Wilkes Forever!'; and in the 1780 Gordon Riots (seeking the repeal of the 1778 Catholic Relief Act, which had ended some forms of legal discrimination against Catholics) 'No Popery!'

Sometimes, the simple 'huzza' was used to attract attention. According to one observer of the Sacheverell riots, huzzaing 'in the case of the mob is sounding the trumpet'. He might have cited the example of Daniel Damare, who, according to one witness, 'did stir up and animate the people by making a noise hollowing and throwing up his hat and wig'. Decades later the French visitor Pierre Jean Grosley noted that the cry of huzza 'is the signal for rallying in all public affrays'.[10] Once the attention of the crowd had been secured, the shouting served the purpose of exciting and rallying people to action. In 1721 a dispute erupted over the building of a wall across a pathway in Hampstead, causing a crowd of at least one hundred people to gather. As one witness testified, the crowd 'with great clamours and loud shouts did excite and encourage one another to hinder the building of the said wall and to demolish the same'. During a riot of a similar size outside a justice of the peace's house in 1768, the crowd was witnessed 'huzzaing and exciting one' another to break into the house.[11]

For those of weak voice or the ambition of attracting even bigger crowds, several other techniques for summoning crowds were available, some of which imitated official practices. The ringing of church bells had long been an official means of attracting attention in order to announce or commemorate major public events, and those with the right connections could get the bells rung on non-official occasions like the demise of the Excise Bill in 1733 and the release of Wilkes from prison in 1768. Those who were unable to get into the parish belfry achieved a similar effect on a smaller scale by ringing a hand-held bell. In 1697 the weavers were summoned to go to Parliament (in support of a bill to prevent the wearing of imported silks and printed calicos) by a poor woman who had been 'hired ... to ring a bell, and ... go about and raise the weavers'. In 1749 sailors bent on destroying the brothel where one of their number had been robbed were seen coming 'ringing a bell, and calling out the host, the host'.[12]

Drums, and sometimes fifes and trumpets, which were commonly used to muster the militia and soldiers, were also used to summon crowds, especially during the industrial disputes of the 1760s. In May 1765, when journeymen weavers planned to lobby Parliament in support of a bill which would prohibit silk imports, 'all the weavers in Spitalfields and the environs thereof ... assembled themselves together by beat of a drum'. A few days later, an informer reported that a weaver had told him that 'they should be out all night, beating their drums in order to collect at a general rendezvous in Moorfields at 5 o'clock in the morning'.[13] Drums were used in a similar manner in 1768 in separate industrial disputes by coalheavers and sailors and in 1780 by the Gordon rioters. Other noise-making instruments used by the latter were a frying pan with a pair of tongs, and a rattle.[14] The power of these tools for summoning crowds is evident in the steps the authorities took to seize the drums carried by marchers during the industrial disorders of the 1760s.

At an election in 1784 a group of rioters was seen 'parading the streets and beating the marrowbone and cleaver amongst the mob'.[15] The discordant sound of marrowbones and cleavers probably had its origins in the 'rough music' used to shame deviants in a traditional riding or charivari, but in the eighteenth century it was used more widely to attract attention and more positively to accompany celebrations. When Robert Harley, Earl of Oxford, was taken to the Tower to await his trial for treason in 1715, his supporters were rallied with marrowbones and cleavers. In 1741, popular opposition to Robert Walpole's foreign policy crystallised around celebrations of the naval exploits of Admiral Vernon. On Vernon's birthday, Walpole's son Horace noted that 'the city shops are full of favours, the streets of marrowbones and cleavers, and the night will be full of mobbing, bonfires and lights!'[16]

Walpole's evocative comment provides evidence of three other means of recruiting support for protests: favours, bonfires and lights. The wearing of emblems of support, such as cockades (rosettes worn on one's hat), was not only a means of expressing loyalty to the cause but also of attracting more followers. White roses were worn by supporters of the Jacobite Pretender in 1715; cockades bearing the motto 'liberty, prosperity, and no excise' were worn by those celebrating the defeat of the Excise Bill in 1733; and blue cockades were sported by supporters of Wilkes in 1768 and by members and supporters of the Protestant

Association in 1780, until the latter were removed by the soldiers who finally put an end to the Gordon Riots.[17] In December 1688 crowds supporting the future King William, then Prince of Orange, marched with oranges on the top of their staves; and in 1715 Whig supporters wore orange ribbons and miniature warming pans (a reference to the alleged illegitimate origins of the Pretender). Such symbols were not always political: on 17 March 1768 (St Patrick's Day) coalheavers wearing shamrocks in their hats 'assembled together and paraded through the high streets and public highways' as part of their labour dispute.[18]

But probably the most effective visual tool used to recruit support was a flag. Along with drums and music, the flag was a traditional part of official celebrations such as the Lord Mayor's procession and at elections. Crowds marching 'with drums beating and colours flying', often on their way to Parliament, were a frequent phenomenon on London's streets, particularly in the third quarter of the century. In May 1765 the journeymen weavers (who as we have seen had been summoned by the beat of a drum) marched through the City and St James's Park to Parliament preceded by nine men, each carrying a black silk flag (imported silk was their primary grievance) to present a petition to the King. A few days later, they once again marched to Parliament, this time in three different contingents, 'carrying flags of various colours before them'.[19] In 1768, the shamrock-wearing coalheavers marched with colours flying, and two months later sailors were seen marching in 'solemn procession with colours flying' on their way to Old Palace Yard in Westminster.[20] Prior to the Gordon Riots, members of the Protestant Association, wearing blue cockades, met in St George's Fields and marched three or four times around the field with flags and music before heading to Westminster. Flags continued to play a significant role in the ensuing riots: Samuel Solomons was seen on 7 June in Whitechapel 'carrying a blue flag at the head of a number of persons who were conducting themselves in a riotous and tumultuous manner'. As John Clawson testified, 'the said flag was used as a standard for the said rioters to repair to and operated as an encouragement to the rioters'. The significance of flags as emblems of support for a cause can be seen in a riot which occurred in 1768 when a procession of Wilkes's opponents carried a flag bearing the phrase 'no blasphemer'. This public insult provoked a violent response from his supporters: a mob knocked a man from his horse, 'took off the wheels of one of the carriages, cut the harness, and broke the glasses to pieces; several other carriages were damaged'.[21]

The two other activities which Walpole expected would accompany 'mobbing' were 'bonfires and lights'. Bonfires were a traditional method of celebrating good news, and throughout the seventeenth and most of the eighteenth centuries they were ordered to be lit by Lord Mayors and justices of the peace on public anniversaries such as those of Queen Elizabeth's coronation or the Restoration of Charles II, or significant events such as the birth of a son to the Princess of Wales in April 1721. Some bonfires were organised by parochial or city officials and royal households, but individual householders were also expected to light fires before their doors. To encourage participation and the drinking of loyal toasts, free drinks were often provided. At the bonfires in April 1721, 'four hogsheads of wine, having the heads beat out, were given to the populace' at Leicester House, while at the Royal Exchange 'the King, the Prince and Princess, and the young prince's healths were drunk, with loud acclamations of joy'. Bonfires were a very successful means of drawing together crowds on London's otherwise poorly-lit streets. Unsurprisingly, keepers of alehouses began to provide them as a means of attracting business as well as demonstrating patriotism.[22]

Bonfires acquired greater significance by what was burned in them. In the 1670s, a new dimension to this type of public celebration was given by the burning of effigies of those who were the targets of popular hatred. During the Exclusion Crisis figures of the Pope and prominent Catholics (including the Duke of York) were paraded through the streets before they were burned, the effect sometimes heightened by the squeals of live cats which had been stuffed into their stomachs to represent a dialogue with the devil. Effigies were burned on political anniversaries such as 5 and 17 November until at least 1745. But it was not only anti-Catholicism and Whig party loyalties which were expressed in the burning of effigies. In 1715 effigies of Oliver Cromwell and Benjamin Hoadly, a Whig clergyman, were burnt, though an attempt to burn an effigy of George I was prevented; and in 1733 effigies of Robert Walpole, Queen Caroline and the murderess Sarah Malcolm were burned in the celebrations which followed the dropping of the Excise Bill. Figures representing a wide range of other popular hatreds were also consumed by the flames as this originally political form of protest was used for other purposes. In 1721, following the successful passage of a bill prohibiting the importation of calico, the weavers celebrated by 'dressing up in effigy a female in callicoes' and burning it; and in 1761 popular hostility to an increase in the tax on porter (strong beer, typically consumed by the poor) imposed by statute led to the burning of effigies of the deviser of the act and of publicans who had raised the price of porter in their establishments.[23] Also in 1761, in a nice example of how important traditional commemorations were to the public, an effigy of a churchwarden was burnt by his parishioners because he refused to allow the parish bells to be rung on the occasion of the King's marriage.[24]

'Lights', or illuminations, refers to the practice of lighting candles in windows or outside doors as a way of celebrating good news or expressing approval for a cause. Along with bonfires, Lord Mayors and justices traditionally ordered householders to illuminate to celebrate military or naval victories and important national anniversaries. But householders did not need to wait for official orders to place candles in their windows, and illuminations became an effective means of demonstrating support for any cause. The celebrations of Vernon's birthday referred to by Walpole were not official, but were nonetheless apparently universal, with houses on London's courts and allies, as well as high streets, illuminated.[25] Such displays must have been as impressive as bonfires on London's poorly lit streets, and they also attracted crowds. On Gunpowder Plot Day in 1686, the Lord Mayor, no doubt fearing politically dangerous expressions of anti-Catholicism, prohibited illuminations. Nonetheless, groups of apprentices (who of course did not have houses from which to display their candles) and others placed displays in several public places. At the Monument, 'a great many candles [were] lighted whereupon a great number of disorderly people were gathered together making great noise and disturbance'. In Fenchurch Street candles hung from a rope across the street from the tops of two houses 'begatt an assembly of several rude people thereabouts'.[26]

Bonfires and lights were clearly intended to create public displays of collective joy and approbation. Lighting up the streets gave the appearance of unanimity, and this was increased by the presence of crowds, often wearing cockades, and the drinking of toasts. Similarly, processions moving through the streets, with drums beating, flags flying and music playing, created public displays of collectively held sentiments, not just among those marching but also among the crowds of spectators. While all these activities had origins among officially sponsored celebrations of royal anniversaries and military victories, late seventeenth- and eighteenth-century Londoners did not wait for official encouragement before engaging in these practices, as is evident in the improvised illuminations staged on the fifth of November 1686. During the eighteenth century political parties, workers' clubs, voluntary societies, groups of neighbours and others frequently used these techniques to call attention to their agendas by creating the appearance of universal support for their cause. In doing so, they attracted crowds, which often became riotous either in support of or in opposition to the views expressed.

Faced with the possibility of prosecution, witnesses who had joined crowds were reluctant to admit when interrogated that they had crossed the subtle line between spectatorship and riot, but the fact that many crowds became involved in breaking windows, destroying property and other coercive activities makes it abundantly clear that this line was frequently crossed. In all these activities the aim continued to be to create the appearance of widespread support for their cause, while at the same time punishing those who did not or could not be part of the community of agreed sentiments they were trying to create. Perhaps the best example of this point comes from the demonstrations in support of John Wilkes in 1768. Wilkes, a radical critic of the government of George III, was prosecuted for the obscene and seditious content of issue number forty-five of his periodical the *North Briton*, and the number '45' came to symbolise support for Wilkes's campaign against the government. One of the techniques of his supporters was to roam the streets, marking '45' in chalk on doors and windows, and even on the coats of pedestrians. When Richard Capel was watching rioters pull down the house of a justice of the peace (who had tried to break up a riot earlier in the day) late at night on 9 May 1768, John Percival 'took him by the collar and said damn you I'll mark you and accordingly he did mark him [with a] large figure number 45 on the cape of his great coat'.[27]

Crowds also sought to enforce the appearance of widespread support by forcing householders to illuminate, threatening to break their windows if they failed to do so. Even where the illuminations had been officially ordered, crowds took it upon themselves to punish those who failed to comply, as a letter to the Lord Mayor complained in 1706: 'they breake windows with stones, fire gunns with pease in our houses to the hazard of peoples lifes or limbs because they do not comply to thare humours'.[28] From this it was but a short step to enforcing illuminations on non-officially sanctioned occasions. During a Tory celebration of the anniversary of the Restoration of Charles II in 1715 crowds broke windows that were not illuminated, including those of the Whig Lord Mayor, the figure who normally ordered illuminations in the City.[29] Similar enforced illuminations occurred throughout the century, celebrating, among other events, the failure of the Excise Bill and the anniversary of the coronation of William and Mary in 1733 and 1735, Vernon's birthday in 1741, Wilkes's victory in the Middlesex election and several similar occasions in his support in 1768–70, the release of the Lord Mayor from the Tower during the City's confrontation with Parliament over the printing of parliamentary debates in 1771, and the election of Wilkes as Lord Mayor in 1774. As the *General Evening Post* reported on 11 October of that year, 'the mob on Saturday evening obliged the inhabitants of the principal streets to illuminate their windows. Many who refused to comply had their windows broken and other mischief done to their houses. The inhabitants of Leicester Fields were great sufferers, as the windows of almost one whole side of the square were demolished'.[30]

The large sash windows found in Georgian houses must have offered a tempting target for protesters, and residents seem to have become resigned to the need to replace broken panes occasionally (the use of wooden shutters inside the windows prevented further damage to houses). In a draft letter written to a friend in France by William Mawhood, a London woollen draper, in 1774, Mawhood joked that he would 'send Wilk's dirty blackgardes to brake all your windows, in which I shall have a double advantage, beside saving my own, which I expect will suffer this even[ing] it being the morn of the election for Middlesex at Bren[t]ford' (an election which Wilkes won).[31] Mawhood indicated that he would not illuminate his windows: it appears that it was more important to him not to show false public support for Wilkes's cause than it was to save his windows. Other householders adopted a different strategy, reluctantly conforming to whatever was demanded by the mob:

during a 1771 demonstration Wilkes was attended by a mob of about 'two hundred persons seemingly of inferior rank and amongst them many boys'. As one witness reported, 'hitherto there were few or no illuminations on this side of Temple Bar, [but] the hollowing of the mob soon made the inhabitants illuminate which was pretty general throughout the Strand'.[32]

On many occasions it could be argued that crowds had something genuine to celebrate, even if their joy was not shared by all of London's householders. But as this last example suggests, in other cases crowds used forced illuminations simply as a method of calling attention to their cause, often as part of a wider arsenal of tactics. In 1736 they were used during the attacks on houses where Irish workers were lodging; in 1768 by rioters who had been dispersed from a demonstration outside King's Bench prison; and on 6 June 1780 during the Gordon Riots, when 'the mob insisted upon lights being put up at every window in joy for the destruction of Newgate [prison]; the illumination accordingly was general'.[33]

A street full of houses with candles in their windows was seen as significant sign of public support for a cause. But in cases where popular opinion was divided, as was particularly the case in the early years of the reign of George I, crowds could find themselves offended by windows that *were* illuminated. By breaking such windows, one undermined the appearance of support for one's opponents. On 28 May 1715, the eve of the anniversary of the Restoration of Charles II, 'a great mob came into Basinghall Street about 11 a clock [at] night, hollowing, and breaking windows that were illuminated'. Three years later, on 1 August, Thomas Lister 'illuminated his door to show his loyalty to the King, it being the anniversary of his Majesty's accession to the crown'. This, no doubt together with the fact that Lister had informed on other rioters, had the consequence that 'a great number of people assembled in a riotous and tumultuous manner [and] threw great quantities of stones and dirt at his household windows and seized and assaulted his person and pulled down his illuminations'.[34] Conflicts over the public display of political loyalties on the streets of London in the early years of George I's reign were intense.

Irrespective of whether or not they were illuminated, breaking windows in the eighteenth century appears to have become a common means of making a political statement or of branding a household as anti-social, labelling the residents as violators of community norms in the same way that a public insult sought to damage the reputation of a deviant. Houses were as much a target of popular shaming protests as those who lived in them. Early in the Sacheverell riots Thomas Gray encountered a man who said the rioters had agreed to 'damnifie' the house of Dr Burgess, a Presbyterian preacher. Accordingly, they went and broke his windows.[35] Numerous other incidents of broken windows occurred in similar contexts of trying to punish and marginalise the occupants for their political views. In 1715–16, the 'mughouses', alehouses in which Whig clubs met (so called because of their practice of toasting the King with mugs of beer), attracted the ire of Tory mobs. The attack on the windows of Read's mughouse in Salisbury Court on 23 July 1716 was well organised, with seven or eight pound stones brought in baskets and thrown at the windows 'so that [there] was scarce a whole pane left below stairs'. In 1768 and 1769 supporters of Wilkes broke the windows of the Mansion House several times in order to punish the Lord Mayor for his opposition to their cause.[36]

More frequently, crowds broke windows in order to punish those whose activities were deemed anti-social. In 1736 anger at Irish labourers working for low wages led to attacks on the houses in which they lodged; at one, in Lemon Street, Whitechapel, John Blundridge was accused of inciting the rioters by saying 'play away, it is an Irish house, I will have every pane of glass down'.[37] In 1738 the use of French actors at the Little Haymarket Theatre (at a time when English actors were out of work due to the Licensing Act of 1737) caused resentment: a mob in the streets took advantage of vendors selling potatoes and pippins and used these to break 'the windows of the house all to pieces'.[38] Crime could also be punished in this way: in 1744 a crowd gathered outside a brothel to which a girl newly arrived from the country had been inveigled. A constable was summoned, who found several bloody clothes in the house, but the woman could not be found. Several arrests were made, but the mob, not being satisfied, 'was so exasperated at the suppos'd murder, that they broke all the windows, shutters, and doors about the house'.[39] Similarly, in 1749 and 1761 brothels were attacked by sailors who had been robbed therein. Crowds also, however, sometimes broke the windows of the houses of those whose testimony was responsible for the conviction and execution of criminals. In 1774, after the funeral of two men who had been hanged for theft, a crowd of mourners went to the house of the prosecutor, broke his windows, and attempted to set the house on fire by 'throwing lighted links up to the windows that were broken'.[40]

Bonfires provided similar opportunities for disorder. Householders did not wait for official orders to light them, and they were lit to celebrate political and other events which were not officially sanctioned. In November 1679, the return of the Duke of Monmouth, an unwelcome turn of events for the King, was welcomed in London in the traditional manner: 'the people were so rejoiced that before daybreak ... they made bonfires in several places ... and at night there were some hundreds of bonfires about the town at which all people cryed God bless the Duke of Monmouth'.[41] On 22 March 1710, during the Sacheverell riots, Michael Messenger, a perfumer, asked several boys to light a bonfire in King Street. According to a witness, the fire, together with the drink he provided, 'soon created a mob that were very riotous in their proceedings'.[42] Instead of an event at which the authorities and elite Londoners could stimulate expressions of loyalty through the provision of alcohol and drinking of toasts, bonfires became occasions when crowds wrote their own scripts by forcibly demanding money from passers-by for charity or in order to drink their own toasts. In 1710, for example, at a bonfire lit in support of Dr Sacheverell, Lady Overkirk's coach was stopped and 'the mob in a rude and insolent manner came and demanded money and being refused called ... 'em Presbyterian bitches and other opprobrious language'. At other times unwilling spectators were forced to provide at least the appearance of support for the cause by taking off their hats, huzzaing, and drinking specified toasts. At a Jacobite bonfire outside a tavern on the birthday of the Prince of Wales in June 1695, John Page, an apprentice, alleged that his wig was 'pluckt off' and he was 'forced to drinke a health upon his knees'.[43]

Just as illuminations caused disorder when public spaces were used for the expression of sentiments crowds disagreed with, bonfires were sometimes the scenes of violent conflict. In 1682 Catholics tried to put out the bonfires lit on 5 November. At the 1695 Jacobite bonfire discussed above, a fight erupted between Jacobites and supporters of William III;

the latter broke the windows of the tavern and threatened to pull it down. In 1715, a loyalist bonfire on the evening before the anniversary of the Restoration of Charles II was disrupted by a mob that 'came down and abus'd several that drank [King George's health]; crying out Ormond, High Church etc ... they hissed the King's health, threw firebrands into the house, and almost murder'd several who were about the bonfire'. A dispute over the healths drunk at a bonfire on the anniversary of the martyrdom of Charles I in 1735 resulted in the 'populace' attacking the tavern 'in a most terrible manner, the frames and the shutters, as well as the glass ...' [44]

Breaking windows and bonfires frequently accompanied a more violent form of crowd protest, the practice of 'pulling down' houses. Like almost every other aspect of public rioting in the eighteenth century, 'pulling down' houses had its origins in traditional festive customs and official practices. In early seventeenth-century London apprentices seeking to purify the town on Shrove Tuesday pulled down brothels and playhouses on a regular basis.[45] The authorities had the power to destroy buildings which were a nuisance, built contrary to regulations, or housed illegal activities, and the government of Charles II used this power against places where dissenters worshipped.[46] Although these official or quasi-official practices were conducted rarely after the 1660s (although eight hundred apprentices did attack brothels in St Giles in the Fields in 1682) [47] this tactic was frequently used by London crowds in the eighteenth century.

The expression 'pulling down' a house was actually something of a misnomer. Since most London housing was built in brick terraces, the physical demolition of an entire house would have caused considerable damage to neighbouring houses, as would setting fire to it. Rather, rioters tended to leave the structure of the house intact and only destroy the windows and doors, interior fittings, and furniture; the debris was burned in the streets. Boitard's 'The Sailor's Revenge' (Figure 14) shows sailors throwing the furnishings out of the windows of a brothel and into bonfires on the Strand in 1749. Not only did the normal practice of lighting bonfires of the wreckage in the streets avoid danger to nearby houses, it also called further public attention to the protest. Although buildings' structures were preserved, the damage could nonetheless be extensive. John Boyle, who witnessed the attack on Read's mughouse

14. Louis-Philippe Boitard, 'The Sailor's Revenge: or The Strand in an Uproar' (1749). (*Guildhall Library, Corporation of London*)

in 1715, reported that the upper part of the house was preserved because soldiers arrived in time to save it, but

> below stairs the windows and sashes were all broke to pieces, the bar and the cupboard, and the post to which the coffee mill was fixt, were broke down, and also the benches and wainscot, and *it look'd just like a house that was pulling down*; and all the goods were broke to pieces and destroyed.

The Gordon rioters systematically destroyed a large number of houses in this manner. On 7 June 1780 the house of Christopher Connor was 'stripped of all the furniture which was burned and much of the timber house destroyed ... the window frames in front and on one side of the dwelling house were then taken out and part of the brick work about such frames was pulled down and demolished'.[48] In 1749, and again during the Gordon Riots, some houses were actually set on fire; this may be because the availability of fire engines meant that neighbouring houses could be protected.

Following the precedent set by the official destruction of the meeting houses of dissenters after the Restoration, the most frequent motivation behind crowds pulling down houses in the eighteenth century was to purge the city of religious nonconformity. Catholic chapels in 1688, dissenting meeting houses during the Sacheverell riots of 1710, a Presbyterian meeting house in 1715, and Catholic chapels and houses in the Gordon Riots in 1780 were all pulled down. In the last, crowds actually searched houses looking for evidence of householders' religious beliefs before commencing the destruction, claiming to enforce a 1549 statute which forbade keeping Catholic books. When rioters came to Elizabeth Currey's house, 'they asked for books, and the deponent showed them a common prayer book, which they made her kiss'. This temporarily convinced the mob to spare her house, but when two women 'gave fresh information to the mob' they cried out the 'house must come down'.[49] But the motivations for pulling down houses were multifarious, including political (attacks on the mughouses in 1715) and economic reasons (attacks on the lodging houses of Irishmen working for low wages in 1736 and the houses of strike-breaking 'undertakers' by coal-heavers in 1768). In addition, crowds took revenge both on those who committed crimes (attacks on St Martin's Round House, where several prisoners died after being crammed into a cell in 1742, and the destruction of brothels by sailors who had been robbed in 1749 and 1761) and on prosecutors in criminal cases where the prosecutions were thought to be unfair. In 1755 crowds gathered nightly for a month outside the house of William Boxal, who was accused of having starved his wife and of living with another woman. Several people shouted 'Pull the house down, break open the door, pull him out and knock his brains out'.[50] In 1794, the house of 'crimps', men who adopted unfair recruiting practices for the armed forces, were targeted.[51] In a kind of ritual expulsion from the community, many forms of deviance were punished by destroying houses where offensive behaviour had taken place.

Anticipating the Luddite attacks of the early nineteenth century, some attacks focused on the removal and destruction of job-threatening equipment and consumer goods while leaving the houses intact. In 1768 a group of 500 sawyers destroyed the inside of a mill because 'the saw mill was at work when thousands of them were starving for want of bread'. Weavers had a particularly long history of this type of direct action. In 1675 groups of weavers who objected to the adoption of an engine loom used for weaving silk ribbons broke into houses, seized the offending machinery, and brought it out into the street 'where it was set afire and destroyed in an atmosphere of celebration'.[52] Actions like this echoed the traditional search and seizure powers of guilds. In 1697 and 1719, when complaints concerned the threat to jobs caused by the popularity of imported silks and calicos, weavers entered houses and shops and destroyed the offending fabrics. In the 1760s an additional focus of discontent was low wages, and new tactics were adopted: journeymen weavers formed secret societies, which sought to punish masters who refused to pay specified wages, or to pay contributions to the societies. Groups of 'cutters' entered houses and destroyed the looms and work of weavers who violated their rules. The offending behaviour included the use of female labour: in December 1769 a body of 'cutters' came to the house of Daniel Clarke on Artillery Lane in Bishopsgate, demanded entrance, and asked whether his wife made any of the work in his loom. He claimed that she no longer did such work, but not believing him they went upstairs and cut the cloth in the loom.[53]

Although this last attack occurred in the middle of the night, these attacks were often very public events, in the sense that crowds frequently called attention to their actions by huzzaing, building bonfires in the street, and parading about with trophies of what they had destroyed. One of the Sacheverell rioters, who acted as captain, grabbed 'part of a curtain of a meeting house that was pulled down' and used it as a flag. In 1715 one of the rioters who attacked Read's mughouse, Thomas Bean, was seen carrying 'part of the sign in his hand, in a great heat, running with it along in the greatest joy and triumph imaginable'. Similarly, the Gordon rioters paraded with parts of a pulpit removed from a Catholic chapel, and one rioter rode a horse 'caparisoned with chains filched from Newgate'.[54] The atmosphere of celebration surrounding these destructive acts is indicative of their genealogy as descendants of officially sponsored public commemorations. It also testifies to a widespread sense of legitimacy among rioters, and to their use of London's streets for the purpose of creating the appearance of widespread public support for their actions.

Riots were generally disciplined, as well as celebratory. Most of the violence that did occur was directed at property (especially houses) or symbols rather than directly inflicted on people. Since the aim of riots was to create the appearance of public support, physical objects were in some ways more important targets than individuals. As the occasionally savage treatment of men standing in the pillory and the cruel murder of an informer, Daniel Clarke, in 1771 suggests, crowds could be extremely brutal. But such occasions were the exception rather than the norm. (Clarke's offence was particularly egregious: his testimony had led to the conviction and execution of a weaver ('cutter') for destroying cloth in looms.) People who were targets of popular hatred were more likely to be burned in effigy than directly attacked, and we have seen that even the destruction of property took place in a selective and disciplined manner, with goods burned in the middle of the streets to avoid setting fire to neighbouring houses. Even during the most violent riots of the century, the Gordon Riots, Horace Walpole commented on

> the mixture of rage and consideration in the mob. In most of the fires they threw furniture into the street, did not burn it in the houses – nay made several small bonfires, lest a large one should spread to buildings. They would not suffer engines to play on the devoted edifices, yet the moment the objects were consumed, played the engines on contiguous houses on each side! [55]

Such behaviour was viewed as largely unthreatening, even in a city which had suffered a massive conflagration in 1666, not just because it was disciplined, but also because the rioters so often appeared in such a positive, celebratory mood, 'rejoycing and jumping' about bonfires, and parading in triumph through the streets. Suffused throughout the actions of eighteenth-century crowds was a sense of legitimacy, which, although perhaps in some cases more an aspiration than an actuality, represents a belief that there was widespread community support for their actions.[56] This claim to legitimacy was reinforced by the use of traditional crowd gathering techniques such as bonfires, illuminations and processions, and by the tendency to stage events on holidays and official anniversaries such as Guy Fawkes Day, royal birthdays, and dates of royal accessions to the crown, when crowds were accustomed to gather. In 1715 riots occurred on the anniversaries of Queen Anne's accession and coronation, Charles II's restoration and George I's birthday.[57] Later in the century riots were less tied to this calendar of royal anniversaries, but we have seen that a celebration leading to a forced illumination did occur on the anniversary of William and Mary's coronation in 1735. At this point, however, this date was perhaps more significant as the day the Excise Bill had been dropped two years earlier.[58]

Another method by which crowds claimed legitimacy for their actions was by mimicking official punishments. Since many of these involved public participation or observation, Londoners were well aware of the vocabulary of punishment and its meanings.[59] In 1681, a pope-burning procession included effigies of three men (whose testimony concerning the 'Popish Plot' had been exposed as false) standing in the pillory. The machinery of hangings, the halter and the gibbet, was also commonly used in crowd protests. In the pope-burnings in 1715 the effigies were paraded with halters around their necks and then 'hung out in chains on a high gallows'. On 4 July 1719, a gibbet was 'hung from top to bottom, with fragments of callicoe, stuffs torn or rather stolen from women by journey men weavers'. Similarly, supporters of Wilkes in 1768 marched to the Mansion House carrying 'a gibbet, with a boot and two petticoats'; the boot was a pun on the unpopular Lord Bute.[60] In April 1771 two very different episodes reflect the widespread use of the symbolism and methods of official punishments to legitimate protests. Early in the month, as part of the City of London's defence of the Lord Mayor from prosecution for protecting a printer of parliamentary debates, two carts were drawn through the Strand, Fleet Street and Cheapside with persons impersonating Jack Ketch (the nickname for the executioner) and four political enemies. Subsequently, the 'last dying speeches of the malefactors executed on Tower Hill' were sold in the streets.[61] Two weeks later, the participants in the riot which led to the murder of Clarke imitated the practices of several public punishments: he was whipped through the streets; a cord was tied around his neck; and he was ducked in a pond.[62]

Although ducking in water had once been used as an official punishment for scolds, from the late seventeenth century this punishment was only used unofficially in London, particularly by crowds punishing pickpockets who had been apprehended in the act. The provision of conduits for the supply of water to the city's inhabitants gave rise to a variant of this practice known as being 'pumped'. As César de Saussure wrote in 1726, pickpockets in London 'are given over to the populace, [and] they are dragged to the nearest fountain or well and dipped in the water till nearly drowned'. By bringing offenders near to death and then releasing them, crowds imitated the way official executions were sometimes reprieved by pardons at the last minute.[63] Other bodies of water in London used for this purpose were ponds, the Thames, or sometimes just a muddy ditch (often filled with urine and excrement, thereby adding symbolic defamation to the punishment). Extortionate bailiffs were subjected to 'the discipline' of the debtors of the New Mint, which involved being stripped naked, whipped, and thrown 'into a deep hole filled with ordure and such like nastiness and obliged to duck under twice'.[64] Later in the century canals were used. Over the century the range of deviant figures punished in this way widened to include informers, leaders of press gangs, and workers who refused to cooperate in labour disputes. In 1768, for example, as part of their campaign for higher wages, the coalheavers required everyone working in the trade to register with a single undertaker and obtain a ticket. As the Middlesex justices complained, the coalheavers 'invented a punishment, [for] those who had not [obtained a ticket], by tying a rope around their bodies and plunging them in the river Thames'.[65]

Other crowd punishments emerged out of popular, community-based traditions, notably the riding or charivari. This form of public shaming, which was more common in rural areas in this period, involved parading the deviant (usually a cuckold) around the streets while sitting facing backwards on a horse, accompanied by 'rough music' (discordant noise made by beating pots and pans or other tools).[66] Although such processions were rare in London in this period (but not unheard of),[67] some of the shaming elements of ridings were part of the vocabulary of urban protest, including rough music, horns (symbolising cuckoldry), and riding backwards on a horse (or substitute). In London these procedures were used for more than just cuckolds. They were found in pope-burning processions (the Tory Sir Roger L'Estrange was depicted riding backwards on a horse), anti-Hanoverian protests (horns evoked the cuckoldry of George I), a procession mocking freemasons, attacks on informers and labour disputes. In 1776 a strike-breaking journeyman sawyer was paraded through Wapping 'tied to a donkey, face to its tail, with a saw tied to his back and placarded "WORKING BELOW PRICE"'. Another punishment used by coal porters and carmen against scab labourers in 1768 involved forcing them to ride the wooden horse, which involved 'carrying them upon a sharp stick, and flogging them with ropes, sticks and other weapons'; this form of punishment added real pain to the shame inflicted by a traditional riding.[68] In contrast, the propensity of Londoners to use public ridicule to punish anyone they disapproved of is treated humorously in Anthony Walker's 'The Beaux Disaster' (Figure 15), where an effeminate 'fop' is hung up on a meat hook by a group of butchers.

The sense of legitimacy evident in the symbolic vocabulary of crowd actions was reciprocated by the attitudes of the authorities and the wider public. As reflected in Mawhood's air of resignation about the inevitability of broken windows, there was a remarkable degree of toleration of public disorder in London, and this explains why rioting was so widespread and so publicly festive. Giving legitimacy to the views of the mob, the opposition leader Lord Carteret said in 1737 'The people seldom or never assemble in any riotous or tumultuous manner, unless they are oppressed, or at least imagine they are oppressed'. Of course, attitudes were ambivalent, depending on the degree of sympathy for the sentiments expressed, the social composition of the crowd and the degree of violence used.[69] But analysis of the views and actions of

15. Anthony Walker, 'The Beaux Disaster' (1747). (*Guildhall Library, Corporation of London*)

the authorities, politicians and newspapers makes the extent of the toleration of rioting, even where some violence was involved, clear. There were frequent complaints that those responsible for keeping the peace failed to suppress, and even encouraged mobs. During the 1715 attacks on Read's mughouse the constables failed to protect the house, and actually supported the rioters. Michael Burrel testified that as he was

> going up to the house he saw two constables and several watchmen in the street before the house, who encouraged the mob, for that he was sure they were able to have dispers'd them, if they had a mind to it ... stones were brought in baskets to the mob, some of 7 or 8 pound weight, and laid down just by the constables and watchmen who suffered the mob to throw them at the house.[70]

In 1721 and 1768 justices of the peace allegedly led riots,[71] and even the Lord Mayor of London did not appear to mind a mob if it served his purposes. Following the disorderly celebrations of the failure of the Excise Bill in 1733 (which involved forced illuminations, broken windows, the Prime Minister and Queen burnt in effigy, and occupants of coaches forced to hand over money), the Lord Mayor allegedly said that, 'no person whatever could have a greater abhorrence of riots and tumults than himself; but that he thought the public rejoicings ... were laudable and highly becoming good citizens and good subjects, as they were testimonies of universal joy'.[72] The fact that it was difficult to draw a line between 'public rejoicings' and 'riots and tumults' meant that praise for one could easily be interpreted as toleration for the other.

Newspapers also appeared to support rioters. During the weavers' riots against calico in 1719 Daniel Defoe wrote in the *Weekly Journal*, in response to a complaint that the paper's support for the weavers encouraged rioting, 'we could advise them to more moderate measures, was it not absurd to dictate patience and forbearance to those in their conditions'.[73] In 1761 newspapers stirred up opposition to an increase in the price of porter, editorialising that 'there is no reason for the Brewers hurrying publicans to raise the [price of] beer ... [there will be] time enough to grind the poor', and by giving considerable coverage to popular attacks on pubs where the price had been raised.[74]

Politicians, whose own experiences of disorder often began with election riots, were of course the most shameless in justifying disorder when it served their purposes. It was Whig politicians who first appealed to the crowd in the late seventeenth century by organising the pope-burning processions, and both Whigs and Tories continued to organise public celebrations of anniversaries well into the eighteenth century. And politicians did not always expect crowds to remain passive. Tory churchmen and politicians played a major role in encouraging the Sacheverell riots in 1710 and anti-Hanoverian riots in 1714–15. In response to the latter, the Duke of Newcastle encouraged loyalist mobs to stage their own demonstrations, and to attack those organised by their opponents, in order to generate the appearance of public support for the King.[75] Half a century later street protest was an important tool in Wilkes's political campaigns, although he was careful to avoid appearing to encourage disorder.

Further evidence of the toleration of rioting comes from the relatively small number of London rioters who were ever prosecuted and punished for their actions. Of the approximately one hundred men and women who were arrested during the Sacheverell riots (out of thousands who rioted), only thirty-three were actually indicted. Smaller riots, which were less likely to strain the resources of law enforcement, also resulted in few prosecutions. The weavers' attacks on women wearing calico, for example, which occurred sporadically for over a year, resulted in only thirty-five prosecutions, only about half of which resulted in guilty verdicts. Participants in only four outbreaks of rioting during the century were convicted at the Old Bailey of offences against the 1715 Riot Act, which made participation in riots involving twelve or more people a capital offence. Most rioters were charged with misdemeanours and most of those convicted were only given moderate fines.[76] Although there were practical reasons why the authorities were reluctant to make arrests (notably the danger that this would provoke further disorder), this reluctance to prosecute and punish rioters reflects the fact that only in cases of considerable violence or subversive political behaviour was rioting perceived to be a serious crime at this time.

The widespread acceptance of riot was reflected in the broad social composition of those who participated. Mobs were composed of both women and men, of all social classes. The mixed crowd of Wilkite supporters celebrating his release from prison in 1770 was described as composed of 'half-naked men and women, children, chimney-sweepers, tinkers, Moors and men of letters, fishwives and females in grand array'.[77] Of 415 rioters bound over by recognizance to appear at the Middlesex Sessions between 1660 and 1779, 72 per cent were female. Women were probably overrepresented in the small-scale riots which dominate this type of prosecution, but this figure nonetheless reflects the fact that women were very much part of London's public life, and they played a major role in many types of street protest, particularly when it concerned the enforcement of moral standards in the community. Thus, women frequently instigated and joined in protests against sexual immorality. In 1664 Frances Trevett, the wife of a labourer, allegedly assaulted Alice Webster and followed 'her in the street, clapping her hands and crying out whore whore whore thereby raising a great tumult of people about her to the endangering of her life'.[78] As with individual acts, women were frequently involved in crowd protests involving the shouting of defamatory words or the performance of defamatory acts such as spitting and throwing dirt and mud. Women also played an important role in the attacks on informers who initiated prosecutions for selling gin in 1736. Believing that such people violated community norms by entrapping their neighbours, women pelted informers with mud and stones, dragged them through sewers and ponds, and otherwise defamed them.[79] Women were also prominent in some economic disputes, where they emphasised their household responsibilities by carrying their children with them in marches to Parliament. In 1697 it was a group of women who hired another woman to ring a bell to summon the weavers to march to Westminster, and this procession involved men, women and children, as did a similar procession in 1765.[80] Although women were less prominent in the political riots of the period, they were by no means absent. Women were involved in both the mughouse riots and the Gordon Riots, where eighty were prosecuted for pulling down houses, extorting money from property owners, and stealing from burning buildings.[81] Women's participation in protest underlined rioters' desires to project the appearance of widespread community support for their actions.

Similarly, Londoners of all social classes participated in mobs. Detailed evidence on this point is difficult to obtain, but, of 125 rioters bound over by recognizance who were identified by status or occupation, there

were seven labourers, fifty low status craftsmen such as butchers, carpenters, and tailors, fifty-one craftsmen of unknown status (including
several victuallers), eleven high status craftsmen and tradesmen including
a goldsmith, linen draper, and merchant, and six gentlemen.[82] Although
these records do not include the poorest rioters, who would have been
committed to gaol because they were unable to find sureties, this demonstrates that the London 'mob' was not composed of the dregs of
society, as the meaning of the term suggests and contemporaries often
alleged. No doubt the most socially elevated disturbances of the century
were the Sacheverell riots, where there were significant numbers of the
self-employed, professionals, and gentlemen among the rioters apprehended. The participation of the latter was remarked upon by
witnesses, who reported seeing several 'gentlelike' men, or men 'in
appearance like gentlemen' participating in, and encouraging the mob,
sometimes by handing out money. But such men did not want to call
attention to themselves, which suggests that surviving evidence does not
adequately record their presence. William Watson reported that 'most
of those who were at Dr Burgess's meeting house the said Wednesday
night were gentlemen in disguise with long wigs and coats to hide their
cloathes'. The riots of 1715 and 1768, however, were probably more typical,
in that those arrested were primarily from lower and lower middle-class
occupational groups including servants, labourers, artisans and petty
tradesmen.[83] Nonetheless, as the evidence concerning toleration suggests,
higher-status Londoners often looked on with approval.

Reflecting the diversity of the composition of the crowd was the
diversity of the views expressed: despite the aspirations of participants,
there was no consistent point of view expressed by a single London
'mob'. As an unsympathetic broadsheet complained in 1710, the mob
'are such a hotch-potch of contradictions and uncertainties, that a body
can't tell what to make of them, or where to have them'.[84] Since the
inhabitants of the city were divided by religious and political allegiances,
occupations and other differences, mobs were often in conflict with one
another. We have seen evidence of this in the conflict between Jacobite
and Whig supporters at a bonfire in 1695 and in the fights between Tory
crowds and the occupants of Whig mughouses in 1715. Similarly, the
views of crowds with respect to the desirability of punishing prostitutes
and brothel keepers were contradictory, with some mobs attacking

brothels and breaking their windows, while others protected them from constables who were attempting to close them down.[85] Later in the century, support for the various causes espoused in 1768 was not universal: groups of sailors were involved in violent confrontations with coalheavers after the sailors started to break their strike by unloading coal from their own ships, and the sailors 'attacked and dispersed' a Wilkite mob, which they encountered when lobbying Parliament for higher wages, as a means of demonstrating their loyalty to the King. Journeymen weavers were also divided, with fights breaking out between those who operated engine looms and those who worked 'single-handed'.[86] Even the participants in a single crowd did not necessarily hold the same views. When a large mob captured Clarke and sought to punish him for prosecuting the cutters in April 1771 there was some uncertainty about what do to with him. According to one witness, 'some cried one thing and some another, some were for hanging him and some for drowning him, and some cried out for mercy, but there were but few of them'.[87] In a culture where street protest was the norm, every Londoner had the opportunity to express their views, and this led to conflicts within the mob as well as between the mob and its enemies.

The notoriously destructive Gordon Riots of 1780 represent the culmination of this widely accepted tradition of Londoners taking to the streets to voice their grievances (Figure 16). A year earlier, the *London Evening Post* had praised the actions of protesters celebrating the acquittal of Admiral Keppel in his court-martial, which included an attack on the Prime Minister's house in Downing Street, where they broke the windows, entered the house, and attempted to destroy the furniture, by lauding 'this spirit of the people without doors'.[88] On Friday 2 June 1780, when an orderly procession of tens of thousands of members of the Protestant Association marched to Parliament to present their petition for the repeal of the Catholic Relief Act, Lord George Gordon told the crowd that 'the Scotch ... had no redress [against the Catholics] until they pulled down the mass-houses'. Later that evening, the first building to be attacked, the Sardinian Chapel, was set on fire. Two days later, as more chapels were attacked, the Lord Mayor, who had been noticeably inactive in suppressing the riots (perhaps because he feared popular retribution), was reported as saying 'the mob had got hold of some people and some furniture they did not like and were burning

16. William Hamilton 'The Devastations Occasioned by the Rioters of London Firing the New Gaol of Newgate' (1780). (*Guildhall Library, Corporation of London*)

them, and where was the harm in that'. By the time the riots ended on
8 June, the 'harm' can be calculated at hundreds of dead (mostly killed
by soldiers), dozens of houses, chapels and public buildings destroyed,
and at least £100,000 worth of property damaged.[89] Attitudes towards
the mob would never be the same again.

Even before the Gordon Riots shook the city to its core, Londoners'
propensity to take to the streets was in decline, as both elites and
ordinary people became concerned about the extent of violence and
disorder, and developed other means of expressing their grievances.
Analysis of the sessions records suggests that the number of small-scale
riots on London's streets declined from the 1750s (Chart 3), and quali-
tative evidence indicates that the nature of crowd protest changed
significantly in the second half of the eighteenth century, making it more
difficult for rioters to project the appearance of public support for their
point of view. Riots which took place towards the end of the century
were more violent, involved greater use of weapons, and were subject
to greater repression by the authorities. Rioters in the early eighteenth
century rarely used weapons more lethal than stones, and those who
did were soldiers and gentlemen wielding swords. But the industrial
disturbances of 1768–69 marked a substantial escalation in the use of
weapons by both protesters and the authorities. Both the coalheavers
and the silkweavers used cutlasses and pistols. The coalheavers' grievances against John Green, a rival 'undertaker' who attempted to break
their strike, led them to attack his tavern repeatedly in April 1768,
breaking his windows and threatening to pull down the house. On the
night of the 20th a cobbler was shot in the street by an unknown person,
and the coalheavers, suspecting that Green was responsible, began to
attack his house more vehemently. Green tried to frighten them off by
firing a warning shot, which caused the rioters to retreat for about fifteen
minutes, but they returned with firearms and ammunition. They laid
siege to the house, and the ensuing gunfight lasted all night, only ending
when Green managed to escape early in the morning. In the coalheavers'
dispute with sailors who broke their strike by unloading their own ships,
shots were fired from both sides 'till at length there was an actual state
of war between these ruffians and the colliers' ships and in the nighttimes
a continual firing was kept up'.[90]

In the case of the silkweavers, a statute passed in 1765 had forced their activities underground by making the destruction of looms and the work on them punishable by death. According to a prosecution brief, this statute

> put no effectual stop to these mischiefs, but it put the offenders upon acting more cautiously and withal more cruelly: knowing their fate if they were apprehended, they disguised themselves and performed their exploits in the dead of night, [and] procured arms and offensive weapons of all kinds ...

In the attack on Thomas Poor's house, about midnight on 7 August 1769, for example, seven cutters entered the house armed with swords, cutlasses and pistols. Following the destruction of silk in his looms, they left the house, firing off two or three pistols in celebration of their successful attack.[91] Another reason for the cutters' use of weapons was that they were also being used by at least one employer, who ordered his employees to refuse to pay strike dues to the journeymen societies and instead issued them with firearms.[92] During the Gordon Riots, pistols were used in the attacks on the Bank of England and firearms were carried by rioters who attacked the house of George Reid, a justice who was active in suppressing the riots.[93] Rioters' growing use of weapons was also, as discussed below, a response to the escalation of violence by the authorities in their attempts to suppress disturbances.

Faced with the possibility of injury or death from these weapons, Londoners may well have chosen to steer clear of popular protests, unless they were particularly committed to the cause. This was not difficult in the case of the cutters, whose actions tended to take place in the middle of the night. But evidence that community involvement and support for protest was declining can also be seen in the decrease in the use and efficacy of the crowd-gathering techniques which summoned the community to participate in demonstrations. As we have seen with public insults, crowds became less likely to gather spontaneously in response to the summons of a shouted insult in the second half of the eighteenth century, and indeed such public insults became less common. Similarly, bonfires, effigy burnings, and flags and cockades were rarely used to assemble crowds after the Gordon Riots.[94] Crowds also became less likely to invoke the symbolism of community protest. The vocabulary of rough music and ridings was rarely present in crowd protests in the final quarter of the century, as was the use of references to official punishments such as the halter and gibbet. Instead, the symbols crowds adopted, such as 'the cap of liberty', expressed more politically divisive (and even subversive) meanings.[95]

These changes reflect a decline in the extent to which crowds used public spaces to express sentiments which were intended to represent the views of the whole community. A nice example of this general trend is the history of May Day rituals in London. Whereas in the seventeenth century this celebration of the advent of spring was a genuinely communal festivity, by the end of the eighteenth century the ritual had become socially divisive, with the primary activity involving chimney sweeps intimidating householders into giving them handouts.[96]

Why did mob protest cease to play such an important role in London's public life? From the point of view of elites, public demonstrations no longer effectively served the purposes they once had, and became perceived as nothing more than a source of disorder. As indicated by the use of weapons, riots appear to have become more violent, and in any case elite standards of order were becoming more demanding. Consequently, elite sponsorship and toleration of street protests was withdrawn. In the second half of the century the annual calendar of celebrations of political anniversaries declined, and from the 1760s more sober celebrations were demanded. Impending commemorations of the arrival of the new Queen and the coronation of George III in 1761 prompted concerns that the mob would use these traditionally festive occasions as an excuse to riot. An editorial in the *London Evening Post* objected to 'bonfires in the streets, to the great annoyance of all passengers, and even to the endangering of lives and limbs; for who can restrain a mob?' Bonfires, it alleged, were 'encouragers of riot', and they allowed gangs to assemble, 'who commit every crime in their power'. On the day of the coronation, the *Public Advertiser* published a letter complaining about the firing of guns and setting off of squibs (firecrackers), practices which normally accompanied 'the usual demonstrations of joy on public occasions'. 'As soon as the Tower guns are fired off', it complained, 'the public consider it a signal for every kind of outrage.' Signalling a new attitude towards the use of public spaces for expressing and reinforcing communal loyalties, the *London Evening Post* published another letter complaining about the 'luxury' of processions, which promoted appearances rather than substance, leading to a situation where 'the external figure shall denominate the man, and glory be founded in the shout of a mob'. By the late eighteenth century royal celebrations became less public, with active participation restricted to those who were directly connected to the court. In 1790 the Queen's birthday was celebrated with ringing church bells, shots fired from military guns in Hyde Park and the Tower, a drawing room and ball at St James's Palace, and 'illuminations in the front of the houses of all the tradesmen of the Royal Family in different parts of the town'.[97]

From 1765 the authorities cracked down on the use of flags, drums and cockades to gather crowds. Facing possible riots from the silkweavers in 1765, a letter from Lord Sandwich to justices of the peace urged them to apprehend 'all persons who by beat of drum and carrying of flags and colours are concerned in gathering together such tumultuous assemblies'.[98] Similarly, in 1768 flags, banners and drums carried by striking sailors and coalheavers were seized by the justices, and in 1780 it became clear that the Gordon Riots were finally coming to an end when, on 8 June, the soldiers pulled down the blue flags hanging from houses and tore the blue cockades from the rioters' hats.[99]

Following the Wilkes and Liberty and industrial protests of 1768, politicians and newspapers appear to have become more cautious in appealing to the crowd. There were attempts to keep crowds from getting involved during the dispute between the City and the government over the printing of parliamentary debates in 1771. In early April, when passions were running high, the Lord Mayor, Brass Crosby, was brought from the Tower to attend court, but it was decided not to turn this into a public occasion. As the *General Evening Post* reported, he was brought to Westminster 'in a private manner'. Three months later, there was some dispute over how the Lord Mayor should present a City remonstrance to the King. Although the King instructed Crosby to bring only a small number of people with him, he attempted to summon a crowd. But newspapers advised masters and parents to keep their children and servants at home, claiming 'those who are cautious will keep out of the way of riot and disorder'. In the end, the day passed off peacefully. In September, the behaviour of crowds was once again called into question when an anti-Wilkite candidate for the next Lord Mayor, Alderman Nash, was 'brutally attacked by the populace' on leaving the Guildhall.

Not only were the people involved censured in the *General Evening Post* as 'unprincipled, uninformed reptiles', but Wilkes, a former promoter of mobs, went out of his way to protect Nash and 'endeavoured by every possible means to calm the fury of the rabble'.[100]

Unsurprisingly, attitudes towards the crowd hardened considerably after the Gordon Riots. Only a few days after they ended an occasion arose which was traditionally the cause of public celebrations: news reached London of the British victory at Charles Town in the American War. Despite the good news, attempts were made to prevent celebrations by distributing a notice which discouraged Londoners from engaging in 'illuminations and other demonstrations of joy', since these 'may give a pretence to ill-disposed and ill-intentioned people to assemble in crowds, and endeavour to renew the late disorders'.[101] Similarly, celebrations of the centenary of the 'Glorious Revolution' in 1788 and of the recovery of the King in 1789 were designed to keep popular participation to a minimum, with the activities in 1788 organised primarily by gentlemen's clubs and societies. While in 1789 specially commissioned transparencies brought elites out in the streets in their carriages, the role of ordinary people was largely confined to acting as spectators and as the recipients of doles. A correspondent to the *St James's Chronicle* in 1794 observed that while 'it will generally be found that a mob is not wrong in its principle', it never abides by it: 'if you once are so weak as to give way to them, they will soon change their ground, and general plunder will be the word'.[102]

Concurrently, greater efforts were made to subdue rioters through the use of the military. Owing to the perceived constitutional threat posed by the existence of a standing army, there had historically been great reluctance to use soldiers to police civil disturbances in the capital. Nonetheless, after the Hanoverian accession soldiers were occasionally summoned when the civil authorities lost control, and in the ensuing decades the procedures for requesting such assistance were gradually streamlined. In the 1760s, under provocation from crowds throwing brickbats and, as we have seen, occasionally using swords and guns, the military began to adopt more offensive tactics, such as charging through crowds on horse and foot, using the flat sides of their swords as weapons and firing into the air. Fatalities began to mount: four were killed suppressing a sailors' attack on a public house in 1763; six or seven were shot in the riot outside King's Bench prison in 1768; and nine 'cutters' were killed in 1769. Three soldiers and one magistrate were prosecuted for murder in the aftermath of the King's Bench shootings. Although none were convicted, this increased officers' reluctance to order soldiers to fire unless they were specifically directed to do so by a magistrate. The absence or inaction of London justices during the Gordon Riots led to a virtual paralysis of the machinery of law enforcement, until on the sixth day the King ordered the military to act directly without waiting for orders from magistrates. In a significant escalation of their role, the military were ordered 'to use force for dispersing the illegal and tumultuous assemblies of the people'. Within days, over 275 rioters had been killed by some of the over 10,000 soldiers deployed to suppress the riots.[103]

Although crowds were not always intimidated by the presence of soldiers (and soldiers were often reluctant to shoot at their fellow citizens), the danger of arrest, injury or death often caused mobs to disperse rapidly when the army appeared, and no doubt dissuaded many potential participants from joining protests. The attack by sailors on a brothel in 1749 ended quickly when 'the guard came with a drum beating' and 'they all took to flight'. When around one thousand journeymen shoemakers assembled outside a magistrate's office in February 1792 to protest at the arrest of twenty-one of their number for organising a strike for higher wages, soldiers were immediately sent for. At their approach, the *Times* reported, 'the mob instantly dispersed'. Responses to the military were more varied four months later when rioting was provoked by the actions of an overzealous justice of the peace who arrested more than forty servants for dancing on the King's birthday. When a watch house was attacked on the first evening, the presence of soldiers failed to intimidate the crowd, even after they fired their weapons. The *Times* reported that 'a great many people must have been wounded, for the soldiers kept a very constant fire for more than half an hour'. The next night, however, when a crowd gathered again and soldiers were once again summoned, 'there seemed a great disposition to riot, had it not been restrained by the appearance of the military'.[104]

By increasing the costs and dangers of participating in disturbances, the presence of the military helped to destroy the spontaneity of London rioting, whereby passers-by had often joined any crowds they happened to come across. By the late eighteenth century the choice of participation had to be made more deliberately, and the opportunity appears to have more frequently not been taken up. Rioters were further marginalised by the use of organisations of householders to suppress riots. These associations dated from the Gordon Riots, when the presence of mobs roaming the streets looking for houses of Catholics to pull down caused attitudes towards the mob to harden and led neighbours to band together to protect their homes. As John Drummond, a gentleman of Lyon's Inn, reported in a letter to Lord Stormont on 7 June praising 'the citizens of London' for acting 'with vigour and spirit', one Mr Thorp of Fleet Street 'first took my hint of uniting with his neighbours to meet in the vestry of St Bride's and patrol the streets in defence of themselves and property ... There are, I am persuaded, many of those who were active in spiriting up the mob to commit devastation that have now changed sides.' The next day, groups of Catholic Irish coalheavers and chairmen in Wapping and residents of the Inns of Court formed similar associations, and within a week Samuel Romilly reported that 'the inhabitants of almost every parish are forming themselves into associations to protect their houses'.[105] These associations continued to be active in preventing disorder after 1780. In September 1800 high food prices led to riots directed at corn dealers, butchers, bakers and cheesemongers in the City. However, according to the *Gentleman's Magazine*, 'the vigour and promptitude of the chief magistrate, aided by the zeal and alacrity of the volunteer associations, prevented the mob (except in two or three instances), from effecting any greater mischief than the breaking of windows and lamps'.[106]

The formation of associations of householders was a key development in the history of the London mob, since communities were now more sharply divided between rioters and those who wished to preserve order. The long-held fiction that crowds expressed the views of the community could no longer be sustained: rioting was now clearly a divisive force. No doubt these divisions were often those of class: the associations were often described as composed of gentlemen, while the mob comprised the 'populace'. But, as the participation of the coalheavers and carmen suggests, those who joined these associations were not all gentlemen. There was a widespread change of attitudes towards street protest, which led Londoners of all social classes to become less willing to use the streets to voice their grievances, as is also evident in the history of the public insult in this period.

Following the debacle of the Gordon Riots, radical politicians also began to distance themselves from the mob. Not only was the anarchic nature of the rioting against their principles, it was also counterproductive, since it provided the authorities with an excuse to close down opportunities for protest. In 1795, Vicesimus Knox, a Whig scholar, argued that 'riots, tumults and popular commotions are indeed truly dreadful, and to be avoided with the utmost care by the lovers of liberty'. By the end of the eighteenth century it was loyalists who were more likely to appeal to the crowd for support. When the radical Thomas Hardy refused to illuminate his house on the occasion of Admiral Duncan's victory over the Dutch Fleet in 1797, he complained that a 'lawless mob' broke his windows.[107]

Radicals and others could afford to abandon crowd protest owing to the development of alternative methods of pressing their case, notably the voluntary society and the public meeting. Voluntary societies, often meeting in public houses, date from the late seventeenth century in England, and were another quintessential feature of eighteenth-century urban life, alongside the mob. But while the mob was in decline at the end of the century, voluntary societies flourished: by 1800 there were up to 3000 clubs and societies in London. In 1715 the 'loyal societies' of Whig loyalists who met in the mughouses organised street demonstrations and attacks on Tory crowds. But as societies developed more sophisticated tactics for pressuring governments over the course of the century they evolved as an alternative method of protest to rioting. Some of the earliest of these organisations in London were primitive trade unions, groups of journeymen and labourers in some trades who used petitions and strikes to push for higher wages or better working conditions. London's tailors formed a union as early as 1700, which sought, often successfully, to regulate employment practices in the trade. Although they were in frequent conflict with the master tailors, they rarely resorted to street protests. The development of this new form of labour relations was facilitated both by the rapid expansion of this trade and the fact that the merchant tailors' guild largely ceased to regulate it, but tailors were not the only group of wage labourers to organise during the century.[108] In 1768 all the major groups involved in industrial protests, including the sailors, coalheavers, and silkweavers, had formed societies, some of which, as with the silkweavers, were secret. Although street protest was part of the repertoire of action of these groups, it was typically used only when other methods failed. As we have seen, the silkweavers enforced a ban on the use of labour-saving 'engine looms', minimum piece rates and the payment of strike contributions through visits of 'cutters' to weavers' houses, but even these riots, taking place as they did in the middle of the night, were not meant to attract public attention. Street protest continued to play a role in labour unrest, supplementing work stoppages, legal actions, and petitions to Parliament until the 1830s, but it was increasingly used as a last resort.[109]

Radical politics adopted the voluntary society, and its tactics of holding indoor meetings, publishing propaganda and conducting petitioning campaigns, in the 1760s. Supporters of Wilkes formed the Society of the Supporters of the Bill of Rights in 1769 and mounted a nationwide petitioning campaign in support of his struggle to be allowed to take up a seat in Parliament. In 1779 and 1780 the Association Movement was formed to press for parliamentary reform. One of the most radical associations was based in Westminster; a newspaper account of its meeting in April 1780 noted that 'no particular riots or disorder had ensued, when this paper went to press'. Of course, such meetings did not always end peacefully: two months later the Gordon Riots erupted following a mass march to Parliament by the Protestant Association. But by discrediting crowd protest, these riots provided further encouragement to political campaigners to focus their efforts on holding meetings, which often took place in alehouses. Legal persecution of landlords who allowed such groups to meet in their premises, however, and the sheer size of the groups involved, often forced the meetings outdoors. The London Corresponding Society (founded in 1792) organised peaceful mass meetings of up to 300,000 supporters in Copenhagen and St George's Fields in 1794–95. These outdoor meetings were very different from the Wilkite demonstrations of the 1760s: they were stationary rather than processions, they took place on the edge of the metropolis, and they were heavily policed. Although such meetings were prohibited by the Seditious Meetings Act in 1795, they re-emerged powerfully after 1815. This 'platform radicalism' marked the development of a new form of popular politics which in seeking respectability avoided disorder in any form.[110]

According to a recent statistical analysis of 'contentious gatherings' in southern England between 1758 and 1834, there was an increase in meetings, demonstrations, gatherings of associations and official assemblies over this period, and a decline in both violent gatherings and shaming punishments which involved the vocabulary of ridings. Although much of this change occurred following the Napoleonic wars, there was an increase in meetings, marches and petitioning in London from 1768. These marked a significant change from early eighteenth-century protests, which frequently occurred within the established traditions of official public celebrations. Meetings were typically planned in advance at the protesters' own initiative rather than simply taking advantage of official occasions when crowds were known to gather.[111] They were more likely to be stationary, rather than moving through the streets, and they sometimes took place indoors. Instead of mounting pressure on the government or their employers by creating the physical and symbolic appearance of widespread community support, the purpose of these events was more likely to be signing petitions, passing resolutions, and deciding to hold further meetings.

By the end of the eighteenth century the age of the mob was over. In 1799 J. H. Meister commented that, despite seeing vast crowds during his stay in London, 'I have met with fewer disturbances and frays than are to be seen at Paris in one morning'.[112] Although street protest was still part of the repertoire of collective action in early nineteenth-century London, its role was much diminished, and its character had changed.[113] Just as Londoners became less likely to participate in policing deviance and shaming convicts punished in public, they were less likely to join demonstrations, and crowds became less likely to form spontaneously from those present on the streets. Many of the traditional techniques for summoning crowds were in decline, as public anniversaries were no longer used as a springboard for popular protest. Instead, protests were planned in advance and participants were recruited with printed handbills and posters.[114] As reputations became established less publicly, crowds became less likely use and manipulate visual symbols to claim public support for their actions. Elites, who had previously sometimes been guilty of encouraging mobs, had become scared of crowds, and many ordinary Londoners were also discouraged from joining by the presence of the military and the threat of damage to life and property posed by both soldiers and rioters. In any case, new methods of voicing protests and exerting pressure on opponents were developing, often involving stationary or indoor meetings. Instead of being one of the first resorts of those with grievances to express, crowd protest became a last resort. The mob, which had become a significant feature on metropolitan streets only a century earlier, had lost its central place in London public life.

# 6

# *Violence*

Violence was never far away on the streets of eighteenth-century London. The behaviour of crowds in riots and public punishments typically involved verbal if not physical intimidation, and threats of force were often realised, leading to property damage, injuries and occasionally death. Yet, when compared with the rest of Europe, visitors were impressed by the lack of serious violence in England. The Swiss visitor Béat-Louis de Muralt wrote early in the century that the English 'abhor all cruel things; duels, assassinations, and generally all sorts of violence are very uncommon in this country'. Specific note was made the lack of violence in London, described by the Frenchman Pierre Jean Grosley in 1770 as 'the only great city in Europe where neither murders nor assassinations happen'.[1] Such comments, of course, may be interpreted as revealing more about street life back in their home countries than about conditions in London, but in fact homicide rates were lower in England than on the Continent in this period.[2] While murder may have been relatively rare, Muralt was wrong to state that other forms of violence were uncommon. In 1799 J. H. Meister observed that though 'murders are very rarely the consequence', 'frequent quarrels arise amongst the populace'.[3] London life was permeated by beatings and fights, but it is important to note that such violence was not indiscriminate or meaningless.[4] Like rioting, violence was governed by informal rules which served both to legitimise it and to limit (but not eliminate) fatal consequences. And like both insults and riots, violence was a fundamentally public activity, at least for men. It was used both to establish and defend reputations, and instrumentally by those who could not get what they wanted by other means. Yet over the course of the century changes in the way reputations were established in London, together with changing attitudes towards violence, rendered public violence increasingly unacceptable and its incidence decreased.

Controlled violence was an integral aspect of masculinity in this period. Men were expected to assert their independence by resorting to violence when their honesty or authority was challenged. Formally embodied in the duel and boxing match (discussed in the next chapter), the use of violence to assert and defend male honour publicly was widespread. In conflicts with other men, men needed to demonstrate their courage, strength and independence – their manliness – by exhibiting their willingness to fight. As the *London Evening Post* described an incident between 'two young fellows' who quarrelled in Marylebone, they 'went out to try their manhood in the fields'.[5] Joseph Blakemore and John Everet were playing skittles at the Coach and Horses in Highgate in 1731 when an argument erupted about a bet. When the company judged that John Everet had won, Blakemore said to him 'What for a man are you?' to which Everet made the only possible reply: 'A man, or piece of man, as well as you' and the fight which occasioned Everet's death started.[6] The bravado men displayed in such disputes often contributed directly to the outbreak of violence. In an argument with Daniel Looney over the behaviour of Looney's wife, Joseph Shanks said 'he would rout' Looney. Faced with this challenge, Looney shot Shanks. As he explained to the court, having had his masculinity questioned, he had no choice but to respond, despite his professed lack of malice towards Shanks:

> Rout me, said I, who shall rout me? I pay ground-rent and all taxes; it is not that man that ever was born that shall rout me. The gun happened to be there, I don't know who loaded her; I had not had it in my hand for weeks before. I said, that man, be who he will, man or woman, shall not rout me. As for any malice, I had none at all; I had no more malice against Captain Shanks than I had against my own heart.[7]

Some men spontaneously claimed superior strength in a way which demanded a response from anyone present with a claim to manliness. In 1754 John Hudson sat in an alehouse with his head on the table as if he was asleep, 'and all of a sudden he started up and clapt his hat down on the table and said he would fight the best man in the house'. He then said to Thomas Moss, 'you I take to be the best man and I will fight you for a guinea'. They fought the next day (but only for a leg of mutton and some turnips, since they were poor men), and Moss died from the injuries he received.[8]

The association of men with violence started at an early age. For boys, fighting was a form of play. François Misson reported that 'apprentices, and all boys of that degree, are never without their cudgels, with which they fight' like prize-fighters, and Grosley observed that the taste for fighting 'is so inherent in English blood, that at Eaton [sic], Westminster school, and other places of the same sort, the children of the greatest noblemen often challenge one another to combats of this kind, and box according to all the rules and punctilios of honour'.[9] The sense of bravado found among adult men is already evident, for example, in an account of a fight in 1749 between a tap house boy and an apprentice, occasioned by some comments about the former's singing. The tap house boy then responded by calling the apprentice and his friend 'monkeys' and said 'he would knock both their heads together'. Groups of boys were easily recruited to join in assaults on figures of authority. In November 1761, for example, 'a number of butchers' boys from Leadenhall Market' joined a mob which 'fell furiously' on a press gang which had been impressing men for the navy, routed them, and forced the officer in charge 'to undergo a severe discipline under a pump'. According to a newspaper report, 'several persons were wounded in the fray'. Eight months earlier a group of apprentices known as the 'Bride-well boys' attacked some constables who were searching disorderly houses in the Strand and rescued the 'disorderly women' the constables had arrested.[10]

Men were frequently provoked into violence when their honour was questioned. Typically, this occurred when they were accused of telling a falsehood; 'giving the lie' was the expression which inevitably escalated a dispute from words to violence. Even a petty dispute about sharing the costs of a drinking session was sufficient. John Chambers and John Milman were drinking together in 1698 when 'some difference happened about the reckoning' and Chambers, 'without any other provocation than a lye, gave the deceased the wound' with a rapier which caused his death.[11] Men accused of dishonesty (by being called a 'scoundrel') or general low life ('rogue', 'dirty fellow') had little choice but to respond, and whereas women tended to respond to similar insults with ever more colourful insults, or by pursuing court cases, men were expected to respond physically.[12] Indeed, insulting words directed at men are often portrayed as so provocative that a violent response was inevitable.

Following an exchange of insults ('hard words passed ... on both sides') between William Payne and Arthur Hancock in 1755, Payne told Hancock 'for your abusive man[ner] you ought to be beat'; Hancock responded to the provocation by knocking him down and almost pushing him into the kennel. The *London Journal* reported an incident in 1731 when an apprentice of 'good character', who was participating in a muster of the trained bands, was 'insulted and treated ... in a very rough manner' by a Mr Longworth, which 'unhappily provoked the young man so far as to stab him with his bayonet'. Quarrels between gentlemen and hackney coachmen more than once ended in the former killing the latter, 'provoked by the villainous tongues of those fellows beyond the extent of their patience'.[13] Violence was also provoked by physical affronts, when a man was jostled, elbowed or obstructed, intentionally or not, and felt obliged to respond. In 1731 Joseph Everet, although an old man, slapped William Shaw on the face after Shaw had insulted him and 'jostled' him with his elbows, saying he 'would not take these affronts'.[14] Reluctant men were provoked into fighting by the threat of being called a coward, the very antithesis of manliness. At 5 o'clock one morning in February 1696, John Sharpe, a soldier, met an old acquaintance, Richard Campion, who invited Sharpe to join him for a drink. They went to a tavern in Lincoln's Inn Fields, where 'between them the lie was given' and Campion asked him to step outside. When Sharpe refused, Campion said that 'unless he followed him ... he would expose him as a coward', so Sharpe accompanied him to Lambs Conduit Fields where a sword fight ensued. In another case, a man who refused to fight was told that if he did not respond his challenger 'would post him in the coffee house for a scoundrel'.[15]

Men were less likely to complain to the courts when insulted or challenged because to do so would be a sign of weakness. Similarly, to apologise for an affront could be seen as unmanly, no doubt because it meant acting in a subservient manner. In 1779 James Proctor, impressed for military service by George Lister, a constable, was about to be released at the intercession of a third party, but he refused to apologise to Lister for 'having run against him in the street'. Instead, Proctor went on the offensive. He proceeded to give Lister 'very opprobrious language ... lifted up his hand against Lister and bragged that he could beat him and several more'.[16] Men had such a high sensitivity to insult and such a keen desire to prove their manliness that fights often arose out of incredibly trivial incidents. The *General Evening Post* ridiculed this practice in a report of an incident on 13 August 1771, during a party at the Mansion House, when a young gentleman, 'who happened to get a little top heavy ... strayed into a dark room, and fancying that someone had affronted him, drew his sword on his supposed antagonist, and ran it through the glass door of a bookcase'.[17]

When cornered during a dispute, violence was preferable to surrender. In June 1771 a dispute between a hackney coachman and a gentleman who had no change to pay his fare turned violent when the coachman grabbed hold of the gentleman and refused to let him go to a nearby coffee-house, swearing 'he would be paid before his quitted his hold'. Put into an intolerable position, 'the gentleman drew his sword, and ran the coachman through the arm ... and got clear off'.[18] Violence was particularly likely when men were threatened with arrest and therefore the loss of their independence. In 1699 Benjamin Barton was in 'a little drinking box' in an alehouse in Red Lion Square when John Jones, a Marshal's Court officer, came to arrest him, telling him there was an action (a lawsuit over a debt) against him. Barton threatened to stab anyone who opened the door, and when Jones did so he was fatally stabbed. When a lawyer, Mac-gwen (sic), was threatened by a justice with imprisonment on a warrant for the peace in February 1735, he reacted angrily, insulting the justice and 'telling him, he did not dare commit him, being a sworn attorney'. Nonetheless the commitment was signed, and Mac-gwen responded by drawing out his penknife and stabbing the man whose testimony had caused him to be arrested.[19]

Unsurprisingly, the practice of impressing sailors to serve in the navy generated some of the most violent opposition. While in some cases the press gangs were thought to have overstepped their powers, in all cases men faced not just with the loss of their liberty but also dangerous conditions in naval service had every reason to resist, and their friends, fellow workers, and neighbours frequently joined the battle in their support. In 1761, after a press gang apprehended some sailors in Whitechapel, the crews of their ships were 'enraged ... they pursued them and beat them in so bad a manner, that it's feared two of the men of war's men will lose their lives by the wounds and bruises they received'. In anticipation of heavy resistance or provoked by insults, the violence was sometimes instigated by the press gangs. When a lieutenant entered an alehouse in Southwark in October 1741 in search of 'skulking seamen', the *London Evening Post* reported, he

> was opposed and insulted by the company that were drinking there; at which his men being exasperated began to exercise their oaken towels [cudgels], and laid about them very briskly. The people in return had recourse to paring [sic] shovels, broomsticks, pokers, tongs, or anything they could lay hold of. In a word, the battle was presently general, and very bloody; here lay a taylor, and there a sailor, and so on ...

The landlord received fifteen wounds, and one of the sailors had a shovel full of burning coals thrown into his chest. Ultimately, as was usually the case, the more heavily armed press gang triumphed and carried off five men.[20]

Men used violence not only to assert their independence from other men but also to claim superiority over women and other dependants. It was common practice for men to use violence to discipline their wives in this period, and heads of households were also entitled to beat their servants and children. Angry that he 'came home hungry to dinner' and his wife was not there, Patrick Noonan, a soldier, went to the pub where she was drinking and struck her on the head with a 'thick stick'. This conduct appears to have been acceptable to those who witnessed it, except for the fact that, although 'he thought it was his wife he corrected', he actually struck the wrong woman. Even so, the victim forgave him, although she later died.[21] Such was the legitimacy husbands were accorded in performing such beatings that they were often carried out in front of witnesses, or with the neighbours' knowledge. Men thereby called attention to the legitimacy of their actions and sought to increase the impact and effectiveness of the discipline.[22] There were limits to the extent of acceptable violence in such contexts, however, and neighbours did sometimes interfere when they believed the violence had gone too far. When the landlord of a public house near Golden Square fell out with his wife in 1721 and 'threw her down, stamp'd on her breast, and broke her sternum', the noise 'drew many of the neighbours together' who rushed into the house.[23]

The 'discipline' meted out to servants by their masters (and occasionally mistresses), and to children by anyone with authority over them, could be equally violent. In 1731 two men were playing billiards when one of the sticks broke and Matthew Morrice, a boy, was sent to get it mended. While he was gone the two men argued about a bet they had placed, and when he returned one of the men, John Piggot, blamed the boy for causing the dispute, and 'gave him a blow on the head with the billiard stick'. Despite the fact all the witnesses claimed the blow was given 'without any violence', Morrice fell down and died shortly thereafter. Revealing just how widespread such allegedly low-level violence was, the other player sought to exonerate Piggot by claiming that 'he had given much greater blows to his own son, to his thinking, without doing him any injury'.[24]

Men also used violence against other men to show women that they were dependent on them for their protection. It was claimed in 1680 that when gentlemen accompanied ladies in the street they were over-protective of their companions, and should another man 'casually ... give her the least jostle, tis ten to one but this zealous gallant, out of an ambition to ingratiate himself and appear a man of mettle ... either he draws [his sword] himself, or gives the other provocation enough to do it'. After a drunken gentleman threw a glass of wine over a lady's head in 'a public garden' in 1771, one of her gentleman companions immediately drew his sword and exchanged a few thrusts with the culprit. Men did not even need to know the victims of these real or pretended insults. In July 1686 a group of women at Whitefriars stairs quarrelled with some watermen about the cost of taking them to White-hall. John Brooks, a soldier standing nearby, took the side of the women. He called the watermen 'puppy and rascal and other names', threw stones at them, and provoked a fight.[25] When women were insulted, men felt compelled to affirm their honour and protect them by fighting or issuing a challenge. In doing so, they affirmed their role as protectors of the weaker sex.

Read outside their contexts, accounts of fights and murders in eighteenth-century London might lead one to conclude that violence was widespread and indiscriminate, but this was not the case. Men used violence only in specific circumstances, when they felt the need to defend or assert their masculine honour and independence, and when it appeared there was no other way to achieve their goals. This is evident in the relatively rare cases in which violence was used during street robberies. Like today, robbery was a crime which caused considerable public concern, and such anxiety was fuelled by reports of such crimes in newspapers and other contemporary writing about crime, where the use of violence was exaggerated. Charles Hitchin claimed in 1718 that Londoners were afraid to visit pubs, coffee houses and shops after dark 'for fear that their hats and wigs should be snatched from off their heads, or their swords taken from their sides, or that they may be blinded, knocked down, cut or stabbed; nay, the coaches cannot secure them, but they are likewise assaulted, cut and robbed in the publick streets'. During a panic over property crime following the end of the War of Austrian Succession, the *Whitehall Evening Post* reported that 'the streets of this city, and the suburbs thereof, are greatly infested with a number of villains confederating in small companies to rob, and, on any the smallest opposition, to maim and murder the passengers'.[26] In practice, however, the amount of violence used by London robbers was actually relatively low, and, while it is impossible to explain every incident in these terms, most of the force that was used was either instrumental or the threat of violence was used to enhance the thief's social prestige. Only 9 per cent of the indictments for theft at the Old Bailey between 1714 and 1799 charged the defendant with violence, and in many of these cases the violence was only threatened, sufficient to put the victim in fear but not actually carried out. Around midnight on 20 December 1724, as William Wasey was walking along Lincoln's Inn Fields, 'he was attacked by three men, one of which clapt a pistol to his head ... and they bid him deliver immediately, threatening if he spoke one word, they would shoot him through the head'. After surrendering his gold watch, a tweezer case, a sword and some money, he escaped without injury.[27]

The tradition of the gentlemanly highway robber, who treated his victims courteously, was mostly a myth, but when mounted robbers had overwhelming force and worked in an isolated location or under cover of darkness they 'indulged in a form of polite interchange' with their victims in order to enhance their claims to gentility.[28] The *General Evening Post* reported on a robbery of some stage coaches committed by 'a single highwayman' in January 1752:

> he behaved with great civility as a highwayman, for being desired ... to withdraw his pistol, he immediately returned it to his bridle hand, desiring

the passengers would not be affrighted, his intent being only to get a little money to supply a present necessity. On his riding off, he dropt 4s. 6d. to treat the passengers in one of the coaches with a breakfast.

Even on the crowded streets of the metropolis, there were occasionally opportunities for robbers to act with 'civility'. As George Lewis Jones was travelling from the City to Cavendish Square at eleven o'clock one night in February 1754, his coach was stopped in St Giles in the Fields by Samuel Dean and William Wilson. Dean put a pistol to Jones's breast, and, according to Jones,

> ordered me to sit down and behave quietly … he said, he would use us like gentlemen … he demanded my watch and money, I gave him a guinea and some silver, I believe about three or four shillings; then he put his hand to my fob, to feel for my watch, but did not find it, although [it was] then in my fob. After this they went away.[29]

When robbers actually used violence, it was typically in order to facilitate the rapid removal of the owner's property, to overcome resistance, or to facilitate their escape. When a robbery was committed on London's streets it usually had to be committed expeditiously, and thieves often initially knocked their victims down in order to remove property from them before they realised what was happening. Sarah Wood was coming through Exchange Alley about eight o'clock in the evening in August 1723 when 'some body came by her side, gave her a violent push, and she fell against the wall, and putting his hand under her petticoat pull'd off her pocket', containing a pair of silver buckles and a considerable amount of money, and ran off. Needless to say, if a victim resisted, cried out for help or chased after the culprit, the violence escalated. As robbery was punishable by death, escape without detection was essential. When James Belford accosted Ann Baker in the middle of Tothill Street and tried to pull the ring off her finger, she 'cry'd out'. As she told the court, he then 'knock'd me down (I believe it was with his fist), cut my hand in three places, and tore off my mob [cap] (and some of my hair with it), and leaving me on the ground, ran away'. When another of Belford's victims, Mary Allen, chased after him and cried out 'murder and stop thief', he knocked her down, pulled out a knife and threatened to cut her throat. When Captain Jasper Johns was robbed by two men in 1747, he initially 'let them go off quietly, but hearing some people coming towards him, he found he had the [culprits] between these people and himself, and he thought it proper to take one or both of them, and he cry'd out, stop thief. Upon which one of them return'd and gave him [a] stab in the body', which proved fatal. Victims who denied having a watch or money, as Richard Harper did when accosted by four men in Moorfields around eight o'clock one evening in January 1754, were likely to regret it. As Harper told the court,

> I said I had no money; then one of them struck me over the head, but [he] had asked me for my watch first, and I said I had never a one; I was stunned with one blow, then they began to rifle me for my watch, which they found in my waistcoat pocket ... then one of them gave me a drive on the head, and said if I offered to call after them they would come back and murder me.[30]

Thieves, like other men, did not like being lied to.

Whereas contemporaries identified ordinary robbers as the most violent group in society, early in the century gentlemen were in fact proportionally the social group most likely to engage in violence leading to death, the consequence of their need to affirm their social position (and their related propensity for carrying swords). Whereas the gentry accounted for only around 3 to 5 per cent of householders in London, 15 per cent of the men accused of murder in London were gentlemen.[31] At a time when the definition of a gentleman was becoming increasingly fluid, those who aspired to gentility were especially anxious to assert their social superiority over their increasingly prosperous middle-class competitors. One way of doing this was to carry a sword; another was to engage in an illegal activity such as fighting that showed that they were above the law. Still another method of asserting difference was to subscribe to a particularly demanding code of honour, in which any questioning of a gentleman's honesty was deemed so offensive that 'satisfaction', either in the form of an apology or a fight, was required.[32] Captain Richard Sowle, indicted for murdering George Paschal at Mayfair in 1751, justified his participation in the fight by saying Paschal 'gave him a great deal of abusive language, which was what a gentleman or officer could not put up with'.[33] The adoption of new codes of elite urban behaviour such as 'politeness' in the eighteenth century, which in some ways threatened to feminise them, may have given some gentlemen added impetus to use violence in order to assert their manliness.[34]

Much gentry violence was driven by social competitiveness. When Francis Newland offended a Mr Thomas by shutting a window on him, calling him 'sirrah' and daring him to come up to him, Thomas responded by saying 'I am a gentleman as well as you' and swords were drawn.[35] In a dispute between two gentlemen over the sale of a horse in 1694 which led to the death of John Dodd, it was allegations of ungentlemanly conduct which turned the dispute violent. Mr Ropington, the purchaser of the horse, complained that Dodd had ordered a bailiff to arrest him, presumably for non-payment. Complaining that the horse was defective, he said to Dodd 'you gave me the horse upon your word, to have no fault and you did not use me like a gentleman'. Dodd responded: 'Do not say so, for you are ungentile [sic] to make all this noise and uproar about it'. 'God damn you', said Ropington, stepping back and drawing his sword, 'I will not take this at your hands.' Dodd also drew, they parried, and Ropington stabbed Dodd, who died instantly.[36] Gentry insecurity about their position led them to use insults and violence to assert their distinctive identity. During an argument which erupted in an alehouse in Chelsea Fields in 1731 Francis Woodmath told the company that 'he himself was a gentleman, and a scholar, and talked Latin, and that they were tradesmen, and did not understand Latin'. After a further exchange of insults, in which Woodmath was called 'a Jew's face', they went out into the yard where Woodmath stabbed Robert Ormesby.[37] Those on the margins of gentility, such as military officers and so-called 'sharpers', were especially likely to use violence to assert their social standing. Army and navy officers, a group which grew considerably during the century as a consequence of almost continuous foreign warfare, accounted for 2.4 per cent of the murders committed by men. Such men were often in a particularly ambiguous social position, since their claims to gentility by virtue of their office could be at odds with relatively humble family backgrounds. 'Sharpers' were pseudo-gentlemen who lived by their wits. As the advice book *The Tricks of the Town Laid Open* (1728) warned country gentlemen newly arrived in the city, these were especially likely to 'draw you into a quarrel, or at least to try whether you will fight'.[38]

Gentlemen further emphasised their membership of a select group by following a rigorous set of rules in the conduct of violence, in which honour demanded particular sensitivity to the requirements of fair play and the needs of their opponents. Swordplay, even when it did not occur in a formally arranged duel, was conducted according to a series of unwritten rules that were meant to ensure a fair fight. Having drawn a sword, one gave one's opponent time (and space) to do likewise, encouraging him to do so (if necessary) by tapping him on the head with one's sword.[39] If one's opponent broke his sword, lost it, or fell down or was wounded, one was expected to stop fighting. When Richard Cary and Benjamin Corbett quarrelled and fought over an old debt in the Mermaid Tavern in Cornhill in 1707, Cary managed to take Corbett's sword from him. Cary thought this ended the fight, but Corbett managed to stab Cary with a piece of his own sword, behaviour that Cary described as unfair and not 'done ... like a man'.[40] If one's opponent did not have a sword, one did not draw one's own, though a sheathed sword could still be used as a stick. César de Saussure observed that 'noblemen of rank, almost beside themselves with anger at the arrogance of a carter or person of that sort, have been seen to throw off their coats, wigs, and swords, in order to use their fists'. When some young gentlemen quarrelled with an unarmed drunken waterman in 1761 and one of the gentlemen drew his sword, a witness 'told the young hero that it was not a point of manhood to draw his sword on a naked man'.[41]

Young adult gentlemen needed to be socialised into the rules of fair play, for they had a particularly aggressive culture of violence, which occasionally involved actively terrorising the streets and attacking and wounding strangers. In the late seventeenth century 'scowring' became a popular sport, in which young gentlemen forcibly cleared taverns, broke windows and assaulted bystanders and the watch.[42] In February and March 1712, a group of young men labelled the 'Mohocks' terrified the inner west end (Holborn, Covent Garden and around the Inns of Court), causing malicious damage and attacking young men and women and the watch without provocation by striking them or cutting their faces and heads with swords and penknives. According to one account, they were equipped with 'short clubs or batts that have lead at the end, which will overset a coach, or turn over a chair, and tucks [rapiers] in their canes ready for a mischief'. Although political circumstances led observers to exaggerate wildly the extent and nature of these attacks,[43] a small number are well documented in the judicial records. John Bouch, a watchman, was attacked on Essex Street on 11 March by around twenty men with swords and sticks, 'they intending ... to nail him up in his watch house, and roll him about the street'. When Mary Ann Kilby, a servant, was walking along Fleet Street near Temple Bar between eight and nine in the evening of 16 March, two persons 'like gentlemen' seized her 'by her head and with a violent force thrust a penknife or some other instrument through the lower part of her face and some small distance from her lower lip into the mouth ... which occasioned her to lose a great quantity of blood' and then knocked her down and left her lying on the ground. As an alewife was delivering a pot of drink to a house in Cecil Street near the Strand about the same time the next evening, five or six men came up to her and 'threw the drink in her face and upon her clothes, and threw her candle and candle stick in the street, [and] threw her all along upon the stones, pulling her head clothes off'. When the door to the house opened, they ran off. The small groups of men who perpetrated these attacks included Lord Hinchingbrooke and Sir Mark Cole, a baronet, and several others who were or appeared like gentlemen. Since these men acted in groups and targeted symbols of authority, such as watchmen, and vulnerable people whom they appeared not to know, the primary motive for the violence appears to have been to impress their friends and confirm their social and gender identity. The 'very well dressed' men who knocked down Sara Jones, a cook maid, cut her lip, and struck her on the side of the head 'laft mittly' (laughed mightily) to each other as they went away.[44]

The outcry over young male violence prompted by the Mohock attacks did not stop the behaviour. On 29 May 1720, Morrice Fitzgerald and three or four other drunk gentlemen decided 'to go scower the watch' and go 'on the rake'. Encountering a watchman in Cecil Street, they kicked his staff and lantern, beat him, and 'then gave him some money, and bid him go about his business'. At the end of street they attacked some chairmen carrying a gentlewoman, saying 'Damn ye, we'll have some fun'. They forced her to get out and struck a chairman with a sheathed sword. When a watchman arrived, he was stabbed twice.[45] Similar attacks occurred later in the century, though they were described in different language. In 1761 the newspapers contained several reports of violent attacks by 'young bloods', including an incident in St Paul's

Church Yard when a female news hawker was attacked by 'a man dressed like a gentleman, who asked her to go with him, but she refusing, he stabbed her in a terrible manner in the head with a tuck he had in a stick, and escaped'. Ten years later three young men were involved in an affray in which a woman was jostled, insulted, and had a hand placed down her bosom. This was described as an episode of 'skylarking', defined as 'playing till it sometimes turns out fighting'. In 1776 John Fielding warned new arrivals to the city of the dangers of walking at night: 'he will sometimes be liable to the more dangerous attacks of intemperate rakes in hot blood; who occasionally and by way of bravado, scower the streets, to shew their manhood, not their humanity; put the watch to flight; and now and then have murdered some harmless and inoffensive person' (Figure 17).[46]

The common themes of these attacks, which were public, unprovoked, committed by elite young men, often targeted at strangers (especially young women), involved an element of playfulness, and were often described using the imagery of blood, suggests that the perpetrators were adolescents, possibly confused about their sexuality, who were seeking to affirm their masculine identity and social position through collective violence. At a time when a male homosexual subculture was forming, there was arguably a need for heterosexual men to assert their masculinity more forcefully.[47] These performances affirmed membership in an elite, though obviously insecure group, evident in their tendency to run away or surrender at the first sign of serious opposition. In December 1693 three men with drawn swords walked down Salisbury Court in the City swearing 'damn them they would kill the next man they met, making responses I will, I will, I will'. Although they eventually lived up to their promise, this was not before two of them ran away when confronted by a householder who was angry because they had broken his windows. These men needed to prove to each other that they could use their swords, but they clearly had trouble doing so.[48]

Ultimately, attempts by the gentry to use violence to defend their privileged social position failed. They did not have a monopoly over the use of swords: 55 per cent of the male defendants charged with causing a death with a sword in London were neither gentlemen nor military men. Moreover, fighting in order to defend one's honour, according to accepted rules of fair play, was a characteristic of men of all social classes

17. 'High Life at Midnight' (1769). (*Guildhall Library, Corporation of London*)

in London.[49] It is possible that the increased use of swords by their social inferiors may help explain why the gentry largely abandoned sword fighting over the course of the century.

Violence was primarily, but not exclusively, a male phenomenon in this period. Men were responsible for 87 per cent of the murders tried at the Old Bailey. Women also appear to have committed far fewer non-fatal violent attacks than men, accounting for less than a third of the recognizances for assault where violence or a weapon was used. In conducting thefts, they were less likely to threaten or attack their victims: women account for only 15 per cent of those accused of committing robberies.[50] While it is likely that female violence was under recorded (men may have been unwilling to admit that they had been attacked by women), the enormous size of these disparities suggests that there were very real differences in the roles that violence played in the lives of men and women in London.[51] Male violence was part of an accepted code of masculine behaviour, offering men a means of affirming their gender and social identities. This explains why so much male violence was committed in public, while women's violence tended to take place inside, or on doorsteps. Women were far more likely to murder (and be murdered) inside private houses (or, less commonly, in other buildings) than on the street. For men, violence was a public method of affirming their honour, even if steps were sometimes necessary to avoid the attention of officers of the peace. At the same time, however, the rules which governed male violence controlled its use in ways which reduced the possibility of injury or death. Given the male need to assert super-iority in a world where public reputation still played a crucial role in determining self worth, the potential for violence was always present, and methods of limiting this form of behaviour were important.

In contrast, violence had a very different significance for women. Whereas violence was an expected, if from some points of view delin-quent, aspect of the male personality, it was simply not seen as a feminine activity, not only because women were assumed to be weaker than men, but due to the expectation that women were more passive and sub-missive, as well as more sensitive to the needs of others. Women who failed to conform to these expectations were deemed unfeminine. Thus a woman who committed a particularly violent assault and robbery was labelled a 'masculine woman', and another who rescued a man who had been impressed was described as an 'amazon' who had received a pension for 'her many manly services by sea and land'.[52] Also important is the fact that women did not carry weapons, which meant that even when they did commit assaults they were less likely to be fatal. Women rarely committed murders with swords, pistols, sticks, canes or staffs. Instead, they used their own fists and feet and any object they happened to be able to grab hold of quickly (such as pots, hammers, mallets and knives). Of course, these impromptu weapons could be lethal. During a quarrel between two women in Covent Garden Market in May 1751 'one struck the other with a bed screw which she had in her hand, by which means she fractured her skull, so that she died on the spot'; later that year, after John Brown struck Margaret Fitch, his former lover, during a struggle in an alehouse, she stabbed him 'with a small knife which she had in her hand paring her nails'.[53]

While female violence was much less common, it was also sometimes more vicious than that committed by men. Since female violence was unexpected, there were no accepted forms of combat that served to contain it. In this context it is fortunate that women were not quick to resort to violence to settle disputes. When Elizabeth Young and Elizabeth Rock quarrelled over half a crown given to Young by a gentleman, they argued about it 'at intervals' from noon till 10.30 in the evening before Rock, trying to prevent Young from entering her house, finally punched her in the stomach and pushed her down.[54] On the other hand, the lack of rules could mean that disputes spiralled out of control. In 1751 two women quarrelled in East Smithfield and, according to the newspaper report, one, 'not knowing any other way to be revenged, cut the throat of the child of the other woman' – an extreme example of the point that since women had no ritualised form of violence for settling disputes, the violence could get out of hand.[55] As a consequence of the lack of agreed forms of staging combat (though women occasionally boxed),[56] women were more likely to engage in one-sided attacks. Whereas male attackers typically gave their antagonists time to prepare for the fight by stripping to the waist or drawing their swords, and warned them that if they did not do so they would be killed directly, fighting for women was more spontaneous, as is evident in their choice of weapons. All this helps explain why women's violence was so often described as passionate and temperamental – it lacked a ritualised form. When two officers came to Ann Andersby's house to arrest her husband on an action for ten pounds, there was a fight in which both sides later claimed they had been violently attacked by the other. According to an officer, she scratched him on the face and acted 'very outrageously'. The other officer blamed her subsequent illness and miscarriage on 'the effects of her rage and the violence of her passion rather than any injury she received' from the officers.[57]

Except in the case of wife beating, there were also few rules governing the violence inflicted by men upon women. Since men and women were not expected to fight, men too sometimes lost control and used unconventional weapons when quarrelling with the opposite sex. When a woman argued with a manservant in a distiller's shop near Salisbury Court in 1741, 'she exasperated him to that extravagant degree, that in his rage he threw a can of boiling liquor over her, which scalded her in so miserable a manner, that ... she died'. Men's violence against women was often spontaneous and brutal. After having been robbed by Eleanor Cross, 'a thieving woman', in a street in Westminster in January 1698, a man (identified in the court records only as L— B—), lashed out and bruised her with his hands, knees and feet, and she instantly died.[58]

Women were far more often the victims than the perpetrators of violence. Given the frequency with which they were attacked, the fact that they so rarely engaged in lethal violence themselves speaks volumes about the relatively insignificant role played by violence in female culture. Despite the large number of provoking insults that women received, evident in the widespread practice of defamation early in the century, it is impressive how *rarely* insults, words which often undermined their character in very damaging ways, provoked women to respond with violence.

Over the course of the eighteenth century, the amount of violence on London's streets declined considerably, part of a much longer historical trend of declining violence in English society dating from the late middle ages.[59] As Chart 4 demonstrates, the number of cases of murder tried at the Old Bailey declined dramatically over the course of the eighteenth century. Since London's population increased by more than half during the period, the per capita rate of decline is even more dramatic: the

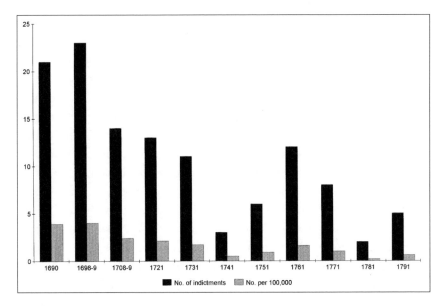

Chart 4. Homicide Rates in London, 1690–1799. (Source: *Old Bailey Proceedings*. For population figures see Chapter 3, n. 48.)

figures suggest that Londoners' propensity to commit murder decreased by more than six times during the century. There is of course no direct correspondence between the number of murders in a society and the amount of violence more generally, but murder is the only form of violence to have been systematically recorded across the ages.[60] In any case, since so many prosecutions for murder in eighteenth-century London derived from fights and disputes where murder was not intended, and the wounds incurred only led to deaths owing to inadequate medical care, levels of indictments arguably do reflect wider patterns of violence. John Mercer died after having been shot by John Munford, a beadle, in 1709, when Mercer was standing on the roof of a house and throwing tiles at the officers of the peace. Munford was acquitted of the murder, not because he acted in self-defence, but owing to evidence that Mercer died 'due to improper care of the wound'. When William Wheatly died after having been beaten and dragged down the stairs by John Bacchus, his death was ascribed to 'an ill state of [his] body'.[61] While the fact that both Munford and Bacchus were charged with murder suggests that the homicide statistics overstate the true number of intentional murders, it also demonstrates that these statistics reflect wider patterns of violence at the time.[62]

Two types of homicide declined most dramatically: deaths resulting from resistance to law enforcement and those involving the explicit assertion or defence of male honour. The former may reflect declining participation in both official and unofficial law enforcement,[63] leading to a greater acceptance by Londoners of police authority exercised by others and a growing unwillingness to interfere with officers enforcing the law. The Prussian visitor D'Archenholz noted in 1791 that the English 'commonly esteem' constables and rarely opposed them (though resistance to bailiffs was frequent).[64] Violent assaults provoked by insulting words also declined. As insults ceased to have the kind of impact, in terms of the potential damage caused to reputations, that they had in the seventeenth century,[65] Londoners felt much less need to respond when they were insulted. This led to a change in the relationship between words and violence in male behaviour, with the former less often directly leading to the latter. Although some murders continued to be provoked by insulting words, from the mid eighteenth century there are increasing reports of men who failed to respond to such language. In 1761 three men stepped into the Ben Johnson's (sic) Head on Russell Street, Covent Garden, to wait until the rain cleared. They happened to sit down next to a 'woman of the town', which occasioned some sailors who felt she belonged to them to insult the men, using expressions involving the words 'spitting in their faces ... shitting in their mouths'. They also threatened to pull one man's nose, and challenged them to fight. Despite all this provocation, the men refused, and tried to leave: only when the sailors prevented one of them from leaving the house was assistance sought from men drinking in a nearby alehouse and a fight begun.[66]

In a growing number of cases bystanders (of all social classes) intervened in disputes and attempted to stop the violence, or at least prevent one combatant from having an unfair advantage. By the second half of the century witnesses had attempted to pacify the dispute in 39 per cent of murder and manslaughter cases tried at the Old Bailey.[67] D'Archenholz observed that in late eighteenth-century London 'when a quarrel happens in the streets, the passengers immediately interfere. Persons of the highest rank do not hesitate for a single moment to become mediators.' He then cites an incident when he grabbed a man who he thought had cheated him. A crowd gathered around him, and he was informed that 'no offence whatsoever could warrant [his] behaviour'.[68] It was not only gentlemen who were involved in stopping fights. When John Rock, holding a knife in his hand, quarrelled with a woman in Covent Garden in 1755, a chairman grabbed hold of Rock, allowing the woman to escape. Rock then chased the chairman into an alehouse and attacked him, upon which Lewis Lewis, another chairman, 'bid him let the man alone'. After striking Lewis, Rock ran off, and another witness, a gentleman, tried to capture him. Although three men (a gentleman and two chairmen) had tried to stop the violence, Lewis died. When two journeymen carpenters, John Garnett and William King, quarrelled in 1761 in a house on Ludgate Hill over their work and the borrowing of chisels, there was some pushing and shoving and they threatened each other with their fists and tools. They appeared to be about to fight when Thomas Bradbourn came between them and pushed one of them back, saying 'Come, come, let us go home, there will be mischief done'. Another journeyman, William Willson, pleaded with King, 'My dear Billy, good boy, go home, do not let us have quarrelling here'. Despite these efforts to prevent violence, Garnett managed to strike King over the head with a plane, upon which he fell down the stairs and later died.[69] Even soldiers prevented fights. When Captain Richard Sowle and George Paschal drew swords on each other at a tavern in 1751, John Malcomb, a soldier, immediately went up to them, 'saying, consider gentlemen, what you are going about is a thing of a very dangerous consequence, and you are both, I suppose in liquor, and when you are sober you will be sorry for it'. Later, when the two clashed again, the soldier only managed to part them after Paschal had received a fatal wound.[70]

The best evidence of efforts to prevent fatal violence comes from depositions in murder cases, which explains why all the efforts just described ultimately failed: where such interventions succeeded they were unlikely to be recorded. Despite the growing number of disputes where observers attempted to intervene and stop the violence, there was no consequent increase in the number of deaths of those who intervened, which suggests that participants in fights became more tolerant of attempts to pacify their disputes. Men, in other words, became less insistent on asserting their independence from any form of authority.

The biggest decline in violent behaviour appears to have been among gentlemen, who shifted from the social group most likely to be accused of murder at the Old Bailey to the least.[71] Incidents of young gentlemen roaming the streets attacking vulnerable women and the watch also declined. Where such attacks did occur, they were increasingly blamed on foreigners or social outcasts, and no longer seen as a product of young elite male culture. When, in 1780, Londoners panicked over the activities of a 'gang of modern mohawks' who roamed the streets 'cutting and ill-treating women', the culprits were thought to be Lascars, who had arrived on ships of the East India Company and who allegedly went about punishing the women of the city after they had been infected with venereal disease by prostitutes in Wapping.[72] Between 1788 and 1790 an even greater panic arose over a series of attacks on female pedestrians committed by a man who used a sharp instrument to slit their clothing and the flesh of their buttocks. Unlike previous episodes, these attacks were attributed to a single man, and the fact that they were now totally outside the pale of acceptable conduct led the perpetrator to be labelled the 'Monster'.[73]

Facilitating and signifying the decline of elite male violence was the decline in the 1720s and 1730s of the habit among gentlemen of carrying swords, the weapon most commonly used to commit murder in this period. Saussure reported in 1726 that 'Englishmen are usually very plainly dressed ... almost all wear small, round wigs, plain hats, and carry canes in their hands, but no swords'.[74] When gentlemen fell out in taverns or coffee houses, they no longer had lethal weapons immediately to hand. Since the fashion of sword-carrying symbolised the gentry's assumption of privileged access to violence, its decline signals a significant change in the understanding of what it meant to be a gentleman. When, in 1761, an officer named Ratsey threatened a Mr Jolley in a tavern in Covent Garden, Jolley 'desired he would behave like a gentleman'. When Ratsey called out for his sword, Jolley told him 'I wore no sword, neither did I know how to make use of one'.[75]

Expectations about how Londoners should behave in public changed among non-gentlemen as well, however, as pedestrians on the crowded streets were expected to act in ways which did not provoke disputes or lead to violence. They were advised to avoid offending others by not using their elbows to make their way through a crowd, surrendering the wall to oncoming pedestrians, and not staring into their faces.[76] Recognizances from quarter sessions indicate that these expectations had firmly taken hold among many sections of the population by the 1760s, when Londoners first began to complain in significant numbers to justices of the peace about the objectionable behaviour of their fellow pedestrians: they complained that they had been pulled, pushed, dragged, grabbed, seized hold of, knocked down and kicked when walking through the streets. In separate incidents in September 1771, for example, women complained of having been knocked down with a fist, seized by the arm and dragged about, and violently kicked and bruised; and men complained of having been pushed, head-butted, pulled about and had their clothes torn.[77] It is unlikely that such acts were a new feature of London street life; what was new was Londoners' desire to complain about behaviour which disrupted their passage and threatened to embroil them in disputes they would prefer to avoid. In 1781 John Bryan, accused of being an 'Irish thief' and chased by a mob, tried to use these new standards to challenge those who sought to apprehend him. After he was struck with an elbow and 'pushed ... off the pavement into the middle of the street', he returned to the pavement and 'asked the said persons what reason they had to molest him and if he had not as much liberty to walk the streets as they had'. Although this did not prevent the mob from chasing him into a nearby house and beating him, Bryan's expectations regarding how pedestrians should be treated are revealing.[78]

With new standards of behaviour beginning to regulate public spaces, violence moved indoors in London. By the end of the century, more than half of reported homicides took place indoors, in private houses, taverns, coffee houses and shops. Moreover, rather than disputes between men over issues of honour, the causes of homicidal assaults were more often domestic, primarily disputes between husbands and wives. This can be seen as part of the long-term historical trend in which homicides involving family members increased from only a few per cent of homicides in the middle ages to about half of all homicides in modern England.[79] It is important to note, however, that there is no evidence that the amount of domestic violence increased. Rather, as public violence declined, domestic violence accounted for a growing *proportion* of all homicide cases. Violence was increasingly hidden behind closed doors.[80]

Why did violence become so much less common on London's streets over the course of the eighteenth century? This was not a product of better policing, since the limited improvements to the watch introduced in this period were directed primarily at preventing property crime.[81] Since most violence was conducted in public, it was changes in the nature of London street life which explain this significant development. Over the course of the century definitions of individual honour came to be less dependent on publicly established reputations. We have seen that the perceived impact of insulting words on the individual diminished during the century, as the role of neighbourly opinion in shaping reputations diminished. While for both sexes these changes undermined the significance of the public defamatory insult, for men, whose identity had historically been constructed around violence, the fact reputations came to be defined less publicly also led to a decline in violence. For most men, public demonstrations of courage and bravado were no longer effective methods of defending their honour and asserting their social and gender identity. To a certain extent, as the evangelical revival celebrated inner virtues, male honour came to be internalised. For those still conscious of their external reputations, there were new and continuing opportunities to create a good reputation through participation in voluntary societies and professional employment. But for those for whom violence was still culturally significant, new standards of public conduct channelled it into more ritualised and less lethal forms of combat.

# Duels and Boxing Matches

When a group of bricklayers and labourers were eating dinner at the Cow and Calf alehouse on Eastcheap in the City on 25 January 1757, a dispute arose over who would pay for a 'pot of hot' which had been brought to their place of work that morning. Thomas Powel said Francis Lenard should pay for it, since he had drunk it. Lenard replied, 'D—n your eyes, you are a liar', prompting Powel to say 'It does not look well of you to give me the lie'. Lenard responded by offering to fight. This was prevented by some of the others present, but Lenard continued to taunt Powel, saying 'You are no more a freeman than I am, and if you do not take care, you shall go and serve your time over again'. Powel replied 'You had better hold your tongue, or worse will come of it'. According to a witness, Lenard replied, 'd—n his body, he'd fight him, and would lick him if he could'. He got up, threw down his hat, pulled off his clothes, went out into the yard, and said 'come out, come out'. Powel agreed, 'I'll have a blow or two with you', tied his handkerchief around his head (to prevent his opponent from grabbing his hair) and went out. Seconds were chosen. As they began to box, people crowded around them. A screen got in the way, so the two fighters jointly picked it up and put it aside. During the fight, Powel was knocked down twice, and each time a witness helped him get up. Then, seeing that Lenard was a good fighter, Powel took off his clothes. Further blows were exchanged, Lenard fell, and his second said he would not fight any more. Powel went inside to wash and put on his clothes, and ordered a glass of the best gin in the house for Lenard. When he learned that Lenard was dead, he cried out 'God forbid!', went outside and picked him up in his arms. As Powel testified at his murder trial, 'I held him in my arms, till with grief I was ready to drop ... I made no attempt to go away, knowing there was no animosity on my side'.[1]

Seven years earlier, Captain Edward Clark and Captain Thomas Innes quarrelled about the testimony Clark had given against Innes at a court martial, and over a period of several weeks Innes repeatedly called Clark 'a perjured rascal', saying he had tried to take away his life. Innes was then warned that 'he had said so severe a thing of Captain Clark, which he could never forget, and that he must be obliged to resent it'. On 11 March 1750, Clark came to Innes's house and the two went into the dining room and ordered Innes's servant, William Newman, to leave. Listening through the keyhole, Newman heard Clark say 'Sir, you have used me very ill', and then insist on fighting with sword and pistol. On leaving, Clark desired Innes to call on him in the morning. Between 6 and 7 the next morning, the two entered Hyde Park, with their servants surreptitiously following at a distance, hoping to prevent the fight. They took up positions five or six yards apart, stood facing each other with their pistols, and Clark fired. Innes fell, and his servant rushed up. Clark was reported to say 'What I have done, I was obliged to do, and I am very sorry for it'. Later that evening, as he was on his death bed, Innes said 'he forgave Captain Clark with all his heart, and all the world; saying, he behaved like a gentleman, but fired too soon'.[2]

Boxing matches and duels were a common feature of London public life in the eighteenth century, and, despite differences in terms of weapons and the social status of the participants, they shared several characteristics. As these examples suggest, both types of fights were provoked by insults which called into question the honour and honesty of one of the participants, leading to a challenge. Both fights followed accepted rules of fair play, which ensured that each party was ready before the fight commenced (although Clark apparently fired too early), and were fought on equal terms. In both cases no animosity remained between the two parties following the fight, and the survivors expressed regret over the slaying. These common features arose out of the shared culture of honour which governed male violence. Yet not everyone believed that such fights were desirable: in both cases there were attempts to prevent the violence. The one important difference between the two types of fights, however, was that while boxing matches were typically conducted in front of crowds, duels were usually conducted privately, early in the morning in out of the way places.

We have seen that much male violence in eighteenth-century London was conducted in public and followed certain rules, but in boxing matches and duels the violence was particularly circumscribed. Fights like these were unlikely to be recorded unless (as in the cases reported above) they led to the death of one of the participants. Despite the fact the rules limited the risk of fatalities, these fights were so frequent that approximately one in seven homicides prosecuted in London resulted from incidents like these.[3] As attitudes towards violence became more intolerant during the century, however, the way such fights were conducted rendered them less dangerous to the participants. Pistols replaced swords for gentlemen duellists (which, surprisingly, *reduced* fatalities), while the commercialisation of boxing largely turned it from a method of resolving disputes into a spectator sport. Arranged fights became more frequent towards the end of the century, but as men's reputations came to depend less on their bravery and physical prowess, such fights took on new meanings.

Duelling was introduced into England from the Continent in the 1570s along with the needle-sharp rapier. Despite attempts to suppress the practice, it became fashionable in the early 1600s and again after the Restoration and into the eighteenth century. As John Cockburn wrote in 1720, 'partly on the account of public differences, and partly out of resentment for private injuries, duels were frequent from the Restoration to the Revolution [1688], and how common they have been since, none can be ignorant'.[4] Duels embedded in ritual some of the basic features of sword fights between gentlemen. Their essential features were: they originated in disputes over honourable conduct; they were preceded by a challenge and there was some delay between the challenge and the actual fight; the fight was conducted on equal terms and often ended as soon as a party was injured; and the wounded party forgave his opponent. The fight was not supposed to begin until both sides were ready: when Andrew Staining and John Corland quarrelled over a woman outside a tavern in December 1700, Staining promised to give Corland 'satisfaction' for something he said. They drank together, and Corland said 'he believed [Staining] a man of honour and would trust himself with him'. They went upstairs, but as soon as they got to the top of the stairs Corland stabbed Staining, prompting Staining to complain that Corland 'had barbarously murdered him before his sword was drawn', though he added in mitigation that 'he hoped he was a gentleman that gave' him the wound. Similarly, if a duellist dropped his sword or it broke, or he fell down, the other party was expected to desist: when Miles Langthorne was stabbed by William Edwards after his foot slipped and he fell and broke his sword, Langthorne said to Edwards, 'are you not a rogue to run me through when my sword is broke?'[5] These were rare examples of gentlemen not conforming to the rules.

Just as patterns of violence committed by gentlemen in London changed significantly over the course of the century, so did the way duels were conducted. First, the swordfight became less lethal, and then pistols replaced swords as the preferred weapon; both changes contributed to a significant decline in the mortality rate. Growing sensitivity to bloodshed appears to have led duellists fighting with swords to become more likely to stop at the first sign of blood, or when an opponent was disarmed, rather than fighting until serious injury or death, and as a result mortality rates in sword duels declined slightly between the first quarter and second half of the century.[6] Critics of the sword duel emphasised duellists' failure to rein in their passions, condemning them as 'being full of rancour and wrath', and characterising them as men who 'strike and thrust in passion and fury'.[7] But the way gentlemen used their swords changed in the early eighteenth century as fencing was reinvented as a defensive art, and as a skill that contributed to the development of a polite gentleman. In 1707 William Hope, the deputy governor of Edinburgh Castle, introduced a 'new method of fencing', which prioritised defence and rendered 'the offensive part or pursuit more slow', explicitly in order to allow a duellist 'a fair opportunity, both as a man of honour, of defending himself, and as a good Christian, of saving his adversary. (Honour, as well as religion, obliging him to both.)'[8]

While throughout the century fencing masters continued to argue that the skill was essential for self-defence, fencing was increasingly promoted as a skill worth practising for more 'polite' reasons. Domenico Angelo, whose school of fencing established at Carlisle House in 1763 and manual *L'école des armes* did much to increase its popularity, emphasised the civilising benefits of fencing for persons of rank, 'giving them additional strength of body, proper confidence, grace, activity, and address; enabling them, likewise, to pursue other exercises with greater facility'.[9] These changes, which made fencing more rule-bound, rendered sword fights less lethal, but they may also have contributed to the declining willingness of gentlemen to use swords in duels. The rules that all hits should strike the opponent's breast and that time had to be allowed for one's opponent to recover after a lunge, for example, were likely to inculcate habits which undermined the ability to triumph over a less refined antagonist. Indeed, from early in the century there was concern among fencing masters that the skills they taught were perceived as no longer suitable for life-threatening combat.[10]

Another factor that led to a reduction in fatalities from sword duels was a change in the role played by seconds. Although these were not consistently used in the early part of the period, when seconds were present they often joined in the fight. In the late seventeenth century many duels were actually group battles. As a commentator wrote in 1680, 'the mode nowadays, is for all the seconds to draw at once with the principal, and among them the engagement is as vigorous as if each were the very person that first gave the affront'.[11] In 1668 a duel involving the Duke of Buckingham and two soldiers on one side and Lord Shrewsbury and two others on the other was fought in the 'French style', in which the two groups of three lined up opposite one another, and at the signal 'came together with clashing blades'. All six participants were wounded, and two died. The seconds on both sides were said to have been chosen on the basis of their fighting skills, and the duel was thought to be the result of a plot to assassinate Buckingham.[12] In the famous duel between Lord Mohun and the Duke of Hamilton which took place in Hyde Park in 1712 (Figure 18), the seconds (who had had their own differences in the past) drew their swords against each other simultaneously with the principals, and clashed, wounding one, Colonel Hamilton. (Allegations that Mohun's second, Lieutenant-General Maccartney, also stabbed the Duke appear unfounded.)[13] In contrast, most reports of sword duels from the 1730s to the 1770s suggest that seconds were not present, or, if they were, they did not join in the fighting.

During the third quarter of the century an even more important change took place: swords were replaced by pistols. Although pistols were occasionally used early in the period (the first duel involving pistols in the London area took place in Tothill Fields in 1711 between Colonel Richard Thornhill and Sir Cholmley Deering),[14] pistols were not commonly used until the early 1760s. Swords were then relatively quickly abandoned, and few were used in London duels after 1785. The main reason for this change appears to have been the decline of fencing skills among gentlemen. The duel was meant to place both participants on an equal footing, but unevenness in levels of sword fighting skills between the participants undermined that equality. It was considered 'base, for one of the sword, to call out another who was never bred to it, but wears it only for fashion's sake'.[15] Whereas the small sword required long practice in order to master it, one could learn quickly how to fire a pistol. When John Knill sent a written challenge to a Mr Stephens in 1766, he wrote 'as I suppose neither you nor I know enough of sharps to risque anything upon 'em I fancy implements which may be carried in the pocket will suit better'.[16] It was thought that using pistols ensured equality and prevented potential duellists from the 'false pride' that their 'strength or agility' would ensure victory. As an anonymous observer commented in 1752, because 'firearms ... leave no inequality between combatants, but of intrepidity, recourse will inevitably be had to these on all momentous occasions'.[17]

This change led to a huge reduction in the mortality rate. More than a fifth of the participants in sword duels, but only 6.5 per cent of the participants in pistol duels, were killed or mortally injured.[18] This was partly because early pistols were very inaccurate. In 1692 Hope advised duellists on horse who fought with pistols to ride up so close that 'you may almost with the fire of your pistol, singe your adversaries doublet or coat' before firing; whereas this method 'will hardly ever fail to do execution', shooting at a greater distance was described as firing 'at random'.[19] With the introduction of the duelling pistol around 1770 and a series of refinements over the ensuing decades, however, pistols quickly became much more accurate. The duelling pistol was lighter than earlier pistols, with a curved stock that fitted easily into the hand and which meant that the barrel lined up naturally as an extension of one's arm. Adjustable hair triggers, roller bearings, gold-lined touch holes, water-proof pans and the patent breech all caused faster firing and straighter shots.[20]

In a context of ever more sophisticated weaponry, the real reason injuries became much less common was the distinctive way in which pistol duels were conducted (though we should note that almost a third of the participants were still harmed in some way). Practical reasons

18. 'Duel between the Duke of Hamilton and Lord Mohun' (1712). (*Guildhall Library, Corporation of London*)

dictated that, in comparison to the sword duel, pistol duels took place after a longer delay. Typically, after a quarrel had taken place and a challenge had been issued, the participants fought their duel early the next morning. Although not all participants could wait that long, some kind of delay was necessary, since gentlemen were not in the habit of carrying a set of pistols around with them. In contrast, early in the century gentlemen normally carried swords, so the delay between the initial quarrel (when, many times, swords were actually drawn) and the actual duel was often minimal. All that was necessary was to step outside, as Theophilus Young and Charles Graham did in 1693 after Young whispered a challenge into Graham's ear following an alehouse quarrel.[21] The delay between the challenge and the actual fight in pistol duels allowed tempers to cool (and the participants to sober up), and gave friends and seconds a chance to settle the dispute before shots were fired.

While gunsmiths competed to produce ever more deadly weapons, cultural constraints severely reduced the likelihood that duellists would actually hit their antagonists; it was changing attitudes towards violence and ideas about the purpose of duels that explain why the level of fatalities in pistol duels was so much lower. Some technical improvements were forbidden: although rifling was becoming an effective means of ensuring a straight shot, it was considered inappropriate to use rifled pistols in duels. Similarly, sights were discouraged, making pistols difficult to aim.[22] Unlike the sword duel, the pistol duel was not meant to be a trial of skill between the participants. When given a chance to aim and shoot deliberately, Lieutenant Samuel Stanton commented in 1790, even a poor marksman had a five to one chance of either wounding or killing his adversary.[23] But developing conventions prevented duellists from benefiting from the increasing accuracy of their pistols and any skills they possessed. It was actually considered bad form consciously to aim the pistol, or to practice beforehand.[24] After Clark shot Innes in their duel in Hyde Park, Innes complained that 'he did not think [Clark] behaved very honourabl[y]', not only because he fired before Innes was ready, but 'he took full aim at him'. Duellists were expected to point their pistol at the ground until just before firing. As Stanton advised, 'it is highly improper for any person to put the pistol across his arm, or to be longer in taking aim than is necessary; a moment or two is full sufficient to view your object, and fire'.[25] Consequently, the duel turned

into an exercise in which the chances of death depended on the inade-
quately directed paths of the bullets, and were thus essentially equal
(and random) on both sides. Of course, none of this actually prevented
the participants from practising beforehand, or of increasing their
chances of survival by tactics such as standing sideways to their antagonist, or of attempting to increase their chances of hitting their
opponent by measuring in advance the 'dispart' or throw of their pistols,
and learning how to load them correctly.[26] No doubt some people will
always try to improve their chances in such situations; what is impressive
is how often the rules for maintaining fair play and reducing the
bloodshed were actually followed.

As an illegal activity, duels were regulated primarily by the expectations of the participants themselves (and their seconds), and especially
in the early years of the pistol duel there was considerable uncertainty
concerning the procedures to be followed. Should the participants fire
together, or in turn? What distance apart should they stand? And how
many shots should they fire? These issues had to be settled prior to the
commencement of a duel. When Lloyd Dulany and Bennet Allen met
at Grosvenor Gate in Hyde Park in June 1781 and were walking with
their seconds towards the appointed spot, 'a conversation passed ... to
know what distance these two gentlemen should stand ... Then the next
question was, How should they fire?'[27]

Most frequently the participants fired together, with the next most
common procedure being that the challenger – the person whose perceived injury led to the duel – fired first. (In other cases the parties
tossed for the privilege, or it was the person challenged who fired first.)
Firing by turn, what one author called 'cool, alternate firing', was more
commonly used in the early years of the pistol duel (when pistols were
less accurate), but later authors argued that, because this procedure
allowed the participants too much time to aim, it led to excessive
fatalities: one wondered 'if ever there was a more bloody system introduced into the world'. In contrast, by shooting on an agreed signal,
such as dropping a handkerchief, the participants were forced to take
their eyes off their opponent until the moment of firing. By 1824, firing
on signal was 'pretty generally determined' to be the best procedure.[28]

The choice of the distance may have evolved in a similar way to reduce
the carnage. In the duel between Deering and Thornhill in 1711 the

parties initially stood apart, and then 'came up like two lions, and with their pistols advanced, when within four yards of each other each discharged'; another account says they fired when their 'pistols near touched'. Unsurprisingly, one (Deering) was killed.[29] In the duel between Clark and Innes described at the start of this chapter the two stood only four yards apart. When the surgeon complained 'it was murder to stand so close', Innes explained it was 'because my pistols were so small'.[30] As pistols became more accurate, distances grew longer. In the second half of the century they ranged from four to fifteen paces, with a median figure of ten (definitions of a pace varied, but were most commonly between two and a half feet and a yard.) Although twelve yards was described as the 'common distance' when Dulany and Allen fought in 1781, this proposal was rejected. A counter-offer of six yards was rejected as 'murdering work', and they agreed on eight yards. A commentator in 1793 complained of 'the bloody distances sometimes given; eight and seven yards are not infrequent ... which, when the parties come to present, will of course bring the mouths of their pistols to no more than four or five'. This was described as 'such a cool, diabolical design as to bring certain death'. From the 1790s most commentators advised ten paces or yards, or twelve in the case of 'trivial disputes'. According to a pamphlet published in 1836, nineteenth-century distances were even further apart: 'Duels are generally fought at 10, 12, and 14 paces.'[31]

The number of shots fired on each side ranged from one to six, but in the vast majority of cases the participants fired only one or two shots each. When at least four shots were fired on each side in the duel between Richard England and William Rowlls in 1784, this was described as contrary to 'those usual modes of satisfaction, which the laws of honour ... have introduced'.[32] Although serious injury to a participant occasionally forced the issue, the small number of shots fired is another crucial reason why the mortality rate of the pistol duel was so low, and provides a significant contrast to the sword duel, which often only ended when one of the participants was injured. Partly because there were often no seconds, the participants in sword duels did not always have a clear sense of when they should stop. When John Sharpe and Richard Campion fought in Lambs Conduit Fields in 1696, they made several passes at each other before Campion disarmed Sharpe, who acknowledged Campion as 'the better man'. According to a witness, they then parted and seemed to be friends, until Campion said to Sharpe 'that unless he would fight again he would stab him and [Campion] threw him his sword, whereupon they fought again, and in two or three passes Sharpe gave Campion a mortal wound'. Twelve years later another fight in the same fields had a similar outcome: a witness told the Old Bailey court he saw James Melton and Thomas Lewis

> strip, take up their swords, and push at one another; that the deceased [Lewis] wounded the prisoner [Melton] in his right side, which bled very much; that they shook hands, the deceased went away, and the prisoner followed him; that the deceased turn'd about, and the prisoner stood ready to receive him; that they fought again, and the prisoner wounded the deceased in the left breast, who died immediately.

In his defence, Melton claimed that the second engagement was the result of a misunderstanding. He testified that 'he did not know that he followed the deceased, till he turn'd and said, I thought I had done your business already; when he (the prisoner) gave back, and the deceased ran on his sword'.[33]

Pistol duels typically ended when one of the principals refused to fire, or fired in the air, or the seconds interfered. In 1793 duellists were advised not to fire at all if they were in the wrong: 'if any clear and decided injury has been done by either of the parties to the other, he will only present [his pistol], in order to interrupt the aim of his adversary; on receiving his fire, he will instantly recover, and then submit himself to the generosity of his enemy'. This is the procedure adopted when Colonel Harvey Aston met Major Picton in 1799 over a comment made by Aston in a private letter that the major had 'acted rather illiberally' toward one of their officers. As the wounded party, Picton fired fist; although his pistol snapped, 'the seconds decided that this was equal to a fire'. Aston then fired his pistol into the air, 'declaring that he had no quarrel with Major Picton'. At this point, according to the *Times*, 'mutual explanations took place, and they shook hands'.[34]

The role of the seconds was clearly another vital aspect in reducing bloodshed in pistol duels. The 'éclaircissement', the process of attempting to defuse an affront and reconcile the parties, became a key role played by seconds. In contrast to their participation in late seventeenth-century duels, seconds in the late eighteenth century were expected to try and prevent the duel from taking place at all, and, if this was unsuccessful, to stop the duel after as few shots were fired as possible. In the dispute in 1773 which came to be labelled the 'Vauxhall Affray', the seconds, having 'reduced the causes of [the] quarrel and defence to writing, the better to understand what ground they were to stand upon', concluded 'from the particulars they had heard on both sides, a trifling acknowledgement that each was wrong would be best, [and] recommended it to the parties'. This temporarily ended the dispute, but the settlement subsequently unravelled and a duel took place.[35] As noted in the British Code of the Duel (1824), the use of pistols, unlike the sword, allowed, between shots, a 'positive pause to the seconds for conciliation ... when the honour of both parties may have been mutually satisfied'.[36] In the duel between Prime Minister William Pitt and George Tierney fought on Putney Heath in 1798, occasioned by a speech Pitt made in the House of Commons, both parties fired twice, with Pitt firing his second shot in the air (Figure 19). As the Times reported, 'the seconds then jointly interfered, and insisted that the matter should go no further, it being their decided opinion that sufficient satisfaction had been given, and that the business was ended with perfect honour to both parties'.[37] As many commentators noted, the actions of the seconds were crucial in determining the outcome of a duel: seconds could exacerbate the conflict by encouraging the principals to fight on, or, as seems to have been most often the case, they could encourage a quick settlement. They could also subvert the intentions of the principals by loading their guns with insufficient powder (thereby weakening the force of the shot), or even by loading them with powder only and no ball. According to one humorous account of a duel in 1771 between 'two Hibernian hairdressers', the seconds 'charged their pistols, unknown to them, with potatoes half boiled'. Reporting yet another duel which ended after each party fired a single shot (and one of those was in the air) in 1790, the Times commented, 'according to the system of modern duels, neither party received any injury'.[38]

These changes in the way duels were conducted not only explain the decline in mortality rates; they also suggest important changes in the reasons why duels were fought. They suggest that the point of participation in a duel was increasingly a demonstration of courage, and the duel was no longer considered a test of fighting skills and of the ability

19. James Gillray, 'The Explanation' (1798), depicting the duel between William Pitt and George Tierney in which Pitt fired into the air. (*Guildhall Library, Corporation of London*)

to inflict injury on one's opponent. In his *Discourse of Duels* in 1687, Thomas Comber explained that 'the accepter of the challenge comes prepared to kill the challenger if he can, and hopes to get the reputation of a braver man by doing so'.[39] A century later the emphasis had shifted subtly from the more active assertion of 'bravery' to the more passive demonstration of 'courage', of standing firm in the face of fire. Lord Talbot fought a duel with John Wilkes in 1762 because Wilkes refused to state whether he had written an attack on Talbot published in the *North Briton.* After they exchanged shots, Wilkes immediately acknowledged authorship. According to Wilkes's account of the duel, Talbot then 'paid the highest encomiums on my courage', and Talbot's second, Colonel Berkeley, told him he 'admired my courage and coolness beyond his farthest idea; that was his expression'. A pistol duel between 'two young gentlemen of fortune' in 1771 also ended after a single pair of shots, when 'the affair was amicably settled as the parties were sufficiently convinced of each other's courage'. Interfering after three shots were fired in the duel between England and Rowlls, Lady D'Arterie cried out 'Gentlemen, is not three times enough to try your courage, or do you want to murder one another?'[40]

Many duellists refused to apologise for the insult which had led to the duel until after they had received their adversary's fire, in order to avoid any implication that they apologised through cowardice. Similarly, many duels were fought because the challenger felt that not to issue a challenge, after an insult, would be taken as a sign of cowardice. In 1804, when a dispute arose between Lord Camelford and Captain Best, 'several overtures were made ... to effect a reconciliation', but they were vehemently rejected. As the *Gentleman's Magazine* reported, 'The fact was, his Lordship had an idea that his antagonist was the best shot in England, and he was therefore extremely fearful lest his reputation should suffer, if he made any concession, however slight, to such a person' in order to avoid having to fight.[41] What drove men such as Camelford to fight duels was not so much the desire to redress an injury or affirm their honesty, but to demonstrate their courage. This was one reason why men were not allowed to fight when inebriated: 'no man's courage is the better established by anything he does in such moments'.[42] In 1791 two attorneys, who were friends, got into an argument while drinking 'freely' and used some 'abrupt language'. Despite the fact the cause of the quarrel was thought to be trivial, and efforts were made to reconcile them, the duel proceeded, a product, the *Gentleman's Magazine* commented, of 'an absurd unwarrantable fear of what might be said and thought, if they did not expose their lives to each other'.[43]

Despite changes in duelling practices which limited the bloodshed, over the course of the century Londoners became increasingly opposed to this ritual and men from all social classes sought to prevent duels from taking place. Even in 1712 the duel between Lord Mohun and Duke Hamilton was almost prevented by the various actions of a footman, tavern drawer, labourer and hackney coachman.[44] When Captain John Laverick and Captain John Dawson quarrelled in 1748, and Dawson attempted to issue a challenge, they encountered numerous obstacles. The messenger bringing the challenge was told by a woman that she thought he 'might have something better to do than bring messages to set gentlemen to fighting'. A maid subsequently persuaded Dawson 'to be cool, and alter his purpose', and she sent a message to Laverick not to come home (so he would not receive the message). Despite these attempts to subvert the duel, it started anyway, but a second, two passing gentlemen and a servant attempted to beat down their passes. Although in the end Dawson was killed anyway, the extensive efforts to prevent this duel are impressive.[45] Similarly, when two Americans duelled in Hyde Park early one summer morning in 1796, around ten people, including a servant to an herb seller, happened to be bathing in the Serpentine. According to the servant, when he saw the gentlemen 'he put on his shirt and ran towards them; several others went naked'. Before they got there, however, the parties exchanged shots and one was killed.[46]

In the 1780s and 1790s ordinary Londoners' attempts to prevent duels were supplemented by the efforts of thief-takers based at rotation offices such as the one at Bow Street. Possibly tipped off by friends of the participants – or even one of the principals themselves – thief-takers occasionally managed to prevent duels by showing up at the appointed time and arresting the would-be participants. In March 1796 two men agreed to fight a duel, but 'the affair was so well known to their friends' that warrants were secured from both the Bow Street and Marlborough Street offices, and the affair was instead 'amicably settled' by 'the good offices of the sitting magistrate'.[47] In some cases, soldiers even attempted to stop duels. When George Townshend and Lord Albemarle were about to fight in Marylebone in 1760, a Captain Caswell, who had been tipped off, stepped out from a coach 'and beg[ged] their pardon, as his superior officers, but told them they were his prisoners'. He sent them home by separate coaches, and acquainted the King, who appointed a mediator.[48] These efforts supplemented longstanding official attempts, which date back to the Restoration, by magistrates, the crown, ministers and the houses of Parliament to prevent duels involving prominent figures.[49]

There had long been opposition to duelling among some sections of the gentry and nobility. Critics, from Francis Bacon in 1614 and Richard Steele in the *Tatler* and *Spectator* in 1711 to the editors of the *Gentleman's Magazine* from its inception in the 1730s, claimed that the notion of honour on which duelling was based was 'false' and dependent on fashion and the fear of shame, as opposed to 'true' notions of honour based on virtue and Christianity. As John Cockburn wrote in his *History and Examination of Duels* (1720), 'things are honourable and base by virtue of their intrinsic nature, however men may judge them'.[50] As with other aspects of public life in eighteenth-century London, honour was increasingly perceived as an inner virtue, rather than a reputation established by public actions judged in the court of public opinion. From the 1770s, critics of the duel stepped up their attack by promoting a new vision of social conduct based on evangelicalism and middle-class values, further undermining the heart of the code of honour, the passion for social approbation.[51] The topic was hotly debated in London's debating societies in the last quarter of the century, and, judging by newspaper reports, the prevailing sentiment was clearly against the practice.[52] Support for duelling in elite society was thus limited. When Lord Byron (great uncle of the poet) was tried for the murder of William Chaworth in a duel in 1765, resulting from a trivial argument over who had more game on their estates, it is not surprising that Horace Walpole reported that 'the bitterness of the world against [Byron] has been great'.[53]

Violent behaviour was increasingly condemned in urban gentry culture. Gentlemen became subject to the ideals of politeness, in which men were expected to control their emotions and be generous and complaisant towards those with whom they interacted, and from the 1760s and 1770s the ideals of sensibility required men to show even greater sensitivity and sympathy to other people's feelings. Reflecting these new values, those who criticised duels evoked the sentiments which would be experienced by duellists who killed their opponents: 'the pangs of self-reproach for having sacrificed the life of a fellow creature to a punctilio [and having ruined] an innocent family by the brutal deed'.[54] Duellists may have increasingly maintained their distance from each other, and communicated only through their seconds, in order to avoid becoming aware of their opponents' feelings.

Duelling consequently became a much more private affair, as the number of people who believed it was a necessary and laudable activity declined. Paradoxically, although duels were allegedly fought to defend reputations, they were increasingly fought in private. When John Wilkes and Samuel Martin duelled in 1763, they went to Hyde Park with their pistols concealed, and when some people walked by them in their chosen location it became 'necessary to retire to a more private place'.[55] Throughout this period the majority of duels were fought away from the public eye, in out of the way places such as 'the backside of Southampton House'.[56] Nonetheless, as efforts to prevent duels escalated, they were increasingly fought outside the built-up area of the metropolis, in Hyde Park or on the heaths, commons, and fields surrounding the metropolis. Whereas many duels fought in the late seventeenth and early eighteenth centuries were fought within the city, inside houses, taverns and coffeehouses, or in streets, squares and alleys including 'old Pall Mall', Covent Garden, Lincoln's Inn Fields, and Falconbridge Court near Soho Square, by the last quarter of the eighteenth century few duels took place in an urban location.[57] This secrecy is not simply explained by practical considerations, such as the fact that pistol shots attracted attention and endangered passers-by, and that duelling was illegal and the participants could be arrested merely for attempting to fight. The real problem was the ever-present danger that friends or witnesses would interfere and prevent the duellists from carrying out their ritual.

Those who fought duels were performing for an increasingly limited audience. Not only was the number of men who were impressed by duelling diminishing, but the way duels were conducted became extremely asocial, as if the duellist was acting primarily for his own benefit. In his *Dissertation on Duelling* (1784), Richard Hey complained about 'the haughty self-importance ... the selfish and excessive regard, paid by the punctilious duellist to his own private feelings of disgrace'.[58] Contact between duellists largely disappeared: challenges now emerged out of exchanges of written correspondence using formulaic expressions,[59] and when they reached the field their seconds made the arrangements, while they stood apart from their antagonists and then attacked each other from a distance. The duellist's mission was now to convince *himself* that he was an honourable and courageous man.

Although it is commonly thought that the custom of duelling spread down the social scale in the late eighteenth century, there is little evidence, beyond complaints in the *Times*, that the social composition of duellists changed significantly. Even at the end of the century only a small minority of duellists came from what might be labelled middle-class occupations, and even these were men with plausible claims to gentry status: lawyers, doctors, merchants and bankers. The vast majority of duellists still came from the nobility, gentry and military.[60] Those lower down the social scale, however, had other methods of settling their disputes. César de Saussure observed in 1727 that when two lower class men

> have a disagreement which they cannot end up amicably, they retire into some quiet place and strip from their waist upwards ... The two champions shake hands before commencing, and then attack each other courageously with their fists, and sometimes also with their heads, which they use like rams.

Noting the similarity with upper class duels, Coustard de Massi commented in 1770 that 'examples of this kind of athletic bruising are to be seen every day ... which may be with the strictest propriety be called duels with the fists'.[61] Both the motivations and the rules governing boxing matches had much in common with the upper-class duel. As a fight between two sawyers in September 1749 suggests, men issued challenges to box when they were accused of cheating or lying, or otherwise behaving dishonourably. When William Burford was sharpening his saw in a carpenter's yard in St Giles in the Fields, Samuel Cross went up to him and asked him 'if he was not a scoundrel and a rogue to leave the yard where he was at work'. He pulled the saw out of Burford's hands, slapped his face, and threw some wood at him.

Challenging Burford, Cross 'immediately stript himself' and prepared for a fight. Seconds were appointed. Told not to fight in the yard, they 'went out into the street and fought together for some time'. Cross knocked Burford down, his face struck a stone, and Burford refused to continue the fight; he later died from his wounds.[62]

Like duels, boxing matches started with the participants on even terms, having appointed seconds and been given time to take off their shirts. The unwritten rules which ensured fair play were frequently commented on by foreign visitors, who noted that they were enforced by the crowds which frequently gathered to watch. According to D'Archenholz, 'the art of boxing has certain rules, from which no one ever departs: whoever attempts to infringe them, becomes immediately exposed to the fury of the populace'. Béat-Louis de Muralt noted that 'by the laws of the play (as they call it) a man is not to strike his adversary on the ground, but must give him time to rise'. Although there was some uncertainty over this point early in the century (François Misson reported that 'he that has got the other down, may give him one blow or two before he rises, but no more'), by the end of the century it was agreed, as D'Archenholz reported, that 'when one party falls, his adversary must not strike him; and the conduct is immediately to cease, on any of them acknowledging himself to have been beaten'.[63] Certain types of hits were also unacceptable. After Simon Small and John Lambert 'stript and fell to boxing', Lambert said to Small, 'D – ye, Small, you are a rogue, you kicked me in the face'. In a fight in Enfield in 1789, Edwin Swaine pulled his opponent by the hair, upon which some witnesses cried 'Foul!' and another said 'Swaine ought to have his liver cut out ... for fighting unfair'.[64] In contrast, after an alehouse argument over some borrowed money in 1751, a fight between Charles Troop and George Bartholomew followed the rules of fair play. They went out into Marylebone Fields, where a lemon was purchased and divided so that each had a half to suck on before the fight began. They then stripped, shook hands twice, 'declared no animosity', and engaged in what a witness described as 'fair boxing'. At least three times one or the other went down, and they stopped and started over again. At the end of the fight (which lasted about twenty-five minutes), they shook hands again. Given the fact that the participants were so drunk 'that as they went to strike at each other they missed their blows', their adherence to the rules is even more remarkable.[65]

Combined with the absence of weapons, the rules of fair play explain why boxing matches led to few fatalities. Despite pummelling each other for long periods and causing numerous falls, restarting the fight after each fall, few boxers actually died from their wounds. In his testimony in a murder case where the deceased had been beaten up by six men, William Baker, a surgeon, argued that the wounds were not serious, noting that 'I have seen people at a boxing match beat a great deal more, and done well again'.[66] Nonetheless, the fighting ethos dictated that combatants should continue to fight until they were physically unable to continue, and this contributed to several deaths. When John Hudson and Thomas Moss boxed in 1754, witnesses reported 'it was a very severe battle'. According to Charles Oakman, when Moss 'was incapable of fighting, [Hudson] asked him if he would fight any more; he answered, he would fight; (he was then standing on his legs, with his hands hanging down) then [Hudson] struck him one blow, upon which he fell down'. He died that evening from head injuries.[67] Moss may have carried on out of concern for the damage that would incur to his reputation if he lost the bout. When Colonel Lennox was defeated by Colonel Tarleton in a match in 1789 the loss was 'invidiously circulated to Colonel Lennox's discredit'.[68]

Men chose boxing as a way of resolving their disputes for a number of reasons. As with other forms of violence, they fought in order to defend and assert their status among men. Matches often arose out of disputes over who was the best man in a group. The fight between Small and Lambert began when they were drinking together 'in a friendly manner' and, 'some dispute arising about wrestling and who was the best man', Lambert told Small, 'D—ye, you are a cramin [coward?], I can either throw you or beat you.' Small dared him to try, so they went outside and boxed.[69] Fights often seemed to occur for no other reason than to see who was the better fighter. The cause of the boxing match between Robert Smith and William Johnson was summarised in court as 'Johnson thought himself a very good fighter, and therefore he wished to beat him, thinking himself a better fighter than [Smith]'.[70] For many, boxing was more a form of recreation than a serious contest for honour or status, and the pleasure was enhanced by laying wagers. According to Pierre Jean Grosley, 'combats frequently happen at London between the lower sort of people, and sometimes between persons of condition, who, by way of recreation, chuse to engage in a bruising match'. John Price and Alexander Miller, two friends who 'never had words together', were drinking beer in a pub at Pelican Stairs in Shadwell in 1759. According to one witness, they 'were in friendship and joking together till [Miller] challenged in a joke John Price to fight him at sticks for a half a gallon of beer'; another reported Miller saying 'I'll give you a touch at sticks for a full pot of beer'. When Miller's stick broke, Price threw his away so as not to take advantage of him, and they fought with their fists. Price became angry when Miller tore his shirt, however, and the fight became more violent. They head-butted each other, and after a direct hit under his chin Miller instantly dropped down dead.[71] Similarly, a fatal fight between two servants in a room in a pub in 1774, although prompted by one having thrown a cat at the other, was described by witnesses as 'only for diversion', 'a bit of fun', and 'nothing but in good nature'.[72]

That such encounters were frequent is suggested by reports that spontaneous boxing matches often accompanied festivities and celebrations in London, such as the Lord Mayor's banquet, entertainments at Vauxhall Gardens, and public holidays. Just after New Year in 1771 the *Public Advertiser* reported that 'Monday being the close of the holidays among the mobility, no less than twenty-two battles were fought in the fields behind Bedford House and the British Museum, when several combatants were carried off speechless without hopes of recovery'.[73] Women also boxed, though observers always emphasised that this applied only among the poor (Figure 20). Following his description of male boxers, Saussure added, 'I have actually seen women – belonging, it is true, to the scum of the people – fighting in this same manner'. Looking back from the 1820s, Francis Place recalled that in the late eighteenth century fighting frequently occurred among the poor women of St Catherine's Lane just east of the Tower, and 'black eyes might be seen in a great many'.[74]

In contrast to the secrecy with which duels were conducted, boxing matches were usually watched by spectators. Crowds quickly gathered around men preparing to fight. According to Misson,

> anything that looks like fighting is delicious to an Englishman. If two little boys quarrel in the street, the passengers stop, make a ring around them in a moment, and set them against one another, that they may come to fisticuffs ...

> During the fight, the ring of bystanders encourage the combatants with great
> delight of heart, and never part them while they fight according to the rules:
> and these bystanders are not only other boys, porters, and the rabble, but
> all sorts of men of fashion; some thrusting by the mob ... others getting
> upon stalls.

When John Daws, a gentleman, and David Davis quarrelled in a street
near the Old Bailey in 1793, Davis 'put himself in the attitude of boxing'.
Quickly 'a crowd gathered around, and they called out, a fight! a ring!'[75]
The observers both ensured fair play and participated vicariously in the
fight by betting on the outcome. Betting on competitions such as
running races and tests of endurance was a popular pastime, and fighting
was no different. Saussure reported that

> everyone who sees [men] preparing for a fight surrounds them, not in order
> to separate them, but on the contrary to enjoy the fight, for it is a great sport
> to lookers-on, and they judge the blows and also help to enforce certain rules
> in use for this mode of warfare. The spectators sometimes get so interested
> that they lay bets on the combatants and form a big circle around them.[76]

Spectators often encouraged the fight in the first place. When disputes
arose observers often encouraged the participants to fight it out by
offering to bet on the outcome. An argument over some missing money
at a 'chair club' in a pub in St John's Street in 1768 apparently ended when
the publican agreed to cover the loss. But in the course of the argument
Robert Knight had bragged that he could 'lick' Robert Ball. Although
Ball and the publican dismissed this comment, another man told Ball 'I
will back you, if you will fight him'. As the publican testified, 'Then
another would back [Knight] for half a guinea, they aggravated [Ball],
and he said he would fight a guinea to half a guinea. The bet was made,
and they agreed to meet the next day'. Similarly, a newspaper complained
in 1726 that boxing matches were 'daily encouraged by the mob in our
streets with impunity; especially in setting poor children to fight it out,
when they perceive them at any variance about their pay'.[77]

Having wagered some money, spectators frequently encouraged the
combatants to fight longer than they might otherwise have wished.
Saussure noted that 'should one of the men fall ... those who have laid
their bets on the fallen man generally encourage him to continue till
one of the combatants is quite knocked up and says he has had enough'.

20. Thomas Rowlandson, 'Miseries of London' (1807). (*Guildhall Library, Corporation of London*)

Some such interventions appear to have prolonged matches to the point of death. After the first fall in the fight between Troop and Bartholomew in Marylebone Fields in 1751, a witness reported, 'there came a parcel of fellows from making bricks, I believe there were twenty of them, [who] said, you will not leave yet'. Troop appeared sick and lay down, but 'these people by main strength got them up again and set them to like two cocks, and made people afraid to attempt to part them'. After another fall, Troop managed to score a direct hit on Bartholomew, who collapsed and hardly spoke a word before he died. Similarly, when William Smith and William Alsop (aged nineteen and twenty) fought after an argument during a game of throwing at oranges, the fight was prolonged by their seconds and the spectators. After an initial exchange of blows, Alsop walked away, but Smith, assisted by 'the mob', brought him back. According to Smith, 'the men ... pulled off [Alsop's] frock ... they told me not be afraid of him, and made a ring for us to fight'. They fought somewhat unenthusiastically, and after twenty-five minutes Smith's second told him 'if he did not mind to hit him a straight punch or two, he could never do for him, nor yet beat him'. According to Richard Brown, after that 'they fought two or three minutes ... Smith gave [Alsop] a blow under the ear, and after that another under his nose, and with one of them blows he killed him'. As Edmund Price observed, 'they were over-persuaded by their seconds to fight longer than they would have done, having both of them enough'.[78]

Boxing was clearly becoming a popular spectator sport, and alongside the custom of fist-fighting as a method of resolving disputes and as a form of popular recreation, the related phenomenon of prize-fighting arose. Following the longstanding practices of staging bull- and bear-baiting and cock-fighting matches, by the late seventeenth century entrepreneurs were organising sword-fights and wrestling matches for prizes performed in front of paying (and betting) audiences, and in the early eighteenth-century boxing matches also began to be staged. In the 1660s Samuel Pepys attended wrestling matches in Moorfields and at Bartholomew Fair and sword fights in theatres and at the Bear Gardens. Several different sharp weapons were used at each sword fight, such as at the New Theatre in June 1663 when 'they fought at eight weapons, three bouts at each weapon'.[79] In the early eighteenth century similar fights took place in the Bear Garden at Hockley in the Hole (Saffron Hill), at Southwark Fair, and in private amphitheatres. In 1710 the Prussian visitor Zacharias von Uffenbach visited the Bear Garden to witness 'a truly English amusement', a fight between an Englishman and 'a Moor' before a mixed audience of the 'common people' and their social superiors, who paid extra for the best seats. His account reveals that many features of these prize fights were derived from duels and boxing matches. Before the fight, 'a properly printed challenge was carried round and dealt out. Not only were all the conditions of the fight there set forth, but also the weapons to be used'. Each combatant had a second, 'to see that there was fair play on all sides'. First they fought with broadswords; then with sword and dagger; then with 'sword and buckler' (broadsword and shield). After each round they shook hands. The fight ended when the Moor 'was slashed from the left eye right down his cheek to his chin and jaw with such force that one could hear the sword grating against his teeth. Straightaway not only the whole of his shirt front but the platform too was covered with blood'.[80] Like sword duels, fights like these typically ended only when one of the participants had drawn blood.

In the early eighteenth century boxing was just one of the types of combat performed by prize fighters. An advertisement for Southwark Fair promised entertainment 'with the manly arts of foil-play, back-sword, cudgelling and boxing'. When James Figg (or Fig), allegedly the first boxing 'champion' of England, opened his academy for instruction and demonstration in 'the noble science of defence' in 1719, he was more famous as a swordsman than as a pugilist (Figure 21). But over the next few decades boxing became the most popular form of prize fighting, and sword fights for prizes died away at about the same time as the sword duel. Captain John Godfrey observed in 1747 that 'in Fig's time, the spirit of [the back-sword] was greatly kept up; but I have been often sorry to find it dwindle, and in a manner, die away with him'.[81] Jack Broughton, author of the first set of written rules for conducting boxing matches (in 1743), also fought battles with a stick and a small sword, but his amphitheatre, opened in the same year on Oxford Street, was best known for the well-advertised boxing matches that were staged there.[82] Boxing matches were also staged at other venues, both indoors and outdoors. In February 1761, the *London Evening Post* reported that a match at the Tennis Court in the Haymarket, on which 'considerable sums' had been bet, had been so popular that ''tis thought that twice the number of people were turned away for want of room, than those who saw the battle'. Two months later it reported that 'a very severe battle between a drover of Smithfield and a soldier, for eight guineas to five that the soldier beat him' was fought at Marylebone Basin and in 1771 papers reported fights in 'a cockpit in Mutton Lane, near Saffron Hill' (for 100 guineas), and in Moorfields (for 50 guineas).[83]

By the 1780s, patronage from the Prince of Wales, together with the emergence of superstar boxers including Daniel Mendoza and Richard Humphries, raised boxing to the height of fashion, much to the disgust of the *Daily Universal Register* (later to become the *Times*), which commented that 'if we may judge from the present progression of this elegant accomplishment, we may venture to presage that black eyes and bloody noses will shortly succeed to [replace] patches and dimples in all beautiful countenances'. Despite its hostility to the practice, the paper reported many prize fights in the late 1780s. These occurred in places including Hyde Park (where a ring had been built in 1720 on the orders of George I), St George's Fields, Stepney Fields, a field on the road to Kentish Town, Finchley Common, and Barnet race course.[84]

Although these matches were essentially a form of commercial entertainment, they shared several characteristics with boxing matches conducted on the streets. Prize fights and street fights were similar activities, each custom influencing the other. Many of the same people who went to see organised fights must have gathered around and laid bets on impromptu matches. It is likely that some of the boxers were also the same: men who won battles conducted on the streets were encouraged (and sponsored) to participate in the ring. Following his description of boxing matches, Muralt wrote, 'such as are pleased [successful] with conflicts of this kind, may easily indulge their taste by turning prize fighters'. In an advertisement for a fight in 1742, one boxer, John Francis ('commonly called by the name of the Jumping Soldier'), claimed he had previously 'fought several bruisers in the street'.[85] In his memoirs, Mendoza describes how he started boxing as a boy, and by the age of sixteen fought with anyone who insulted his master and mistress. When a porter challenged his master to a fight following a quarrel about his fees, Mendoza stepped in. He recalled that his victory

21. 'James Figg, Master of the Noble Science of Defence'. Business card drawn by William Hogarth. (*University of Sheffield*)

'excited the general applause of the spectators ... and became the general subject of conversation in the neighbourhood for some time after'. Shortly thereafter, a friend entered him in a fight for money, and before long men were sponsoring him whenever an opportunity for a fight arose, either owing to a dispute which arose on the street or purely for entertainment.[86]

The rules first codified by Broughton for his new amphitheatre in 1743 clearly grew out of popular boxing customs, particularly rules 1, 4 and 7:

1. That a square of a yard be chalked in the middle of the stage; and every fresh set-to after a fall ... each second is to bring his man to the side of the square, and place him opposite the other; and till they are fairly set-to at the lines, it shall not be lawful for the one to strike the other.

4. That no champion be deemed beaten, unless he fails coming up to the line in the limited time [30 seconds]; or that his own second declares him beaten ...

7. That no person is to hit his adversary when he is down, or seize him by the ham, the breeches or any part below the waist; a man on his knees to be reckoned down.

By specifying the starting positions for a fight, the amount of time boxers were allowed for recovering after a fall and returning to the line, and certain types of hit which were unacceptable, the rules were more prescriptive than prevailing customs, however, and their influence can be seen in the conduct of both informal boxing matches and prize fights for the remainder of the century. In 1791 an observer of the fight between Smith and Johnson complained that Smith gave blows 'below the waist-band of the breeches', and this point was taken seriously at his murder trial, where the surgeon was actually asked if he had observed 'any blows on the private parts'. But the main reason for the introduction of written rules was not so much to regulate fighting as to prevent disputes among those laying bets. The rest of Broughton's rules specified who was allowed on stage, how umpires were to be appointed, and the division of money thrown on stage by the crowd.[87]

At least as publicly stated, the motives for participation in prize fights were also similar to those which prompted boxing matches on the streets. To heighten popular interest, quarrels between the fighters were sometimes stressed. An advertisement for a fight between Jack Broughton and John Slack claimed that 'as Mr Broughton some time since took leave of the stage, it may not be improper to acquaint the publick that nothing but an insult, which to let pass unresented would highly impede his manhood, could ever have provoked him again into the lists'.[88] Like street fights, prize fights were described as 'trials of manhood', in which men sought to defend their reputations as strong, courageous and honourable men. This is evident in the language of the challenges (written, apparently, by the 'principal bet holders' rather than by the fighters themselves) published in the newspaper advertisements which announced the fights.[89] In his challenge to Patrick Henley in 1742, John Francis claimed he 'always had the reputation of a hearty fellow ... nor am I afraid to mount the stage, especially at a time my manhood is called into question'. Inviting Henley to fight him for two guineas, Francis concluded with the statement that 'I doubt not I shall give him the truth of a good beating'. In his challenge to John James in August 1747, Joseph Line, from Hertfordshire, claimed 'I am the terror of all around, having fought and beat the best men the country could produce'. Sometimes, as with recreational fighting, boxers just wanted to show they were the best fighter around. Rowland Bennet claimed that he 'never intended to have engaged on the stage any more, but hearing of the fame of Mr [Joseph] Johnson, and believing I have a right of seniority therein, hereby invite him to meet me in the time and place above mentioned' (Broughton's amphitheatre, July 1745).[90]

Ultimately, however, profit was without a doubt the main motivating force behind commercial boxing matches. Although street battles were often fought for a pot of beer or a few shillings, money was not what primarily motivated the fighters. According to D'Archenholz, the combatants 'are generally instigated by hatred alone', but we have also seen that men fought to defend their masculinity or simply for amusement.[91] In contrast, the prizes at commercial matches ranged from a few guineas to over a hundred. These were made possible by the sponsorship and attendance of royalty, nobility, and gentry. Broughton built his amphitheatre with support from the Duke of Cumberland and other noblemen, and was sponsored by the Duke when he fought Slack to the extent that the Duke was said to have bet £10,000 on him (Figure 22). When Broughton lost the battle, the Duke in a fit of pique closed down the amphitheatre and switched his patronage to Slack. Aristocrats 'discovered' fighters and brought them to London to fight. Figg was found in Oxfordshire around 1720 by the Earl of Peterborough, who brought him to London and set him up in a building on Oxford Road; and in 1733 William Pulteney brought a Venetian gondolier back to London in order to fight one of Figg's protégés.[92] In 1788 it was claimed that 'the science of boxing is now become so fashionable, that some of the first personages of the kingdom are known to patronize it'. These included the Prince of Wales, who sponsored several fighters including Mendoza, whom he backed in a fight with Sam Martin in April 1787 to the tune of £50 before the fight and £500 after his victory. Other aristocrats, gentlemen and wealthy merchants followed his lead.[93] Later that year Mr Hollingsworth, a corn factor, sponsored Tom Johnson, a porter, in a fight with Michael Ryan for 100 guineas, on which £4000 of bets were said to have been made. After Johnson's victory, the *Daily Universal Register* reported, Hollingworth 'settled £20 a year for life on his victorious servant'.[94]

As boxing became fashionable to watch, some gentlemen sought to practise it, and teaching boxing became another lucrative activity. Virtually all the famous boxers ran academies where they staged demonstrations and offered lessons to gentlemen. This was facilitated by the use of padded gloves, first introduced by Broughton, which prevented injuries to their fair complexions during practice. Boxing was dignified with the label of a 'noble science' and could be taught as a polite skill just like fencing. John Jackson, victor over Mendoza in a 1795 fight, joined Angelo's academy in Bond Street to teach boxing alongside fencing. Some gentlemen 'did not feel ashamed of being seen in the ring, or acting as umpires at a manly boxing match'.[95] Other elite men even used boxing to resolve their disputes. In 1771 a quarrel erupted in the City 'between a Captain of a trading vessel and a merchant, owner of the vessel; after many high words, they fell to blows, and fought nearly five minutes with great spirit, when some gentlemen present parted them'. Later, in proper gentlemanly fashion, 'the affair was amicably adjusted over a bottle'.[96]

Entrepreneurs also attracted audiences by staging the unusual spectacle of fights between women. Like male prize fights, those which took place early in the century involved swords, and were advertised with printed

The BRUISER BRUIS'D: Or, the Knowing-Ones Taken-in.

22. 'The Bruiser Bruis'd: or The Knowing Ones Taken-in' (1750). The fight between Jack Broughton and John Slack, in which the Duke of Cumberland was said to have bet £10,000 on Broughton. A purse containing prize money is on the stage. Broughton's unexpected defeat led to suspicions that the match was fixed, as indicated by the title of this print. (*Guildhall Library, Corporation of London*)

challenges from the fighters. Accounts of these fights stress their eccentricity and rarity, and the manliness of the participants. Having gone to see 'the gladiators' fight in February 1728, Saussure describes 'an extraordinary combat' he witnessed, 'two women being the champions':

> As soon as they appeared on the stage … they boasted that they had a great amount of courage, strength and intrepidity. One of them regretted that she was not born a man, else she would have made her fortune by her powers; the other declared she beat her husband every morning to keep her hand in, etc.

After three rounds, the fight ended when one woman 'received a long and deep wound all across her neck and throat'. 'Fortunately', Saussure concluded his account, 'it is very rarely one hears of women gladiators.'[97] The first report of a prize boxing match involving women dates from 1722, when the *London Journal* reported that

> Boxing in publick … is what has lately obtained very much amongst the men, but till last week we never heard of women being engaged in that way, when two of the feminine gender appeared for the first time on the theatre of war at Hockley in the Hole, and maintained the battle with great valour for a long time, to no small satisfaction of the spectators.

In the printed challenges, one of the women promised 'to give her [opponent] more blows than words'. Accounts of boxing prize matches between women later in the century are rare but not unheard of. In 1795 the famous fighters Mendoza and Jackson acted as seconds in a fight between Mrs Mary Ann Fielding and 'a Jewess of Wentworth Street' for a prize of eleven guineas.[98] While the participants of these fights may have been attracted by the prospect of transcending conventional gender roles, audiences must have been primarily attracted by the fact they were so unusual, which is why sponsors staged them.

Boxing was not the only sport to become commercialised in the eighteenth century: similar changes occurred in cricket and horse racing. In each case, the promotion of matches for prizes in front of paying and betting audiences stimulated changes in the way the sport was conducted, notably the codification of sets of rules.[99] Boxing, however, was unusual in that the sport, whether conducted on the streets or in prize fights, incurred considerable disapproval throughout the century.

It was largely elite sponsorship which saved it from being suppressed. Initially there were two lines of attack: first, that the activity was unsuitable for gentlemen; and, secondly, that it promoted disorder among the poor. A published 'letter to a young gentleman' in defence of duelling in 1752 included a section, entitled 'the bruiser, or an inquiry into the pretensions of modern manhood', which criticised gentlemen for 'vainly' attempting to emulate 'the hardiness of the labourer' by boxing. Contrary to duelling, fist-fighting was not 'a fair trial of manhood', since the parties were not necessarily equal in size or strength; nor did it require true courage, since the risk of death was so low. Moreover, since opponents were often not gentlemen, it encouraged 'an inglorious inequality with the meanest rabble', leading to insolence and insubordination among the lower classes. Later in the century 'the vulgar mode of boxing' was criticised as totally opposed 'to the ideas of a gentleman, whose manners are refined by education and habit'.[100]

Concern about the alleged disorder caused by assemblies of large numbers of spectators led magistrates to attempt to suppress boxing matches using the licensing provisions of the 1752 act 'for regulating places of entertainment'.[101] Although staged fights were often accompanied by additional contests between men in the audience who spontaneously challenged each other ('bye-battles'), the actual threat of disorder posed by boxing matches appears to have been minimal. It is remarkable how easily magistrates were able to disperse planned fights, even when thousands of expectant spectators had already gathered. The first attempt to stage the 1787 fight between Mendoza and Martin, on Ealing Common, was broken up when magistrates arrived and read the Riot Act. Despite the fact that the fight had been 'the subject of every blackguard's conversation for some days', the *Daily Universal Register* reported, 'the mob, in number perhaps ten thousand, dispersed quietly'. (The fight took place three weeks later in Barnet.)[102]

Towards the end of the century three new lines of criticism were introduced. As part of the revived movement for a reformation of manners in the 1780s, there were complaints about Sabbath-breaking, since so many matches took place on Sundays when working people had the day off.[103] Secondly, the view was increasingly expressed that fist-fighting was barbaric and unsuitable for a civilised country. In a series of editorial comments in the late 1780s the *Daily Universal Register* and then the *Times* described boxing as 'savage', 'barbarous', 'brutal', 'shameful' and 'unnatural'. One correspondent, identified as 'a friend in the community', wondered how men with 'fine feelings of humanity' could watch their fellow creatures 'fighting like dogs'. In December 1787 the paper demanded that magistrates suppress this 'brutal amusement', 'unless we all suddenly decline all pretension to that of being a polite, civilized, enlightened nation'. Introducing a third line of attack in 1792, the paper questioned the honesty of the participants, alleging that fights were often fixed beforehand.[104]

Despite this opposition, and several successful attempts by magistrates to prevent fights from taking place, many Londoners of all social classes continued to enjoy prize fighting into the 1820s, though prestige fights were staged at increasing distances from London in order to evade the authorities.[105] Indeed, facilitated by elite sponsorship, the period between 1780 and 1820 was probably the golden era of bare-knuckle boxing, when successful boxers mingled with royalty and became popular heroes. Following the fight between Mendoza and Humphries in 1788, boxing came into 'general notice':

> the newspapers teemed with anecdotes concerning them – pamphlets were published in favour of pugilism – and scarcely a print shop in the metropolis but what displayed the set-to in glowing colours, and portraits of those distinguished heroes of the fist ... Boxing became fashionable – followed, patronized, and encouraged.

Mendoza was the subject of at least twenty-five portraits, and seven medals were issued in his honour.[106] At a time of military threats from abroad, boxing usefully contributed to the celebration of 'manly' martial and heroic qualities as national characteristics, and criticisms of boxing were derided as the 'trifling squibs' of 'Frenchified ... effeminate scribblers'.[107]

A withdrawal of aristocratic support, together with growing concern about fixed matches, caused a decline in support for prize boxing in the 1820s.[108] Yet many people's attitudes had already shifted decades earlier. By the 1790s 'sparring' (demonstration fights with gloves) was becoming a popular alternative spectator sport to boxing matches for those who found the latter too violent. In 1791 Mendoza opened a theatre on the Strand for public exhibitions of sparring, where 'the manly art of boxing would be displayed, divested of all ferocity, rendered equally as neat and elegant as fencing [and] conducted with the utmost propriety and decorum'. At about this time the 'Fives Court' in Leicester Fields advertised demonstrations of sparring in similar terms: 'those persons, whether from want of inclination or inconvenience who do not witness the combats of the ring, may ... see the science illustrated in every point of view with gloves ... with all the minutiae of a regular match, and without offending the most fastidious advocates of humanity'.[109]

Concurrently, the practice of boxing on the streets to resolve quarrels appears to have declined, particularly among the upper class. In 1770 de Massi observed that instances of boxing 'practised in the higher life' are 'not to be seen so often'. When John Daws encountered David Davis and 'a little man' quarrelling and about to fight in a street near the Old Bailey in 1793, Daws, a gentleman, was ambivalent about the merits of fighting. He successfully prevented the fight, saying to the other man, 'go on my good little fellow, and go about your business, for this man is too strong for you, he will lick you; he would kill you, if you was to fight with him'. Having thereby provoked resentment and a challenge from Davis, Daws admitted that 'he understood boxing', but said he 'believed, in such cases, people generally come off second best'. Yet he was willing to fight, but not 'in such a public manner'. He told Davis: 'I would not attempt to fight you here, [but] if you could lick me in a room, I would give you a crown bowl of punch, but I am not a fighting man'. Daws was willing to fight, either for fun or to defend his honour, but he did not think he should do it in public. Some people also lost interest in watching fights. When a baker and a gentleman began fighting at a Freemasons' Lodge at the Cock and Lion Tavern in 1756, 'the rest of the company retired to avoid seeing the quarrel'.[110] D'Archenholz suggested that the decline of elite boxing also led to a decrease in lower-class boxing when he wrote in 1791 that boxing 'is not, however, so much in fashion as formerly. Even persons of quality were not heretofore ashamed of engaging in such quarrels. They have of late, however, left the glory of them entirely to the populace, who being no longer animated by their example, begin now to have less relish for them'.[111]

In early 1791 the *Times* reported that in the previous year there had been thirty-three duels (of which fourteen were fatal) and twelve boxing matches in Great Britain and Ireland.[112] While these figures are not to be trusted, the fact that the two phenomena were reported together is significant. Contemporaries were aware that duels and boxing matches were complementary rituals for resolving disputes, since they involved similar patterns of behaviour and were prompted by similar concerns. These similarities were not simply the result of the lower classes imitating their social superiors (as D'Archenholz suggested), but were instead the product of shared understandings of masculinity and honour.

Certainly there are many examples of lower-class boxers imitating the rituals of the gentlemanly duel. It was not only prize fights where boxers issued formal challenges to each other: when Thomas Brown, a black servant, fell out with a fellow servant who had thrown a cat at him, he was told he 'should send a challenge like a gentleman'. Being unable to write, he was forced to try and find someone else to write it for him. Although he challenged his opponent to fight him using a sword and pistol, they ended up fighting the way lower-class men normally fought, with their fists. Describing the quarrel that led to his fight with Francis Lenard, described at the start of this chapter, Thomas Powel (a brick-layer) used the gentlemanly expression that Lenard had given him 'the lie'. When boxing matches ended the injured forgave their opponents, just as gentlemen did: a carpenter's apprentice, dying after a scuffle with a fellow apprentice in a workshop in Dorset Gardens, was reported to have said that 'if he should die he freely forgave and excused' his antagonist.[113] These men were not, however, just imitating their social superiors. Embedded in the practices of both boxing matches and duels were commonly held attitudes towards honour, manliness and fair play.[114] Arguably it is these shared values which explain why juries, typically composed of tradesmen, shopkeepers and artisans, were so reluctant to convict gentlemen who killed their opponents in duels of murder, finding them guilty of manslaughter instead.

Gentlemen also imitated their social inferiors. Standards of fair play dictated that when they quarrelled with those who did not possess swords or pistols, they had to put aside their weapons and fight with their hands. Muralt reported that 'persons of quality lay aside their swords, wigs, and neck-cloths to box, when they are insulted by mean people, against whom they must not draw their swords'.[115] After a coachman quarrelled with and then struck a gentleman in 1771 at Vauxhall, the latter removed his sword, 'deposited it in the hands of a friend, and resting his defence on the power of his arm, showed so much agility and skill in the art of boxing, that the fellow was forced to beg pardon in a submissive manner, and the spectators were much pleased to see the aggressor beat at his own weapons'. We have seen that, as boxing became a fashionable spectator sport, some gentlemen began to take lessons. Although critical of the practice, the *Daily Universal Register* thought it was preferable to duelling, and actually wished that duels would be replaced by boxing matches, a 'mode of combat, infinitely more characteristic of old English prowess, and less destructive of human life'.[116]

Over the course of the eighteenth century, however, the common culture of violence and honour which sustained both these rituals changed dramatically. Violence was increasingly socially unacceptable, and male honour came to depend far less on public displays of bravery and courage. The practices of duelling and boxing survived and even prospered into the early nineteenth century, but in each case by the late eighteenth century their conduct and significance had been fundamentally transformed. The introduction of the pistol duel, with its far lower fatality rate, allowed duelling to flourish in spite of widespread criticism.[117] But at another level the duel at the turn of the nineteenth century was a pale reflection of its former self. Men's emotional and physical involvement was much reduced, and the central actors in the ritual became the seconds. The honour affirmed had changed its meaning, and had a much more restricted constituency, encouraged by the fact that duels were increasingly conducted in out of the way places. The duel would not disappear from English soil for another fifty years,[118] but arguably in London it had been fatally undermined in the eighteenth century by changing understandings of the role of violence and honour in definitions of elite masculinity.

Concurrently, boxing became largely a spectator sport, conducted more frequently as a form of commercial entertainment than as a means of resolving disputes. For most men the violence was displaced onto the stage, where the sport for the spectators lay as much in the betting as in the actual fighting. Even then, some spectators preferred the less bloody sparring matches with gloves. Prize fighters became like modern superstars, praised for their physical strength and beauty as much as for their fighting ability. Louis Simond, a French visitor to England in 1810 and 1811, noted that 'the windows of print shops are decorated with engraved full-length portraits of the favourites of the pugilistic art ... naked; displaying their well-formed limbs, the fine entrelacement of their muscles, and the graces of strength'.[119] Like duellists standing in the face of fire, one of the most valued qualities of boxers became their passive ability to withstand repeated attacks. Reflecting changing attitudes towards violence, boxers were praised not so much for their strong arms and powerful fists, as for their 'bottom', defined as 'a high degree of passive courage or fortitude, which consists of bearing blows and wounds, attended with the most dreadful sufferings, without flinching or yielding, as long as there is breath'. One boxer, for example, was said to possess 'rare bottom, spirit, and manliness, which would bear a great deal of beating'.[120] Like duels, prize matches were increasingly conducted in places remote from London in order to escape the unwanted attentions of magistrates. The popularity of prize boxing peaked in the first two decades of the nineteenth century, but it soon entered into a period of decline. Cut off from the day-to-day practices of publicly resolving disputes on the streets or in alehouses, the golden ages of both boxing and duelling were coming to an end.

# *Going to Law*

In a letter published in the *Times* in February 1800, a correspondent identified only as 'Anti Duelist' wrote to Lord George Cavendish, thanking him for having responded to an insult given to him by an officer by filing a lawsuit in King's Bench. The letter concluded, 'I consider your appeal to the laws as a more effectual means of preventing this detestable alternative of duelling, than all the logic that can be used'.[1] Contemporary observers (as well as many later historians) believed that duels were prevented because gentlemen increasingly chose to resolve their disputes peacefully in the courtroom rather than on the field of battle. The Reverend John Trusler wrote in 1804 that 'I am happy to find that gentlemen, men of honour, and even military men in some cases, appeal to the civil laws of their country, when challenged, instead of the sword; and they appear to be countenanced in so doing'. Similarly, Charles Moore wrote in 1790 that since men began to prosecute their wives' lovers for damages through actions for criminal conversation, 'lighter matters alone are productive of the duel'.[2] This idea, that the violence of the duel was replaced by litigation, fits nicely into the standard account of a long-term transition in English history from an 'honour and shame' society (characterised by violence) in the medieval and early modern periods to a modern commercial society, where wrongs are compensated for by the payment of damages negotiated through the courts.[3]

The law did replace, or supplement, the duel as a means of conducting *some* late eighteenth-century disputes. Following an incident at a horse race at Epsom in which George Dive beat John Howe with a cane after Howe allegedly made sexual advances, Howe sued Dive for assault and defamation. In addressing the assizes jury, Howe's counsel demanded significant damages for his client in order to send a signal that going to law in such a situation would be rewarded. If not, he argued, the jury would be saying that 'if he is injured, [his client] must in defiance of the laws of God and man carve out his own satisfaction, by plunging his sword into the heart of the offender'. The jury responded by awarding £150 to Howe, who donated the money to charity.[4] In other cases, duellists went to law after duels had failed to resolve their disputes. Following the discovery, in 1795, that John Townshend, son of Viscount Townshend, had had an adulterous relationship with the wife of William Fawkener, clerk of the Privy Council, the two men fought a duel in Hyde Park in which neither party was injured. Fawkener nonetheless prosecuted an action of criminal conversation at King's Bench. At the trial, Thomas Erskine, Townshend's lawyer, told the jury that it should not give 'vindictive damages', since the plaintiff had already 'received satisfaction for the injury done to his honour'. It disagreed, however, and awarded him £500 damages. Other duels, however, occurred fol-lowing an unsatisfactory verdict in the courts. Following an unsuccessful lawsuit in 1775, John Chapman delivered a written challenge to William Morgan, steward of the manor of Abergavenny in Monmouth, at his house in Marylebone: 'After another robbery committed upon me Wednesday last of £6 19s. 8d. by the Court Baron of Abergavenny ... I put into my pockets the only proofs [pistols] remaining for that purpose'.[5]

As, over the course of the eighteenth century, Londoners became less willing to conduct their disputes in public by engaging in defamation, demonstrations and violence, did the law take over? Did the court-room replace the streets as the preferred venue for resolving conflicts and restoring reputations? Although this is a tempting narrative, it is not what happened in eighteenth-century London. Throughout the century Londoners remained sceptical of the ability of the law satisfac-torily to resolve their disputes, and if anything over time they became *more* reluctant to go to law. This was a litigious society, but attitudes towards the law were deeply ambivalent. As reflected in the fact that crowds often imitated official forms of punishment when inflicting their own sanctions on perceived deviants, legal ideas permeated popu-lar culture, but the law was also often rejected in favour of (or supplemented by) more direct forms of waging conflict.[6] Alongside a deeply-held belief in the rule of law, there lay both the general conviction that the judicial system could be an effective tool for advancing one's interests *and* a widespread belief that it was inefficient, expensive and often corrupt.

One of the most enduring legacies of the constitutional conflicts of the seventeenth century, especially the Revolution settlement in 1689, was the belief that the historical tradition of the common law was the guarantor of English rights and liberties, the bulwark which protected Englishmen against the threat of arbitrary government. As a correspondent to the *Universal Spectator* affirmed in 1731, no law 'hath or can have juster or better principles than the common law of England, since it consists in nothing more than the impartial dictates of reason, settled by wise men, and confirmed by custom'.[7] One of the most potent legitimating myths of the eighteenth-century state was the claim that all Englishmen were protected by the rule of law. Not only did it defend Parliament's authority against encroachments by the King, it gave even the poorest Englishman protection against mistreatment by his social superiors.[8] As the Prussian visitor D'Archenholz commented in 1791, even 'the first man in the kingdom is cautious of striking his domestics ... for they not only may defend themselves against him, but also commence an action in a court of justice: in such a case, a pecuniary recompense, and many disagreeable circumstances are sure to follow'.[9] As attempts to fight impressment for service in the navy through the courts suggest, Englishmen did believe that the law could be used effectively to secure their rights and limit abuses of power by agents of the state. Similarly, when a gang employed to enlist men for service with the East India Company attempted to kidnap a cooper in an alehouse and beat him, many of the neighbours interfered. As the *General Evening Post* reported, these 'reputable housekeepers ... are determined to prosecute the offenders, for the sake of public justice'.[10]

What litigants sought to obtain from the courts, however, varied considerably, depending on the nature of the wrong, the circumstances and perspective of the victim, and the identity of the opponent. Many prosecutors of serious crimes (felonies) sought the finality of a formal conviction and punishment. Indeed, any attempt to settle felony accusations with private apologies, or the payment of damages, was illegal. Nonetheless, particularly for less serious crimes and civil cases, there was widespread belief that the purpose of litigation was to facilitate the settlement of disputes, not the systematic punishment of those who violated the law. In a case of slander heard by Judge Dudley Ryder at the Middlesex assizes 'the plaintiff offered that if [the] defendant and wife would beg pardon and declare [the] plaintiff innocent, [the] plaintiff would be content and satisfied', and the suit was dropped.[11] For many people, influenced by the belief that litigation was viewed as 'a breach of proper neighbourly relations', the main purpose of going to law was to facilitate informal agreements between the parties concerned.[12] Indeed, judicial practices were frequently designed to encourage such settlements.

When hearing petty criminal complaints, for example, the first instinct of most justices of the peace was to *avoid* a formal prosecution. A notice placed by John Fielding in the *Public Advertiser* in 1763 announced the establishment of an office in Westminster where magistrates would be available at set times 'to hear the complaints and redress the grievances of the inhabitants', since 'making of peace, reconciling of differences, and preventing expensive prosecutions on frivolous accounts, [are] the true characteristics of candid magistrates'.[13] This office merely formalised long-standing procedures. When complaints of assaults were brought before Justice Henry Norris of Hackney in the 1730s, his main concern was to settle them informally, typically with apologies or the payment of damages. As he recorded in his notebook, when Hamilton Smith complained that Thomas, Nicholas and John Batmaker had 'assault[ed] him ... in the yard of the King's Arms in Kingsland ... beating him in a severe manner', Norris issued a warrant for their arrest. Five days later they were brought before him, together with Smith and other witnesses, and 'after a long hearing they agreed the matter' and the prosecution was dropped.[14] Justices also used the procedure of binding over by recognizance to encourage the parties in criminal complaints to settle their differences. Because failing to meet the conditions of a recognizance could be expensive, this was an effective method of resolving disputes. Relatively few cases proceeded to further legal action; in most cases either the parties reached a mutually satisfactory settlement or the plaintiff concluded that merely requiring the defendant to appear at sessions was sufficient punishment for the offence.[15] Many other disputes and accusations, of course, were settled by other authority figures before they even reached a justice. In 1704 Mary Faulkner was struck 'in a grievous manner' on the back by a gentleman, Philip Walgrave, with a stick as she was standing at a door on London Bridge. Asked to apprehend Walgrave, a constable went up to him and asked him 'to go back to make satisfaction for what [he] had done'.[16] Respected local inhabitants also resolved disputes: recollecting the time when he was a breeches maker living on Wych Street (near the bottom of Drury Lane) in the 1790s, Francis Place claimed 'I had many matters brought to me for adjudication, arbitration or arrangement'.[17]

Even after formal prosecutions were initiated, it was common practice for the courts (except in felony cases) to encourage the parties to settle the dispute and drop the prosecution. Cases in the church courts, the common law courts in Westminster, and quarter sessions were all frequently resolved in this way. Many matrimonial suits at the consistory courts were settled privately or dropped before they reached the sentencing stage. Judges hearing civil suits frequently suggested agreements to the litigants or referred cases to arbitrators. Lord Mansfield referred numerous cases at King's Bench to arbitration, particularly those where the law and facts of the case were clear cut, and he was displeased when the parties refused to cooperate. In one case of breach of covenant for not repairing a house in Red Bull Alley in Thames Street, he wrote in his case notes 'I tried all I could to have the whole [case] referred and settled, but plaintiff would agree to nothing'.[18]

Prosecutions for petty crimes such as indictments for assault at the Middlesex quarter sessions were frequently settled out of court when defendants agreed to pay damages to the victim, typically in exchange for formal written releases not to prosecute. Since the offence was vaguely defined in law and charges could arise out of any conflict in which a person felt physically threatened, indictments for assault could be used in a wide variety of disputes, and were often used in essentially civil disputes where plaintiffs were seeking damages. The large number of indictments which were dropped before trial or which resulted in formal releases indicates that negotiated settlements frequently occurred. Plaintiffs agreed to such arrangements because they usually received significant financial compensation, whereas if the case went to a final verdict any fine levied on the defendant would go to the King instead. Both parties benefited additionally from not having to undergo the expensive and time-consuming process of a trial.[19] After Thomas Richardson and his

wife repeatedly abused and threatened Elizabeth Jacobs and other neighbours, Jacobs prosecuted Richardson for assault and his wife for
being a common scold. Upon the Richardsons promising to give Jacobs
'some satisfaction for the abuse' and move out of the neighbourhood,
the London sessions suspended judgment on Richardson and respited a
fine of 20 marks imposed on his wife 'till such promises [have] been
fulfilled'.[20]

There were, however, significant disadvantages to the widespread
practices of arbitration and informal settlements in the English courts.
Many agreements, such as the last one, were subsequently broken,
generating new litigation. Only wealthy defendants were able to provide
the kind of financial 'satisfaction' which made such settlements worth-
while. Moreover, not everyone agreed that private settlements were
desirable, particularly in cases of egregious wrongs. After Sir Alexander
Leith MP was maliciously prosecuted by Benjamin Pope at the Old
Bailey on a felony charge in 1778 (and acquitted), he negotiated 'private
compensation' for the injury he received. But for some this was an
insufficient punishment of Pope and did not compensate for the injury
done to the public. It was discussed at a London debating society whether
Leith,

> in his capacity as one of the legislative body, can be justified, either to his
> constituents or the public at large, in perverting the course of justice against
> a most atrocious violator of private peace, by accepting any private compen-
> sation as a satisfaction for the injury he sustained in being arraigned and
> tried for his life, at the Old Bailey.[21]

Most importantly, the frequent 'private compensations' paid out in
lieu of formal prosecutions, verdicts, and punishments encouraged vexatious and malicious prosecutions, a problem which plagued the English
courts and undermined confidence in the law. The threat of a trial, with
all its attendant costs, inconveniences and embarrassment, forced many
people who had been indicted or sued, or who were threatened with a
lawsuit, to buy off their prosecutors, regardless of the merits of the
case. In a system which depended almost entirely on private citizens
for bringing prosecutions with, in criminal cases, only minimal vetting
of charges by grand juries, it was relatively easy to instigate false charges,
litigation which was often designed as blackmail or to exacerbate conflicts

rather than to resolve them. Some Londoners were very adept at this practice. When one Horton, a glazier, repeatedly insulted the former churchwarden of his parish in a pub by telling him he was 'perjured', he was told to desist. When he refused, 'something was said about taking the law', but Horton claimed he was not intimidated, for he 'liked a little law now and then'. Another person prosecuted for slander who also knew how to take legal revenge allegedly said 'she knew the way to Westminster Hall [the location of the central courts] and she had money to go there again, and she would do so'.[22] In order to prevent the cost and trouble of litigation, those sued or indicted were often willing to negotiate with their antagonists, even when the charge was unjustified. Consequently, such suits were frequently instigated in order to pressure plaintiffs who had filed other prosecutions into dropping the charges.[23]

Malicious and vexatious litigation was endemic in London, given the close proximity of several courts, operating under three different legal systems (common law, equity and canon law). Perhaps the simplest way of using the law to harass enemies was for men or women to go to a justice of the peace and swear that that they had been assaulted, or that their antagonists had threatened to put their life in danger in some way, thereby forcing them to enter into a recognizance to appear at sessions. The active justice of the peace Thomas De Veil noted how easy it was for someone accused of a crime to turn around and 'swear (by way of revenge) anything that comes into his head, to defeat the prosecution of his adversary; whereby a stop is entirely put to justice'. Should a justice refuse to hear such a charge, there were usually other justices nearby who would welcome the business. Thomas Jeffreys told Justice William Moore in 1721, 'if he could not have law here he would go where he could have law'. Consequently, 'cross warrants', where both sides in a dispute were forced to enter into recognizances at the other's request, were common. These were frequently issued by 'trading justices', who supported themselves partly on the fees received from such business.[24] Those arrested were often willing to drop any prosecutions they had initiated in order to avoid being bound over. After William Boxal, a constable, was arrested for debt, he managed to get Sarah Longslow, the person responsible, arrested on a warrant for a riot. When she was brought before the justice, Boxal reportedly said, 'if

Mrs Longslow would give him a free discharge and take him out of the [debtors' commons], he would discharge the warrant against her'.[25]

Prosecutions (both civil and criminal) for assault and slander were frequently vexatious, facilitated by the fact that these offences were so broadly defined. The vague legal definition of assault meant that 'any injury done to a man in an angry insolent manner, be it ever so small, is actionable; for example spitting in his face, jostling him, treading on his toes, or any way touching him in anger'.[26] In a fictional, but resonant, account of A Trip Through London in 1728, the narrator tells of having accidentally bumped into someone while walking through Temple Bar: 'the man did not complain of any injury done him ... but by the time I reached to the end of Wood Street in Cheapside, two fellows came up to me, and I was arrested in an action of £1000 for assault and battery, a North Country solicitor having, it seems, advised the plaintiff to this surprising proceeding'.[27] It was not difficult to find a pretext for prosecution. In 1751 a woman who had been arrested for debt and then absconded was reapprehended by the men who had provided security for the debt, who carried 'her away by a kind of violence'. She prosecuted them for assault at King's Bench and won. In 1760 Eleanor Steed, a widow, was convicted of petty theft and sentenced to be publicly whipped. Because, when complaining about the theft, her victim had 'three or four times [had] a mob before her door', she retaliated by serving the prosecutor with 'an action of scandal'.[28] Another option was to get one's antagonist arrested for a small debt. Debtors' courts were, a commentator wrote in 1716, 'for the most part, used for vexation and revenge, and generally known to favour the plaintiffs in the vilest and most scandalous litigation', and conditions in debtors' prisons such as the Marshalsea were notoriously unpleasant. Thus when Jane Garton preferred two indictments for assault in February 1709, her husband was at the instigation of one of the defendants 'arrested and he is now a prisoner in the Marshalsea Prison in Southwark'. According to his wife, the defendants were 'all letigious people and have caused her husband to be arrested on purpose to putt her to further charge'. Presumably the ultimate aim of this 'sham action' was to get the Gartons to drop the original indictments.[29]

Even prosecutions for felony, where compounding prosecutions was illegal, were used vexatiously. Accusations of sodomy, which not only

put the accused at risk of a death sentence or the pillory but were also
extremely embarrassing, provided a perfect opportunity for blackmail.[30] But prosecutions for theft, the most common offence charged
at the Old Bailey, could also be malicious. In the 1730s after John
Drinkwater, once a servant to John Warwick, fell out with him for
unknown reasons, the two, along with several others, instigated a series
of prosecutions against each other at the Old Bailey and other courts
for a period of at least five years. In April 1735 Warwick, who allegedly
had once lived with Elizabeth Sayer 'as man and wife', removed some
goods from her house. According to Sayer, he 'called me bitch, and said
if I took the law of him, he would cut my throat, or get fifty people to
swear my life away'. He then got her arrested on an action for debt of
£140, and while she was in prison he removed more goods. When Sayer
then indicted Warwick for theft, he complained that Drinkwater had
caused his wife, while she was a spectator in court, to be arrested for a
robbery. In later indictments, Warwick and four acquaintances were
charged with conspiring falsely to charge Drinkwater with highway
robbery, Drinkwater was charged with perjury and with receiving stolen
goods, and Drinkwater charged another man with barratry, the offence
of falsely instigating lawsuits. For one witness at the trial of this last
charge this was a case of the pot calling the kettle black; referring to
Drinkwater, he said 'I don't think there is such another litigious fellow
in London'. As the judge summed up another of the cases, 'why truly
I think we are in very bad company on all sides' (the evidence suggests
that, in addition to felonious crime, most of the participants were
involved in prostitution or running brothels).

Although at this distance it is impossible to sort out fact from fiction
in these cases, the courtroom testimony suggests just how easy the
participants thought it was to procure perjured testimony and initiate
false charges. When Warwick and his friends were informed that Drinkwater was about to prosecute him for robberies committed in his house,
'they all contrived to get [Drinkwater] out of the way' by falsely charging
*him* with a robbery. They suborned a witness to make a fictitious
complaint to a justice; when the justice refused they simply found
another one who was willing to cooperate. According to Drinkwater's
wife, 'their intent was to distress my husband in jayl, in order to bring
him to sign releases, so that they might not be prosecuted for what they

had done' (the robberies committed in Warwick's house). Drinkwater claimed that they later confessed to him that 'you have been cruelly and wrongfully charged'. A few years later, prompted by a prosecution Drinkwater had initiated against another man for keeping a bawdy house, several people agreed to prosecute him for barratry in order to 'perplex Drinkwater and bring him to terms'.[31]

Two of the central features of the English legal system, its reliance on private prosecutors and its encouragement of private settlements, thus opened the courts up to widespread abuse. These cases demonstrate that Londoners of both sexes and all social classes understood the law and knew how to manipulate the legal system for their own ends. In this sense, going to law was widely seen as a useful means of advancing one's interests. But the frequency of malicious prosecutions also undermined respect for the law; because such tactics were available to all, litigants knew that each lawsuit was only one battle in what was potentially a long war. Although plaintiffs knew the law was an effective tool for harassment, they must have had little confidence that they would obtain justice from the courts.[32] These considerations may have discouraged many people from going to law at all, while for others it meant that lawsuits were supplemented by direct action. When Katherine Allen fell out with John Davis in 1708, she both went to his door 'in a tumultuous manner threatening and abusing [him] several times in a violent man- ner', *and* threatened 'to ruin [him] with vexatious actions, and to that purpose ... employed a bailiff to arrest him'. In 1731 the debtors in the Fleet Prison, believing they were being mistreated, initiated an action against the warden at the Court of Common Pleas, but they also 'caused a riot and insulted the keepers' directly.[33] Because it could not be relied upon to provide the desired results, the law supplemented, rather than replaced, street conflict.

In the eighteenth century the reputation of the English legal system, as opposed to belief in the rule of law as an abstract principle, was at a low ebb. There was, according to the French visitor J. H. Meister, 'no country in Europe where suits at law may be maintained on slighter grounds, nor where you are more certain to be ruined by gaining them'.[34] Complaints about malicious lawsuits and the costs, delays and complex- ities of going to law are endemic throughout English history, but they reached a peak in this century, when commentators frequently worried that ordinary people preferred to suffer wrongs rather than take the trouble to go to law. In his *Historical Treatise of an Action or Suit at Law* (1766), Richard Boote complained that, owing to 'the obscurity and expense which necessarily attend the conducting a suit at law', 'people are often deterred from having recourse to the law in order to recover what is ever so unjustly withheld from them'.[35]

There was substance in all these complaints. For several reasons, the overall cost of civil litigation doubled between 1680 and 1750. In 1694 stamp duty was imposed on legal actions above the value of 40 shillings, leading to an immediate and significant decline in litigation. In addition, both the number of court officials and the fees they charged increased. Since they had often purchased their posts and they collected fees for each step in the legal process, they tended to prolong cases in order to ensure an adequate return on their investment. Solicitors also found new ways of increasing their fees, as a fixed tariff system was replaced by charges for the amount of time actually spent on a case, and they found more tasks to perform before cases went to trial. Their clerks were paid by the page, and as litigation declined they augmented their income by writing in increasingly large handwriting with generous margins.[36] Commenting on a case in 1777 where the plaintiff's declarations amounted to 2506 pages, Lord Mansfield complained 'in a severe and angry tone, upon the common practice of drawing up numerous long and voluminous affidavits of various people ... which answers no other end, but by the number of stamps, sheets and lines, to swell the attorney's bill'. As a contemporary pamphlet complained, 'by the turns and managements of the inferior practitioners in the courts, our approach to them is made so intricate and expensive, that they, who are obliged to sue ... are frequently undone'.[37] In 1757 an impoverished gentlewoman, who claimed that a man who had raped her was on the verge of avoiding trial 'from the strength of his money' and his 'powerful friends', actually placed an advertisement in a newspaper seeking donations so she could afford to hire 'proper council'.[38] Contemporary views about lawyers' charges are nicely summed up in a satirical print published in 1770 in which a lawyer shares an oyster with the two parties in a lawsuit: the lawyer eats the oyster, while each litigant gets an empty half shell (Figure 23).

The fact that lawyers exploited complex court procedures and the intricacies of the law also led to frequent complaints. Writing about 'the tediousness and delays' of civil suits in 1730, Sollom Emlyn, editor of the first published collection of state trials, noted especially 'the nicety of special pleadings, whereby the justest cause in the world, after having with great trouble and expense been conducted almost to a period, may through the mistake of a letter (often occasioned by an attorney's clerk) be irretrievably lost, or at least turned round to begin again'. A quarter of the suits heard at Chancery in 1685 took longer than a year to complete, and a century later this figure had increased to more than a third. Lawyers' tactics were often seen as devious and dishonest: in debates in London's debating societies over whether it was hardest to find an honest lawyer, a pious clergyman or a disinterested doctor, the lawyer always won.[39] An editorial in the *Old England Journal*, complaining about 'the unhappy state and condition which the subjects of this kingdom are reduced by the law', argued that 'if I consult with a lawyer I consult with a mistaken guide, who leads me into a wilderness, or rather a waste of brambles and briers which tears my clothing into rags, and bewilders my understanding, and confounds me with disappointment'.[40] In sum, the law was perceived as sacrificing the interests of justice in order to satisfy the greed of lawyers.[41]

Perhaps the most damning of all these criticisms was the high cost of going to law, which denied access to the courts to a significant proportion of the population. In a system reliant on privately initiated prosecutions, this limited significantly the number of both criminal and civil lawsuits filed. When the constable William Boxal was harassed by his estranged wife and her friends, whom he claimed staged nightly riots outside his house and got him imprisoned for debt, he consulted an attorney, who advised him 'to make it up', since pursuing an action would cost 'a great deal of money'. 'If you fight them', he said, 'the expense will ruin you.'[42] As Henry Fielding complained with respect to felonies, when all the costs of prosecution are added up, 'the whole amounts to an expense which a very poor person, already plundered by the thief, must look on with such horror (if he should not be absolutely incapable of the expense) that he must be a miracle of public spirit, if he doth not rather choose to conceal the felony'.[43] Provisions were established to reimburse the costs of poor prosecutors in certain circumstances, but these had a

23. 'A Sharp Between Two Flats: A Pearly Shell for Him and Thee, the Oyster
is the Lawyer's Fee' (1770). (*Guildhall Library, Corporation of London*)

limited impact. Before 1752 prosecutors of those convicted of the most serious crimes could earn statutory rewards or valuable 'Tyburn Tickets' (exempting the holder for life from the obligation of serving in parish offices), but this applied to only a minority of prosecutions. Statutes passed in 1752 and 1778 gave the courts discretionary power to order reimbursement of the costs of prosecution in all felony cases, and by the end of the century around two-thirds of prosecutors received some compensation. But such payments did not cover all the costs prosecutors incurred: they were, for example, unlikely to reimburse the expense of finding the suspect in the first place, or of counsel. Moreover, they were only paid following the completion of the trial, leaving prosecutors out of pocket for a time before they received compensation. Consequently, the arrangements for paying expenses did not significantly alter the fact that the costs of prosecution were a major disincentive to initiating prosecutions.[44]

The costs of prosecuting petty crimes were lower, but the fee for filing an indictment still amounted to more than a week's wages for a labourer, and no compensation was available. As a justice of the peace commented in 1816, 'though the expense of an indictment is no more than 2s. 6d. or 3s., yet it turns aside the intentions of justice in even the most miserable cases, ninety-nine times out of an hundred'. Consequently, those living in the poorest parts of the metropolis (east of the City) were only a third as likely to prosecute indictments as those living in the west end.[45] This discrepancy was also a product of distance, since journeying to and from the court houses in Clerkenwell and Westminster was time consuming. The same applies to the initial trip victims needed to make to a magistrate's house or courtroom for a preliminary hearing. As Francis Burton told the House of Commons when he introduced the Middlesex Justices Bill in 1792, 'those who [are] robbed of trifles, or slightly injured in their persons, if at a considerable distance from Bow Street, put up with their injuries, rather than involve themselves in the trouble of a prosecution of the offenders'.[46] It was not only the poor who were dissuaded from prosecuting misdemeanours: shopkeepers who were victims of fraud or who were paid with counterfeit money faced potentially complex and expensive prosecutions, and they could not benefit from the legal aid provided in felony cases.[47]

Costs were considerably greater in civil cases, which is why gentlemen, professionals and merchants were significantly over-represented among the litigants in the Westminster courts.[48] It was possible for defendants in the common law courts, church courts and the Court of Chancery who were worth less than £5 to litigate 'in forma pauperis' (as a pauper), which meant that all expenses were paid by the other party regardless of the outcome, but it is unclear how often this right was used. Meister thought this compensated 'in some measure' for the greater access to the law enjoyed by the rich, but he was concerned that it encouraged vexatious prosecutions, since the poor litigant had little to lose: 'this regulation, however, appears to encourage chicanery and every device of the most cruel injustice'.[49] To prevent abuse, the right was hedged with qualifications, such as that petitions to sue in this manner needed to be signed by a lawyer, and some fees still had to be paid.[50] Despite its title, this form of prosecution was not therefore available to the very poor. One type of lawsuit, for small debts, was more accessible to 'the lower class of people'. Courts of request, such as the City of London's, heard suits for small debts inexpensively and rapidly without the need for a lawyer. Once again, however, there were complaints of difficulties encountered by litigants, including chaos, delays and difficulties in getting decisions enforced. No form of litigation was unproblematically available to the poor.[51] Overall, as a recent survey of seamen's resistance to impressment concluded, while the lower class were knowledgeable about the law, they frequently lacked the money and social networks necessary to use it effectively unless they were assisted by their social superiors.[52]

Going to law was also more difficult for women than it was for men. Not only did women generally have access to fewer financial resources, but the world of litigation was controlled entirely by men, and suits instigated by women were likely to be treated sceptically. The Middlesex grand juries rejected misdemeanor indictments prosecuted by women proportionally far more often than those prosecuted by men.[53] In civil suits, married women were disabled from prosecuting on their own in the common law courts by the principle of coverture, which placed their property in the control of their husbands (though there were some ways of evading these restrictions). Women had greater opportunities under the laws of equity, which allowed married women to own property in 'separate estates'. They participated in between 14 and 21 per cent of suits filed in Chancery, and were frequent litigants in courts of request, which accepted testimony from married women acting as their husband's 'agents'. Nonetheless, women remained a small minority among litigants in civil cases, and usually when they did litigate they did so jointly with men.[54]

In contrast, women found it easier to prosecute in the ecclesiastical and criminal courts. In the early eighteenth century female plaintiffs outnumbered men by a considerable margin at the London Consistory Court and the Court of Arches (the court of appeal for the church courts), mostly initiating prosecutions for defamation and the enforcement of marriage contracts, but this was reversed over the century as defamation cases declined and marriage litigation shifted towards attempts to secure separations (usually initiated by men).[55] In criminal prosecutions women dominated the most informal method of prosecution. More women than men in London instigated recognizances, the simple and inexpensive procedure by which defendants were bound over to appear in court to answer charges and often to keep the peace in the meantime. (The reverse was true in rural areas, where women's lives were not as independent as they were in the metropolis.) Over 80 per cent of recognizances issued at the behest of women were for offences against the peace, particularly minor assaults, defamation and simple binding over to keep the peace, indicating that women used this procedure in situations where men may have chosen to resort to fisticuffs or sword fights. In contrast, women accounted for less than a third of the indictments prosecuted at the Middlesex sessions, though most of these were also for offences against the peace.[56] Even fewer women were listed as plaintiffs in Old Bailey trials, partly because theft was the most common offence and goods stolen from married women were deemed the property of their husbands. Nonetheless, women accounted for only 10 per cent of Old Bailey plaintiffs who prosecuted offences against the peace. With the significant exception of the recognizance, even the criminal courts, where the laws of coverture did not apply, failed to provide women with feasible methods of conducting their disputes.

Despite the considerable disadvantages of going to law, the large numbers of criminal and civil suits for assault, riot, and slander prosecuted by Londoners suggests that for many people the courts did provide an

alternative (or a supplement) to street conflict. The widespread encouragement of arbitration and informal settlements by the courts was
perfectly suited to the types of conflicts which normally arose on the
streets and in pubs and coffee houses, which also often led to public
insults and violence. But there was growing scepticism in the eighteenth
century of the ability of the legal system to provide efficient, predictable
and just outcomes, and rising costs meant access to litigation became
difficult not just for women and the poor, but also for artisans, shopkeepers and the urban middle class more generally. Consequently, as
Londoners became increasingly reluctant to resort to insult, violence
and street protest, they did not all rush to the courts instead. Patterns
of litigation in London's many courts varied considerably depending on
the type of litigation heard, but overall per capita levels of litigation fell
over the course of the century. Business in some courts increased, but
rarely in line with the massive increase of London's population between
1700 and 1800, and in many others the number of prosecutions actually
declined.

The church courts experienced the most significant collapse in business. Although weakened by the loss of their disciplinary powers in
the late seventeenth century, these courts continued to hear private
prosecutions, notably matrimonial cases and defamation, throughout the
next century. As the public insult lost its power and significance, however,
victims of insult became less likely to prosecute, and defamation cases
declined dramatically, particularly after 1725.[57] Matrimonial cases decreased about the same time, but then recovered significantly after 1770
to become the most frequent type of suit heard by the courts. Nonetheless, in the last decade of the century the total number of suits heard at
the London Consistory Court was less than half that heard in the first
decade, and the types of suits and identities of the litigants had changed.
Not only were marriage suits now most frequently initiated by men, but
rising legal costs meant that by the end of the century most litigants
were from the upper middle class and above.[58] For the rest of the
population, the once feared church courts had become an irrelevance.

The central Westminster courts also experienced a catastrophic decline
in business in the early eighteenth century, though compared to the
church courts they staged a more significant, if still partial, recovery at
the end of the century. The courts of Common Pleas and King's Bench

handled a variety of wrongs, including unpaid debts, broken contracts, slander, malfeasance, negligence, disputes over land, and various types of trespass (including assault, false imprisonment, damage to property and criminal conversation).[59] Although these were the types of disputes which often led to violence or insults on the streets, these courts do not appear to have benefited from the decline of public conflict in London. Business in both courts collapsed in the first half of the century as the costs of litigation rose. Between 1670 and 1750 the number of cases in advanced stages at King's Bench fell by 72 per cent and at Common Pleas by 90 per cent. A 1744 pamphlet observed that 'if you look into Westminster Hall, the lawyers are together by the ears with one another, and nothing but complaints against the badness of the term, and want of money, is heard amongst them'.[60] While Common Pleas never recovered, business at King's Bench picked up in the late eighteenth century, especially in the 1790s and even more so in the 1810s and 1820s. Nonetheless, per capita the number of cases in these courts in 1830 was still only 57 per cent of the number in 1640. These figures concern the entire country, but, even when we allow for the fact that the proportion of cases filed from London and Middlesex increased, it is unlikely that the per capita level of metropolitan litigation in these courts in the late eighteenth century reached the level of the previous century.[61] A similar pattern of litigation occurred in the courts of Chancery and the Exchequer.[62] Once again, the revival of litigation towards the end of the century occurred primarily amongst the wealthy. In the 1820s litigants unanimously reported to parliamentary investigators that those involved in trade and commerce were discouraged from using the courts by their high costs and intricate procedures.[63] We have seen that the criminal courts provided a cheaper method of redress, while often also providing the opportunity for plaintiffs to obtain financial compensation for their legal costs. Nonetheless, the number of indictments filed for trespass did not increase: after fluctuating considerably throughout the century, per capita indictment levels in Middlesex declined in the early 1790s. Early in the nineteenth century the number of indictments did increase significantly, partly due to increased reimbursement of prosecutors' expenses, but the inability of the courts to scrutinise them adequately led to growing complaints about the number of vexatious prosecutions.[64]

A more attractive option for many prosecutors was the recognizance,

since, as we have seen, convincing a justice of the peace to bind a
defendant over to appear at sessions was simple and inexpensive.
Recognizances were issued in response to a wide variety of complaints
which also often led to public conflict on the streets, including accusations of theft, fraud, threatening behaviour, assault, riot and slander.[65]
In eighteenth-century London some justices, known as 'trading justices',
turned the task of issuing recognizances into a business, with some even
reputedly encouraging custom by granting warrants on credit or em-
ploying a clerk to stand outside their door, touting for business.
According to one observer in 1758, the Middlesex justices 'are no sooner
appointed than some of them open shops, contiguous to their trade and
employments, for the distribution of justice'. In a city where there were
dozens of active justices, access to this type of law was relatively easy
for anyone who could afford the cost of a warrant (one or two shillings)
to bring the accused before a justice.[66] This was the cheapest legal
procedure available in London, and trading justices in particular attracted large numbers of female and low-status defendants. The *Times*
called the office of justice of the peace the poor's 'principal court'.[67]
This may, however, overstate their accessibility: the fact that the per
capita number of recognizances emanating from the poorer east end
parishes was less than half that of the west end suggests that the cost
was still prohibitive for many.[68]

As always happened when cheap or subsidised legal procedures facilitated large numbers of prosecutions, trading justices acquired a bad
reputation. Already in 1716 a common proverb was 'as corrupt as a
Middlesex justice'.[69] Among other charges, trading justices were thought
to issue large numbers of vexatious recognizances, particularly by signing
'cross warrants'. They were also accused of creating business for themselves by encouraging complainants to request recognizances in even
the most trivial disputes. A contemporary observer complained that 'the
common people' applied to trading justices 'upon every trivial occasion,
to gratify their own spleen and malice against their neighbours'.[70] A
pamphlet describing the foibles of Londoners in the 1730s included a
story of a woman who emptied a chamber pot outside her window.
It landed on a passing woman, who immediately ran to 'Justice Twelve-
penny's to fetch a warrant'.[71] The reputation of trading justices has,
however, been recently somewhat rehabilitated. Analysis of court

business has identified some justices who attracted many poor and female complainants and who issued large numbers of recognizances, but there is no evidence that they acted improperly. One Middlesex justice, Edward Chamberlaine, defended his popularity by claiming that 'all in our parish and in several adjacent parishes chose rather to make their addresses to me because I never treated any roughly and insultingly but endeavoured reconciliation and saving charges especially amongst the poorer sort in a mild way'.[72]

As a result of the activities of trading justices, 'the recognizance list swelled'.[73] From the late 1760s the number issued to attend the Middlesex and Westminster sessions each year increased dramatically, till it reached a peak of 7322 in 1791, five times the average annual total in the 1750s. In 1792, however, the Middlesex Justices Act, Parliament's response to widespread concern about the activities of trading justices, effectively abolished them in London by stipulating that only stipendiary justices sitting at rotation offices could charge fees for judicial services, and these fees would go to the Treasury, not the justices. These new justices were apparently far less interested in hearing the time-consuming (and often vexatious) complaints of the poor. Immediately the number of recognizances fell by over half, and remained low well into the early nineteenth century. A supporter of the new system commented that the act had 'contributed to quell a spirit of litigation among the lower classes'; alternatively one could argue that one of the most accessible sources of legal redress for the poor had been radically constricted.[74] Nonetheless, even if they had to pawn their clothes in order to take out warrants, they continued to bring their complaints of breaches of the peace, assaults and disputes with landlords before justices: according to one who testified before Parliament in 1816, 'we have a hundred complaints of that sort in a week'.[75]

While the recognizance was often the only legal act arising out of petty criminal complaints brought before justices, victims making complaints about felonies were supposed to be bound over to repeat the charge to a grand jury and, if the indictment was found a 'true bill', to prosecute the case at the Old Bailey. While many accusations, particularly of minor felonies, were nonetheless settled out of court, justices were alert to the fact they could be sued if they failed to bind over victims of felonies to prosecute.[76] According to Henry Fielding, however, there were many reasons why victims were often reluctant to prosecute, including the cost, fear of intimidation by members of criminal gangs, 'tender-hearted' concern that the culprit might be sentenced to death, and the 'extremely great' difficulties of securing a conviction, caused by the rule that evidence from accomplices had to be corroborated and by defendants' successful use of alibis provided with perjured evidence.[77]

The growing use of defence counsel also made life difficult for plaintiffs. Permitted in felony trials from the 1730s as a consequence of both the increasing use of prosecution counsel and worries about the reliability of some prosecution evidence (particularly that provided by thief-takers), defence counsel were not used in a significant number of trials until the 1780s, when there were twice as many defence counsel as counsel for the prosecution. Whereas trial procedures favoured the prosecution early in the century, by the 1740s defence lawyers were beginning to turn the tables. In aggressive cross-examinations they questioned the motives of prosecutors and their witnesses (particularly when they stood to benefit from a reward for a conviction), exposed contradictions in their testimony, and highlighted ways in which their own misbehaviour contributed to the alleged crime.[78] When Lawrence Potts prosecuted John Smallwood for highway robbery in 1748, for example, Smallwood's counsel exposed differences between what Potts had told the magistrate at the preliminary examination and what he now told the court, noting that the magistrate had committed Smallwood only for assault, not robbery. More damningly, he questioned whether Potts had been drunk when the incident in which he lost his wig and hat occurred, forcing him through persistent questioning to admit that he was:

[Smallwood's] Counsel: Was you drunk or sober?
Potts: I was quite perfectly sober.
Q: You was just come from an alehouse, was not you?
Potts: Yes.
Q: You was a little reeling, I suppose?
Burton, the watchman: He was as sober as he is now.
Prisoner: I had been drinking at a publick-house, and was going home to bed; I was very much fuddled, and run against this man, and fell down ...

Needless to say, Smallwood was acquitted.[79] In 1787 Sir John Hawkins worried that fear of such cross-examinations deterred victims from prosecuting, since they were concerned that they 'may be entangled or made to contradict themselves, or each other, in a cross-examination, by prisoner's council'.[80] Potential plaintiffs may have also been put off by the fact that it seems likely that the presence of defence counsel led to an increase in rates of acquittal.

The growing presence of defence counsel, together with the decline in judicial activity revealed in the fall in the number of recognizances issued after 1792, may have contributed to the slight decline in the number of trials held at the Old Bailey in the 1790s, though one should not ignore the impact of war, which reduced unemployment and sent many potential criminals overseas. Over the course of the eighteenth century the number of trials increased only marginally, and did not come close to matching London's population growth. Once again, the courts failed to provide an attractive alternative to other forms of dispute resolution. Starting in the 1810s, however, the number of Old Bailey trials began to increase dramatically, stimulated not only by the end of the Napoleonic Wars but also by more generous provisions for the payment of prosecutors' expenses.[81] From the advent of the Metropolitan Police in 1829, however, the task of prosecution was increasingly taken over by the police, reducing the ability of private prosecutors to file indictments as a means of conducting personal disputes.[82]

The changing position of the law in English culture, particularly in the metropolis, meant that, when they became reluctant to fight their conflicts on the streets, Londoners did not choose instead to go to law. As the constitutional conflicts of the seventeenth century faded in memory, the celebration of the law as the guarantor of English liberties seemed less immediately pertinent, although radicals such as John Wilkes made dramatic new claims for these ideals.[83] At the same time, growing frustration at the cost, delays and complexities of the legal system, together with the seemingly unending tide of malicious prosecutions, served to alienate many people from the law. The courts seemed increasingly remote from the preoccupations of the urban middle classes, who found Parliament, voluntary societies and the press more effective institutions for getting what they wanted. Consequently, the significance of the law in English culture was reduced. In novels, for example, the law was increasingly experienced from a greater cultural distance: more as an outside force than as part of day-to-day life. Whereas the novels of Daniel Defoe and Henry Fielding include numerous episodes in which the main characters are caught up in the law and attempt to manipulate it to their own advantage, the works of William Godwin and Ann Ratcliffe portray the law as an oppressive system which terrified those caught up in it.[84]

This change was encouraged by the fact that participation by ordinary Londoners in the workings of the courts declined. By 1700 local, community-based courts, such as the manorial courts and wardmotes in the City of London, had already ceased to play a significant role in regulating urban life.[85] In the eighteenth century, as we have seen, the role of householders in policing diminished as they ceased to serve by rotation as constables and watchmen, and victims of crime increasingly relied on advertisements and thief-takers to find the culprits rather than seeking the assistance of passers-by, by calling out 'stop thief!'[86] As a form of evidence in the criminal courts, the judgement of the community lost its legal force. Whereas evidence of 'common fame' had previously been a sufficient basis for initiating formal accusations, the veracity of such evidence was called into question. Cautioning justices of the peace against binding people over by recognizance on this basis, Richard Burn warned in 1755 that 'it may be hard to prove such evil fame ... because in fact it is not always true, for many a good man hath been evil spoken of'.[87] Indicative of the changing role of community based accusations is the almost total disappearance of prosecutions at the Middlesex sessions for being a 'common disturber'.[88] In the courtroom, testimony by witnesses and defendants was increasingly controlled by lawyers or supplanted by expert professionals, especially surgeons.[89] As the role of ordinary people in day-to-day policing and prosecution was marginalised, it is not surprising that the law lost its central place in Londoner's thoughts when they considered how to respond to perceived wrongs.

Paradoxically, this cultural shift occurred at a time when the public visibility of the courts was dramatically increased in London by the creation of public magistrates' courts for the conduct of preliminary examinations of suspects and by the widespread publication of reports of trial proceedings. Starting in the City of London in 1738 and at Thomas DeVeil's house in Bow Street in 1740 (later taken over by Henry and

John Fielding), magistrates in the metropolis began to sit in specially designated rooms at fixed times to hear criminal complaints. In the 1760s these were supplemented by two additional 'rotation offices' and in 1792 by the creation of seven 'police offices' under the terms of the Middlesex Justices Act. Since hearings at these offices took place at advertised hours, they could easily attract spectators; indeed the hearings were intended for 'the *public* administration of justice'.[90] Accommodation for spectators was provided: a contemporary print shows John Fielding conducting an examination at Bow Street with a fashionably dressed audience sitting on both sides of the room and in a balcony (Figure 24). Sensational trials such as those of Daniel and Robert Perreau and Mrs Rudd in 1775 also drew huge audiences to the Old Bailey. But this was a very different form of public participation in justice: while the views of those present no doubt on occasion influenced the proceedings, the audience were for the most part only observers, who treated the events as a form of entertainment. In February 1780, following reports that some of the 'Lascars' who had been attacking women in the streets with sharp instruments were going to be examined, 'the public office, and the avenues leading to it, were remarkably crowded'.[91]

A second type of new publicity for the courts derived from the explosion of printed trial accounts in the eighteenth century. From the late 1670s pamphlet reports of the trials held at the Old Bailey, the *Old Bailey Proceedings*, were regularly published after every meeting of the court (eight times a year), and these were widely read by Londoners seeking news, entertainment and moral instruction. According to Béat-Louis de Muralt, the *Proceedings* were 'in the opinion of many people one of the most diverting things a man can read in London'.[92] Printed reports of trials conducted in other courts, notably adultery cases and actions for criminal conversation, were even more entertaining. The 'trickle' of publication of these in the 1690s had reached a 'flood' by the 1770s.[93] In addition to separate publications, the more notable trials held at the Old Bailey, quarter sessions, the church courts and the courts of common law, as well as reports of preliminary examinations held at magistrates' courts, were reported in the newspapers, as they began to devote increasing space to domestic news. In their homes, coffee houses and alehouses, Londoners could read about the latest sensational trial, and debate the rights and wrongs of judges' rulings and jury verdicts,

24. 'View of the Public Office Bow Street, with Sir John Fielding Presiding and a Prisoner under Examination' (1779). (*By permission of the British Library*)

but this was a very different way of participating in the legal system from their earlier active roles in policing and prosecution.[94]

While Londoners clearly enjoyed consuming these new forms of 'public justice', litigants, who did not necessarily wish to see their dirty linen aired in public, were not always so pleased. Lieutenant Samuel Stanton rejected the courts as an alternative to duelling since the law 'subjects the party to numberless malicious taunts, by rendering that public, which was before known only to a few'.[95] Even in criminal cases, where plaintiffs generally had less to fear from the publicity, since the spotlight tended to be more firmly focused on the alleged criminal, there was concern about the new publicity generated by public preliminary hearings. One of the reasons listed by Fielding why victims were reluctant to prosecute was that they were 'delicate, and cannot appear in a public court'. There may have also been concerns that the publicity damaged the prospect of a fair trial. In January 1781 the Westminster Forum debated the question, 'Whether the practice of examining persons accused of crimes publicly before magistrates, and afterwards publishing the examinations and evidence before trial, ought to be discontinued?'[96] While the publicity accorded to trials may have occasionally encouraged victims of other crimes to prosecute, in many more cases it could well have discouraged Londoners from going to law at all, encouraging them to choose, for example, to arrange a private separation rather than pursue an action of criminal conversation in order to obtain a divorce. The decline in civil suits initiated by the gentry may thus be partly due to the fact that some may have thought it dishonourable to have their private affairs discussed in public.[97] Similarly, the decline in matrimonial suits initiated by women may, as with the decline of defamation cases, reflect the growing reluctance of women to have their personal lives publicly scrutinised, at a time when they were subjected to more stringent expectations of chastity. The increasing publicity accorded to legal proceedings in the eighteenth century is one of many reasons why the courts did not replace the streets as the preferred venue for conducting disputes in London.

# 9

# *Print*

In August 1695 John Stubbs, a merchant, threw 'a great many' copies of a single sheet advertisement into a shop on Fleet Street (Figure 25), labelling Mainwearing Davis as a sodomite.

> At the Golden-Turk's-Head in Fleet Street ...
> Is a Suck-Prick Hoberde-Hoy, Pimp and Atheist,
> to be seen with a Barr gown on,
> Bugger'd Davis the Pimp and Sodomite.
> Also Blank warrants to the Assessors, printed there for
> Christopher Conningsby,
> Allice Conningsby, &
> Susan Conningsby.

Davis had previously had several altercations with Stubbs, in which Stubbs had allegedly 'very much abused' Davis, and had once assaulted and drawn his sword on him.[1] The distribution of this printed libel represented a new tactic in a long-running dispute. Using print to expose one's enemy to public derision was potentially an effective method of pressuring one's antagonists, and could possibly supplement or supplant more traditional techniques of waging conflict such as the public insult and the duel, or going to law. A pamphlet attack on duelling published in 1779 recommended that those who questioned another's honour should be dealt with instead by 'exposing them in the public prints, as incorrigible slanderers and bullies'.[2] When Charles Daubeny became involved in a dispute with Thomas Meade over accusations that Meade had forged Daubeny's sister's will, Daubeny reluctantly followed this advice, since 'family considerations' prevented him from fighting a duel, and he had lost a court case brought by Meade for defamation. Daubeny published a long pamphlet, including extensive transcripts of family correspondence, stating his side of the case and defending his reputation, and Meade responded in kind.[3]

The use of print to attack and defend reputations became possible on a significant scale for the first time in the eighteenth century, owing to the expiration of press licensing in 1695, a huge expansion of the press, and a big increase in popular literacy. As had already occurred in seventeenth-century London during periods when control of the press lapsed (during the Civil War and Interregnum, and between 1679 and 1682 during the Exclusion Crisis), in the eighteenth century the city was flooded with printed literature in numerous formats, from the more respectable books, pamphlets, newspapers and periodicals to more ephemeral broadsides, ballads, cartoons, and single-sheet libels like the one scattered by John Stubbs. By 1700 there were already sixty-two printers and 188 bookshops in the metropolis, as well as numerous book stalls. Less substantial items were also hawked and sung through the streets, posted on walls and doors, and flung just about everywhere. Clearly one did not need to spend money in order to be exposed to at least some forms of printed material.[4] Virtually all Londoners born after the Restoration could read or knew someone who could. Since reading was typically a sociable rather than a solitary experience, whether in coffeehouses, alehouses or at home, and hawkers frequently sung ballads on the streets, few Londoners were untouched by the written word.[5] The influence of print among women and the lower class was not simply confined to the consumption of texts but also extended to their production. At least two pamphlets produced during the weavers' protests in 1719 and 1720 outlined the grievances of the 'poor weavers' against calico.[6]

How effective was print as a means of conducting public disputes? Legal recognition of the growing power of the printed word to destroy reputations came with the emergence of written libel as a separate and more serious offence in the late seventeenth century, distinct from oral slander. Written libel was seen to be a greater wrong since it inherently involved premeditation and malice on the part of the author, it could inflict more widespread and lasting damage on reputations than an oral insult, and it was thus more likely to provoke a breach of the peace. It was argued in a King's Bench case in 1687 that whereas libels and writings 'are public ... words are private offences'.[7] This legal development

# Advertisements.

At the Golden-Turk's-Head *in* Fleet-ftreet, *a Stationers-Shop over-*
*againft St.* Dunftan's *Church,* *up one pair of Stairs* *forward,*

I S A

𝕾𝖚𝖈𝖐 = 𝕻𝖗𝖎𝖈𝖐 *Hoberde-Hoy*, 𝕻𝖎𝖒𝖕
and 𝕬𝖙𝖍𝖊𝖎𝖋𝖙, to be feen with
a *Barr Gown* on,

Bugger'd *Davis* the 𝕻𝖎𝖒𝖕
and 𝕾𝖔𝖉𝖔𝖒𝖎𝖙𝖊.

A L S O

Blank Warrants to the
*Affeffors,* printed there for

𝕮𝖍𝖗𝖎𝖋𝖙𝖔𝖕𝖍𝖊𝖗 𝕮𝖔𝖓𝖓𝖎𝖓𝖌𝖘𝖇𝖞,
𝕬𝖑𝖑𝖎𝖈𝖊 𝕮𝖔𝖓𝖓𝖎𝖓𝖌𝖘𝖇𝖞, &
𝕾𝖚𝖋𝖆𝖓 𝕮𝖔𝖓𝖓𝖎𝖓𝖌𝖘𝖇𝖞,

25. Libel against Mainwearing Davis (1695). (*Corporation of London Record Office*)

clearly reflected prevailing ideas. Already in 1656, Edward Reyner had written in his *Rules for the Government of the Tongue* that 'a man may do more good or more hurt by writing than by speaking, because what is spoken is transient, and passeth away, but what is written is permanent, and spreads itself further by far for time, place and persons, than the voice can reach'.[8] Although eighteenth-century charges by justices of the peace to grand juries very rarely mention slander, several instruct the juries to pay particular attention to libels. For one Middlesex justice, the key feature of printed defamation was that, in contrast to the arguments made before King's Bench in 1687, libels spread scandal *privately*, 'creeping from hand to hand, in a mean clandestine manner', making them harder to oppose than the publicly delivered oral insult.[9] Commenting on the power of written libel in 1770, Robert Morris wrote 'there are men who dread the lash of public writings, and who fear not any other censure, human or divine'.[10]

Contemporaries were most concerned about the use of libel for political purposes. The growing role of public opinion in politics meant that printed libel became an effective political tool, while the rise of party conflict early in the century provided ample incentives for such attacks. A Whig paper, the *Freeholder*, complained in 1716 about 'the personal slander and reflection which was slung out so freely by the libellers of the last reign', and blamed the Tories, who it alleged were bereft of any valid arguments: 'when they cannot refute an adversary, the shortest way is to libel him; and to endeavour at making his person odious, when they cannot represent his notions as absurd'. In 1728 Justice John Gonson observed that 'this offence is grown so common, that if a man goes into a coffee house, it is uncertain whether he lays his hands upon a newspaper or a libel'.[11] Such complaints continued in the second half of the century: in his sermon on 'the folly and guilt of satirical slander' in 1763, John Tottie noted that 'the unhappy political divisions in our country' led writers to 'enlist themselves on each side of the dispute as champions of the cause; and they exert all the learning and ingenuity they are masters of to the purposes of defamation'.[12]

While political libel attracted more attention, private slander (both handwritten and printed) was also widespread, with arguably more serious consequences, since many victims did not have sufficient resources to fight back.[13] Although graffiti was endemic in eighteenth-century London, the little evidence of it which survives suggests that it was rarely used for personal attacks.[14] But circulated copies of manuscript verses, ballads, newsletters, squibs and other libels through 'scribal publication' had long complemented oral methods of spreading personal slander.[15] With the lapsing of press licensing many of these acquired broader circulation through print; one no longer needed to go to a coffee house or alehouse, or find a ballad singer, in order to hear or read them. Ballads, handbills, pamphlets and newspapers were all used for libel.

Ballads were particularly effective because they combined oral and written methods of disseminating slander. Placing insulting words in verse linked to a tune allowed them to be sung through the streets by the numerous pauper ballad singers and sellers, and for the words to be easily remembered and repeated by others.[16] Thus, when the weavers sought to recruit support for their campaign against women wearing calico dresses, they published a broadside, *The Spittle-Fields Ballad: or The Weavers Complaint against the Callico Madams*, to be sung to the tune of 'For an Apple of Gold'. This justified the weavers' attacks on women wearing the fabric, branding them as whores:

> Now our trade is so bad
> That the weavers run mad,
> Thro' the want of both work and provisions,
>
> ...
>
> Then well may they tare
> What our ladies now wear,
> And as foes to their country upbraid'em,
> Till none shall be thought
> A more scandalous slut
> Than a taudry callico madam.[17]

The marketing of ballads like this was a commercial enterprise. Another ballad, *The Weaver's Delight, Tune of Pretty Sally* (1719), was printed by Thomas Norris, who claimed he did it 'only to make a profit'. Similarly, John Sharpe, who bought about a hundred of them, claimed he distributed them to make money. Although he had been a weaver, he said he had lately 'taken up the employment of singing love songs about the street for his livelihood'.[18] Ballads were sold from stands as well as by hawkers and continued to be a profitable and effective method of disseminating slander throughout the century (Figure 26). In 1781 it was reported:

> If a man has an enmity to a particular person or family, there is a house of call where a set of men are ready to write on any subject or business. If you have a mind to have a ballad on a treasonable subject, or one which injures the peace of society, you have but to apply at this house with seven and sixpence, and you may have it sung in the course of three hours from your time of payment in St Paul's Churchyard, or the corner of Fleet Market.[19]

After a failed courtship, Robert Wright, a butcher, procured a ballad in 1779, lampooning the chastity of his intended and her mother. Entitled 'A Copy of Verses Made on a Young Lady in W—E C—L M—T' (Whitechapel Market), it described the girl's promiscuous behaviour and its causes and consequences:

> But her father has lately found out their fun,
> By which I'm persuaded, his daughter's undone.
> Her mother cries, Hussey, how could you do so?
> And Betsy says, Mammy, you very well know,
>
> When you was in your youth you the like game did play ...

Sold for a halfpenny a piece, these ballads were 'industriously spread about in the market' and in a nearby alehouse, the Bull's Head. Wright reportedly said 'he would give any body five dozen of them for nothing that would sing them up and down the market'. As the girl's father reported, 'it has done me a great deal of prejudice among my customers'.[20]

Handbills, which were stuck up on walls and distributed by hand in the streets (or thrown into a shop like those by John Stubbs), could also spread accusations widely. A man who published a seditious libel during the Gordon Riots hired a boy 'to deliver them out to people that passed and repassed' through the streets; 'great quantities' of handbills were distributed this way. In 1808 William Pyne celebrated the contributions of the bill sticker to 'the general improvement of civilization'. Through his efforts, 'within six hours, by the means of printed bills, the inhabitants of a great city can be advertised of a thousand things necessary to be publicly known'.[21] Whether all bills were recognised as contributing to the public good or not is debatable. While frequently

26. Henry Walton, 'A Girl Buying a Ballad' (1778). (© *Tate, London, 2004*)

used for official purposes, and to advertise goods and services, handbills could also be used to spread slander. Richard Plumbland was accused in 1684 of 'making a scandalous libel against one Elizabeth Alsop widow, and fixing it on the post of her door, which hath caused much difference amongst her neighbourhood'. Isaac Broderick, who was tried, convicted and pilloried for what he claimed was a false charge of sexual assault on two boys, suffered further when his prosecutor published some 'papers ... to be cry'd about the streets' which alleged 'that, thro' a sense of guilt, I had murdered myself'. In 1772 handbills were distributed in Whitechapel falsely charging Thomas Powel, a pencil maker, and his accomplice with fraud, in order to 'deprive [Powel] of his just honest name and character'.[22] Libellous satirical prints were also published (Figure 27).

Some people even went so far as to write and publish entire pamphlets defending their reputations and attacking those of others. Although such works were primarily used to advance political causes, they were occasionally also used in other disputes. In 1712 a dispute involving both personal reputations and politics arose concerning the craftsmen working on St Paul's Cathedral. Following petitions to the Archbishop, Parliament and the Queen, and investigations by a master of Chancery (all of which clearly failed to resolve the conflict), the dispute entered the realm of print, not only with 'advertisements printed and posted up on the public entrances to that Cathedral' but also in a pamphlet war, starting with the publication of a forty-two page pamphlet, *Frauds and Abuses at St Paul's: In a Letter to Parliament.* This alleged that Richard Jennings, a carpenter, had failed to pay his workmen's wages; that the clock and bell made by a named clock-maker and bell-founder were faulty; and that the architect Sir Christopher Wren had obstructed attempts to correct these abuses. Jennings and his fellow artisans responded with four pamphlets containing a detailed defence of their work, and appended copies of indictments, accounts and an agreement. This generated further accusations (backed up by more reprinted documents) by the anonymous author of the original pamphlet. Jennings and his fellow workers submitted their published defences 'to all candid and unbiased persons'; Londoners who read these works were invited to draw their own conclusions about the guilt or innocence of the parties on each side of the dispute.[23]

Writers of pamphlets like these sometimes justified their publication by claiming the need to restore their reputations following private attacks by their adversaries. Dr Richard Russell, bitter at having been shunned 'as a person void of proper medicinal education' by a fellow physician in Henley, Dr Addington, because his degree was not from Oxford or Cambridge, published a letter to Addington in which he sought to do 'justice to my own character'. Russell was further annoyed when, rather than responding in public, Addington stooped 'to the low office of handing about, in a clandestine manner, a letter written against me, by one Mr Bigg', a surgeon. Russell then published another pamphlet which contained details of the whole affair, including copies of extensive private correspondence between the parties, despite the fact this was by his own admission 'a dispute relating solely to physicians'.[24] Similarly, William Woolley, angry at his former patron Richard Hill for his role in preventing him from obtaining a bishopric, was provoked into printing a libellous letter to Hill by the fact that he believed Hill had spread lies about him, wounding his character.[25]

It is difficult to imagine that such pamphlets, which were often lengthy and included tedious details concerning petty private disputes, attracted many readers. On the other hand, newspapers, which contained numerous letters, reports and advertisements which could damage or enhance reputations, reached a much wider audience. As a consequence of the expiration of press licensing, the modern newspaper was created in eighteenth-century London. Whereas Londoners in the late seventeenth century had only manuscript newsletters and the turgid official publication, the *London Gazette*, available, those in the next century were increasingly spoiled for choice. The first successful daily paper, the *Daily Courant*, began in 1702, and the number of newspapers published, and their circulation, increased dramatically during the century. From a dozen papers (daily, tri-weekly, and weekly) in 1712, the number of titles increased to eighteen by mid century and twenty-three in 1790. Increases in total national circulation (from 44,000 copies weekly in 1704 to 200,000 in 1773) were accompanied by greater social diffusion: it has been estimated that in the 1780s one-third of the capital's residents read a paper. In addition to being found in most coffeehouses and many alehouses, some papers, particularly those including large numbers of advertisements, were posted in public places.[26]

Dr. Hill.

not to know me
argues thy self
unknown.

27. John June, 'Lusus Naturae or Carracaturas of the Present Age' (1752). A
group of caricatured figures set in Whitehall, including Dr John Hill (on the
left, with a prostitute) and Sir Samuel Prime (on the right, looking directly at

at the viewer). Prime was mocked for marrying his cook, referred to in the news sheet held in front of him. (© *The British Museum*)

As César de Saussure commented, 'by reading these papers you know of all the gossip and of everything that has been said and done in this big town'. In a rapidly expanding metropolis, inhabitants had no more effective way of learning the latest news. According to the Reverend Robert Kirk, writing in 1690 before newspaper availability was commonplace, 'Few in [London] know the fourth part of its streets, far less can they get intelligence of the hundredth part of the special affairs and remarkable passages in it, unless by public printed papers, which come not to everyone's notice'.[27] But while Londoners depended on the papers for the news, paradoxically the papers relied on Londoners for their content. Lacking full-time reporters, newspapers depended to a much greater extent than today on their readers and part-time news-gatherers to supply them with the letters, reports and advertisements which filled their pages. Papers actively solicited letters from their readers, which presented Londoners with a golden opportunity to publicise their gripes (most were published anonymously).[28] Printers, however, were ambivalent about having their pages used to conduct private quarrels. In his *Weekly Journal*, Nathaniel Mist claimed to 'have been as careful as he could possibly be, not to hand forward the piques and quarrels of private persons, desiring not to be the tool or instrument of any man's malice'. Yet papers needed content, and criticisms of individual behaviour could be justified as being in the public interest. Responding to complaints that too many people were censured in newspapers, the *London Evening Post* argued in 1761 that 'admonitions well founded are of great use, and appear no where so properly as in newspapers; which passing through many hands, have the best chance of producing sometime or other, a good effect'. From the 1770s some newspapers, notably the Reverend Henry Bate's *Morning Post*, sought to increase their readership by devoting increasing space to aristocratic scandal.[29]

Letters published in the papers could be used both to attack and defend reputations. A letter published in Mist's *Weekly Journal* in 1718 (which prompted his defensive comments cited above) criticised 'two beautiful young ladies (sisters) who of late frequented a certain church in this city; and by their ill carriage there in time of Divine Service, have given great offence to most of the congregation'. The letter censured their 'fleering, gigling, antick carriage', accused them of ogling and winking at one another 'in the height of their devotion', and suggested that 'impure thoughts and desires must be at the fountain from whence flow such filthy streams'. Its author, 'T.L.', begged Mist to publish the letter, so that 'it may be of service to those for whom it is designed, to reprove them, and also to many other impudent negligent Christians', but these high-minded motivations were called into question by his postscript, which pointed out that the women 'are great Whigs; that indeed their carriage too plainly demonstrates'.[30] Although those attacked were rarely explicitly named, readers obviously speculated on the identity of the intended targets. In April 1752 a column in the *London Daily Advertiser* titled 'The Inspector' included a letter from 'Cloudy', giving a purported autobiography of a French rake which made fun of his lack of a title (though he went under the name of 'Lord Anglois'), his inability to cheat on his mistress without being caught, and his cowardice. Subsequently the author, Dr John Hill, was assaulted by a group of men headed by Mountfort Brown who claimed that Brown was the man defamed in the original article, and that Hill had identified him as such in a coffee house. The paper then printed a defence of Hill's original article, criticised Brown's assault, and called into question Brown's claim to be a gentleman. In response, Henry Fielding defended Brown's actions and gentlemanly status in his *Covent-Garden Journal.* The affair did not end there, however, as Hill was subsequently attacked in a number of satirical pamphlets and prints (Figure 28).[31] In some cases those attacked in the papers were directly named. In 1779 the *Morning Post* ran a series of articles on the 'characters of some leading men in the present rebellion' in America, one of which claimed that the Dulany family had hedged its bets, with part of the family supporting the crown and the other staying in Maryland, 'to take care of their property, and to be ready to close with the winning side'. When Lloyd Dulany complained, the *Post* published his denial, but distanced itself from the 'anonymous correspondent' who had written the piece.[32]

Often articles like these were 'puffs': reports which appeared to be news items but were in fact paid for like advertisements. This suggests just how easy it was to get libels into the papers. As the clerk to the *Morning Herald* testified during a libel action concerning an article which attacked the editor of a rival newspaper written by a Mr Finney (an occasional writer for the *Herald*), 'I received the article in question from Mr Finney. [It was] paid for as an advertisement by Finney'.[33] Those objecting to a vicious anonymous attack on the Earl and Countess of Mexborough (who were not named) published in the *Morning Post* in 1775, alleging the Countess had had an incestuous relationship with her sister's husband with the Earl's consent, were particularly outraged that the accuser hid behind a pseudonym ('Camlin'), and that 'the printer of the paper [was] *paid* for inserting it'.[34] Printers did not necessarily check the veracity of the reports they received; within the limits of the libel laws some allowed their papers to serve as a forum for competing accusations. In this dispute the printer of the *Morning Post*, claiming to maintain 'the strictest regard for impartiality', published numerous letters from both Camlin and his opponents.[35] Others adopted a more judgemental approach. In 1781 Henry Bate, at that point editor of the *Morning Herald*, printed several pieces accusing Robert Haswell of sodomy with J. Perry, the printer of a rival paper. When Perry complained, Bate said he

> did not then know that Mr Perry's character stood so clear that he, as a gentleman, could give him any answer, but that when his character should stand clearer in the estimation of the world, he would cooperate with him in setting that character in a clearer point of view by inserting anything that tended to his exculpation in the *Morning Herald*.[36]

The perceived power of the press to shame wrongdoers is evident in the fact that merely *threatening* to expose people in print was thought to be a useful tactic in disputes. In 1721 John Ellis, a justice of the peace annoyed by the overzealous activities of some reformation of manners informers, threatened to put them 'in all the news papers in towne'. In 1741 the *London Evening Post* reported that an exhibitionist had been repeatedly exposing his 'bare backside' to women in Lincoln's Inn. It reported with satisfaction that a servant had 'discharged a gun, well loaded with small shot, at his bare breech, and handsomely pepper'd him, upon which he walked pretty hastily off, but seemingly with some uneasiness, and it's supposed that he scarcely sat down to dinner that day'. After describing his clothing, the item concluded, 'if any one knows who this person is, it would be kind to publish his name, that the persons who have been so nastily annoy'd by him, as well as others, may now have the pleasure of laughing at him'.[37] Such threats could be used to force the offending behaviour to stop, and as a form of blackmail.

28. 'A Night Scene at Ranelagh' (1752). In the ampitheatre of Ranelagh Garden
Mountfort Brown is shown pulling off Dr John Hill's wig and challenging him
to a duel. (*Guildhall Library, Corporation of London*)

In 1796 Michael Robinson threatened to publish some manuscript verses accusing James Oldham of having murdered his master by poison twenty years earlier. Although Oldham had successfully brought an action for slander in the court of Common Pleas against those originally responsible for distributing the verses, Robinson issued this new threat in order, he claimed, to obtain funds to support the deceased's widow and children. Oldham took the threat seriously, but instead of handing over the money successfully prosecuted Robinson for extortion at the Old Bailey.[38]

'Puffs' could also be used to enhance reputations, as explained in a 1737 satirical pamphlet:

> All mankind, from the highest to the lowest, seem to be running into the new method of puffing their fine parts, performances, and notable achievements in newspapers, a practice altogether unknown to our ancestors. These are what the printers call, paid for paragraphs.[39]

Advertisements, whether labelled as such or not, often accounted for more than half the content of eighteenth-century newspapers, even those without the word 'advertiser' in the title, while papers such as the *Daily Advertiser* ('a paper calculated for advertisements of all kinds, being taken in by all the public houses in London') devoted over three-quarters of its space to them. Defending their prominence in his paper, Mist wrote in 1725, 'it is certain, that in a great and populous city like this, where the inhabitants of one end of the town are strangers to the trade and way of living of the other, many things which prove of singular use and benefit could never be known to the world by any other means but this of advertising'.[40] Still possessing an element of the word's original meaning of a public notice, advertisements were used for a much wider variety of purposes than today, including, as we have seen, notices seeking the return of stolen goods.[41] A claim by the publisher of *Fog's Weekly Journal* in 1736 suggests that they could attract widespread interest:

> I look upon them as pieces of *domestic* intelligence, much more interesting than those paragraphs which our daily historians generally give us, under the title of home news ... the advertisements are filled with matters of great importance, both to the great, vulgar and small.[42]

Advertisements were thus a useful method of responding to slander. In 1680 an advertisement denied that a 'Lady of Quality in London' had 'lately been brought to bed of an untimely squint-ey'd female child', contrary to what had 'been maliciously and most industriously reported'.[43] Perhaps because the space had so obviously been purchased, however, they were not used to make accusations. After one of its members had been 'swindled out of some plate and a diamond locket by the Baroness Minckwitz' in 1796, the Society for Prosecuting Felons, Forgers, Etc. considered placing an advertisement to 'caution the public against giving credit to the Baroness', but decided against it when the secretary expressed 'some doubts in the propriety of his signing such an advertisement'.[44]

Advertisements were frequently used to publish apologies for insults and a variety of other wrongs committed in London. Defendants in lawsuits often agreed to publish such apologies as part of negotiated settlements. The *Daily Advertiser* carried 1274 apology notices between 1745 and 1795. In 1745, for example, a notice from Abraham Burton, a porter, was published, apologising for insulting 'a lady in the publick streets for wearing a painted gown'. He asked pardon of all concerned, in the hope that 'out of compassion to my wife and numerous family now unprovided for, they will not prosecute me according to my deserts, promising to behave myself peaceably and quietly'. In an advertisement apologising for distributing the handbills against Thomas Powel discussed earlier, Raphael Solomons apologised for harming Powel's 'just honest name and character' and averred 'that the said bills and malicious aspersions are groundless, fictitious, and without any foundation'. Not only did these notices seek to restore the reputations of those who had been insulted, they also warned the public to avoid engaging in such illegal behaviour. William and Mary Franckly and John Hill placed an advertisement in the *Times* in 1786 apologising for assaulting and raising a mob of at least sixty people about a sheriff's officer who had arrested William. Thus 'publicly acknowledging our rashness in opposing the officers of justice in the execution of the King's writ' and having paid the legal costs, the case against them was dropped.[45]

Usually resulting from agreements reached after a legal prosecution had commenced, such printed apologies supplemented, and to some extent supplanted, formal legal action. What was the relationship between print and other methods of conducting disputes in eighteenth-century

London? Did the printed word provide a more effective method of waging conflicts than actions which took place on the streets or in the courtroom? Was it more accessible to women than street violence, which was dominated by men? In some respects, the wider and more lasting impact of print did undermine the impact of oral insults, public punishments, duels, riots and even court decisions. Yet in a number of respects print did not (and could not) replace these other activities. It was people guilty of slander, for example, who featured most prominently in the apologies published in newspaper advertisements, which used print to restore the reputations of Londoners originally defamed orally. Yet analysis of the sexual and social composition of both those who placed these advertisements and the recipients of the apologies shows that this tactic was used predominantly by middle-class men and for only a limited range of insults, primarily those which either undermined the recipient's financial and business reputation or called into question the competence of law enforcement officials. Gentlemen and the poor (with the exception of servants apologising to their employers) were rarely involved. The most common form of oral public insult, made between women over issues of chastity, figured relatively infrequently, suggesting that print was not seen as an effective method of countering this type of insult.[46]

Print potentially played a more significant role in shaping the conduct and effectiveness of public punishments, often undermining the damage intended to be inflicted on the convict's reputation. Some printed flyers were used to summon spectators to the pillory and encourage them to pelt the victim mercilessly. One broadside (Figure 29), apparently distributed just before a man convicted of sodomy was killed in the pillory, included a cartoon depicting a man standing there with mostly female spectators preparing to pelt and flog him, and a ballad condemning 'a race so detested, of honour divested'. It invited 'the daughters of Britain ... to well flog'em with birch'.[47] But those punished used this tactic more frequently, both by distributing handbills in advance in order to attract a friendly audience, and by handing them out at the pillory in order to persuade the spectators of their innocence. When John Sweetman and Thomas Howard stood in 1771 for compounding a penal statute, the General Evening Post reported that 'at first, the populace, who were very numerous, began to pelt them, but handbills being

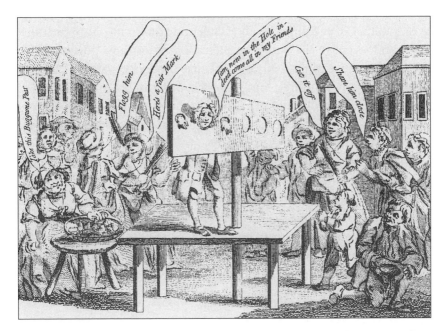

29. 'This is Not the Thing: or Molly Exalted' (1762). (*London Metropolitan Archives*)

dispersed, signifying that they were drawn into the affair by another person, who made off with the best part of the cash, the pelting ceased, and they stood quietly the rest of the time'.[48] Publications could also be published afterwards, to counteract the long-term damage to reputations sustained by those who had been pilloried. Following his severe treatment on the pillory in 1731, Isaac Broderick published a pamphlet, *An Appeal to the Public*, seeking to restore his reputation. Claiming the prosecution had been malicious, he went on to argue that during his stint on the pillory his 'enemies' had behaved unfairly, having 'hired a great number of the populace to assault and wound me, insomuch that I was almost cut to the skull'. An indication of just how powerful such a printed defence might be is the fact that Broderick claimed his antagonists had sent him threatening letters in order to try and prevent him from publishing his side of the story. Although Broderick had suffered greatly on the pillory, he clearly thought that he could restore his reputation through the use of print.[49]

Even in the case of hanging, where print could not prevent or alter the fact of execution, an extensive gallows literature both justified some punishments and implicitly undermined the impact of others by celebrating the convict's crimes or treating the death lightly. The exploits of Jack Hall, executed for theft at Tyburn in 1707, were celebrated for decades after in a ballad which included the following lines which describe his crimes and execution light-heartedly:

> I furnish'd all my rooms, with mops, brushes, and hair brooms,
>    Wash balls and sweet perfumes, them I stole, them I stole.
>    . . .
> I sail'd up Holborn Hill, at St Giles's drunk my fill,
>    And at Tyburn made my will, in a cart, in a cart.[50]

Print had the power both to accentuate and to undermine the intended public impact of official punishments, both during the event and long afterwards.

Print had a similar complex relationship to male violence, serving at different times to stimulate it and to counteract its long-term significance. In some cases, as with the assault on Hill by Brown in 1752, allegations in print led to violent retribution from those insulted. Following the publication of the letter criticising the behaviour of two women at church in his paper, Nathaniel Mist was confronted in a tavern by 'two men armed with swords, canes, and pistols' who forced him to draw up 'a scandalous writing of submission and acknowledgement'. Reporting that an Irish printer had 'acquitted himself in single combat, as a gladiator, at Figg's Ampitheatre with great honour' in 1729, *Fog's Weekly Journal* commented that he was 'a wise man, for as the world goes, it seems necessary for all printers to practice the noble science of defence'.[51] In many cases, the status and sense of honour of the person insulted meant that newspaper articles led to formal challenges and duels. John Wilkes fought a duel with Lord Talbot in 1762 following an article in the *North Briton* which questioned Talbot's management of the royal household. The article in the *Morning Post* in 1779 questioning the loyalty of the Dulany family caused Lloyd Dulany to write a letter published in the same paper demanding that the author should either identify himself or acknowledge himself to be 'a detestable liar and cowardly assassin'; effectively, this was a challenge to a duel. Three years later, Bennet Allen wrote to Dulany, acknowledging authorship and seeking 'to punish your insolence'; later that evening they fought a duel in Hyde Park.[52] The threat of exposure in print could also be used to pressure men into fighting duels, or to penalise them for failing to do so. When eighty-two-year-old Philip Thicknesse refused to fight a duel with John Crookshanks in 1790, Crookshanks took revenge by having posters accusing him of being the much despised London 'Monster' printed and pasted up on walls throughout the city.[53]

If what was said in print could give rise to duels, printed accounts published after duels took place could exacerbate conflicts and publicise them more widely. Having required the protagonists to demonstrate their courage on the field of battle, duels were supposed to bring closure to disputes, but in practice duellists (or their seconds) often carried on disputes by publishing accounts of how their antagonists had behaved before and during the duel. Some seconds jointly submitted accounts of duels to the papers to ensure that the public was informed of the honourable conduct of both principals, but not all accounts were bipartisan. Following the 1711 duel in which Sir Cholmley Deering was killed by Richard Thornhill, four pamphlets were published, including an anonymous defence of Thornhill's actions (claiming that Deering had threatened to shoot him in the head if he refused to fight) and a broadsheet apology written by Thornhill while he was in prison. Another pamphlet blamed the duel on Thornhill. It was this last view which in a sense prevailed, for despite the printed defences of Thornhill's reputation he was subsequently murdered by Deering's friends.[54]

Similarly, a spate of newspaper articles and broadsides published following the duel between the Duke of Hamilton and Lord Mohun in 1712 (which led to the deaths of both principals) charged that the duel was the result of a Whig plot to murder Hamilton, and that Mohun's second, Lieutenant-General Maccartney, actually killed him. In response, Daniel Defoe attempted to restore 'the injur'd memory of a noble person dead' (Mohun) by refuting these allegations in a pamphlet: 'let the unbiased part of the world judge', he wrote, 'whether there is the least appearance here of any foul play'.[55] Following his duel with Talbot in 1762, Wilkes published his account of the affair, thereby further promoting the reforming agenda which had led him to make the original charge in the *North Briton* which prompted the duel. Talbot was so angry he attempted to fight another duel, but this was prevented.[56] A similar cycle of duelling and attacks in print occurred in 1789. Following a duel between Colonel Charles Lennox and the Duke of York, Theophilus Swift published a pamphlet which criticised Lennox for challenging a member of the royal family and claimed that the duel was part of a conspiracy to murder the Duke. Lennox then challenged Swift, who was injured in the ensuing duel. While recuperating, Swift responded with an attack on Lennox in another pamphlet, and he spread a rumour (reported in the *Morning Herald* and the *Times*) that had the duel been fought with swords (rather than pistols) he would have been victorious. It was even reported that he would fight Lennox again after he recovered from his wounds.[57]

The use of print ensured that, by themselves, duels did not necessarily settle disputes while preserving the honour of both parties. By exposing the participants' conduct to public scrutiny, authors appealed to the court of public opinion for a decision over which party was in the right. Following an argument at Vauxhall Gardens in 1773 in which Henry Bate chided some soldiers who were 'ogling' a woman, a boxing match took place in Richmond Park (it was claimed that, since he was a man of the cloth, Bate could not fight with swords or pistols). Bate's opponent, however, turned out to be a servant, not a gentleman as Bate felt he had a right to expect. What followed was an extraordinary series of letters to the newspapers in which each side gave its version of the events and consciously submitted it to 'the tribune of the public'. Other correspondents joined in what came to be known as the 'Vauxhall Affray', and the whole collection of letters was reprinted in a single volume, which was so popular it went into a second edition. Rather the ending the dispute, the boxing match served merely as the starting point for an extensive exchange of printed insults, and it is debatable whether the reputations of any of the parties gained from the affair.[58] Similarly, a long-running dispute between Colonel Thomas McCarthy and Lieutenant Patrick Leeson in 1790, which started in a playhouse when McCarthy commented that he had seen Leeson acting as a servant, involved a duel, a brawl, three court cases and several letters to the *Times*. The duel, which was not fought according to accepted rules, only exacerbated tensions. In the end, the participants seem to have decided that the courts and the press offered the best means of winning the dispute. In his 'final' letter to the *Times*, McCarthy could not resist further insults (he called Leeson 'in implication at least an assassin') before 'confidently rest[ing] my cause on the public judgement [particularly] as the principal facts will receive a speedy elucidation in a *Court of Justice*'.[59] The complicated relationship between duelling and print in the second half of the century, and the overarching importance of the latter, is evident in the duel fought between Charles James Fox and William Adam in 1779. Adam demanded an explanation following a speech Fox made in the House of Commons which ridiculed him. Although Fox assured him 'he meant no personal invective', Adam felt forced to pursue the issue after 'he had read a very injurious detail of the affair in the newspapers'. Since the insult was now in print, Adam insisted that Fox's explanation of the affair also be printed. Fox refused, and the duel, in which Fox was slightly wounded, took place in Hyde Park. Needless to say, the exchange of letters which preceded the duel, as well as accounts of the duel itself, was covered in several papers.[60]

Even the world of popular protest was infiltrated, and increasingly shaped, by print during the eighteenth century. Printed handbills were frequently used to recruit support and stimulate action, for example during the weavers' attacks on women wearing calico dresses, when a printed 'sham proclamation' supplemented the ballad discussed earlier.

In May 1720 Jane Elward (who could not sign her name) was arrested for crying and selling this proclamation through the streets of Spitalfields. Formatted to look like an official proclamation, it outlined the weavers' grievances against 'Madam Callico', and 'command[ed] all hang-men, bailiffs, yeomen, and all other officers to secure her, and bring her to Spitalfields, where she shall undergo the punishment our law in such cases provides'. Over the previous eleven months, that 'punishment' had consisted of vandalising the women's dresses with knives, ink and nitric acid, and these practices continued into the summer.[61] In 1736 a virulent broadside entitled *Spitalfields and Shoreditch in an Uproar* stirred up hostility against Irish workers, and may have been included in the 'large parcels of printed papers ... found scattered on Tower Hill' during the riots, in which some of the houses in which the Irish lodged were pulled down.[62] In 1773 handbills were distributed to weavers, coalheavers, watermen, porters and carmen encouraging them to assemble in Moorfields in order to march to Westminster and inform the King and Prime Minister of their distress owing to the high price of provisions and the poor state of trade. According to Justice Wilmot, these were effective: after a handbill addressed 'To the Weavers in General' was distributed in Spitalfields on the night of 25 April, 200 to 300 gathered the next morning.[63] Handbills were also used to encourage protesters to assemble before and during the Gordon Riots in 1780, in protests against the New Militia Bill in 1794 and during protests over the high price of food in 1800. Following the distribution of one of the 1794 bills, 'several thousand persons, many of them having no concern in the business ... assembled in Guildhall'.[64]

The importance attached to protest posters is evident in the fact that attempts to remove them sometimes triggered riots, as was the case with a coalheavers' riot and the riot by supporters of Wilkes at King's Bench Prison, both in 1768. In the former, the coalheavers had pasted some bills, attacking an 'undertaker' who was undermining their campaign for higher wages, on walls near the house of one of his agents, John Green. After one of his servants removed one, within fifteen minutes up to a hundred coalheavers gathered around Green's door. According to Green, they 'cried, by Jesus they would have my life if I offered to meddle with any of their bills ... one of them cried, by Jesus he shall have a bill put up at his own window; he took up a handful of dirt, and put it upon the window, and put the bill upon it'. That evening, Green's house came under sustained attack from several hundred rioters wielding bludgeons and broomsticks.[65]

Since riots often supplemented more formal political action in this period, it is not surprising that newspapers and printed pamphlets, often used in politics, also accompanied and sought to legitimise popular protests. During the weavers' campaign against calico numerous pamphlets were published, as well as a special newspaper, the *Manufacturer*, sponsored by the Weavers' Company and written by Daniel Defoe. Apologising for the 'warmth' of the weavers' attacks, Defoe sought to use 'the violence of persuasion' instead. Yet at a time when extra-parliamentary lobbying on the part of labourers was still unacceptable ('some tell us, printing is a kind of mobbing; and so they say, the weavers are but playing the street game over again'), he had to defend even the use of print.[66] There was, indeed, widespread concern that print had the power to mislead the mob and stimulate disorder. During the campaign against the Excise Bill in 1733, which included large disorderly demonstrations outside Parliament, it was alleged that 'ebullitions of popular resentment' by two newspapers, the *Craftsman* and *Fog's Weekly Journal*, had 'ballad-sung the mob out of their senses'.[67] Yet if the mob was on the same side, there was little reluctance on the part of elites to use print to recruit popular support. Riotous attacks on 'crimp' houses in 1794, taverns where men were forcibly held before being inducted into the armed forces, were allegedly stimulated by numerous 'false and iniquitous inflammatory handbills and pamphlets [intended] to prejudice the minds of the public against' the new Militia Bill. On 18 and 19 August, for example, 'handbills were distributed, telling the people that men and children were kidnapped and sent off to Canada and elsewhere', and on the 22nd 'a most inflammatory hand-bill was … dropped about the different courts and alleys in the metropolis, which … was drawn up in such a stile, as could only be intended to work up the lower class of people to immediate rebellion against the existing government'.[68]

Of course, printed handbills and pamphlets were also used to try to discourage rioting. During the calico riots in 1719 the master weavers published a short paper addressed to their journeymen, which begged them 'to consider coolly the consequences of such outrages as have lately been committed' and reminding them that Parliament provided 'proper methods for redress of grievances'.[69] Following the defeat of the bill to prevent the importing of calico in the Lords in May 1720, the Weavers' Company resolved 'that something might be prepared to be printed and dispersed speedily throughout the trade in order to prevent any disorders and to keep quietness among the journeymen of the trade'. This, however, failed to prevent further riots.[70] Similarly, a 'printed request' in 1794 from the Lord Mayor to householders, asking them to keep children and servants off the streets and reminding them of a proclamation against riots and the provisions of the Riot Act, did not prevent further anti-militia riots.[71] On the other hand, papers distributed following the attacks on houses inhabited by Irish labourers at the end of July 1736 may have contributed to the end of that rioting. The 'beadles of several parishes delivered a printed paper to most of the house keepers of Spittle-fields, White-Chapel, and thereabouts, intituled *A Kind Caution to Rioters* ... the same was affix'd up at Aldgate, Bishopsgate, and several other publick places in that part of town'. This paper warned potential rioters that those found guilty of violating the Riot Act could be sentenced to death. Whether by coincidence or consequence, the riots ended almost immediately.[72] That print could have a significant influence over rioters is suggested by Justice Thomas DeVeil's successful use of a newspaper to divert popular hostility aroused by the deaths of four female prisoners at St Martin's Round House away from him in 1742. By getting a copy of the warrant under which the women had been committed published in the *London Evening Post*, the responsibility for the fiasco was placed on the constables and the keeper of the Round House instead. The advertisement did not prevent a riot, but it diverted the mob's anger towards different targets.[73]

In other cases later in the century printed notices may have successfully prevented disturbances. In the week following the Gordon Riots, fears that celebrations of the victory by General Clinton in America might be disorderly (as such celebrations often were) led to cards being circulated recommending 'to all persons to forbear such demonstrations upon this occasion, as they might, at the moment tend to affect the public peace'; the same notice appeared in a newspaper. This seems to have worked, and the town appears to have remained quiet. Similar fears in 1794 led to the distribution of handbills and publication of an advertisement requesting inhabitants to refrain from illuminating their houses.[74] Printed notices could not prevent many disturbances, but after a riot they could be used to shape its long-term impact. As we have seen with William Franckly, some rioters were forced to issue printed public apologies for their actions. Following a riot on Cheapside on the evening of John Wilkes's birthday in 1769, Jacob James was forced to place an advertisement saying, 'I do hereby in this public manner most humbly confess my crime and ask pardon of my prosecutor and the public'.[75]

Ultimately, print had a wider and more long-lasting influence than most other methods of public conflict and dispute resolution. Even legal decisions were shaped by, and subsequently discussed in, newspapers and pamphlets. The guilt or innocence of the Perreaus and Mrs Rudd (charged with forgery in 1775) was extensively discussed in print before their trials took place; supporters of both sides clearly sought to use the press to influence the juries' decisions.[76] Verdicts could be evaluated and criticised by the readers of the numerous published accounts of civil and criminal trials, such as the *Old Bailey Proceedings* and accounts of trials at the church courts. Those convicted sometimes went further and published pamphlets maintaining their innocence. In October 1725 Foster Snow was found guilty of murdering Thomas Rawlins with a knife. Shortly afterwards, an article entitled 'The Case of Foster Snow', published in the *Postman*, gave rise to an official complaint, as it represented 'his case very different from what it appeared to be, upon the evidence given at his tryal; thereby to extenuate his own guilt, and reflect upon the justice of the nation'. Similarly, in his *Appeal to the Public*, Isaac Broderick claimed that his prosecution had been malicious. He further argued that the account of his trial in the *Old Bailey Proceedings* had omitted his side of the case, which he then provided.[77] Some participants in actions for criminal conversation and slander, such as Charles Daubeny and Thomas Meade, also published pamphlets supporting their positions.[78] Following the controversial 1770 trial at King's Bench of John Almon for libel (for selling a magazine containing seditious letters by 'Junius'), three publications criticised how the trial was conducted. A published account of the trial questioned the motives behind the prosecution and the rulings of Lord Mansfield in court, and the latter were further attacked in a second pamphlet. In the third, Robert Morris, who had testified in support of Almon, complained that a judge, Sir Robert Aston, had 'cast a very injurious reflection on my character in court' (by accusing him of perjury). In stating his side of the case, and then leaving its resolution 'to the determination of the public', Morris felt confident that his pamphlet would damage the reputation of the judge, not himself. He wrote, 'I am now appealing to a tribunal where we are both equal, a tribunal to the full as awful and just' as King's Bench.[79]

Some authors appear to have believed that appealing to the court of public opinion was at least as powerful a tactic as a formal prosecution. William Woolley also used legal metaphors in his published attack on Richard Hill: 'I shall drag you forth into the open face of day ... You cannot make any appeal from the tribunal, before which I mean to bring you: it is the tribunal of the English nation ... I boldly call you to the bar; and ... I shall leave your country to sit in judgement on you'. (Hill, however, had the last word when Woolley was convicted of libel.) For those who, due to the nature of their grievances, could not obtain legal redress, print was seen as the only available option. Richard Russell claimed that his only remedy against Thomas Bigg was 'to accuse the aggressor, and to bring him before the bar of the public, as the most proper judge' by publishing his letter to Bigg.[80]

Printed literature outlining grievances and defending and attacking reputations, whether in the form of ballads, handbills, newspaper reports or full-scale pamphlets, clearly had the potential to replace or neutralise other methods of public conflict, since the impact of printed materials was wider and longer-lasting than anything which took place on the streets or in a courtroom. Nonetheless, the use of such literature for these purposes was limited. Leaving aside political libels, the number of letters and reports in newspapers affecting the reputations of named individuals was actually relatively low, as was the number of surviving pamphlets and handbills which served the same function. Moreover, some publications had a very limited circulation. A pamphlet published in response to the libellous attacks in the *Morning Post* on the Earl and Countess of Mexborough allegedly had to be forced on readers by the Countess, who 'sent a servant ... to every person's house, whom she thought of any consequence; whilst the compiler attended at the Haymarket masquerade, and then distributed the pamphlet, as he formerly had done his handbills'.[81] The small number of disputes which produced long-running exchanges of letters in the newspapers, such as this one and the exchanges between Patrick Leeson and Thomas McCarthy, took on a life of their own, and popular interest must have focused on the new insults levelled by the participants in each issue while the original dispute was forgotten. Even newspaper apologies averaged only twenty per year in the *Daily Advertiser* between 1745 and 1795 (considerably below the number of court cases and street altercations), and from the 1770s the number published declined significantly.[82]

This is not to say that newspapers and other publications were un-interested in gossip, slander and wrongdoing – it is just that they were reluctant to name names. The newspaper and periodical press which developed in the late seventeenth century treated morality as one of its central concerns, but the new publications sought to censure actions, not individuals. Several papers with variations on the title *Poor Robin's Intelligence*, published in the late 1670s and early 1690s, for example, satirised the follies of the lustful but failed to name delinquents. A typical example, from 1691, describes a 'youngster' who lived near Temple Bar, 'being out late ... finds in the street a female, but arriving at one of the city watches, the constable was so kind, as to provide them both a hard bed in the counter' (a lock-up). The next day, while they drank a glass of wine together, she picked all the money out of his pocket.[83] John Dunton's *Nightwalker* (1696–97), a monthly magazine devoted to expos-ing vice (while also titillating readers with accounts of the author's 'evening rambles in search of lewd women') and Ned Ward's *London Spy* (1698–1700) adopted the same strategy: in Dunton's words, 'our design is to reform, not expose'.[84]

Eighteenth-century newspapers also avoided naming those they ac-cused of bad behaviour, particularly when the accused was not a public figure, using instead vague references such as 'a certain nobleman', 'a tradesman', or giving only initials. In 1721 the *Weekly Journal: or British Gazetteer* carried a report of an incident involving wife beating and possible murder without giving much information about the identities of the culprits: 'Last Tuesday about noon, two men who were brothers in law quarrelled in Leicester Fields, one by an accidental blow on the ear immediately dropt down dead; the quarrel was occasioned by the deceased beating his wife, sister to the other'. In 1741 the marriage of a very old man to a young woman, a type of behaviour that sometimes was punished by the rough music of crowds, was instead lampooned in the papers, but without identifying the names of the culprits. According to the *Daily Post*,

> Mr S——, a surgeon in Deadman's Place, Southwark, in the seventy-eighth year of his age, phrensical with love, was married at St Mary Overy's Church to his servant, a brisk young woman in her bloom. It were almost to be wish'd that a commission of lunacy might, in like cases, be granted to the next heirs, and take effect.[85]

In 1771 the *General Evening Post*, reporting a delicious piece of gossip, also refrained from giving any names:

> On Monday evening a person, who has been employed as a man cook in a family of reputation near eight years, was on the point of being delivered of a child in the necessary of a house near Long Acre. The woman has, it seems, worn breeches ever since she was eight years of age, and is so good a servant, and so great a favourite with the family, that they have ordered her to be properly taken care of, and mean to continue her in their service.[86]

Duelling, an illegal activity, was also typically reported with only the initials of the participants. In April 1781 the same paper reported that 'the duel which happened on Sunday last, in Hyde Park, was between Mr W——n, a member of the Irish Parliament, and Mr B——k, of the same kingdom. It arose from a conversation relative to Lord H——'s political conduct on the affairs of Ireland'.[87] Even some of the people who advertised apologies in newspapers were allowed to remain semi-anonymous, using only their initials. One 'R.M.' thanked his antagonist for allowing him to apologise 'without exposing my name'.[88] Politicians and other public figures were also sometimes referred to using code names or initials, but, despite the dangers of prosecution for seditious libel, they were more often named. Towards the end of the century newspapers, periodicals such as the *Town and Country Magazine* and the *Bon Ton Magazine*, and radical pamphlets began to report the delinquencies of the aristocracy in greater detail, but this often had a political purpose, to promote Jacobin reforms.[89]

For those who knew the participants even vaguely, these semi-anonymous reports may have conveyed some useful personal information, but these readers probably already knew about the scandal. All most readers will have learned is that such incidents of wrongdoing took place. Lurking behind this general unwillingness to name names, of course, were the libel laws. Those defamed could bring an action for libel in the common law courts, though in civil actions the truth of the accusation was a valid defence. In 1728 the printer of the *Daily Journal* was prosecuted for reporting that John Hopkins had been apprehended for stealing 'great numbers of tiles and stones', and we have seen that the editor Henry Bate was tried for accusing Robert Haswell of sodomy in 1782; Bate was convicted and fined £100 and sentenced to three months imprisonment. Significantly, a conviction was obtained despite the fact Bate's paper used euphemisms such as 'tender advances' to refer to attempted sodomy and it did not name Haswell (who was referred to as the 'amorous printer'). It was successfully argued in court that the real meanings of these terms were clear.[90] Such libel actions were, however, relatively rare, and it was charges of seditious libel (a criminal offence, where truth was not a defence) arising from political reports which publishers feared more. Those accused faced arrest, the seizure of their papers and substantial legal costs, while those convicted could be fined, imprisoned and have their presses destroyed.[91]

It was actually newspapers' own sense of their mission, and the broad unfocused audience reached by this form of print, which played a more important role in limiting their use for pursuing private disputes. Many papers argued that their public function precluded reporting material relating to private feuds. Although the *London Evening Post* acknowledged in 1761 that 'admonitions well founded are of great use', it added an important qualification: what was reported in the paper 'never had any other object than that of publick utility'. In 1779 an announcement of the impending publication of a new paper, the *London Courant*, stated its intention to

> prevent the insertion of any articles of falsehood, malignancy, and private scandal. In the conduct of this publication, it shall be a fixed principle to meddle with no private character, of either sex. But public characters in public stations will be treated with freedom yet always with liberality.[92]

Similarly, an early correspondent to the *Daily Universal Register* (later to become the *Times*) argued that the purpose of newspapers was 'the conveyance of important intelligence, which concerns the public in general'. This prompted the editor to ask, rhetorically, 'what have we to do with the ridiculous disputes of whimsical ladies, or the infamous assurance of bullies and swindlers, at public places and gaming houses?' This letter was an attack on fashionable 'west-end sheets', including the *World* and the *Morning Post*, which it accused of engaging in just such reporting, but many papers conformed to this correspondent's advice. When an anonymous author tried to get a letter libelling the coroner of the City printed in 1767 he was unsuccessful. As the author acknowledged in a letter to the *Public Advertiser*: 'as anonymous correspondents are dangerous to rely on, I cannot help thinking but that your caution is deserving of applause ... I was in some hopes to have seen it in print, and therefore circulated it to all the papers, from whence I have met with a general objection'. On 30 March 1771 the *General Evening Post* included an announcement that 'the letter signed x z is far too virulent and personal to find room in this paper, as our aim is to reform the times and to attack manners not men'.[93]

Moreover, from the point of view of many disputants, newspapers and other forms of print reached too wide and unfocused an audience to influence the right people. Poor women concerned about the sexual delinquencies of their neighbours, for example, had no need to spread their accusations beyond the courts and alleys in which those who knew the offenders lived and worked. (In any case, women were increasingly reluctant to discuss this type of issue in public.) For those who had been defamed, publishing a printed defence could do more to spread awareness of the insult than to restore one's reputation amongst those who had already heard it. As William Woolley wrote in his pamphlet attack on Richard Hill, 'however forcible and convincing his defence may be ... he foresees the danger of spreading a blaze around it which may attract the public eye'. Similarly, 'Camlin' alleged that the pamphlet published in response to his attacks on the Earl and Countess of Mexborough 'exposed *them* more'. Some authors of defamatory material sought, perhaps unrealistically, to limit their audience. In the exchange of pamphlets between Meade and Daubeny (following a slander trial) referred to previously, Daubeny addressed his 140 page pamphlet, which sought to restore his character, to his 'friends ... not to the world'. But the logic of print was such that it was impossible to limit its audience, and Meade's reply was 'written for the public eye'.[94]

But was the public interested? Because the reputations of those who were not public figures in late eighteenth-century London were increasingly established among more narrowly defined reference groups than those reached by print, the publication of libels could be counterproductive, generating hostility towards the author without necessarily reaching the intended audience. Print was a public medium, while personal reputations were increasingly established in more private circumstances. This is why it was not only advertised apologies which declined so dramatically at the end of the century, but also another item often found in the newspapers: personal (but often anonymous) appeals for charity.[95] It may also help explain the dramatic decline in ballad singers found on London's streets between the 1770s and the 1810s, reflecting both more active policing and declining public interest in their wares.[96] By the turn of the century the realm of print was deemed too public to allow discussions of personal needs and individual reputations to be effective, unless those involved were public figures. As with litigation, print ultimately did not offer a satisfactory alternative to conducting disputes on the streets. While handbills, newspaper reports and pamphlets could encourage, supplement or undermine other forms of public conflict, including litigation, printed literature was largely unsuitable on its own for the task of shaping and defending reputations in a modern city.

30. 'Renwick Williams, Commonly Called the Monster' (1790). (*Guildhall Library, Corporation of London*)

# *The Monster*

On 12 May 1790 a German visitor, Georg Forster, noted in his diary that London was in an uproar about a 'Monster' who was terrorising the streets, insulting women and stabbing them with sharp instruments, usually in their buttocks (Figure 30). This man 'disguises himself, goes about in various different guises, wounding beautiful women with specially invented instruments, with hooks hidden in bouquets of flowers, with knitting pins, etc.' Londoners, he reported, were talking about little else:

> The newspapers are full of him; the playwrights entertain audiences with his exploits from the stage; the ladies are afraid of him; the mob gives every pedestrian a keen look in case he is the Monster; all the walls are covered with posters advertising a reward for the apprehension of the Monster; a fund has been opened to finance the hunt ... [1]

Between May 1788 and June 1790 there were reports of over fifty women who had been attacked and wounded in public by men wielding sharp instruments.[2] Although the details vary (which strongly suggests that there was in fact more than one 'Monster'), the assaults shared several characteristics: they were generally unprovoked and carried out by men who did not know their victim, the culprit used insulting and threatening language, and he used a sharp object to cut through the victim's clothes and into her flesh, typically in the thigh or bottom, but sometimes on the face. He then lingered, clearly enjoying watching his victim suffer. The instruments, which were often disguised and sometimes designed to cause particularly horrific injuries, included knives hidden in canes or attached to legs (for use when kicking), sharp pins disguised inside bouquets (which the victim was urged to smell), and claws with several sharp prongs. Some women were also kicked or punched on the breast or head.

It was not until April 1790 that organised efforts to apprehend the culprit began. Newspapers, the Bow Street Runners, neighbourhood associations and a private philanthropist joined the pursuit. After several false arrests, in June a suspect, Rhynwick Williams, a twenty-three-year-old artificial flower maker, was identified by several victims and arrested. He was tried at the Old Bailey in July and convicted of attacking Anne Porter, but the conviction was overthrown for legal reasons so he was retried on a different charge and convicted again in December. Many people, however, believed he was innocent, a possibility enhanced by the fact the attacks continued to occur following his arrest.

For many Londoners, these attacks were unprecedented and unexplainable. Why attack a woman in this way if there was no intent to rob her? As the prosecuting attorney Arthur Pigot told the jury in the first trial, attacks like this were

> a scene so new in the annals of mankind; a scene so unaccountable: a scene so unnatural to the honour of human nature, that it could not have been believed ever to have existed, unless it had been demonstrated by that proof which the senses cannot resist.[3]

In fact, such attacks were not entirely without precedent: Williams was first indicted under the 1721 statute passed to stop the weavers' attacks on women wearing calico dresses, though he was apparently only the third person to be prosecuted under that act and ultimately the conviction was overturned because his intent was clearly to inflict injuries rather than damage clothing.[4] More relevant were the attacks by 'Whipping Tom' in 1681, the 'Mohocks' in 1712, 'Young Bloods' in 1761 and 'Lascars' in 1780, all of which involved young men carrying out similar unprovoked assaults, mostly on women.[5] Sadistic attacks like these are an enduring, but fortunately relatively rare, phenomenon in European history.[6]

Yet this unusual episode can shed considerable light on London street life at the end of the eighteenth century. Comparison of the activities of the Monster, and even more so Londoners' responses to them, with earlier incidents reveals just how much the activities of the mob had changed over the previous century. The nature of the violence committed by the Monster and his use of insult were radically different from the violence and insult which were so characteristic of early eighteenth-century street life. Similarly, Londoners' reluctance to get involved in apprehending the Monster reflects the declining role of ordinary people in policing the streets. And although print and the law played a major role in creating the panic and shaping its outcome, ultimately neither was able to provide a satisfactory resolution to the case. An examination of the Monster panic thus provides an excellent opportunity for highlighting the major themes of this book, as well as a chance to consider why these dramatic transformations in the city's public life took place over the course of the eighteenth century.

For the most part, the 1788–90 attacks were committed by single individuals acting on their own. In contrast, the Mohocks, young bloods and Lascars acted in groups, and the violence of the young men served in part to confirm their masculine prowess to each other. This is confirmed by the role of laughter and playfulness in these earlier attacks. It is true that the culprits also laughed in three of the Monster attacks, such as when three men attacked Maria Smyth near Covent Garden in May 1790. After punching her and cutting her upper lip with a thumbnail, they 'immediately broke into a loud horse laugh, and walked away'. But these attacks, which all involved groups of men, were untypical of the assaults carried out by the Monster. They took place at the height of the panic, when the immense publicity seems to have generated copycat attacks.[7] The Monster mostly acted on his own, and usually on quiet streets at night. The only example so far identified of serial unprovoked attacks on women by a single individual before 1788 took place more than a century earlier when a man labelled 'Whipping Tom' 'lurked about in alleys and courts' on the western border of the City, seizing women and spanking their bottoms, but this episode appears to have been unique, and the evidence for it is limited.[8]

Violence in the late seventeenth and early eighteenth centuries was much more often a social phenomenon, which often served to confirm the participants' social and gender identity both to each other and to onlookers. Other forms of collective violence against women, such as the weavers' attacks on the 'Calico Madams', were committed in public and the participants claimed legitimacy for their actions.[9] By the end of the century public violence was much less acceptable. Attacks like those of the Monster were committed individually and surreptitiously, and the perpetrators were seen as so beyond the pale that they were thought to be foreigners (as with the 'Lascars', supposedly from India, in 1780) or 'Monsters'. The latter label may have come from the frequent exhibitions of deformed animals and humans staged in London. In contrast, although Mohock was a foreign name (thought to be derived either from Native Americans or a tribe of 'cannibals' in India), it appears to have been self-ascribed and it was widely recognised that the men involved in these attacks were in fact elite English men, including some young members of the nobility and gentry – the participants were simply playing with the notion of the wild savage. Unprovoked knife attacks on women occasionally also occurred in nineteenth-century London, but, like the Monster attacks, they were typically committed by individuals acting on their own, as was the case with the Jack the Ripper murders.[10]

The unacceptability of public violence in late eighteenth-century London is further evident in the way Londoners responded to the Monster. The story of how Williams was apprehended, by John Coleman (a twenty-year-old fishmonger), shows how unwilling Londoners had become to use violence when confronting suspected criminals. Coleman was out walking with two of the Monster's victims, Anne and Sarah Porter, in St James Park on 13 June 1790, when Anne identified Williams among the crowd of pedestrians as the man who had attacked them five months earlier. Rather than summoning assistance and attempting to arrest him, Coleman simply followed him at a safe distance over a long journey through the streets of St James. As he testified at the trial, 'I followed him behind; and I behaved in this kind of way[11] ... and I was going to knock him down once or twice', but he didn't. Instead, he decided to provoke an altercation by insulting him. He told the court that as he was walking along Bond Street,

> I did everything that laid in my power to insult him, by walking behind him, and walking before him, looking at him very full in the face, and making a noise behind him; I used every art I could do to insult him; he would not take any insult; he never said a word ...

According to a correspondent in a newspaper, Williams 'patiently suffered every insult, and only endeavoured to avoid him'. Williams's failure to respond to this provocation was interpreted in different ways. For his prosecutors, this was evidence of his guilt, but for many observers it was entirely normal behaviour. As the correspondent wrote, Williams's response was

> no more than what every prudent man would have done in the same situation. He endeavoured to shun a quarrel with a stranger, who the more he seemed determined to insult him, the more reason he had to suspect of some sinister intention.

The implication here was that Coleman was a homosexual; no normal Londoner would act in that way.[12]

When Williams went into a house, Coleman waited outside until he came out again. After Williams went into another house (inhabited by a Mr Smith), Coleman lurked outside until he was invited in and forced to confront his prey. Coleman then explained that he believed Williams had insulted some female acquaintances and stated 'I want the satisfaction of a gentleman'. Normally this would be interpreted as a challenge to a duel, but instead all Coleman wanted was Williams's name and address, which was politely provided.[13] Coleman's reluctance to confront Williams was typical of the responses of both men and women when the possibility of apprehending the Monster arose. In contrast, in 1681 the response of female Londoners to 'Whipping Tom' was more aggressive. When they needed to be out on the streets late, they went 'armed with penknives, sharp bodkins, sizzars, and the like, resolving if they meet with him, to turn the comedy into a tragedy' if he should attack.[14] In the late seventeenth century, violence was to be met with violence.

Just as the use of public violence in the Monster attacks was very different from that earlier in the century, so was the use of insult. A common theme in the attacks was the Monster's use of threatening and insulting language. When the Monster kicked Mrs Payne on the steps of Lord Howe's house in March 1790, he said 'Damn you b—h, I would enjoy a particular pleasure in murdering you, or in seeing you murdered, and in shedding your blood'. Such threatening language frequently accompanied attacks on women throughout the century, going back to the Mohocks. But the Monster's use of sexual insult was different from common practice earlier in the century. Victims and witnesses never reported his precise words, which is in itself revealing. Instead, his language was described in general terms, as 'improper', 'indecent', 'shocking', 'gross', 'insulting', 'indelicate', 'scandalous', 'rude', 'infamous', 'dreadful' and 'inhuman'. It was alleged that to have given specific examples would have offended the sensitive ears of polite society, especially the women. Exploiting the prevailing image of genteel femininity as pure and delicate, Pigot told the jury in the second trial, referring to the Porter sisters, 'I shall undoubtedly forbear to desire young women to pollute their mouths with the repetition of that language which issued from him, but it was most the horrid, and the least sufferable to human ears'.[15]

It was in fact to the advantage of the prosecution not to provide any specific evidence, for what would have emerged is that, contrary to most Monster attacks, Williams actually knew the Porters, and in previous encounters (acknowledged by Williams) he had abused Anne because she rejected his sexual advances. Accusing her of having slept with a Captain Crowder, he said 'Madam, I do not see that my person is not as good as the captain's, who you went off with from the bagnio'. In fact, every time Williams and Porter met they exchanged insults, which included Williams calling her a bitch and a whore. It transpires that Williams, having a large sexual appetite but few social skills, was accustomed to accosting women who 'appeared to be on the town' and then cursing them with obscene language if they rejected his advances.[16] Although the language may have been similar, such insults served a very different purpose from the public insults which were so common in early eighteenth-century London.[17] Whereas earlier insults were typically conducted in front of an audience, and were intended to invoke the power of community opinion to shame and discipline the victim, Williams was conducting a private quarrel, and he used sexual insults simply to offend his victim in revenge for having been rejected (and perhaps also in the hope that she would change her mind).

Another indication of just how much street life had changed by 1790 can be seen in Londoners' failure to make any serious efforts to apprehend him, although there were several opportunities. In response to the attacks by 'Whipping Tom' in 1681, men dressed up in women's clothes and tried to catch him. When he attacked a gentlewoman and she cried out for help, a watchman immediately came to her assistance. Although these attempts were unsuccessful, the failure to catch him was not for lack of trying, and his escapes were blamed on his supernatural powers.[18]

The success rate in apprehending the Mohocks was also low, but victims and passers-by did manage to facilitate some arrests. Lucia Goddard was assaulted in Covent Garden by John Hare, who 'as she stepped aside to give him the way ... held up his cane and swore he would knock out her brain' in March 1712. After the attack she managed, together with another female victim, to get a warrant from a justice of the peace and 'with great pains and care ... found him and charged a constable with him'.[19] By the end of the century victims and bystanders were much more reluctant to get involved. Complaining about the failure of victims to confront the Monster, a correspondent in the *Public Advertiser* felt compelled to state the obvious: 'those women who feel themselves cutting [should] immediately ... turn on the wretch, and follow him with their cries till assistance comes – by no means to fly from them, as it prevents justice being executed on him'.[20] Influenced by the fashionable cult of sensibility, female victims presented themselves as so traumatised by the attacks that they were unable to act. But men were not much more effective. We have already seen how reluctant Coleman was to take decisive action, despite the fact there was a £100 reward on offer if the Monster was caught and convicted. He was joined by a fellow fishmonger during his feeble pursuit, but after a short period his colleague abandoned the chase.[21] Similarly, when three women were attacked in Bishopsgate Street in April 1790, a man followed the culprit but as he was 'timid of making any alarm [the Monster] was suffered to abscond'.[22]

Victims of attacks were remarkably unwilling to summon help, perhaps because they thought it would not be given. When Mary Forster was harassed by an agitated gentleman on her way home from the Haymarket Theatre in September 1789, she 'hesitated for some time, whether she would not call for assistance and protection from two labouring men who then happened to be near. However she determined to walk home, without creating any alarm'. (When she was attacked shortly thereafter, she did call out to the two men after she recovered from 'her astonishment'. Although they pursued him, it was too late).[23] When the Porter sisters were attacked (in January 1790) they failed to summon help and there was a delay before their father ordered two servants to pursue the culprit.[24] Although passers-by sometimes did come to the assistance of victims when summoned, many cries for help

went unanswered. Susan, servant to a Mrs Colings, who was attacked
in Piccadilly in May 1788, 'screamed out three times as loud as she could,
but no one came to her assistance', while Eleanor Dodson, attacked one
night near Charing Cross by a man who cut her hip, 'instantly screamed
out', but 'no one came to her assistance, or seemed to notice her calling
out for help'.[25] Twice women who had been attacked knocked on nearby
doors but were denied assistance: in one case, a servant 'not knowing
who it was, and intent only upon the preservation of his master's house,
shut the door again' and in the other, a landlady, not recognising
the voice and thinking 'it was a common prostitute ... did not open the
door directly'.[26]

Whereas Londoners early in the century were accustomed to responding to cries for help such as 'Stop thief!' and 'Murder!', they appear to
have been reluctant to come to the aid of the victims of the Monster,
just as they had become reluctant to arrest felons more generally.[27]
Consequently, the role of the mob during the panic was very different,
and less significant, than what it might have been had the incidents
occurred earlier in the century. Mobs were raised against the Monster
on a small number of occasions, but in each case they had been misled.
In 1788 a young woman, Kitty Wheeler, was walking in St James's Park
when she saw a man who had previously harassed her with indecent
language at Ranelagh Gardens. When he began to follow her, she pointed
him out to her father, Parsloe Wheeler, who grabbed him. A crowd
gathered around the struggling pair. However, since Parsloe, a tavern
keeper, was disliked by the crowd, it sided with the alleged monster and
attacked Parsloe, who was forced to let go of him and he escaped. In
May 1790 the Monster was in fact totally absent when a group of
pickpockets robbed a gentleman and then, to facilitate their escape, called
out 'This is the Monster, he has just cut a woman'. As the *World* reported,

> A vast number of people immediately pursued the gentleman, some calling
> out 'The Monster', others 'Stop Thief!', till at length he was knocked down
> and surrounded by near a thousand people, by whom he was very ill treated
> and probably would not have escaped with his life, had he not been, by some
> gentlemen, taken into the Gray's Inn Coffee House.[28]

Mobs occasionally still gathered when summoned, but they were
misinformed and failed to apprehend the right person. Crowds also

assembled a few times at Bow Street when suspects including Williams were examined, and at the Old Bailey when Williams was tried. On at least one occasion a large crowd, armed with stones and bludgeons, attempted to adopt the mob's older role of punishing criminals, but Williams was given strong police protection. When he appeared at Bow Street he suffered only to the extent of being struck by a rotten vegetable.[29] Through strong policing, a lack of reliable information, and the reluctance on the part of most of the Monster's victims to summon its assistance, the crowd's role had largely been reduced to the level of spectators.

Instead of chasing the Monster or summoning help from passers-by, Londoners' first response when they saw him was to seek help from Bow Street, just as the Fieldings had requested them to do at mid-century. One evening in May 1790 a watchman followed a man who had attacked and wounded a woman. When the man stopped at a house on Castle Street and knocked on the door, the watchman, thinking the man would go into the house, 'ran for assistance from justice, while the villain calmly made off'.[30] Actually, until the Monster's attacks were written up in the papers, Londoners *first* response was to do nothing. Maria Smyth, one of the first victims in 1788, initially failed to report the crime because it was so unusual. Similarly, after the Porter sisters were attacked in January 1790, Mr Porter went to Bow Street a *few days* later, and requested that the matter be dealt with privately, in order to protect the family's reputation.[31] The expectation was that this was a police matter, and that the runners, not victims or passers-by, would arrest the culprit.[32] When they failed to do so, they were criticised in the press. On 8 April 1790 an anonymous letter (by Dr Smyth, Maria's husband) to the 'Bow Street Justices', published in the *Morning Herald*, complained that although they had been 'furnished with a train of leading circumstances necessary to detect' the Monster, they had failed to act because they were worried that the anonymous tipsters might have given them false information. So diminished had the role of private citizens become in identifying and arresting criminals that Smyth argued that informants should not even have to identify themselves, telling the justices that 'on a business of so dark and mysterious a nature, you should pay regard to anonymous information'.[33]

Ultimately, reflecting the growing importance of print, it was the press that played the most important role in facilitating the apprehension of suspects. As correspondents told the *Herald,* by publishing Smyth's letter the paper had validated the existence of the Monster, and it offered the best hope of apprehending him:

> Until your known authenticity stampt credit on the report that there existed a Monster ... I can assure you, that there were several otherwise credulous people who imagined the whole a fiction.

> It is with great pleasure I perceive, that a paper of the extensive circulation of the *Herald,* has taken up the cause of the fair; as I have no doubt, if it perseveres, that it will prove the best instrument to bring the unnatural villain to justice.[34]

The papers were then used by Smyth and the philanthropist John Julius Angerstein to assemble evidence about the identity of the Monster by placing advertisements urging victims to send them details of the attacks.[35] In contrast, in response to attacks by the Mohocks in 1712, the Middlesex justices stepped up efforts to apprehend the culprits *before* the press got ahold of the story.[36]

Angerstein's sponsorship, with the support of twenty-one other gentlemen, of the £100 reward for the Monster's capture and conviction indicates that private entrepreneurs and organisations also played a significant role in responding to the attacks. The award was advertised in the papers on 16 April and shortly thereafter in 'large posting-bills [placed] on every corner of the streets', and this publicity dramatically increased awareness of the Monster's attacks and encouraged people to report them.[37] Three weeks later another group of men, householders in St Pancras, formed an association 'for the prevention of such assaults in the future'. Unlike most other inhabitants' associations formed for the prevention and prosecution of crime in the late eighteenth century, this group saw its role as temporary (they thought the Monster would either be captured or driven away within three months), and they resolved to take turns patrolling the streets themselves.[38] But like the roles accorded to the Bow Street runners, newspapers and private rewards, the fact that this association was perceived to be necessary demonstrates just how reluctant ordinary Londoners had become to respond directly to criminal incidents when they occurred.

Both the publicity and the offer of a reward were successful, in the sense that a suspect, Williams, was arrested and put on trial at the Old

Bailey. But, as in so many other cases during the century, the judicial system was unable to bring this conflict to a tidy conclusion. Williams was convicted in July 1790, but because he had been improperly indicted under the obscure 1721 statute in order to make the offence a felony (thereby increasing the severity of the punishment) the conviction was quashed, and he had to be retried (and reconvicted) on a misdemeanour charge in December. From the moment of his first conviction, however, doubts were raised about his guilt. A long letter to the *Diary* on 27 July raised several questions about the evidence given by the Porter sisters and Coleman, and other doubts were raised in other papers. By far the most damning critique of the trial came in a polemical pamphlet by Theophilus Swift, *The Monster at Large: or The Innocence of Rhynwick Williams Vindicated*. Swift listed several procedural defects which had undermined Williams's defence: his witnesses were treated with hostility by the judge (and some had been discouraged from testifying by threats that they would be maliciously prosecuted for other crimes); other members of the Porter household who had witnessed the attack were not summoned by Williams's poorly prepared counsel (Swift alleged the testimony of these other witnesses would have called into question the identification of Williams as the culprit); the sisters failed to explain the nature of their previous interactions with Williams; they lied when they claimed they had 'swooned' and 'fainted' when Coleman brought Williams back to their house for identification; there were inconsistencies in the testimony of Anne Porter between what she said during the preliminary hearing at Bow Street and in her testimony at the Old Bailey; and the Porter sisters wore veils at the trial, thus preventing the jury from seeing their blushes when they lied.

Swift argued that there were two reasons why the Porters had deliberately falsely accused Williams: they sought the reward; and they wanted revenge for the verbal insults he had made to them. 'Public justice', he concluded, 'as it is sometimes administered, is but another word for private revenge … reward is the mother of perjury.' As had been apparent throughout the century, while the use of rewards successfully encouraged prosecutions, they were often malicious. The other obvious problem with the trials, as even the judge and prosecuting counsel recognised, was that the publicity the affair had received made it difficult to conduct a fair trial: Swift argued that Williams had been convicted by 'prejudice'. The huge public interest in the case led newspapers (except the *Times*) to name Williams following his arrest, so by the time the first trial took place Williams had been extensively portrayed in print as *the* Monster.[39]

Swift's pamphlet was calculated to cause an uproar, and it did just that, contributing to already existing scepticism in some papers about whether the Monster had ever existed.[40] Arguments raged about this and about the guilt or innocence of Williams; both topics were discussed at one of London's debating societies.[41] Following his second conviction (he was sentenced to six years in prison and then to provide sureties for his good behaviour for seven years), Williams published his own defence, an *Appeal to the Public*, which repeated some of Swift's arguments and claimed that he had been 'completely and irrevocably pre-judged'. He even printed an oath he had taken before John Wilkes (then City Chamberlain) swearing to his innocence. Although the publication of this pamphlet suggests that Williams hoped that the printed word could triumph over the courts, he was not confident. While he claimed 'I am every day gaining friends', he worried that the pamphlet would cause him to be 'if possible, more abused than ever in the newspapers'.[42]

Print was no more able to resolve this dispute than the law; what was written about the case itself generated conflict. Like the Mohocks, the whole Monster panic was to a considerable extent created by the press. In both cases, violent assaults had occurred periodically for months before the press latched onto the story; its explosion into print appears to have done more to stimulate copycat violence and other conflict than it did to secure the arrest of the culprits. In the case of the Mohocks, the publicity only erupted following the sensational arrest of seven young men, including two aristocrats, on the night of 11 March 1712. The following day the 'Grubstreet papers [flew] about like lightning'. In a series of newspaper reports and pamphlets, the story was exaggerated and manipulated as ammunition for party conflict between Whigs and Tories.[43] In contrast, reflecting the increased power of the press in the late eighteenth century, efforts to apprehend the Monster only became serious *following* the story's appearance in print, both in newspaper reports and with the pasting up of handbills offering a reward for his capture on every street corner. Once again, it is likely that the publicity generated copycat attacks; certainly the frequency and diversity of assaults in the period following the first printed reports suggest that more than one Monster was now at work.[44] In addition, some women may have faked having been attacked, since it was well known that the Monster only targeted beautiful, genteel young women. Swift argued that 'many ladies declared they were assaulted, who had never been assaulted at all: it made them talked of and brought them into fashion'. Similarly, the *Times* claimed that 'several women have reported themselves to have been wounded, merely in the hopes of partaking in the large reward, or for some other sinister purpose'.[45] Like other 'moral panics' created by the media, the extensive printed reports of the Monster appear to have stimulated some of the very attacks about which they complained.[46]

As with the Mohocks, printed commentary on the Monster was used to fight other battles, but the more widespread influence of the press in the late eighteenth century meant that its impact was more varied. Among the comical, ribald and satirical prints published at the time were some which scored political points (the Monster was depicted separately both as Prime Minister William Pitt and as his opponent Charles James Fox), but others libelled non-political figures. Captain John Crookshanks and Captain Philip Thicknesse were old enemies, and when, after some insults, Thicknesse refused a challenge to a duel, Crookshanks had posters printed and distributed, imitating those which offered the reward for the capture of the Monster, identifying Thicknesse as the culprit. Given the degree of popular hostility which had been whipped up against the Monster, this was, according to the *World*, 'certainly ... not altogether a pleasant joke'. In response, Thicknesse convinced Isaac Cruikshanks to draw up a print, entitled 'The Monstrous Assassin: or the Coward turn'd Bill Sticker' (Figure 31), which identified the eighty-two-year-old Crookshanks as responsible for the 'joke' and lambasted him as a coward. Crookshanks is shown standing on the stocks and pasting a bill on a wall saying 'Monster Detected'.[47] Hammering the point home, the text ironically states

> The public are requested to take notice, this is not the Captain Straitshanks who was broke for cowardice, and who afterwards offered to enter into the French Service not to fight against his native country, and who has kept his wife and two children upon 13 pounds a year in Wales till the youngest child was 44 years of age, and who with one leg in the grave, is endeavouring to

do all the mischief he can with the other – this is not that their [sic] Captain Straitshanks.

As occurred increasingly during the century, printed materials were used during the Monster panic as a means of supplementing other methods of conflict and for pursuing unrelated disputes. While print was relatively rarely used for private disputes, the highly unusual nature of these attacks meant they attracted immense public interest. Overall, as Swift's vicious attack on Coleman and the Porter sisters suggests, the primary effect of print seems to have been to exacerbate tensions rather than resolve them.

The attacks on women which gave rise to the Monster scare were atypical, but the way Londoners responded to them highlights several aspects of London life in the late eighteenth century, revealing just how much it had changed over the preceding century. For the most part Londoners refused to use the city's public spaces to respond to the threats posed by the Monster. Instead of attacking men they believed to be the Monster with insults or violence, they expected the Bow Street runners to deal with the problem. When that failed, they resorted to print, and although London's buildings were pasted with handbills warning of the Monster's activities and offering a reward for his capture, the resulting accusations against Rhynwick Williams were hotly debated in courtrooms, the pages of newspapers and pamphlets, and debating societies, as much as they were on the streets.

Ultimately, neither the conviction of Williams nor the pamphlet debate which followed brought closure to the dispute. If the arguments of Swift and Williams are to be believed, this was essentially a private dispute over allegations of sexual misconduct between Williams and a woman he courted, but developing notions of propriety meant that the nature of that dispute could not be discussed in public. By the late eighteenth century such disputes could not be effectively resolved on the streets, in the courtroom or in print. They could only be dealt with privately. It was only the extraordinary nature of the attacks which brought this case out into the public, and that only two years after they first occurred. Londoners had become reluctant to use public spaces for private disputes. This is not to say that such conflicts no longer occurred, but to argue that for the most part they disappeared from the public eye – and therefore from the majority of the surviving sources normally

31. 'The Monstrous Assassin: or the Coward turn'd Bill Sticker' (1790). (*By permission of The British Library*)

available to historians. Insults and violence more often took place indoors, which meant they were less likely to be recorded.[48] Like the Monster's first victims, Londoners decided to avoid the mob and keep their interpersonal disputes private.

How do we explain why London's public spaces became so much more orderly? Explanations of what is sometimes called 'the civilising process' tend to see it as working from the top down, emanating from the growing powers of the state or the cultural practices of the aristocracy and the gentry. A variant of this approach identifies the growing socio-economic and cultural infiuence of the ever-rising middle classes as the key motor of change.[49] Few scholars assign much agency to the lower classes in the ordering of public life, and yet it was the actions of the mob – those who walked London's streets, predominantly ordinary working Londoners – which changed the most. If any explanation of this complex set of changes is to be convincing it must recognise this fact.

The English state, from Westminster down to the parish, was becoming increasingly sophisticated and powerful in the eighteenth century, but it appears to have played only a limited role in the creating order on London's streets. Governments became increasingly adept at raising taxes and fighting foreign wars, but their domestic powers remained limited. Parliament passed numerous statutes in attempts to curb disorderly activities, including the 1715 Riot Act and eight acts regulating the sale of gin, but enforcing those laws required the cooperation of local officers and the populace and this was often difficult to obtain.[50] The statutory rewards offered for the conviction of felons had some impact in encouraging prosecutions, but many of these turned out to be based on false and malicious accusations. In the domestic arena, Parliament was only really effective when it was responding to local initiatives and pressure groups.[51]

Perhaps Parliament's greatest contribution to regulating London life was the passage of enabling statutes which gave individual parishes, or groups of parishes, the power to set up commissions to employ men to watch, pave and light the streets, thereby relieving householders of these communal responsibilities. As we have seen, the improvements to the watch (together with the rewards for convicting felons) led Londoners to rely increasingly on watchmen and thief-takers, like the Bow Street runners, for apprehending suspected criminals. Paradoxically, by encouraging most Londoners to withdraw from active policing, these changes removed one of the main sources of public disorder.[52] Whether salaried watchmen, whose duties were still restricted to the hours of darkness, were any more effective at policing is debatable, but they may have become more efficient in arresting thieves. Certainly the runners played a prominent role in apprehending those suspected of the most serious crimes. Perhaps the biggest improvement to London policing came from the growing use of deputy constables and soldiers to police crowds at the pillory, and to disperse them at boxing matches and during major riots, further discouraging Londoners from participating in public life. Yet none of these improvements to policing can be given direct credit for the decline in minor day-to-day disorder like public insults, fights and small-scale rioting, or the changing character of duelling, since the presence of law enforcement officers on the streets was still very limited.

Foreign observers, used to the more powerful police forces on the continent, were not impressed. The Swedish historian Gustaf Geijer, who visited London in 1809–10, commented that 'the police force in London is worthless, a few decrepit watchmen ... constitute the whole establishment. That, with such a provision, there is not more violence in this immense London is a great testimony to the good character of the people.'[53] Where did this self-discipline of the city's pedestrians come from? Should it be interpreted as a result of cultural changes such as the growing influence of the elite ideal of 'politeness'? This set of ideas and practices, building on earlier ideals of civility and based on the philosophy of the Earl of Shaftesbury (1671–1713), was widely disseminated in periodicals such as the *Tatler* and the *Spectator* and in conduct books. Intended to lubricate social interactions, particularly in an urban setting, politeness permeated English cultural life in the eighteenth century, especially in London and among the gentry and those who aspired to genteel social status.[54] Rejecting all forms of public conflict, politeness certainly had the potential to reform urban life. The expectations that men should engage in affable and refined sociability and avoid extremes of emotion, for example, undermined the traditional gentry culture of drinking and fighting. Thus, when two army officers quarrelled over 'affairs of gallantry' in Hyde Park in 1722, and 'one of them said you're a scoundrel', 'the other answered, use me with good manners sir, and not with ill manners'. Although he didn't, and a fatal sword fight ensued, the fact officers were making such comments suggests that politeness potentially did have an impact on those involved in the male culture of violence.[55] Later in the century, the cult of sensibility and the evangelical revival reinforced politeness for both gentlemen and the middle classes by characterising the ideal man as sensitive, charitable and refined. Arguably the reserved character of the male responses to the Monster, notably that of Coleman, but also Williams's calm response to his accusers, was shaped by these ideals. Meanwhile, we have seen that sensibility's image of femininity, emphasising purity, sensitivity and delicacy, shaped female responses.[56] It was not only the Porter sisters, who clearly took advantage of these expectations to avoid detailed scrutiny of their allegations, but most of the Monster's other victims who adopted this image, refusing to discuss the nature of his indecent language, and frequently reporting that they had fainted and swooned after the attacks and whenever they saw him. One woman even almost fainted when she saw a man who, although she did not think he *was* the Monster, looked *like* him.[57]

The ideals of politeness and sensibility no doubt contributed to the decline of public insult and violence among the gentry in London. Ladies who refused even to talk about sex in public lost the vocabulary of public insult (though they had never been its primary users), while new expectations of refined conduct may explain why violence by gentlemen declined faster than that of all other social classes during the century, facilitated by the decline of sword-carrying. Gentlemen had new means of asserting their distinctiveness from their social inferiors without needing to resort to violence. Although duelling continued, the combination of courage with self-control found in ideals of male sensibility promoted the adoption of a more ritualised, less lethal and less public version of the custom, the pistol duel. While gentry support for boxing increased at the end of the century, this was largely a spectator sport, and most gentlemen who practised it (as a form of recreation) used padded gloves. But the decreases in violence and insult among gentlemen and ladies only account for a small proportion of the dramatic declines in both on London's streets over the course of the century – clearly there were huge changes in non-elite behaviour as well.

How far down the social scale did the influence of politeness and sensibility extend? A range of conduct books targeted at middle-class Londoners promoted similar ideas of affability and refinement. For example, William Winstanley's compendium of advice, The *New Help to Discourse*, included in its 1684 and subsequent editions throughout the eighteenth century a set of 'rules of civility and decent behaviour' which proscribed insult and violence. These included advice on how to handle criticisms of others: 'be not too hasty to believe in flying reports, to the disparagement of any'; 'use no reproachful language against any man; neither curse nor revile'; and, if reprehending someone, 'do it with all sweetness and mildness'. If insulted, one should turn the other cheek: 'when you are bitten, or injured, by words answer not or endeavour your defence, but rather seem to take them in jest, and slight them ... for as the proverb [says], *Each question deserves not an answer*'.[58] Similarly, religious conduct books promoted restraint, magnanimity and charity.[59] Shorter pamphlets containing similar ideas were either sold very cheaply or distributed free of charge to the poor. Published by the Society for the Promotion of Christian Knowledge and the reformation of manners societies, these condemned vice and promoted piety, benevolence and self-discipline: readers were advised to maintain 'a strict watch over their thoughts' and to 'avoid idleness'. Slander was criticised as a breach of charity and as ill-mannered, demonstrating a 'manifest defect in breeding or in sense'.[60]

Polite ideals were disseminated in various formats to Londoners of all social classes. It is doubtful, however, how much influence such prescriptive literature had over its readers. Polite behaviour could also be learned in many different contexts in London including the master-servant relationship and by frequenting coffee houses or pleasure gardens.[61] But the difficulties of teaching the poor a polite code of behaviour are evident in a satirical publication of 1737, *The Man of Manners: or Plebeian Polish'd*, which purported to teach 'plain and familiar rules for modest and genteel behaviour' to 'persons of mean births and education, who have accountably plung'd themselves into wealth and power'. Its precepts governing behaviour on the streets include the following:

> To gape into any dining room, or parlour, where company is assembled, as one passes along, is a most impertinent curiosity.

It is indiscreet and vulgar, when two people meet in the street, to discourse so high, as to be heard up to the garret windows, and to converse in such a vociferous manner, as to make the passers-by loiter about to hear them.

It is unbecoming a person of tolerable appearance to discover any curiosity, when a riot or disorder happens in the streets, by stopping to ask what's the matter, and mixing with the mob; because it may be attended with the loss of a watch or a snuff-box.

It is not decent, indeed, to run and hurry along the streets, like a stay-maker to a ready-money customer ... neither does it look well at all, to hang, loiter, and stare at every wheelbarrow and sign-post, like a printer's errand boy, when he's going with a proof-sheet to an author.[62]

While theoretically seeking to reform lower-class behaviour, in making fun of plebeian incivilities this book showed just how great a task it would be to instruct ordinary people in the ideals of politeness.

Indeed, the trial testimonies in the *Old Bailey Proceedings* suggest that ordinary people rarely used this discourse. It was used once in Rhynwick Williams's trials, when a character witness described him as 'the most amiable character for good nature, amiable behaviour and politeness',[63] but polite language was rarely used in the 45,000 trial accounts published between 1714 and 1799, containing some ten million words. Although the frequent testimonies by defence witnesses to the good character of the accused might be expected to include the language of politeness, they do not. The words 'elegance' and 'refinement' (in its polite sense) never appear; 'polite' and 'politeness' occur in only thirty-nine trials; 'complaisant' and/or 'complaisance' in sixteen trials; 'good manners' in fourteen trials; and the older word 'civility' in ninety-one trials. In total, less than four trials in every thousand use the language of politeness and many of these cases involved the middle and upper classes. Of the few that included working people, some include descriptions of such people as polite, while in others they themselves use that language. A printer's apprentice accused of theft was described by his master as having 'behaved extremely well; he had a very good character, and was extremely useful; he acted so politely and civilly to all the customers, that they all spoke of him with very great commendation'. Similarly, a cabinet maker who kept an alehouse was described as 'the most civil, complaisant publican as ever I saw.

A young fellow shot him in the face, and he forgave him'. And when the wife of a bird seller told the court she shoved a man who had attacked her husband, the court asked, 'what sort of a shove?' She replied, 'only with very good manners'.[64] These cases provide tantalising hints of how politeness might have helped limit violence and insult among the lower classes, or at least how such people may have learned how to use the language of politeness strategically, but the fact they are so rare suggests just how limited that influence actually was.[65]

This is significant, for the changes in London public life described in this book involved men and women of all social classes, and, given their numerical superiority among the mob, it was non-elite Londoners who played the biggest role in effecting these transformations. In the case of public insult, the greatest change in behaviour occurred among tradesmen, craftsmen, labourers and servants, and especially their wives, widows and daughters: these were the people who ceased insulting each other so publicly on the streets of London. Similarly, lower-class men played a key role in the decline of public violence. While they continued to be enthusiastic about boxing, most switched from participating in impromptu street battles to observing commercially sponsored matches. Not only did they increasingly refrain from committing violence themselves, but they bound over those who jostled and kicked them while they were walking through the streets and they broke up fights and prevented duels whenever they were about to happen. In 1772 the Frenchman Pierre Jean Grosley noted 'the great care' which 'those of the lowest rank ... take to prevent the frays almost unavoidable, amidst the eternal passing and repassing of carriages'.[66] When coaches collided with each other in the narrow streets, or were unable to pass, it was ordinary Londoners who often rushed in to keep the peace. Finally, it was predominantly lower-class men and women who fell out of the habit of raising mobs and joining crowds on a daily basis to express their grievances. Many of the people whose behaviour changed were those unaffected by the literature of politeness.

In order to understand why Londoners of all social classes contributed to the decline of public conflict, we need to consider how urban growth radically altered patterns of public social interaction in eighteenth-century London. Owing to the rapid pace of population growth, economic change and social mobility, a new kind of urban environment was created in which relationships formed in neighbourhoods and on the streets became less important than those forged in less public contexts. City life did not become anonymous, but the way Londoners related to each other changed significantly. They did not know their neighbours or take an interest in their activities as much as they had used to: to know someone 'as a neighbour' came to mean one knew him or her only by sight.[67] They were even less likely to interact with those who passed by in the crowds which thronged the streets. Indeed, even people they knew seemed like strangers when encountered in public: when Coleman followed Williams through the streets of St James in order to apprehend him, they did not recognise each other. But when they finally came face to face in Mr Smith's house they each said 'I think I know you!': they had in fact previously met each other in assembly rooms and pubs.[68] The streets had become arteries characterised by movement, making it much harder for pedestrians to linger and mobs to form. Charles Moritz, a German gentleman, observed in 1782 that 'everyone, with hasty and eager step, seems to be pursuing either his business or his pleasure; and everywhere making his way through the crowd'. From the 1770s foreign observers frequently commented on Englishmen's obsession with maintaining their privacy while in public spaces, particularly in London. In order to avoid conflicts arising in crowds, Geijer commented that 'the English manner sets as it were a ring around everyone, within which he can be at his ease'. When walking the streets, he noted, 'if you should bump into anyone it is advisable not to look back. It appears then to have happened intentionally'.[69] We have seen that pedestrians were advised to avoid eye contact, and, by manoeuvring with their elbows rather than their hands, minimise physical contact with passers-by. When the Frenchman La Rochefoucald commented in 1780 that London's squares had 'rather a deserted air', one wonders if this wasn't so much because few people were present as because pedestrians acted as if they were invisible to each other.[70]

In this new urban environment social relationships were more likely to be established and conducted in confined contexts such as workplaces and pubs than on the streets.[71] Reputations in these circumstances were established in new ways, and in these more private contexts violence and disorder became less useful. In addition to work and leisure activities, there were new opportunities to create a good reputation through participation in the numerous clubs and voluntary societies which catered to Londoners of all social classes, including political, religious and charitable societies and trade associations; those involved did not necessarily live near one another, but they could form close personal relationships.[72] In a letter to a potential business partner in 1799, the artisan Francis Place dismissed hostile criticism by noting he would only listen to those whose character he respected, and he did not care what other people said:

> I can bear anything with equanimity from any one whom I think unworthy of my friendship, or whose character is unknown to me, and is not therefore entitled to my particular regard. To such persons I never explain any part of my conduct, whilst to him to whom I have given my confidence I am always ready to explain myself in every way.[73]

For all but the poorest denizens of the streets, what one said or did in public, or what others said about you, became less important than what happened behind closed doors, or indeed one's own individual self-examination. Increasingly, the individual was able to shape his or her own reputation without reference to the wider public. In early modern society, life was often conducted as a public performance, in which individual identity was shaped by a public audience and individuals manipulated that identity through a process of 'self-fashioning', nowhere more so than in London. Over the course of the eighteenth century, however, the significance of purposely manipulating one's public image in this way declined. A more modern notion of the individual developed, as reflected in the development of the novel and a new focus on the 'individualist self' in autobiographies, in which identity was determined by the inner, 'true' self, regardless of public opinion.[74]

As an increasingly firm distinction was drawn between public and private life, the petty issues of insult and individual reputations largely ceased to be addressed in public (whether on the street in the court-room, or in print), except where questions of honour became weapons in political or religious debate. Symptomatic of this change is the fact that adultery, previously a frequent topic of public insult, became perceived as a private problem rather than an offence against the community; the issues of sexual conduct raised in the panic over the Monster were kept for the most part firmly below the surface. Street life came to consist of 'privatised individuals' who came together in public spaces for a more limited set of largely political or civic purposes.[75] Although public life continued to impinge on the private, it did so in new and more limited ways, such as through the power of print.[76]

As public opinion played a declining role in shaping reputations in London, collectivities such as neighbourhoods and crowds lost their powers to shape individual reputations and behaviour. The need for public demonstrations of honourable behaviour, and for publicly censuring dishonourable behaviour, declined. Official efforts publicly to shame deviants in the pillory, as well as unofficial imitations of such punishments, began to lose their power and effectiveness. Public defamatory insults (for both men and women) and demonstrations of violence and courage (for men) ceased to play significant roles in shaping reputations. With the decline of all these forms of engagement in public life, as well as the reduction in popular participation in policing, it became more difficult to recruit support for popular protest. In any case, the use of the streets to create the appearance of widespread community support through illuminations, bonfires and processions was no longer as powerful a tactic as it once was. The views of the community became less important, and other collectivities, such as voluntary societies, provided Londoners with new means of making their views known. Quite simply, Londoners fell out of the habit of taking to the streets to express their grievances.

While the streets *were* better policed, and elite and middle-class behaviour *was* increasingly governed by polite ideals, it is the transformation of London's public life caused by the changing relationship between the individual and the community which best explains the decline of the multifaceted activities of the mob in the second half of the eighteenth century. Rather than being imposed from above, these changes were primarily carried out by the mob themselves at their own initiative as they adapted to a new social environment. Londoners' peculiar response (both panic-stricken but also reluctant to get involved) to the relatively minor attacks comitted by the 'Monster' between 1788 and 1790 underlines just how much had changed in the city since the word 'mob' was coined to describe the disorder on its streets over a century earlier.

# APPENDIX

# *Sources and Methods*

The volume and variety of the surviving primary sources with evidence concerning violence and disorder in eighteenth-century London is simply enormous, and it would take several lifetimes to read it all. Yet much of the material is repetitive, and the number of sources which provide evidence from the point of view of those labelled as the 'mob', as opposed to that of the authorities or other often hostile observers, is limited. In order to make the research for this book both manageable and productive it was necessary to develop a strategy for selecting sources to examine in detail. This appendix describes the most important of the wide range of sources consulted, and the sampling strategies adopted. While contemporary and modern catalogues, indexes, reprints and digital editions facilitated many aspects of the research, it proved necessary to sample many manuscript and printed sources where only limited finding aids exist.[1]

The extent of the research conducted for this book would not have been possible before the information technology revolution, which has made it possible rapidly to search vast bodies of primary sources for relevant material. The creation of the electronic *Eighteenth Century Short Title Catalogue*, for example, which lists virtually every book published in the eighteenth century, has meant that one can search for every work with keywords such as 'mob', 'duel' or 'libel' in the title, and find a large number of publications on these subjects (but of course not everything that might be relevant). Similarly, the digitised catalogues of the manuscript collection at the British Library and of documents at the National Archives (formerly the Public Record Office) and other archives allow one to find many relevant documents on these topics out of the millions kept in these repositories, which are organised according to the identity of the previous owners of the documents or by the government departments which created them, not by subject. It must be noted, however, that these electronic resources are ultimately only as useful as the original descriptive calendars of the documents which they reproduce, and these are often not very detailed. The use of resources like these has not located every document which contains references to mobs and related activities, but it has identified numerous relevant records which would never have been found through simple browsing of the printed catalogues or the records themselves.

Even more useful, of course, are the complete digital editions of printed primary sources which are now being created. Once it becomes possible to search an entire collection of sources by keyword or character string you can find virtually every piece of relevant evidence in a huge body of text virtually instantaneously. (One does need to know what keywords to search for, however, and how to use wild cards and Boolean operators to include variant spellings.) The most useful for this book has been the *Old Bailey Proceedings Online*, which contains printed accounts of some 50,000 felony trials which took place at London's central criminal court during the eighteenth century, providing millions of words of text which can be searched in several different ways. Eighteenth Century Collections Online (ECCO), which was becoming available just as this book was completed, will be another valuable resource, as it promises to provide searchable digitised texts of every 'significant monograph' published in the British Empire between 1701 and 1800.

The eighteenth century is a period rich in visual evidence, particularly satirical prints, and much of it can now be examined on two websites. The Guildhall Library's COLLAGE website contains digitised copies of their excellent collection of images of metropolitan life, which can be searched by artist, place and subject. A broader searchable collection of national and international paintings and drawings can be found in the Tate Collections website. Other prints were consulted in the modern printed collections listed in the bibliography.

Many records, of course, remain largely untouched by the digital revolution. Printed accounts of foreign visitors, which provide valuable eyewitness accounts of public life in London, were primarily consulted in the British Library (those that are available in English), but some have been published in modern editions and are listed in the bibliography. The richly descriptive diaries, memoirs and correspondence of Londoners provide another immensely useful source for evidence of day-to-day street life. The papers of Francis Place (1771–1854), an artisan who painstakingly recorded his memories of late eighteenth-century London, were consulted in the British Library. His autobiography, however, is available in a modern edition.[2] The diaries and correspondence of Samuel Pepys, Horace Walpole and Dudley Ryder were consulted in modern editions; the first two contain comprehensive indexes.

Two types of evidence which survive in enormous quantities have been sampled: newspapers and manuscript court records. This is the century in which English newspapers first provide a consistently published source of domestic news. While indexes of the *Times* (first published in 1785) were searched using the cd-rom edition of *Palmer's Index* (the text itself will soon be available in a digital edition), the huge number of other eighteenth-century newspapers are only available on microfilms in their hundreds. With reports of crimes and other current events, advertisements, announcements and correspondence, newspapers are a vast, largely untapped resource of evidence about eighteenth-century London life, but the sheer volume of the text and the fact that this evidence is distributed among a far greater mass of irrelevant material means that no single scholar can ever look at more than a tiny proportion of the newspapers published. For the purpose of this study, one title for one year of each decade for most decades in the century has been searched systematically for evidence concerning street life.[3] These papers were supplemented by looking at at least one other title in a less systematic way for each sample year to ensure that the coverage of domestic news in the principal title was strong. Other newspapers, of course, were consulted for their coverage of important events and when references to them were found in other sources. The eighteenth century was also the first significant century for the periodical, and several have provided valuable evidence for this book. Most useful was the *Gentleman's Magazine*, founded in 1731, which reprinted many newspaper articles as well as including its own essays and chronicle of events. The valuable contemporary index facilitated searching.[4]

Given the difficulty of efficiently finding relevant material, collections of selections from newspapers proved very helpful. A collection of advertisements and reports of debates held in London's debating societies in the late eighteenth century, which provide valuable evidence of popular attitudes, has recently been published (with an excellent index).[5] Two fantastically rich multi-volume collections of newspaper clippings from the period are available in the British Library. Collected by Sarah Sophia Banks and Daniel Lysons, these include reports, advertisements and illustrations, and cover a range of fascinating topics including the London Monster, boxing matches, running races and other popular recreations, exhibitions of oddities, ballooning and much more.[6]

Manuscript judicial records provide the most important resource for the study of violence and disorder in London, but they are also the most difficult to research. The key criminal offences studied for this book were defamation (tried in the church courts and at quarter sessions), assault (at sessions), homicide (at the Old Bailey) and riot (at sessions and the Old Bailey). The most valuable legal records for the social and cultural historian are depositions, informations and examinations, which provide eyewitness accounts of suspicious, disorderly and criminal activities, more or less directly in the participants' or witnesses' own words. Given their importance, those pertaining to relevant offences have been read in their entirety wherever they have been fully catalogued. Most are kept in the sessions papers of the London Metropolitan Archives (LMA) and the Corporation of London Record Office.[7] Some coroner's inquisitions (which include witnesses' depositions) are also kept in the Westminster Abbey Library Muniment Room; one year in ten of these was sampled. The number of depositions in the London Consistory Court records (kept at the LMA) and the lack of a comprehensive listing meant that they also had to be sampled. Those for approximately 150 defamation cases were examined, from all or part of thirty-nine years spread over the period from 1679 to 1792.[8] Serious cases of riot frequently occasioned correspondence with the Secretaries of State, which is kept in the National Archives. For those rioters prosecuted at the behest of the Attorney General, some prosecution briefs also survive, which contain valuable summaries of the evidence to be presented in court. These were located by searching the electronic catalogue by offence.[9]

Records of the legal process, which are often voluminous but typically only provide very brief descriptions of the offending behaviour, were all sampled. In order to count the number of defamation prosecutions initiated at the consistory court, the Act Books, Acts of Court, and Allegation, Libel and Sentence Books were examined for approximately one year in every ten between 1670 and 1790.[10] A comprehensive account of those tried for serious crimes is available from the Old Bailey Proceedings Online, but petty crimes were not prosecuted at the Old Bailey and few sessions papers survive pertaining to these cases. The best evidence is in the sessions rolls: bundles of indictments, recognizances and other documents arising from each meeting of the court. While the indictments, written according to prescribed formulas, provide little descriptive evidence, the recognizances, legal promises by the accused to appear in court to answer a specified charge, often provide valuable (if brief) evidence of victims' complaints.[11] The sheer volume of these documents, however (approximately 350,000 were issued between the Restoration and 1800 to attend the Middlesex court alone), meant that only a small proportion could be examined. Evidence on defamation and riot cases was gathered systematically from the recognizances issued to attend every August or September sessions of the Middlesex court for approximately every second year between 1660 and 1781.[12] After 1781 the sheer number of cases owing to the increased activity of 'trading justices' and the lack of detail on these justices' recognizances made the task unrewarding. Since the court met eight times a year, one out of every sixteen Middlesex sessions was examined up to 1781, or 6 per cent of the total. Because the Westminster, City of London and Surrey sessions rolls were not included, and the jurisdiction of these courts covered about one third of the population of the metropolis (less early in the period, more later as the metropolis expanded south of the river), the recognizance sample was derived from approximately 4 per cent of the total number of relevant court records from the metropolis. It identified for analysis a total of 767 recognizances for riot and defamation. Due to the much larger number of recognizances issued for assault, only one sessions of the court per decade was analysed in detail. Defamation could also be prosecuted as a civil offence at King's Bench and the Court of Common Pleas. Owing to the small number of such cases, the limited details provided in the records and the fact that there are no indexes, this research was confined to roughly one roll in every twenty years.[13]

Evidence concerning the use of shaming punishments is available from the Old Bailey Proceedings Online for those convicted of felonies, and from the LMA for those convicted of misdemeanours in Middlesex.

A typescript calendar of the Middlesex sessions books (with index) covering 1709 to 1751 was very useful.[14] In addition, one year in every ten of the manuscript sessions books and sessions process books was examined.[15] Evidence of how punishments were actually carried out was found in the Sheriff's 'cravings' (bills of expenses) and in petitions and reports sent to secretaries of state, both kept in the National Archives,[16] and in newspapers. Certificates of penance, which survive erratically, were found at the Guildhall Library and the British Library.[17]

Unsurprisingly, some of the most detailed evidence concerning prosecutions comes from those who ran the judicial system, but these sources survive erratically. Records such as legal reports and judges' notes provide important evidence not only of legal attitudes and practices but also of the offences which were tried. Reports of important civil and criminal cases were found in the 178 volumes of the *English Reports* (now searchable on cd-rom), while the manuscript notes of judges Dudley Ryder and Lord Mansfield shed light on cases of slander, libel, assault and riot; Mansfield's notes have now been published in a modern edition. Recently published editions of the notebook of Middlesex justice of the peace Henry Norris (which includes some complaints of disorderly activities which never led to formal prosecutions) and a collection of charges (speeches) given by judges and justices to grand juries at quarter sessions were also useful.[18]

Many promising opportunities remain for conducting new primary source research into the activities of the mob and London street life more generally in the eighteenth century. In particular, little use has been made here of the rich collections of literature published during the century, notably novels, plays, poems and ballads. While the sources chosen for this study constitute a substantial, wide-ranging and largely representative selection of what is currently available, other scholars, no doubt aided by further advances of the digital revolution, will find much new and valuable evidence which it was not possible to include in the present study.

# Notes

## Notes to Preface

1. Henry Fielding, *The Covent Garden Journal*, 47 (13 June 1752) and 49 (20 June 1752); reprint ed. B. A. Goldgar (Oxford, 1988), pp. 259–64, 268–73.
2. Thomas Shadwell, *The Squire of Alsatia* (London, 1688), p. 59.
3. Roger North, *Examen: or An Enquiry into the Credit and Veracity of an Intended Complete History* (London, 1740), p. 574.
4. Early English Books Online, http://ets.umdl.umich.edu/e/eebo/; Robert B. Shoemaker, 'The London "Mob" in the Early Eighteenth Century', *Journal of British Studies*, 26 (July 1987), pp. 282–84.

## Notes to Chapter 1: Street Life

1. *Lichtenberg's Visits to England*, trans. and annotated by Margaret L. Mare and W. H. Quarrell (Oxford, 1938), pp. 63–65.
2. William Hutton, *A Journey from Birmingham to London* (Birmingham, 1785), p. 24; Daniel Defoe, *A Tour Through the Whole Island of Great Britain* (1724–26; reprint Harmondsworth, 1983), p. 327.
3. *Hell upon Earth: or The Town in an Uproar* (London, 1729), p. 3; *Low-Life: or One Half of the World Knows Not How the Other Half Live* (2nd edn, London, [1750]), pp. 32–33; Tim Hitchcock, *Down and Out in Eighteenth-Century London* (forthcoming).
4. Mark S. R. Jenner, 'Circulation and Disorder: London Streets and Hackney Coaches, c. 1640–c. 1740', in T. Hitchcock and H. Shore, eds, *The Streets of London: From the Great Fire to the Great Stink* (London, 2003), pp. 45–46.
5. [Daniel Defoe], *Some Considerations upon Street-Walkers* (London, [1726]), p. 2; M. Grosley, *A Tour to London: or New Observations on England and its Inhabitants*, trans. T. Nugent (London, 1772), p. 55. See also Tony Henderson, *Disorderly Women in Eighteenth-Century London: Prostitution and Control in the Metropolis, 1730–1830* (London, 1999), pp. 106–8; Randolph Trumbach, *Sex and the Gender Revolution*, i, *Heterosexuality and the Third Gender in Enlightenment London* (Chicago and London, 1998), pp. 153–55.

6. [Béat-Louis de Muralt], *Letters Describing the Character and Customs of the English and French Nations ... Translated from the French* (London, 1726), pp. 38–39; *Low-Life*, p. 78.

7. CLRO, Misc. MS 18.40; *Hell upon Earth*, p. 10; César de Saussure, *A Foreign View of England in 1725–1729*, trans. and ed. M. van Muyden (1902; reprint London, 1995), p. 129; *A Trip from St James's to the Royal Exchange* (London, 1744), p. 4.

8. *Low-Life*, p. 77; W. S. Lewis, ed., *Horace Walpole's Correspondence* (48 vols, London, New Haven, and Oxford, 1937–83), xvii, p. 434.

9. [Muralt], *Letters*, pp. 38–39; Ned Ward, *The London Spy*, ed. Paul Hyland (4th edn, 1709; reprint East Lansing, Michigan, 1993), p. 223.

10. See below, Chapter 5.

11. *A Trip Through the Town: Containing Observations on the Customs and Manners of the Age* (London, [1735]), p. 32; Henry Fielding, *An Enquiry into the Causes of the Late Increase of Robbers*, ed. M. R. Zirker (1751; reprint Oxford, 1988), pp. 167–69.

12. See below, Chapters 2 and 4.

13. For more on rough music, see Chapter 5.

14. *Daily Post*, 13 November 1741; Fielding, *Enquiry*, p. 131; John Gay, *Trivia: or The Art of Walking the Streets of London* (London, [1716]), reprinted in *John Gay: Poetry and Prose*, ed. Vinton A. Dearing, 2 vols (Oxford, 1974), i, p. 151.

15. For the emergence of shops, see Hoh-Cheung Mui and Lorna H. Mui, *Shops and Shopkeeping in Eighteenth-Century England* (London, 1989); Nancy Cox, *The Complete Tradesman: A Study of Retailing, 1550–1820* (Aldershot, 2000).

16. Deirdre Palk, 'Private Crime in Public and Private Places: Pickpockets and Shoplifters in London, 1780–1823', in Hitchcock and Shore, eds, *Streets of London*, p. 136.

17. Jürgen Habermas, *The Structural Transformation of the Public Sphere* (1962; reprint trans. T. Burger, Cambridge, 1989).

18. William Maitland, *The History and Survey of London from its Foundation to the Present Time*, 2 vols (London, 1760), ii, p. 719; Saussure, *Foreign View of England*, p. 119; John Black, 'Illegitimacy, Sexual Relations and Location in Metropolitan London, 1735–85', in Hitchcock and Shore, eds, *Streets of London*, p. 106; Peter Clark, *The English Alehouse: A Social History, 1200–1830* (London, 1983), chaps 10 and 13.

19. Maitland, *History and Survey of London*, ii, p. 719.

20. Both cited by Jessica Warner, *Craze: Gin and Debauchery in an Age of Reason* (London, 2003), pp. 13, 15. See also Jonathan White, 'The "Slow

but Sure Poyson": The Representation of Gin and its Drinkers, 1736–1751', *Journal of British Studies*, 42 (2003), pp. 35–64; Patrick Dillon, *The Much-Lamented Death of Madam Geneva: The Eighteenth-Century Gin Craze* (London, 2002).

21. Richard Sennett, *The Fall of Public Man* (1977; reprint London, 1993), p. 81; Thomas Brown, *Amusements Serious and Comical, Calculated for the Meridian of London* (2nd edn, London, 1702), p. 28; *Hell upon Earth*, p. 39; Lawrence E. Klein, 'Coffeehouse Civility, 1660–1714: An Aspect of Post-Courtly Culture in England', *Huntington Library Quarterly*, 59 (1996), p. 37; Clark, *English Alehouse*, p. 13; Saussure, *Foreign View of England*, p. 102; Brian Cowan, 'What was Masculine about the Public Sphere? Gender and the Coffeehouse Milieu in Post-Restoration England', *History Workshop Journal*, 51 (2001), pp. 127–57.

22. *Low-Life*, esp. p. 22. See also *Hell upon Earth*.

23. E. A. Wrigley, 'A Simple Model of London's Importance in Changing English Society and Economy, 1650–1750', *Past and Present*, 37 (1967), p. 44. These estimates are subject to a wide possible margin of error, as explained in Vanessa Harding, 'The Population of London, 1550–1700: A Review of the Published Evidence', *London Journal*, 15 (1990), pp. 111–28; and L. D. Schwarz, *London in the Age of Industrialisation: Entrepreneurs, Labour Force and Living Conditions, 1700–1850* (Cambridge, 1992), pp. 125–28.

24. For London's economic growth in the eighteenth century, see George Rudé, *Hanoverian London, 1714–1808* (Berkeley, 1971), chaps 1–2; Peter Earle, *The Making of the English Middle Class* (London, 1989), chap. 2; M. Dorothy George, *London Life in the Eighteenth Century* (1925; reprint Harmondsworth, 1979), chap. 4; Schwarz, *London in the Age of Industrialisation*, chaps 1–2.

25. Defoe, *Tour*, p. 317.

26. *The London Directory for the Year 1791* (London, [1791]); Rudé, *Hanoverian London*, p. 25.

27. On migration, see Wrigley, 'Simple Model', pp. 44–47; Peter Clark, 'Migration in England during the Late Seventeenth and Early Eighteenth Centuries', *Past and Present*, 83 (1979), pp. 70–71; David Souden, 'Migrants and the Population Structure of Later Seventeenth-Century Provincial Cities and Market Towns', in P. Clark, ed., *The Transformation of English Provincial Towns, 1600–1800* (London, 1984), pp. 133–68.

28. Sir John Fielding, *A Brief Description of the Cities of London and Westminster* (London, 1776), p. xxiv; John Beattie, *Policing and Punishment in London, 1660–1750* (Oxford, 2001), p. 65.

29. For historical background and bibliography on this topic, see Tim

Hitchcock and Robert Shoemaker, 'Community Histories: The Minority Communities of London', *Old Bailey Proceedings Online*, http://www.oldbaileyonline.org/history/communities/.

30. Daniel Defoe, *The Complete English Tradesman* (1725; reprint Gloucester, 1987), p. 72; George, *London Life*, chap. 6; Hitchcock, *Down and Out in Eighteenth-Century London*.

31. Guy Miège, *The New State of England under our Sovereign Queen Anne* (1703), p. 264; N. Bailey, *Dictionarium Britannicum* (London, 1730), under gentleman.

32. *M. Misson's Memoirs and Observations in his Travels over England*, trans. J. Ozell (London, 1719), p. 201; *The Cheats of London Exposed: or The Tricks of the Town Laid Open to Both Sexes* (London, [1770]), pp. 87–88. For fops, see Philip Carter, *Men and the Emergence of Polite Society: Britain, 1660–1800* (Harlow, 2001), chap. 4.

33. N. McKendick, et al., *The Birth of a Consumer Society: The Commercialization of Eighteenth-Century England* (London, 1982), esp. pp. 52–60, 94–96.

34. Penelope J. Corfield, 'Walking the City Streets: The Urban Odyssey in Eighteenth-Century England', *Journal of Urban History*, 16 (1990), pp. 155–58; idem, 'Dress for Deference and Dissent: Hats and the Decline of Hat Honour', *Costume*, 23 (1989), pp. 64–79.

35. *Cheats of London Exposed*, p. 87; Terry Castle, *The Female Thermometer: Eighteenth-Century Culture and the Invention of the Uncanny* (Oxford, 1995).

36. *Cheats of London Exposed*, p. 89; *The Tricks of the Town: or Ways and Means for Getting Money* (London, 1732), p. 23; Craig Muldrew, *The Economy of Obligation: The Culture of Credit and Social Relations in Early Modern England* (Basingstoke, 1998), pp. 328–29.

37. *The Tricks of London Laid Open: Being a True Caution to Both Sexes in Town and Country* (London [1780]), p. 56. See also, [John] Trusler, *The London Adviser and Guide: Containing Every Instruction and Information Useful and Necessary to Persons Living in London, and Coming to Reside There* (London, 1786), pp. 146–47.

38. *Cheats of London Exposed*, p. 90.

39. See below, especially Chapters 3, 6 and 7.

40. J. R. Kellett, 'The Breakdown of Gild and Corporation Control over the Handicraft and Retail Trades of London', *Economic History Review*, 2nd series, 10 (1958), pp. 381–94; Rudé, *Hanoverian London*, p. 25; Earle, *Making of the English Middle Class*, pp. 25, 28–29; George, *London Life*, chap. 4; C. R. Dobson, *Masters and Journeymen: A Prehistory of Industrial Relations, 1717–1800* (London, 1980), esp. p. 22.

41. *A Trip Through the Town*, p. 23; Tim Meldrum, *Domestic Service and Gender, 1660–1750: Life and Work in the London Household* (Harlow, 2000), pp. 60–64.

42. Grosley, *Tour to London*, pp. 84, 108, 110; *Tricks of the Town*, p. 2.

43. Saussure, *Foreign View of London*, p. 101; see below, Chapter 9.

44. Charles P. Moritz, *Travels, Chiefly on Foot, Through Several Parts of England in 1782* (London, 1795), p. 61; Nicholas Rogers, *Whigs and Cities: Popular Politics in the Age of Walpole and Pitt* (Oxford, 1989); idem, *Crowds, Culture and Politics in Georgian Britain* (Oxford, 1998); Kathleen Wilson, *The Sense of the People: Politics, Culture and Imperialism in England, 1715–1785* (Cambridge, 1995). See also below, Chapter 5.

45. Valerie Pearl, 'Change and Stability in Seventeenth-Century London', *London Journal*, 5 (1979), pp. 25–27.

46. E. G. Dowdell, *A Hundred Years of Quarter Sessions* (Cambridge, 1932); Norma Landau, 'The Trading Justice's Trade', in idem, ed., *Law, Crime and English Society, 1660–1830* (Cambridge, 2002), pp. 46–70; Sidney Webb and Beatrice Webb, *English Local Government from the Revolution to the Municipal Corporations Act: The Parish and the County* (London, 1906), pp. 228–58. For trading justices, see also below, Chapter 8.

47. Norman G. Brett-James, *The Growth of Stuart London* (London, 1935), chap. 12.

48. Defoe, *Tour*, pp. 286–87.

49. Heather Shore, 'Mean Streets: Criminality, Immorality and the Street in Early Nineteenth-Century London', in Hitchcock and Shore, eds, *Streets of London*, pp. 151–54, 157.

50. Brown, *Amusements*, p. 22; Fielding, *Brief Description*, p. xv; M. D'Archenholz, *A Picture of England: Containing a Description of the Laws, Customs and Manners of England* (Dublin, 1791), p. 77.

51. Robert B. Shoemaker, 'Reforming the City: The Reformation of Manners Campaign in London, 1690–1738', in L. Davison et al., eds, *Stilling the Grumbling Hive: The Response to Social and Economic Problems in England, 1689–1750* (Stroud, 1992), pp. 99–120; Leonard W. Cowie, *Henry Newman: An American in London, 1708–1743* (London, 1956), pp. 55–59. For later efforts, see Joanna Innes, 'Politics and Morals: The Reformation of Manners Movement in Later Eighteenth-Century England', in E. Hellmuth, ed., *The Transformation of Political Culture: England and Germany in the Late Eighteenth Century* (Oxford, 1990), pp. 79–118.

52. Grosley, *Tour to London*, pp. 48–50; see below, Chapter 2.

53. E. L. Jones and M. E. Falkus, 'Urban Improvement and the English Economy in the Seventeenth and Eighteenth Centuries', in P. Borsay, ed., *The*

*Eighteenth-Century Town: A Reader in Urban History, 1688–1820* (London, 1990), pp. 116–58; Beattie, *Policing and Punishment in London*, pp. 207–25; Miles Ogborn, *Spaces of Modernity: London's Geographies, 1680–1780* (London, 1998), pp. 91–96.

54. Elizabeth McKellar, *The Birth of Modern London: The Development and Design of the City, 1660–1720* (Manchester, 1999), chap. 8.

55. *OBP*, May 1768, trial of Daniel Saxton (t17680518–23); December 1772, trial of Edward Brocket (t17721209–99).

56. John Gwynn, *London and Westminster Improved* (London, 1766), p. 1; [Muralt], *Letters*, p. 79; Sennett, *Fall of Public Man*, pp. 54–56.

57. John Spranger, *A Proposal or Plan for an Act of Parliament* (London, 1754), preface; David Garrioch, 'House Names, Shop Signs, and Social Organization in Western European Cities, 1500–1900', *Urban History*, 21 (1994), p. 37.

58. Gay, *Trivia*, p. 135; *London Magazine: or Gentleman's Monthly Intelligencer*, May 1780, p. 197.

59. Michael Harris, 'London Guidebooks before 1800', in Robin Myers and Michael Harris, eds, *Maps and Prints: Aspects of the English Booktrade* (Oxford, [1984]), pp. 31–66; Corfield, 'Walking the City Streets', pp. 136–42.

*Notes to Chapter 2: Stop Thief!*

1. John Gay, *Trivia: or The Art of Walking the Streets of London* (London, [1716]), reprinted in *John Gay: Poetry and Prose*, ed. Vinton A. Dearing, 2 vols (Oxford, 1974), i, p. 162.

2. *OBP*, January 1761, trial of Thomas Pearce (t17610116–23).

3. [Spencer Perceval], *The Duties and Powers of Public Officers and Private Persons with Respect to Violations of the Public Peace* [London, 1792], pp. 8–9.

4. *OBP*, April 1761, trial of John Cuthbertson (t17610401–21).

5. For similar responses to crime in the seventeenth century, see Cynthia Herrup, 'New Shoes and Mutton Pies: Investigative Responses to Theft in Seventeenth-Century East Sussex', *Historical Journal*, 27 (1984), pp. 811–30.

6. *OBP*, May 1735, trial of John Sutton and Thomas Godson (t17350522–19); *London Evening Post*, 13 May 1735.

7. *OBP*, February 1761, trial of Charles Reynolds (t17610225–1).

8. For evidence of the decline of the hue and cry, see Cynthia Herrup, *The Common Peace: Participation and the Criminal Law in Seventeenth-Century England* (Cambridge, 1987), pp. 70–72; John Styles, 'Sir John Fielding and

the Problem of Criminal Investigation in Eighteenth-Century England', *Transactions of the Royal Historical Society*, 33 (1983), p. 127.

9. *OBP*, January 1731, trial of Alexander Russel (t17310115–62).

10. Ibid., June 1733, trial of William Sidwell (t17330628–18).

11. Ibid., December 1755, trial of John Furgerson (t17551204–48).

12. Ibid., May 1733, trial of Henry Hart (t17330510–10).

13. Ibid., September 1747, trial of Anne Williams (t17470909–21).

14. Ibid., January 1732, trial of Robert Hallam (t17320114–9).

15. Ibid., October 1781, trial of Robert Evans (t17811017–61).

16. *Weekly Journal: or British Gazetteer*, 29 July 1721.

17. *London Evening Post*, 25 June 1751.

18. *OBP*, April/May 1731, trial of Elizabeth Coventry (t17310428–65; emphasis added).

19. *General Evening Post*, 7–9 November 1771.

20. *OBP*, February 1766, trial of Anne Sullivan (t17660219–11).

21. John Beattie, *Policing and Punishment in London, 1660–1750* (Oxford, 2001), pp. 192–207, quote from p. 200; Elaine A. Reynolds, *Before the Bobbies: The Night Watch and Police Reform in Metropolitan London, 1720–1830* (Stanford, 1998), chaps 2–3; Ruth Paley, '"An Imperfect, Inadequate and Wretched System"? Policing London before Peel', *Criminal Justice History*, 10 (1989), p. 115.

22. *OBP*, June 1761, trial of Mary Smith (t17610625–10).

23. Ibid., July 1748, trial of William Clarenbolt (t17480706–21).

24. Ibid., December 1743, trial of Samuel Moses, Michael Jude and Solomon Athorn (t17431207–62).

25. *General Evening Post*, 21 December 1771.

26. *OBP*, January 1743, trial of Mary Williams (t17430114–38).

27. Ibid., October 1764, trial of Ann Wade (t17641017–19).

28. Ibid., December 1761, trial of Cicily Hicky (t17611209–36).

29. Malcolm Gaskill, 'The Displacement of Providence: Policing and Prosecution in Seventeenth- and Eighteenth-Century England', *Continuity and Change*, 11 (1996), pp. 348–51; Styles, 'Sir John Fielding', pp. 127–49; idem, 'Print and Policing: Crime Advertising in Eighteenth-Century Provincial England', in *Policing and Prosecution in Britain 1750–1850*, ed. D. Hay and F. Snyder (Oxford, 1989), pp. 55–111.

30. *OBP*, December 1736, trial of George Sutton and Robert Campbell (t17361208–39).

31. Ibid., April 1781, trial of Henry Drury (t17810425–8).

32. Ibid., April 1781, trial of Edward Fennell (t17810425–17); see also *General Evening Post*, 12 December 1780.

33. *OBP*, February 1757, trial of John Howland (t17570223–18).

34. Ibid., April 1721, trial of Margaret Allcock (t17210419–28).

35. Beattie, *Policing and Punishment*, pp. 315–18, 386–83, 401–17; 4 & 5 William & Mary, c. 8, cited by Leon Radzinowicz, *A History of English Criminal Law* (5 vols, London, 1948–90), ii, p. 29.

36. Tim Wales, 'Thief-Takers and their Clients in Later Stuart London', in *Londinopolis: Essays in the Cultural and Social History of Early Modern London*, eds Paul Griffiths and Mark S. R. Jenner (Manchester, 2000), pp. 67–84; Beattie, *Policing and Punishment*, chap. 5 and pp. 401–17; Gerald Howson, *Thief-Taker General: The Rise and Fall of Jonathan Wild* (London, 1970); Ruth Paley, 'Thief-Takers in London in the Age of the McDaniel Gang, *c.* 1745–1754', in *Policing and Prosecution in Britain*, ed. Hay and Snyder, pp. 301–40.

37. *OBP*, October 1720, trial of Thomas Tompion and Ann Tompion (t17201012–5).

38. Ibid., May 1739, trial of Joseph Casey (t17390502–54).

39. Howson, *Rise and Fall of Jonathan Wild*; Paley, 'Thief-Takers'.

40. *OBP*, September 1742, trial of George Anderson, Richard Studder and Henry Hinton (t17420909–25).

41. Beattie, *Policing and Punishment*, p. 415.

42. Henry Fielding, *An Enquiry into the Causes of the Late Increase of Robbers* (1751; Oxford, 1988, ed. M. R. Zirker), section 7, pp. 151–54.

43. Gilbert Armitage, *The History of the Bow Street Runners, 1729–1829* (London, 1932), pp. 47–59; Anthony Babington, *A House in Bow Street: Crime and the Magistracy in London, 1740–1881* (London, 1969), pp. 74ff; Radzinowicz, *History of English Criminal Law*, iii, pp. 54–58; Martin C. Battestin with Ruthe R. Battestin, *Henry Fielding: A Life* (London, 1989), pp. 502, 576–80.

44. The first use of the term 'runner' to refer to men employed by Justice Fielding in the *Old Bailey Proceedings* was in 1764 (September, trial of Edward Cook and William Miller [t17640912–15]), and the term was in common usage by the early 1770s.

45. Henry Fielding, *Covent Garden Journal*, 7 (25 January 1752); reprint ed. B. A. Goldgar (Oxford, 1988), p. 401.

46. *Public Advertiser*, 17 October and 20 December 1754.

47. John Fielding, *An Account of the Origin and Effects of a Police Set on Foot by His Grace the Duke of Newcastle in the Year 1753* (London, 1753), p. 34.

48. *OBP*, May 1756, trial of Charles Cane and Thomas Williams (t17560528–22); February 1781, trial of Ann Hunt (t17810222–7). John Fielding died in 1780, but the following year officers at Bow Street were still being referred to as 'his' men.

49. Ibid., April 1757, trial of John Gaul (t17570420–45); September 1757, trial of Brent Coleman et al. (t17570914–29).

50. Ibid., December 1765, trial of James Wilkins and Robert Scott (t17651211–6).

51. Ibid., May 1745, trial of Margaret Greenaway and Ann Rush (t17450530–20); February 1781, trial of Elizabeth Williams (t17810222–10; emphasis in original); John Fielding, *A Plan for Preventing Robberies within Twenty Miles of London: With an Account of the Rise and Establishment of the Real Thief-Takers* (London, 1755), p. 13.

52. *OBP*, February 1760, trial of Saunders Solomon (t17600227–33).

53. Ibid., December 1772, trial of Joseph Harrison and John Mitchell (t17721209–44).

54. *General Evening Post*, 29 April 1780.

55. P. Colquhoun, *A Treatise on the Police of the Metropolis* (1796; 7th edn, London, 1806; reprint edn, Montclair, New Jersey, 1969), p. 383.

56. Peter Clark, *British Clubs and Societies, 1580–1800* (Oxford, 2000).

57. [John] Trusler, *The London Adviser and Guide* (London, 1786), pp. 152–53.

58. David Philips, 'Good Men to Associate and Bad Men to Conspire: Associations for the Prosecution of Felons in England, 1760–1800', and Peter King, 'Prosecution Associations and their Impact in Eighteenth-Century Essex', in Hay and Snyder, ed., *Policing and Prosecution*, pp. 113–207; Adrian Shubert, 'Private Initiative in Law Enforcement: Associations for the Prosecution of Felons, 1744–1856', in Victor Bailey, ed., *Policing and Punishment in Nineteenth-Century Britain* (New Brunswick, New Jersey, 1981), pp. 25–41.

59. Radzinowicz, *History of English Criminal Law*, ii, p. 354; Peter D'Sena, 'Perquisites and Pilfering in the London Docks, 1700–1795' (M.Phil. thesis, Open University, 1986), pp. 107, 131; *London Evening Post*, 17 January 1751.

60. Philips, 'Good Men to Associate and Bad Men to Conspire', pp. 122, 168; CLRO, Misc. MS 115.9; Radzinowicz, *History of English Criminal Law*, iii, pp. 45–46.

61. Philips, 'Good Men to Associate and Bad Men to Conspire', pp. 152–66.

62. Fielding, *Enquiry into the Causes of the Late Increase of Robbers*, p. 151; *London Evening Post*, 24 December 1751; Colquhoun, *A Treatise on the Police of the Metropolis*, p. 510.

63. Saunders Welch, *Observations on the Office of Constable* (London, 1754), p. 6.

64. *OBP*, April 1763, trial of Charles O'Neal (t17630413–13).

65. Ibid., December 1772, trial of Joseph Harrison and John Mitchell (t17721209–44).

66. Ibid., January 1781, trial of Thomas Hodges (t17810110–24).

67. *London Evening Post,* 26 December 1741.

68. Ibid., 28 July 1741; *General Evening Post,* 25–27 April and 13–15 June 1780.

69. Fielding, *Plan for Preventing Robberies within Twenty Miles of London,* pp. 7–8.

70. *General Evening Post,* 28–30 May 1751; *Country Journal,* 4 April 1741; *London Evening Post,* 25–27 August 1761; *Morning Chronicle and London Advertiser,* 4 January 1780; *General Evening Post,* 25 January 1780.

71. *OBP,* December 1771, trial of Lyon Backeruc and Isaac Usher (t17711204–48); April 1781, trial of Charlotte Walker (t17810425–42).

72. LMA, OB/SP, July 1781, no. 54; *OBP,* July 1781, trial of Benjamin Fitter et al. (t17810711–5).

73. See below, Chapters, 4 and 5.

74. See below, Chapters 6 and 7.

75. Beattie, *Policing and Punishment,* pt 1; Reynolds, *Before the Bobbies,* chaps 1–5; Patrick Colquhoun, *A Treatise on the Functions and Duties of a Constable* (London, 1803), p. x; Faramerz Dabhoiwala, 'Sex, Social Relations and the Law in Seventeenth- and Eighteenth-Century London', in M. Braddick and J. Walter, eds, *Negotiating Power in Early Modern Society* (Cambridge, 2001), pp. 85–101.

## Notes to Chapter 3: Public Insults

1. LMA, DL/C 243, fol. 302v, *Smith* v. *Whitfield.*

2. Henry Hooton, *A Bridle for the Tongue* (London, 1709), p. 50.

3. Laura Gowing, *Domestic Dangers: Women, Words and Sex in Early Modern London* (Oxford, 1996); Randolph Trumbach, *Sex and the Gender Revolution,* i, *Homosexuality and the Third Gender in Enlightenment London* (Chicago and London, 1998); Tim Meldrum, 'A Women's Court in London: Defamation at the Bishop of London's Consistory Court, 1700–1745', *London Journal,* 19 (1994), pp. 1–20. For London defamation around the turn of the nineteenth century, see Anna Clark, 'Whores and Gossips: Sexual Reputation in London, 1770–1825', in A. Angerman et al., *Current Issues in Women's History* (London and New York, 1989), pp. 231–48.

4. Hooton, *Bridle for the Tongue,* p. 45.

5. CLRO, Sessions Papers, April 1729.

6. LMA, DL/C 631, fol. 127, *Dyke* v. *Parker.*

7. LMA, DL/C 255, fos 235, 362, *Brockett* v. *Seyrie.*

8. Ibid., fol. 238.

9. LMA, DL/C 147, fol. 238, *Branch* v. *Palmer.*

10. LMA, DL/C 144, fos 51–60, *Tamett* v. *Fletcher*.

11. For the political uses of such actions, see Mark S. R. Jenner, 'The Roasting of the Rump: Scatology and the Body Politic in Restoration England', *Past and Present*, 177 (2002), p. 98.

12. LMA, MJ/SR/2409, R.31 (August 1723), 2599, R.59 (September 1733), 2803, R.252 (September 1743).

13. See below, Chapter 4.

14. LMA, MJ/SR/1820, R.160 (September 1693).

15. LMA, MJ/SR/1762, R.173–74 (September 1690), 2762, R.139 (September 1743), 2845, R.231 (September 1745), 2884, R.255 (September 1747). Many of these activities were carried out by crowds: see below, Chapter 5.

16. Hooton, *Bridle for the Tongue*, pp. 40, 43.

17. Based on a sample of 125 cases for which depositions survive between 1679 and 1792, as described in the Appendix.

18. *The Art of Governing a Wife, with Rules for Batchelors* (London, 1747), pp. 87–88; Clark, 'Whores and Gossips', p. 238.

19. Faramerz Dabhoiwala, 'The Pattern of Sexual Immorality in Seventeenth- and Eighteenth-Century London', in Paul Griffiths and Mark S. R. Jenner, eds, *Londinopolis: Essays in the Cultural and Social History of Early Modern London* (Manchester, 2000), pp. 86–106.

20. LMA, MJ/SR/1289, R.114 (July 1664).

21. Trumbach, *Sex and the Gender Revolution*, p. 45.

22. LMA, DL/C/156, fol. 83, *Heard* v. *Wilkinson*, 262, fol. 160, *Merchant* v. *Ingram*, 147, fol. 228, *Smith* v. *Walsh*.

23. These figures are based on a sample of 358 cases recorded in the consistory court act books, allegation, libel and sentence books and deposition books, as described in the Appendix. See also Trumbach, *Sex and the Gender Revolution*, pp. 25–26.

24. Keith Thomas, 'The Double Standard', *Journal of the History of Ideas*, 20 (1959).

25. LMA, DL/C 156, fol. 48, *Fletcher* v. *Hilson*, 171, fol. 354, *Gaskell* v. *Lever*.

26. LMA, DL/C 156, fos 126–27, *Marlow* v. *Bruce*. See also Trumbach, *Sex and the Gender Revolution*, pp. 41–44.

27. Jennine Hurl, '"She Being Bigg with Child is Likely to Miscarry": Pregnant Victims Prosecuting Assault in Westminster, 1685–1720', *London Journal*, 24 (1999), p. 29.

28. LMA, MJ/SR/2369, R.115 (July 1721), 2096, R.49–51 (September 1707).

29. LMA, MJ/SR/3118, R.327 (September 1761); Gowing, *Domestic Dangers*, pp. 80, 103.

30. LMA, MJ/SR/1651, R.175 (September 1684).

31. LMA, DL/C 240, fol. 50, *Winterbottom v. Burton*.

32. LMA, MJ/SR/2488, R.113 (August 1727).

33. LMA, DL/C 276, fol. 1, *Alendon v. Hiam*.

34. LMA, MJ/SR/1273, R.131, 111 (August 1663).

35. Daniel Defoe, *The Complete English Tradesman* (1726; Gloucester, 1987), p. 134; Donna Andrew, 'The Press and Public Apologies in Eighteenth-Century London', in N. Landau, ed., *Law, Crime and English Society, 1660–1830* (Cambridge, 2002), pp. 220–23; Trumbach, *Sex and the Gender Revolution*, pp. 53–54; Julian Hoppit, 'The Use and Abuse of Credit in Eighteenth-Century England', in N. McKendrick and R. B. Outhwaite, eds, *Business Life and Public Policy* (Cambridge, 1986), pp. 64–65; Craig Muldrew, *The Economy of Obligation: The Culture of Credit and Social Relations in Early Modern England* (Basingstoke, 1998).

36. LMA, MJ/SR/1651, R.173 (September 1684).

37. LMA, MJ/SR/1434, R.305 (September 1672), 2016, R.105 (September 1703), 1651, R.195 (September 1684); Jessica Warner and Frank Ivis, '"Damn You, You Informing Bitch": *Vox Populi* and the Unmaking of the Gin Act of 1736', *Journal of Social History*, 33 (1999), pp. 299–330.

38. LMA, MJ/SR/1472, R.66 (September 1674).

39. CLRO, Sessions Papers, May 1692. See also below, Chapters 6 and 7.

40. [Richard Allestree], *The Ladies Calling, in Two Parts* (Oxford, 1673), p. 48; [Richard Allestree], *The Government of the Tongue* (Oxford, 1674), p. 73.

41. Hooton, *A Bridle for the Tongue*, pp. 5, 37; [Béat-Louis de Muralt], *Letters Describing the Character and Customs of the English and French Nations ... Translated from the French* (London, 1726), p. 83; Defoe, *Complete English Tradesman*, pp. 133–34.

42. See also Trumbach, *Sex and the Gender Revolution*, pp. 31–32; Anna Clark, *The Struggle for the Breeches: Gender and the Making of the British Working Class* (Berkeley, 1995), p. 56.

43. Andrew, 'The Press and Public Apologies', p. 220.

44. J. S., *A Brief Anatomie of Women: Being an Invective Against, and Apologie for, the Bad and the Good of that Sexe* (London, 1653), p. 2; *The Ladies Cabinet: or A Companion for the Toilet* (London, 1743), pp. 10–15.

45. *An Account of a Great and Famous Scolding Match* (London, 1699). In 1721 the *Weekly Journal: or British Gazetteer* reported on 22 July that 'some time next week a match of scolding is to be had at Battersea, between four women for a Holland smock'.

46. *Low-Life: or One Half of the World Knows Not How the Other Half Live* (2nd edn, London, [1750]), pp. 74, 92.

47. Patricia M. Spacks, *Gossip* (New York, 1985), chap. 6.

48. LMA, DL/C 31, 33–34, 36–54, 79, 81, 145–85; *Parliamentary Papers*, 199 (xxiv) (1831–32), Report of the Royal Commission to Enquire into the Practice and Jurisdiction of the Ecclesiastical Courts, pp. 63, 379. Estimates for population were derived from: Vanessa Harding, 'The Population of London, 1550–1700: A Review of the Published Evidence', *London Journal*, 15 (1990), p. 112; E. A. Wrigley, 'A Simple Model of London's Importance in Changing English Society and Economy, 1650–1750', *Past and Present*, 37 (1967), p. 44.

49. *Parliamentary Papers*, Report of the Royal Commission, pp. 63, 379; 18 & 19 Victoria c. 41.

50. Lawrence Stone, *Road to Divorce: A History of the Making and Breaking of Marriage in England* (Oxford, 1990), p. 428; Trumbach, *Sex and the Gender Revolution*, p. 25.

51. It has been argued that the decline in church court prosecutions was the result of an increasing unwillingness by officials to have allegations of bad language and vulgar sexual behaviour discussed in their courtrooms. But no evidence of this alleged change of attitudes among court officials has been provided. See Trumbach, *Sex and the Gender Revolution*, p. 24; Meldrum, 'A Women's Court in London'.

52. Robert B. Shoemaker, 'The Decline of Public Insult in London, 1660–1800', *Past and Present*, 169 (2000), pp. 106–8. The trial notes of Lord Mansfield, which cover the period from 1756 to 1786, include about eight defamation cases a year, but some were from outside London: James Oldham, *The Mansfield Manuscripts and the Growth of English Law in the Eighteenth Century*, 2 vols (Chapel Hill, 1992), i, p. 187.

53. LMA, MJ/SBB/408, p. 47 (October 1683).

54. Joseph Shaw, *The Practical Justice of Peace*, 2 vols (London, 1728), i, p. 189; Hooton, *Bridle for the Tongue*, p. 40.

55. See below, Chapter 5.

56. Ruth Perry, 'Colonizing the Breast: Sexuality and Maternity in Eighteenth-Century England', *Journal of the History of Sexuality*, 2 (1991), pp. 208–13; Robert B. Shoemaker, *Gender in English Society, 1650–1850: The Emergence of Separate Spheres?* (London, 1998), pp. 61–65.

57. LMA, MJ/SR/2522, R.43 (September 1729), 2721, R.82 (August 1739).

58. See below, Chapter 6.

59. LMA, WJ/SP/1772/January/21.

60. LMA, MJ/SR/2332, R.90 (September 1719).

61. LMA, DL/C 638, fol. 63, *Callthrup* v. *Bowman*, 283, fol. 566 *Jarman* v. *Sanders*.

62. LMA, DL/C 240, fol. 49r, *Field* v. *Holgate*, fol. 59r, *Davis* v. *Simpson*.

63. LMA, DL/C 283, pp. 683–89, *White* v. *Bower* (emphasis added).

64. Elizabeth Foyster, *Manhood in Early Modern England: Honour, Sex and Marriage* (Harlow, 1999), p. 154.

65. Lincoln's Inn Library, Transcript of Dudley Ryder's law notes by K. L. Perrin, document 16, fol. 19; Oldham, *Mansfield Manuscripts*, i, p. 187.

66. *The Trial of the Cause wherein Richard Kempster ... was Plaintiff, and John Farhill, Esq. ... was Defendant, for Defamation of Perjury* (London, 1795), p. 5.

67. LMA, DL/C 284, fol. 12, *Barmore* v. *Morris*.

68. LMA, DL/C 638, fol. 45, *Branham* v. *Pratt*.

69. LMA, DL/C 276, fol. 453, *Littlejohn* v. *Forshaw*; 283, fol. 683, *White* v. *Bower*. See also Karl Westhauser, 'The Power of Conversation: The Evolution of Modern Social Relations in Augustan London' (Brown University Ph.D. thesis, 1994), p. 380.

70. Whitlocke Bulstrode, *The Second Charge of Whitlocke Bulstrode, Esq.: To the Grand Jury and Other Juries of the County of Middlesex* (London, 1718), repr. in *Charges to the Grand Jury, 1689–1803*, ed. Georges Lamoine, Camden Society, fourth series, 43 (London, 1992), p. 118.

71. William Gearing, *A Bridle for the Tongue: or A Treatise of Ten Sins of the Tongue* (London, 1663), epistle dedicatory; *A Bridle for the Tongue: or A Curb to Evil Discourse: Published to Regulate the Great Abuses in Coffee Houses, Taverns, Ale-Houses, etc.* (London, 1678), p. 4; Hooton, *Bridle for the Tongue*, p. 36.

72. [George Berkeley], *The Ladies' Library*, 3 vols (London, 1714), i, pp. 421, 425; *The Whole Duty of Woman: or An Infallible Guide to the Fair Sex* (London, 1737), p. 96; Spacks, *Gossip*, p. 145.

73. [Berkeley], *Ladies' Library*, i, p. 429; Josiah Woodward, *The Baseness and Perniciousness of the Sin of Slandering and Back-Biting* (London, 1706; 3rd edn, 1729), pp. 16–17.

74. *Gentleman's Magazine*, 37 (April 1767), p. 158; *The New Whole Duty of Man* (London, 1745), p. 308; William Hutton, *A Journey from Birmingham to London* (Birmingham, 1785), p. 193; OBP, December 1793, trial of David Davis (t17931204–64); Robert B. Shoemaker, 'Reforming Male Manners: Public Insult and the Decline of Violence in London, 1660–1740', in T. Hitchcock and M. Cohen, eds, *English Masculinities, 1660–1800* (London, 1999), pp. 147–48; John Tosh, *A Man's Place: Masculinity and the Middle-Class Home in Victorian England* (London, 1999), p. 112.

75. See below, Chapter 9.

76. Judith Walkowitz, 'Male Vice and Feminist Virtue: Feminism and the

Politics of Prostitution in Nineteenth-Century Britain', *History Workshop Journal*, 13 (1982), p. 86

77. Polly Morris, 'Defamation and Sexual Reputation in Somerset, 1733–1850' (University of Warwick Ph.D. thesis, 1985), p. 217; Barry Till, 'The Ecclesiastical Courts of York, 1660–1883: A Study of Decline' (unpublished typescript, Borthwick Institute, 1963), p. 250; *Parliamentary Papers*, Report of the Royal Commission, p. 63.

## Notes to Chapter 4: Shaming Punishments

1. LMA, MJ/SBB/408, p. 47 (October 1683). Despite this plea, the ducking stool was not used in this period.

2. Guildhall Library, MSS 9180, 9846, 11,168 (orders of penance, 1720–24, 1727–30, 1763–1805); BL, Add. MS 38715, fos 1–24 (certificates of penance).

3. BL, Add. MS 27826, fol. 172.

4. *OBP*, December 1717, trial of Jasper Arnold and William Goddard (t17171204-33).

5. A. Knapp and W. Baldwin, *The New Newgate Calendar* (London, [1819]), ii, pp. 83–85.

6. *Morning Chronicle, and London Advertiser*, no. 5468, 22 November 1786.

7. *The Life and Infamous Actions of that Perjur'd Villain John Waller* (London, 1732), p. 28; *M. Misson's Memoirs and Observations in his Travels over England*, trans. J. Ozell (London, 1719), p. 218.

8. William Hawkins, *A Treatise of Pleas of the Crown*, 2 vols ([London], 1716–21), ii, p. 445.

9. *OBP*, January 1737, trial of John Warwick, Christopher Baws and John Wills (t17370114-27); May 1752, trial of Thomas Jones alias James Derrick (t17520514-34).

10. Faramerz Dabhoiwala, 'Sex, Social Relations and the Law in Seventeenth- and Eighteenth-Century London', in M. Braddick and J. Walter, eds, *Negotiating Power in Early Modern Society* (Cambridge, 2001), p. 91.

11. LMA, MJ/SBP/14 (December 1741).

12. *OBP*, January 1768, trial of Elizabeth Bond (t17680114-42).

13. See, for example, the sentence carried out on Robert Raw in 1797: TNA, T90/168.

14. César de Saussure, *A Foreign View of England in 1725–1729* (trans. and ed. M. van Muyden, 1902; reprint edn London, 1995), p. 212; *M. Misson's Memoirs*, p. 218.

15. J. M. Beattie, *Crime and the Courts in England, 1660–1800* (Princeton, 1986), p. 463; LMA, MJ/SBB/1058, pp. 49–50 (December 1748); [S. Emlyn, ed.], *A*

*Complete Collection of State Trials*, 6 vols (London, 1730), i, p. xi. When a man convicted of defrauding several tradesmen in 1752 was ordered to be severely whipped, the authorities ensured that the punishment would be properly carried out by placing the high constable in the cart to oversee the work of the executioner, and two constables in front of the horses to prevent the driver from going too fast: Henry Fielding, *Covent Garden Journal*, 5 (18 January 1752); reprint ed. B. A. Goldgar (Oxford, 1988), p. 460.

16. LMA, MJ/SP/1691/Feb/8; *An Appeal to the Public: or The Case of Mr Isaac Broderick* ([London], 1731), p. 56.

17. LMA, MJ/SP/1725/Jan/36.

18. G. Parker, *A View of Society and Manners in High and Low Life*, 2 vols (London, 1781), ii, p. 75.

19. James Boswell, *Life of Johnson* (1791; reprint edn, ed. R. W. Chapman, Oxford, 1970), p. 965.

20. LMA, WJ/SP/1768/10/35. See also MJ/SP/1749/07/17; MJ/SP/1751/01/19; MJ/SP/1760/10, bundle six (petition of George Steed).

21. *London Journal*, 10–12 and 12–15 September 1741.

22. Peter Linebaugh, 'The Tyburn Riot against the Surgeons', in D. Hay et al., *Albion's Fatal Tree: Crime and Society in Eighteenth-Century England* (Harmondsworth, 1977), pp. 67, 116.

23. BL, Add. MS 61618, fol. 91.

24. 25 George II, c. 37.

25. Robert B. Shoemaker, *Prosecution and Punishment: Petty Crime and the Law in London and Rural Middlesex, c. 1660–1725* (Cambridge, 1992), p. 162.

26. Guildhall Library, MSS 9180, 9846, 11,168 (orders of penance 1720–24, 1727–30, 1763–1805); BL, Add. MS 38715, fols 1–24 (certificates of penance).

27. For such punishments a century earlier, see M. Ingram, *Church Courts, Sex and Marriage in England, 1570–1640* (Cambridge, 1987), p. 294.

28. LMA, DL/C/175, fos 3–16 (*Arrowsmith v. Waterhouse*); 255, fol. 461 (*Brown v. Atwell*); 276, fol. 313 (*Elliott v. Babtezta*).

29. LMA, DL/C/118, fol. 15v (*McManus v. McManus*), fol. 55r (*White v. Bower*); *Parliamentary Papers*, 199 (xxiv) (1831–32), 'Report of the Royal Commission to Enquire into the Practice and Jurisdiction of the Ecclesiastical Courts', p. 63.

30. TNA, E197/32–4; T64/262; T90/146–47, 165–69.

31. 2 George II, c. 25; R. McGowen, 'From Pillory to Gallows: The Punishment of Forgery in the Age of the Financial Revolution', *Past and Present*, 165 (1999).

32. 56 George III, c. 138 (1816); 1 Victoria, c. 23 (1837). For the events which

led to the 1816 Bill, see G. T. Smith, 'Civilised People Don't Want to See That Kind of Thing: The Decline of Public Physical Punishment in London, 1760–1840', in C. Strange, ed., *Qualities of Mercy* (Vancouver, 1996), pp. 35–37.

33. LMA, MJ/SBB/728–956 (1715–38) and MJ/SPB14 (January-December 1741), passim. The first example of the phrase 'private whipping' in the *Old Bailey Proceedings* was in October 1723 (trial of Jane Kelley, t17231016–14), and the first instance I have found in the sessions records occurred in 1733: MJ/SBB/912, p. 71 (October 1733). For the use of this distinction in the City of London in 1734, see J. M. Beattie, *Policing and Punishment* (Oxford, 2001), p. 444. For similar developments in other counties, see Beattie, *Crime and the Courts*, pp. 461, 614; J. S. Cockburn, 'Punishment and Brutalization in the English Enlightenment', *Law and History Review*, 12 (1994), p. 172; P. King, *Crime, Justice and Discretion in England, 1740–1820* (Oxford, 2000), pp. 272–73; and Gwenda Morgan and Peter Rushton, *Rogues, Thieves and the Rule of Law: The Problem of Law Enforcement in North-East England, 1718–1800* (London, 1998), p. 134. Although there was initially some uncertainty about the legality of this punishment for felons, it was given statutory approval in 1779: Cockburn, 'Punishment and Brutalization', p. 172; Beattie, *Crime and the Courts*, pp. 544–45.

34. See, for example, the description of a whipping in Bridewell in Ned Ward, *The London Spy* (1698–99; East Lansing Michigan, 1993, ed. by P. Hyland), p. 110.

35. LMA, MJ/SBB/827, p. 50 (1724); 829, pp. 59–61 (1725).

36. Sheriff's Cravings for London and Middlesex, TNA, T64/262 (1757), T90/166 (1788).

37. Robert B. Shoemaker, 'Streets of Shame? The Crowd and Public Punishments in London, 1700–1820', in P. Griffiths and S. Devereaux, ed., *Penal Practice and Culture, 1500–1900* (forthcoming), table 1.

38. Parker, *A View of Society and Manners*, ii, p. 75.

39. *OBP*, June 1783, trial of William Jenkins (t17830604–3); TNA, T90/167 (1790).

40. *OBP*, May 1727, trial of John Aberall (t17270517–31); April 1719, trial of Augustine Moore (t17190408–24); December 1761, trial of Mary Cowen (t17611209–35).

41. LMA, MJ/OC/III, fol. 160; TNA, T90/167.

42. Andrea MacKenzie, 'Lives of the Most Notorious Criminals: Popular Literature of Crime in England, 1675–1775' (Ph.D. dissertation, University of Toronto, 1999), chap. 9.

43. P. Rawlings, *Crime and Power: A History of Criminal Justice, 1688–1988*

(London, 1999), pp. 51–53; Bernard Turner and Thomas Skinner, *An Account of Some Alterations and Amendments Attempted in the Duty and Office of the Sheriff of the County of Middlesex and Sheriffs of the City of London* (London, 1784), p. 29; S. Wilf, 'Imagining Justice: Aesthetics and Public Executions in Late Eighteenth-Century England', *Yale Journal of Law and the Humanities*, 5 (1993–94), pp. 70–74.

44. J. A. Sharpe, *Judicial Punishment in England* (London, 1990); Beattie, *Crime and the Courts*, chaps 9–10; C. Emsley, *Crime and Society in England, 1750–1900*, 2nd edn (London, 1996), chap. 10.

45. Randall McGowen, 'The Body and Punishment in Eighteenth-Century England', *Journal of Modern History*, 59 (1987), pp. 651–79.

46. J. M. Beattie, 'Violence and Society in Early-Modern England', in A. N. Doob and E. L. Greenspan, ed., *Perspectives in Criminal Law* (Aurora, Ontario, 1985), pp. 50–51; D. T. Andrew, 'The Code of Honour and its Critics: The Opposition to Duelling in England, 1700–1850', *Social History*, 5 (1980), pp. 409–34. For duelling, see also below, Chapter 7.

47. Beattie, *Crime and the Courts*, pp. 138, 616. See also R. McGowen, 'Punishing Violence, Sentencing Crime', in N. Armstrong and L. Tennenhouse, ed., *The Violence of Representation* (London, 1989), pp. 140–56; J. Sharpe, 'Civility, Civilizing Processes and the End of Public Punishment in England', in P. Burke et al., eds, *Civil Histories: Essays Presented to Sir Keith Thomas* (Oxford, 2000), pp. 215–30; G. T. Smith, 'The State and the Culture of Violence in London, 1760–1840' (Ph.D. dissertation, University of Toronto, 1999), chap. 7.

48. P. Colquhoun, *A Treatise on the Functions and Duties of a Constable* (London, 1803), p. 18; *Parliamentary History*, 21 (London, 1814), col. 389.

49. *Gentleman's Magazine*, 26 (1756), p. 166.

50. 56 George III, c. 75; Shoemaker, 'Streets of Shame?', table 2.

51. *OBP*, June 1783, trial of Mary Siddon alias Field (t17830604–5).

52. *The Laws Respecting Women* (London, 1777), p. 344; V. A. C. Gatrell, *The Hanging Tree: Execution and the English People, 1770–1868* (Oxford, 1994), pp. 336–38; King, *Crime, Justice and Discretion*, p. 286; Ruth Campbell, 'Sentence of Death by Burning for Women', *Journal of Legal History*, 5 (1984), pp. 44–59; A. D. Harvey, 'Research Note: Burning Women at the Stake in Eighteenth-Century England', *Criminal Justice History*, 11 (1990), pp. 193–95.

53. 57 George III, c. 75; Emsley, *Crime and Society in England*, p. 249; David Bentley, *English Criminal Justice in the Nineteenth Century* (London, 1998), p. 12.

54. Cockburn, 'Punishment and Brutalization', pp. 177–78; King, *Crime, Justice*

*and Discretion*, p. 273; L. Radzinowicz and R. Hood, *The Emergence of Penal Policy in Victorian and Edwardian England* (Oxford, 1990), pp. 689–711; J. R. Dinwiddy, 'The Early Nineteenth-Century Campaign against Flogging in the Army', *English History Review*, 97 (1982), pp. 319–20.

55. Gatrell, *Hanging Tree*, pp. 595–97.

56. [R. Holloway], *The Phoenix of Sodom: or The Vere Street Coterie* (London, 1813), newspaper clipping pasted in front of British Library copy (shelf-mark: Cup.364.p. 12).

57. *Mr William Fuller's Trip to Bridewell: With a True Account of his Barbarous Usage in the Pillory* (1703), pp. 2–4; TNA, SP35/44, 30 July–3 August 1723; *London Evening Post*, 27–29 May 1755.

58. TNA, SP35/44, 30 July–3 August 1723; SP 44/290, p. 56.

59. R. Paley, 'Thief-Takers in London in the Age of the McDaniel Gang, c. 1745–1754', in D. Hay and F. Snyder, ed., *Policing and Prosecution in Britain, 1750–1850* (Oxford, 1989), p. 335.

60. [Emlyn, ed.], *Complete Collection of State Trials*, i, p. xi.

61. *Daily Universal Register* (*The Times*), 23 November 1786, p. 2b, and 28 November, p. 2c.

62. TNA, T90/165 (London and Middlesex, 1787); *General Advertiser*, 22 November 1786.

63. Cockburn, 'Punishment and Brutalization', pp. 171–72.

64. Linebaugh, 'Tyburn Riot against the Surgeons', p. 101.

65. Gatrell, *Hanging Tree*, pp. 602–4; *The Times*, 1 August 1788.

66. *Original Weekly Journal*, 25 July 1719; B. R. Burg, *Sodomy and the Perception of Evil: English Sea Rovers in the Seventeenth-Century Caribbean* (New York and London, 1983), pp. 35–36. According to the *Weekly Journal: or Saturday's Post* (25 July 1719), he was also pelted with cats.

67. Shoemaker, 'Streets of Shame', table 3.

68. TNA, SP35/44, 30 July–3 August 1723; *Mr William Fuller's Trip to Bridewell*, pp. 1–7; *Phoenix of Sodom*, newspaper clippings pasted in front; *The Life and Infamous Actions of that Perjur'd Villain John Waller*, p. 29.

69. *Gentleman's Magazine*, 50 (1780), p. 243; 51 (1781), p. 61; TNA, T1/556/390; Smith, 'Decline of Public Physical Punishment in London', p. 33.

70. Colquhoun, *Treatise*, p. 18. See also *The Duty of Constables* (Gloucester, 1790), p. 35.

71. *General Evening Post*, 31 August 1780.

72. P. R. Backscheider, *Daniel Defoe: His Life* (Baltimore and London, 1989), p. 118; TNA, SP35/12, fol. 225; *Gentleman's Magazine*, 35 (1765), p. 96.

73. *Gentleman's Magazine*, 26 (1756), p. 166.

74. BL, Add. MS 27826, p. 180.

75. BL, Add. MS 27826, p. 179. Frost's ill health was used to justify this decision: TNA, T90/168 (1793); *The Times*, 6 and 19 December 1793; J. Epstein, 'Spatial Practices/Democratic Vistas', *Social History*, 24 (1999), p. 300.

76. King, *Crime, Justice and Discretion*, p. 351; Fielding, *Covent Garden Journal*, 14 (18 February 1752), p. 469; *OBP*, July 1735, trial of John Brown (t17350702–61).

77. Gatrell, *Hanging Tree*, pp. 100–1; *Weekly Journal: or British Gazetteer*, 15 July 1721; *London Journal*, 3–5 June 1735 (for his trial, see *OBP*, May 1735, trial of Samuel Gregory, t17350522–20) and 29 May 1725.

78. Peter Linebaugh, *The London Hanged: Crime and Civil Society in the Eighteenth Century* (London, 1991), pp. 363–64. These riots are discussed below in Chapter 5.

79. Henry Fielding, *An Enquiry into the Late Increase of Robbers* (London, 1751; reprint edn, ed. M. R. Zirker, Oxford, 1988), p. 167; Linebaugh, 'Tyburn Riot against the Surgeons', pp. 66, 112; Saussure, *Foreign View of England*, p. 77; Bernard Mandeville, *An Enquiry into the Causes of the Frequent Executions at Tyburn* (London, 1725), pp. 20–24; Fielding, *Covent Garden Journal*, 55 (18 July 1752), p. 447.

80. Thomas Laqueur, 'Crowds, Carnival and the State in English Executions, 1604–1868', in A. Beier et al., eds, *The First Modern Society* (Cambridge, 1989), pp. 305–56; Linebaugh, 'Tyburn Riots against the Surgeons', pp. 109–10; Gatrell, *Hanging Tree*; McGowen, 'The Body and Punishment'.

81. Fielding, *Enquiry into the Late Increase of Robbers*, p. 168; *General Evening Post*, 21–23 November 1780.

82. King, *Crime, Justice and Discretion*, p. 351; *Daily Universal Register (The Times)*, 7 June 1786.

83. *R. v. Ford*, 2 Salk. 390, in *The English Reports*, 178 vols (London and Edinburgh, 1900–32), xci, p. 595. In 1755 the same principle was extended to those punished by whipping: *Pendock v. MacKender*, 2 Wils. 18, *English Reports*, xcv, p. 662.

84. McGowen, 'From Pillory to Gallows', p. 123.

85. *London Evening Post*, 4–6 March 1756; LMA, OB/SP/October 1786, no. 64; *OBP*, September 1790, trial of Samuel Clarke (t17900915–98).

86. BL, Add. MS 27826, fos 172–73.

87. *Exaltation! The Throne. The Pillory* [1820?] (emphasis in original).

88. *OBP*, December 1781, trial of Luke Hughes (t17811205–21; emphasis added).

89. Guildhall Library image database, http://collage.cityoflondon.gov.uk, especially image numbers 6354, 18297, 18842, 18849–51; and 'The Pillory at Charing Cross' by Thomas Rowlandson and Augustus Pugin (1809), LMA, SC/PZ/WE/02/167.

90. For the role played by print in undermining the impact of the pillory, see below, Chapter 9.

91. BL, Add. MS 27826, fol. 174.

92. TNA, SP35/44, 30 July–3 August 1723.

93. *The Times*, 27 July 1796, p. 3c, and 6 July 1797, p. 3a.

94. *London Evening Post*, 27 October 1761; *An Appeal to the Public: or The Case of Mr Isaac Broderick*, p. 60.

95. *Daily Universal Register* (*The Times*), 17 February 1786, p. 3d.

96. *London Journal*, 12–15 September 1741; Turner and Skinner, *Account of Some Alterations and Amendments*, p. 23; Gatrell, *Hanging Tree*, pp. 96, 101–2 and chapter 8.

97. *Gentleman's Magazine* 54 (1784), pp. 18–19; *M. Misson's Memoirs*, pp. 123–24. See also Saussure, *Foreign View of England*, pp. 77–78.

98. Turner and Skinner, *An Account of Some Alterations and Amendments*, pp. 25–26; John Scott, *Observations on the Present State of the Parochial and Vagrant Poor* (London, 1773), p. 134; Randall McGowen, 'Civilizing Punishment: The End of the Public Execution in England', *Journal of British Studies*, 33 (1994), p. 260; Gatrell, *Hanging Tree*, pp. 259–72, 282.

## Notes to Chapter 5: Crowds and Riots

1. This chapter builds on a vast body of distinguished scholarship on this subject (see, in addition to this chapter's notes, the Select Bibliography). Most work, however, has studied popular protest from the viewpoint of its role in the history of political radicalism, and has concentrated on the largest and most dramatic riots of the century, neglecting in the process the much more frequent smaller scale riots (expressing a much wider variety of grievances) which were more characteristic of the London mob, and which formed the essential background to the better-known disturbances. Historians have rarely stepped back from their analysis of individual instances of riot and the content of the grievances expressed to examine the phenomenon of crowd protest *per se*; that is, to examine these repeated patterns of behaviour as a common phenomenon, and to explain why this habit of taking to the streets developed and why it changed over the course of the century. That is what this chapter seeks to do.

2. Edward Chamberlayne, *Angliae Notitia* (18th edn, London, 1694), p. 458; Robert Ferguson, *The History of All the Mobs, Tumults and Insurrections in Great Britain* (London, 1715), p. 53.

3. Nicholas Rogers, 'Popular Protest in Early Hanoverian London', *Past and Present*, 79 (1978), pp. 91–94.

4. BL, Add MS, 61610, fos 95, 111.

5. LMA, DL/C/272, fos 232–33, testimony of Sarah Miller.

6. See above, Chapter 2.

7. CLRO, Sessions File 758, October 1738, cited by Jessica Warner and Frank Ivis, '"Damn You, You Informing Bitch": Vox Populi and the Unmaking of the Gin Act of 1736', Journal of Social History, 33 (1999), p. 299.

8. OBP, July 1719, trial of John Larmony (t17190708–57).

9. OBP, September 1716, trial of Robert Read (t17160906–1).

10. BL, Add. MS 61610, fos 8, 98; M. Grosley, A Tour to London: or New Observations on England, and its Inhabitants (London, 1772), p. 88.

11. TNA, KB 1/1, 3 February 1720/1, deposition of John Fuller; T1/468, fos 265–73, testimony of Wood.

12. Journals of the House of Commons, xi, pp. 682–83, 29 January 1696/97; OBP, September 1749, trial of John Willson, Bosavern Pen Lez and Benjamin Launder (t17490906–4).

13. BL, Add. MS 34712, fos 49, 109.

14. General Evening Post, 4–6 July 1780; TNA, KB 8/79, fol. 140.

15. LMA, OB/SP/1784/May/49.

16. W. S. Lewis et al., eds, Horace Walpole's Correspondence (48 volumes, London, 1937–83), xxvii p. 196 (12 November 1741).

17. A. J. Henderson, London and the National Government, 1721–42 (Durham, North Carolina, 1945), p. 155; J. Paul de Castro, The Gordon Riots (London, 1926), p. 156.

18. Tim Harris, 'London Crowds and the Revolution of 1688', in E. Cruickshanks, ed., By Force or Default? The Revolution of 1688–89 (Edinburgh, 1989), p. 56; LMA, MJ/SP/1768/Sept/47; Rogers, 'Popular Protest in Early Hanoverian London', pp. 73, 79.

19. London Evening Post, 14–16 and 16–18 May 1765.

20. P. D. G. Thomas, 'The St George's Fields "Massacre" of 10 May 1768: An Eye Witness Report', London Journal, 4 (1978), p. 223.

21. de Castro, The Gordon Riots, p. 30; TNA, TS 11/981, fol. 25; Annual Register, 28 March 1768.

22. David Cressy, Bonfires and Bells: National Memory and the Protestant Calendar in Elizabethan and Stuart England (London, 1989), pp. 80–87; Weekly Journal: or British Gazetteer, 22 April 1721.

23. O. W. Furley, 'The Pope-Burning Processions of the Late Seventeenth Century', History, 44 (1959), pp. 16–23; Sheila Williams, 'The Pope-Burning Processions of 1679, 1680, 1681', Journal of the Warburg and Courtauld Institutes, 21 (1958), pp. 104–18; James L. Fitts, 'Newcastle's Mob', Albion, 5 (1973), pp. 42, 46; Rogers, 'Popular Protest in Early Hanoverian London',

pp. 77–78, 80; John Stevenson, *Popular Disturbances in England, 1700–1832* (2nd edn, London, 1992) p. 77; *Weekly Journal: or British Gazetteer*, 11 March 1721; *London Evening Post*, 23–25 and 25–27 June 1761.

24. *London Evening Post*, 8 September 1761.

25. *Daily Post*, 13 November 1741.

26. CLRO, Misc. MS 3.5.

27. TNA, T1/468, fos 265–73. See also John Brewer, 'The Number 45: A Wilkite Symbol', in S. B. Baxter, ed., *England's Rise to Greatness* (Berkeley, 1983), pp. 349–80.

28. Bodleian Library, Rawl. MS D.862, fol. 83, cited by Nicholas Rogers, *Whigs and Cities: Popular Politics in the Age of Pitt* (Oxford, 1989), p. 361.

29. Rogers, 'Popular Protest in Early Hanoverian London', p. 72.

30. *General Evening Post*, 8–11 October 1774.

31. E. E. Reynolds, ed., *The Mawhood Diary*, Catholic Record Society (London, 1956), p. 83.

32. TNA, SP 37/8, fol. 101.

33. de Castro, *The Gordon Riots*, p. 92.

34. *OBP*, September 1715, trial of Bolton Freeman and Thomas Page (t17150907–7); TNA, SP35/12/96, fol. 218.

35. BL, Add. MS, 61610, fol. 97.

36. *OBP*, October 1716, trial of John Nash (t17161010–1); May 1768, trial of Daniel Saxton (t17680518–23); July 1768, trial of Thomas Woodcock (t17680706–62); February 1769, trial of John Williams (t17690222–63).

37. TNA, SP 44/130, fol. 111.

38. *London Evening Post*, 7–10 October 1738.

39. Ibid., 2–5 June 1744.

40. *General Evening Post*, 6–8 December 1774.

41. TNA, ADM 77/1, no. 39 (newsletter dated 2 December 1679).

42. BL, Add. MS 61610, fol. 15.

43. Tim Hitchcock, *Down and Out in Eighteenth-Century London* (forthcoming); Rogers, *Whigs and Cities*, p. 360; BL, Add. MS 61610, fol. 15; LMA, MJ/SP/1695/July/45–51 (it was alleged that Page was a Catholic and may have participated in this ritual voluntarily); *OBP*, July 1768, trial of Woodcock.

44. Cressy, *Bonfires and Bells*, p. 183; LMA, MJ/SP/1695/July/45–51; *OBP*, September 1715, trial of Thomas Cotton and Charles Warren (t17150907–13); *London Evening Post*, 30 January–1 February 1735.

45. K. J. Lindley, 'Riot Prevention and Control in Early Stuart London', *Transactions of the Royal Historical Society*, 5th series, 33 (1983), pp. 109–10.

46. Harris, 'London Crowds and the Revolution of 1688', pp. 53–54.

47. James Sutherland, *The Restoration Newspaper and its Development* (Cambridge, 1986), p. 75. In addition, there were politically motivated attacks on London brothels on Easter Sunday in 1668: Tim Harris, 'The Bawdy House Riots of 1668', *Historical Journal*, 29 (1986), pp. 537–56.

48. *OBP*, October 1716, trial of Nash (emphasis added); TNA, TS 11/981/3592, fol. 25 (testimony of Samuel Solomons).

49. de Castro, *The Gordon Riots*, p. 123; TNA, KB 8/79, fol. 199.

50. Lincoln's Inn Library, Transcript of Dudley Ryder's law notes by K. L. Perrin, document 16, p. 54, *Longslow* v. *Boxal*.

51. Tim Hitchcock, '"You Bitches ... Die and be Damned": Gender, Authority and the Mob in the St Martin's Round-House Disaster of 1742', in T. Hitchcock and H. Shore, eds, *The Streets of London from the Great Fire to the Great Stink* (London, 2003), p. 77; *OBP*, December 1769, trial of Nathaniel Norris (t17691206–23) and September 1794, passim.

52. *OBP*, July 1768, trial of Edward Castle (t17680706–47); R. M. Dunn, 'The London Weavers' Riot of 1675', *Guildhall Studies in London History*, 1 (1973), p. 17.

53. TNA, TS 11/818, *King* v. *William Eastman and Thomas Haddon*.

54. *OBP*, September 1716, trials of John Love et al. (t17160906–2); de Castro, *The Gordon Riots*, pp. 58, 141.

55. Lewis et al., eds, *Horace Walpole's Correspondence*, xxv, p. 63 (14 June 1768).

56. E. P. Thompson, 'The Moral Economy of the English Crowd in the Eighteenth Century', *Past and Present*, 50 (1971), p. 78.

57. Rogers, 'Popular Protest in Early Hanoverian London', p. 72.

58. *London Evening Post*, 10–12 April 1735.

59. See above, Chapter 4.

60. Williams, 'Pope-Burning Processions', p. 111; Rogers, 'Popular Protest in Early Hanoverian London', p. 77; TNA, SP 35/21, fol. 57; *Weekly Journal; or British Gazetteer*, 4 July 1719; *OBP*, July 1768, trial of William Hawkins and Joseph Wild (t17680706–61).

61. *General Evening Post*, 4–6 April 1771.

62. LMA, OB/SP/1771/10

63. César de Saussure, *A Foreign View of England in 1725–1729*, trans. and ed. Madame van Muyden (London, 1995), p. 80; Peter King, *Crime, Justice and Discretion in England, 1740–1820* (Oxford, 2000), p. 27.

64. *OBP*, January 1725, trials of William Green and Richard Edwards (t17250115–67 and 68); TNA, SP 35/53/40, 30 October 1724; E. P. Thompson, *Whigs and Hunters: The Origin of the Black Act* (1975; reprint London, 1990), pp. 248–49.

65. LMA, MJ/SP/1768/Sept/47.

66. E. P. Thompson, 'Rough Music: *Le Charivari Anglais*', *Annales E.S.C.*, 27 (1972), pp. 285–315.

67. *M. Misson's Memoirs and Observations in his Travels over England*, trans. J. Ozell (London, 1719), p. 129; Robert B. Shoemaker, 'The London "Mob" in the Early Eighteenth Century', *Journal of British Studies*, 26 (July 1987), p. 291.

68. Williams, 'Pope-Burning Processions', p. 109; V. A. C. Gatrell, *The Hanging Tree: Execution and The English People, 1770–1868* (Oxford, 1994), p. 93; C. R. Dobson, *Masters and Journeymen: A Prehistory of Industrial Relations, 1717–1800* (London, 1980), p. 90; *St James Chronicle*, 14–17 May 1768.

69. *Gentleman's Magazine*, 7 (1737), p. 374; Tim Harris, 'Perceptions of the Crowd in Later Stuart London', in J. F. Merritt, ed., *Imagining Early Modern London: Perceptions and Portrayals of the City from Stow to Strype, 1598–1720* (Cambridge, 2001), pp. 250–72.

70. *OBP*, October 1716, trial of John Nash.

71. LMA, MJ/SP/1721/May/5; MJ/SP/1768/Sept/47.

72. *London Magazine*, 2 (1733), pp. 240–42; Rogers, *Whigs and Cities*, pp. 53–54.

73. *Weekly Journal: or Saturday's Post*, 8 August 1719.

74. *London Evening Post*, 27–29 January to 2–4 July 1761, passim, quote from 29–31 January. See also John L. Bullion, 'The Monitor and the Beer Tax Controversy: A Study of Constraints on London Newspapers of 1760–1761', *Journal of History and Politics*, 7 (1989), pp. 89–117.

75. Fitts, 'Newcastle's Mob'.

76. Geoffrey Holmes, *The Trial of Doctor Sacheverell* (London, 1973), pp. 175–76, 320; Shoemaker, 'London "Mob"', pp. 294–97; *OBP*, passim.

77. *Lichtenberg's Visits to England*, trans. and annotated by Margaret L. Mare and W. H. Quarrell (Oxford, 1938), p. 45.

78. LMA, MJ/SR/1289, R.48 (July 1664).

79. Warner and Ivis, '"Damn You, You Informing Bitch"'.

80. *Journals of the House of Commons*, xi, pp. 682–83; *London Evening Post*, 16–18 May 1765.

81. Nicholas Rogers, *Crowds, Culture and Politics in Georgian Britain* (Oxford, 1998), chap. 7.

82. These figures include women who were identified as married to men with a specific status or occupation.

83. Geoffrey Holmes, 'The Sacheverell Riots: The Crowd and the Church in Early Eighteenth-Century London', *Past and Present*, 72 (1976), pp. 72–78; BL, Add. MS 61610, fos 87, 92, 112, 137; Rogers, 'Popular Protest in Early Hanoverian London', pp. 85–87; George Rudé, *Paris and London in the Eighteenth Century: Studies in Popular Protest* (London, 1970), pp. 261–62.

84. *Character of the London Mobb* (London, 1710).

85. Shoemaker, 'London "Mob"', p. 300.

86. *Annual Register*, 25 May 1768; Dobson, *Masters and Journeymen*, pp. 83, 85; Rudé, *Paris and London*, p. 253.

87. LMA, OB/SP/1771, fol. 10d.

88. Kathleen Wilson, *The Sense of the People: Politics, Culture and Imperialism in England, 1715–1785* (Cambridge, 1995), pp. 256–69; *London Evening Post*, 11–18 February 1779, quotation from 16–18 February.

89. de Castro, *The Gordon Riots*, pp. 39, 56; Stevenson, *Popular Disturbances in England, 1700–1832*, p. 102.

90. TNA, TS 11/818, brief against Murphy and others for Murder of John Beaty [Beattie], a sailor.

91. TNA, TS 11/818, *King v. Doyle and Valline*, *King v. Horsford*.

92. Dobson, *Masters and Journeymen*, p. 86.

93. de Castro, *The Gordon Riots*, pp. 145, 160.

94. For similar findings, see Charles Tilly, *Popular Contention in Great Britain, 1758–1834* (Cambridge, Massachusetts, 1995), pp. 102–3.

95. James Epstein, 'Understanding the Cap of Liberty: Symbolic Practice and Social Conflict in Early Nineteenth-Century England', *Past and Present*, 122 (1989), pp. 75–118.

96. Charles Pythian-Adams, 'Milk and Soot: The Changing Vocabulary of a Popular Ritual in Stuart and Hanoverian London', in D. Fraser and A. Sutcliffe, eds, *The Pursuit of Urban History* (London, 1983), p. 104.

97. Nicholas Rogers, 'Crowds and Political Festival in Georgian England', in T. Harris, ed., *The Politics of the Excluded, c. 1500–1850* (Basingstoke, 2001), pp. 244–47; *London Evening Post*, 3–5 and 15–17 September 1761; *Public Advertiser*, 22 September 1761; *General Evening Post*, 16–19 January 1790.

98. BL, Add. MS 34712, fol. 51.

99. de Castro, *The Gordon Riots*, p. 156.

100. *Middlesex Journal*, 6–9 July 1771; *General Evening Post*, 7–11 July and 28 September to 5 October 1771.

101. *General Evening Post*, 15–17 June 1780.

102. Rogers, 'Crowds and Political Festival', pp. 251–52; Rogers, *Crowds, Culture, and Politics*, pp. 177, 185–86; *St James's Chronicle*, 23–26 August 1794.

103. Stanley H. Palmer, 'Calling Out the Troops: The Military, the Law, and Public Order in England, 1650–1850', *Journal of the Society for Army Historical Research*, 41 (1978), pp. 198–214; Tony Hayter, *The Army and the Crowd in Mid-Georgian England* (London, 1978), quote from p. 184; Dobson, *Masters and Journeymen*, p. 86.

104. *OBP*, September 1749, trial of Willson, Pen Lez and Launder; *The Times*, 25 February and 6–7 June 1792.

105. de Castro, *The Gordon Riots*, pp. 125, 162, 178, 197 (sources of quotations not acknowledged). Rogers points out another motivation for forming associations: to render the military presence on the streets unnecessary: Nicholas Rogers, 'Crowd and People in the Gordon Riots', in Eckhart Hellmuth, ed., *The Transformation of Political Culture: England and Germany in the Late Eighteenth Century* (Oxford, 1990), p. 47.

106. *Gentleman's Magazine*, 70 (1800), p. 895.

107. Rogers, 'Crowd and People in the Gordon Riots', pp. 51–55, quoting V. Knox, *The Spirit of Despotism* (1795; repr. New York, 1796), pp. 43–44; Linda Colley, *Britons: Forging the Nation, 1707–1837* (New Haven, 1992), pp. 217–28; David Vincent, ed., *Testaments of Radicalism: Memoirs of Working-Class Politicians, 1790–1885* (London, 1977), pp. 90–94.

108. Peter Clark, *British Clubs and Societies, 1580–1800: The Origins of an Associational World* (Oxford, 2000), p. 131; Dobson, *Masters and Journeymen*, esp. chap. 5.

109. Malcolm Chase, *Early Trade Unionism: Fraternity, Skill and the Politics of Labour* (Aldershot, 2000), chs 2 and 3; Marc W. Steinberg, *Fighting Words: Working-Class Formation, Collective Action and Discourse in Early Nineteenth-Century England* (Ithaca, New York, 1999), chap. 1, esp. pp. 29–30.

110. Rogers, *Crowds, Culture and Politics*, p. 212.

111. Tilly, *Popular Contention in Great Britain*, quotes from pp. 96, 191, 349, 358.

112. [J. H. Meister], *Letters Written during a Residence in England, Translated from the French* (London, 1799), p. 20.

113. Stevenson, *Popular Disturbances in England, 1700–1832*, chs 8 and 9.

114. See below, Chapter 9.

*Notes to Chapter 6: Violence*

1. [Béat-Louis de Muralt], *Letters Describing the Character and Customs of the English and French Nations* (London, 1726), pp. 69–70; M. Grosley, *A Tour to London: or New Observations on England and its Inhabitants*, trans. T. Nugent (London, 1772), p. 61.

2. M. Eisner, 'Modernization, Self-Control and Lethal Violence: The Long-Term Dynamics of European Homicide Rates in Theoretical Perspective', *British Journal of Criminology*, 41 (2001), p. 629.

3. J. H. Meister, *Letters Written during a Residence in England* (London, 1799), pp. 169–70.

4. Anton Blok, 'The Meaning of "Senseless" Violence', in his *Honour and Violence* (Oxford, 2001), pp. 103–14.

5. *London Evening Post*, 24 March 1761.

6. *OBP*, September 1731, trial of Joseph Blakemore (t17310908-15).

7. Ibid., December 1761, trial of Daniel Looney (t17611209-19).

8. CLRO, Sessions Papers, January 1754, death of Thomas Moss; *OBP*, January 1754, trial of John Hudson (t17540116-40).

9. F. Misson, *M. Misson's Memoirs and Observations in his Travels over England*, trans. J. Ozell (London, 1719), pp. 307–8; Grosley, *Tour to London*, p. 58. See also M. V. Wallbank, 'Eighteenth-Century Public Schools and the Education of the Governing Elite', *History of Education*, 8 (1979), p. 7.

10. LMA, MJ/SP/Sept 1749, no. 135; *London Evening Post*, 12 March and 3 November 1761.

11. *OBP*, February 1698, trial of John Chambers.

12. Another method of redeeming dishonour was suicide: Michael MacDonald and Terence R. Murphy, *Sleepless Souls: Suicide in Early Modern England* (Oxford, 1990), pp. 275–78, 281–82.

13. Lincoln's Inn Library, transcript of Dudley Ryder's law notes by K. L. Perrin, document 13, p. 34, *King* v. *Payne*; *London Journal*, 21 August 1731; *Daily Post*, 18/19 August 1731; *The Tricks of the Town: or Ways and Means for Getting Money* (London, 1732), p. 15.

14. *OBP*, February 1731, trial of William Shaw (t17310224-42).

15. LMA, MJ/SP/February 1696, no. 16; MJ/SP/April 1748, no. 54.

16. CLRO, Sessions Papers, September 1779, death of James Proctor.

17. *General Evening Post*, 13 August 1771.

18. *General Evening Post*, 4–6 June 1771.

19. *OBP*, May 1699, trial of Benjamin Barton; *London Journal*, 25 February 1735.

20. *London Evening Post*, 17 December 1761 and 17 October 1741. See also John Stevenson, *Popular Disturbances in England, 1700–1832* (2nd edn, London, 1992), pp. 49–51.

21. LMA, Acc. 1268, 3 January 1759, depositions re death of Mary Noonan.

22. Margaret Hunt, 'Wife-Beating, Domesticity, and Women's Independence in Early Eighteenth-Century London', *Gender and History*, 4 (1992), p. 23.

23. *London Journal*, 15 July 1721.

24. *OBP*, July 1731, trial of John Piggot (t17310714-27).

25. *Honours Preservation without Blood: or Sober Advice to Duellists* (London, 1680), pp. 15–16; *General Evening Post*, 17–20 August 1771; CLRO, Sessions Papers, July 1686, information of Richard Redman.

26. Charles Hitchin, *A True Discovery of the Conduct of Receivers and Thief-Takers in and about the City of London* (London, 1718), p. 8; *Whitehall*

*Evening Post*, 4–6 December 1750; N. Rogers, 'Confronting the Crime Wave: The Debate over Social Reform and Regulation, 1749–1753', in L. Davison et al., ed., *Stilling the Grumbling Hive: The Response to Social and Economic Problems in England, 1689–1750* (Stroud, 1992), pp. 78–81.

27. *OBP*, January 1724, trial of John Allen (t17240117–70).

28. J. M. Beattie, *Crime and the Courts in England, 1660–1800* (Princeton, 1986), p. 152.

29. *General Evening Post*, January 1752, cited in Henry Fielding, *The Covent Garden Journal*, 9 (30 January 1752); reprint edn, ed. B. A. Goldgar (Oxford, 1998), p. 463; *OBP*, February 1754, trial of Samuel Dean and William Wilson (t17540227–10).

30. *OBP*, April 1724, trial of Edward Joire (t17240415–10); January 1734, trial of James Belford (t17340116–25); October 1747, trial of Hosea Youell and Jacob Lopez (t17471014–13); February 1754, trial of Francis Wessbrook (t17540227–6).

31. Robert B. Shoemaker, 'Male Honour and the Decline of Public Violence in Eighteenth-Century London', *Social History*, 26 (2001), p. 197 (all statistics from this article were calculated on the basis of a 10 per cent sample of Old Bailey prosecutions); Peter Earle, *The Making of the English Middle Class* (London, 1989), pp. 80–81.

32. Steven Shapin, *A Social History of Truth: Civility and Science in Seventeenth-Century England* (Chicago, 1990), pp. 65–74, 107–14.

33. *OBP*, July 1751, trial of Richard Sowle (t17510703–18).

34. Anna Bryson, *From Courtesy to Civility: Changing Codes of Conduct in Early Modern England* (Oxford, 1998), pp. 269–74. For attempts to 'reform male manners' in the eighteenth century, see G. J. Barker-Benfield, *The Culture of Sensibility: Sex and Society in Eighteenth-Century Britain* (Chicago, 1992), chaps 2 and 5; Lawrence Klein, *Shaftesbury and the Culture of Politeness* (Cambridge, 1994); Philip Carter, *Men and the Emergence of Polite Society: Britain, 1660–1800* (Harlow, 2001). For the feminine aspects of politeness, see Lawrence Klein, 'Gender, Conversation and the Public Sphere in Early Eighteenth-Century England', in J. Still and M. Worton, ed., *Textuality and Sexuality: Reading, Theories and Practices* (Manchester, 1993), pp. 100–15.

35. LMA, MJ/SP/April 1695, nos 21–24.

36. LMA, MJ/SP/August 1694, no. 17.

37. *OBP*, April 1731, trial of Francis Woodmath (t17310428–72, under name Woodmash).

38. *The Tricks of the Town Laid Open: or A Companion for Country Gentlemen* (London, 1728; 2nd edn, London, 1747), p. 31.

39. CLRO, Sessions Papers, September 1675, depositions re death of Jervis Stroope.

40. CLRO, Sessions Papers, June 1707, depositions re death of Richard Cary.

41. César de Saussure, *A Foreign View of England in 1725–1729*, trans. and ed. M. van Muyden (London, 1995), p. 113; *London Evening Post*, 4 July 1761.

42. Bryson, *From Courtesy to Civility*, pp. 248–50.

43. *The Town Rakes: or The Frolicks of the Mohocks or Hawkubites* (London, 1712); Daniel Statt, 'The Case of the Mohocks: Rake Violence in Augustan London', *Social History*, 20 (1995), pp. 179–99; Neil Guthrie, '"No Truth or Very Little in the Whole Story?" A Reassessment of the Mohock Scare of 1712', *Eighteenth-Century Life*, 20 (1996), pp. 33–56; Ian Bell, *Literature and Crime in Augustan England* (London, 1991), pp. 53–54.

44. *A Compleat Collection of Remarkable Tryals*, 5 vols (London, 1721), iii, pp. 105–7; LMA, MJ/SP/April 1712, nos 2–32 (quotations from 4, 27, 28); MJ/SBB/702, pp. 44–46 (April 1712).

45. *OBP*, July 1720, trial of Morrice Fitzgerald (t17200712–15).

46. *London Evening Post*, 24 February, 4 July and 4 August 1761; *OBP*, February 1771, trial of Joseph West, Stephen Paris and Samuel Randall (t17710220–27); John Fielding, *A Brief Description of the Cities of London and Westminster* (London, 1776), p. xxx.

47. Randolph Trumbach, *Sex and the Gender Revolution*, i, *Homosexuality and the Third Gender in Enlightenment London* (Chicago and London, 1998).

48. CLRO, Sessions Papers, December 1693, depositions re deaths of Henry Hutton; *OBP*, December 1693, trial of John Breames, Arnold Breames and Richard Benley.

49. See below, Chapter 7.

50. *OBP*. Calculations concerning assault based on a one session per decade sample of recognizances for assault between 1663 and 1791.

51. For evidence of violence committed by women, see Hunt, 'Wife Beating', pp. 22–23; Fielding, *Covent Garden Journal*, pp. 443–45. On the order recording of female violence, see Garthine Walker, *Crime, Gender and Social Order in Early Modern England* (Cambridge, 2003), chap. 3.

52. *London Evening Post*, 29 March 1735; *General Evening Post*, 29 December 1770.

53. *London Evening Post*, 23 May and 14 December 1751.

54. CLRO, Sessions Papers, July 1778, re death of Elizabeth Young; *OBP*, July 1778, trial of Elizabeth Rock (t17780715–86).

55. *London Evening Post*, 24 October 1751.

56. See below, Chapter 7.

57. See, for example, CLRO, Sessions Papers, October 1698 (depositions against Ann Andersby for assault).

58. *London Evening Post*, 11 August 1741; *OBP*, January 1698 [1697?], trial of L— B—.

59. Lawrence Stone, 'Interpersonal Violence in English Society, 1300–1980', *Past and Present*, 101 (1983), pp. 22–33; T. R. Gurr, 'Historical Trends in Violent Crime: A Critical Review of the Evidence', *Crime and Justice: An Annual Review of Research*, 3 (1981), pp. 295–353; J. S. Cockburn, 'Patterns of Violence in English Society: Homicide in Kent, 1560–1985', *Past and Present*, 130 (1991), pp. 70–106; Eisner, 'Modernization, Self-Control and Lethal Violence', pp. 621–23.

60. Shoemaker, 'Male Honour and the Decline of Public Violence', p. 191. For the limitations of homicide statistics, see Malcolm Gaskill, *Crime and Mentalities in Early Modern England* (Cambridge, 2000), p. 266; J. A. Sharpe, 'The History of Violence in England: Some Observations', and L. Stone, 'A Rejoinder', *Past and Present*, 108 (1985), pp. 206–24.

61. *OBP*, December 1709, trial of John Munford; March 1721, trial of John Bacchus (t17210301–47).

62. Despite the fact that victims of violent assaults were increasingly taken to hospital during this period, there is no evidence that improved medical care explains the decline in homicides.

63. See above, Chapter 2.

64. M. D'Archenholz, *A Picture of England: Containing a Description of the Laws, Customs and Manners of England* (Dublin, 1791), p. 157.

65. See above, Chapter 3.

66. LMA, Accession 1268, 14 October 1761; *OBP*, October 1761, trial of Stephen Dane (t17611021–30).

67. Shoemaker, 'Male Honour and the Decline of Public Violence', p. 206.

68. D'Archenholz, *Picture of England*, p. 211.

69. LMA, MJ/SP/January 1755, depositions re death of Lewis Lewis; *OBP*, September 1761, trial of John Garnett (t17610916–39).

70. LMA, MJ/SP/May 1698, no. 61; *OBP*, July 1751, trial of Richard Sowle (t17510703–18).

71. Shoemaker, 'Male Honour and the Decline of Public Violence', p. 205.

72. *General Evening Post*, 3–10 February 1780.

73. Jan Bondeson, *The London Monster* (London, 2000). This episode is further discussed below, in Chapter 10.

74. Saussure, *Foreign View of England*, p. 70. See also Anne Buck, *Dress in Eighteenth-Century England* (London, 1979), pp. 57–58; *Universal Spectator*, 1730, cited by C. Willet Cunnington and Phillis Cunnington, *Handbook of*

*English Costume in the Eighteenth Century* (revised edn, London, 1972), p. 100. I am indebted to John Styles and Penelope Corfield for advice and references on this issue.

75. *OBP*, October 1761, trial of Dane. See also LMA, Accession 1268, 17 May 1761, depositions re murder of Richard Jasper.

76. *Monthly Intelligencer*, May 1780, p. 197; Penelope Corfield, 'Walking the City Streets: The Urban Odyssey in Eighteenth-Century England', *Journal of Urban History*, 16 (1990), p. 154.

77. LMA, MJ/SR/3246, R.107, 234, 264, 399, 462, 562 (September 1771).

78. LMA, OB/SP/July 1781, no. 54. Bryan, however, managed to get his attackers convicted of stealing a handkerchief and some money from him: *OBP*, July 1781, trial of Benjamin Fitter, George Bolton, and John Lumley (t17810711–5).

79. Barbara Hanawalt, 'Violent Death in Fourteenth- and Early Fifteenth-Century England', *Comparative Studies in Society and History*, 18 (1976), p. 309; J. A. Sharpe, 'Domestic Homicide in Early Modern England', *Historical Journal*, 24 (1981), p. 34.

80. A. J. Hammerton, *Cruelty and Companionship: Conflict in Nineteenth-Century Married Life* (London, 1992), chs 1–4, passim; Anna Clark, *The Struggle for the Breeches: Gender and the Making of the British Working Class* (Berkeley, 1995), pp. 259–63.

81. Elaine A. Reynolds, *Before the Bobbies: The Night Watch and Police Reform in Metropolitan London, 1720–1830* (Stanford, California, 1998), p. 164.

## Notes to Chapter 7: Duels and Boxing Matches

1. *OBP*, February 1757, trial of Thomas Powel (t17570223–32). See also CLRO, Sessions Papers, February 1757, informations at the inquisition concerning the death of Francis Leonard [sic].

2. *OBP*, April 1750, trial of Edward Clark (t17500425–19); *The Trial of Captain Edward Clark, Commander of His Majesty's Ship the Canterbury, for the Murder of Captain Thomas Innes, Commander of His Majesty's Ship the Warwick, in a Duel in Hyde Park* (London, 1750).

3. Robert B. Shoemaker, 'Male Honour and the Decline of Public Violence in Eighteenth-Century London', *Social History*, 26 (2001), p. 195.

4. Lawrence Stone, *The Crisis of the Aristocracy, 1558–1641* (Oxford, 1965), pp. 243–44; John Cockburn, *The History and Examination of Duels: Shewing their Heinous Nature and the Necessity of Suppressing Them* (London, 1720), pp. 351–52.

5. CLRO, Sessions Papers, December 1700, inquisition concerning the death

of Andrew Staining; December 1678, inquisition concerning the death of Miles Langthorne.

6. Robert B. Shoemaker, 'The Taming of the Duel: Masculinity, Honour and Ritual Violence in London, 1660–1800', *Historical Journal*, 45 (2002), p. 530.

7. Cockburn, *History and Examination of Duels*, p. 190.

8. William Hope, *Hope's New Method of Fencing* (2nd edn, Edinburgh, 1714), pp. 18, 40.

9. Domenico Angelo, *L'École des Armes* (London, 1763), translated as *The School of Fencing* (London, 1787), preface; J. D. Aylward, *The Small-Sword in England: Its History, its Forms, its Makers and its Masters* (London, 1960), pp. 107–10; idem, *The House of Angelo* (London, 1953); Arthur Wise, *The History and Art of Personal Combat* (London, 1971), chs 7–8.

10. Aylward, *House of Angelo*, p. 29; William Hope, *A Vindication of the True Art of Self-Defence* (Edinburgh, 1724).

11. *Honours Preservation without Blood: or Sober Advice to Duellists* (London, 1680), p. 24.

12. R. Latham and W. Matthews, eds, *The Diary of Samuel Pepys*, 11 vols (London, 1970–83), ix, pp. 26–27; J. H. Wilson, *A Rake and his Times: George Villiers, Second Duke of Buckingham* (London, 1954), pp. 93–98.

13. BL, Add. MS 52,474, fol. 56; Victor Stater, *Duke Hamilton is Dead! A Story of Aristocratic Life and Death in Stuart Britain* (New York, 1999), pp. 234–36, 246–70; H. T. Dickinson, 'The Mohun-Hamilton Duel: Personal Feud or Whig Plot?', *Durham University Journal*, June 1965, pp. 159–65.

14. *The Life and Noble Character of Richard Thornhill, Esq. who had the Misfortune to Kill Sir Cholmley Deering, Bart … in a Duel in Tuttle-Fields, on Wednesday 9th of May, 1711* (London, 1711); *A True Account of What Past at the Old Bailey, May the 18th, 1711 Relating to the Tryal of Richard Thornhill, Esq. Indicted for the Murder of Sir Cholmley Deering, Bart* (2nd edn, London, 1711).

15. Cockburn, *History and Examination of Duels*, p. 137.

16. TNA, KB 33/17/2, Trinity 6 George III. As the indictment goes on to say, he was therefore challenged to fight 'with pistols'. See also W. S. Lewis, *Horace Walpole's Correspondence*, 48 vols (London, New Haven, and Oxford, 1937–83), xvii, p. 246; xxiii, p. 255.

17. *The British Code of the Duel* (London, 1824), p. 44; *A Hint on Duelling, in a Letter to a Friend: To Which is Added The Bruiser, or an Inquiry into the Pretensions of Modern Manhood* (1751; 2nd edn, London, 1752), p. 34.

18. Shoemaker, 'Taming of the Duel', p. 528.

19. William Hope, *The Compleat Fencing-Master: In Which is Fully Described*

*the Whole Guards, Parades and Lessons, Belonging to the Small-Sword* (London, 1692), pp. 124–25.

20. John A. Atkinson, *The British Duelling Pistol* (London, 1978); J. N. George, *English Pistols and Revolvers* (Onslow County, North Carolina, 1938), pp. 68–76.

21. CLRO, Sessions Papers, January 1693, inquisition concerning the death of Charles Graham. See also Shoemaker, 'Male Honour', pp. 193–98.

22. Robert Baldick, *The Duel: A History of Duelling* (1965; reprint London, 1979), p. 42; *The Art of Duelling, by a Traveller: Containing much Information Useful to Young Continental Tourists* (London, 1836), p. 49.

23. Samuel Stanton, *The Principles of Duelling: With Rules to be Observed in Every Particular Respecting it* (London, 1790), p. 69.

24. Antony Simpson, 'Dandelions on the Field of Honour: Duelling, the Middle Classes and the Law in Nineteenth-Century England', *Criminal Justice History*, 9 (1988), p. 113.

25. *The Trial of Captain Edward Clark*, p. 7; Stanton, *Principles of Duelling*, p. 77.

26. Abraham Bosquett, *The Young Man of Honour's Vade-Mecum: Being a Salutary Treatise on Duelling* (London, 1817), pp. 7–10.

27. *OBP*, June 1782, trial of Bennet Allen and Robert Morris (t17820605–1).

28. *Advice to Seconds: General Rules and Instructions for all Seconds in Duels. By a Late Captain in the Army* (Whitehaven, 1793), pp. 28–33; *British Code of the Duel*, p. 48.

29. *A True Account ... Relating to the Tryal of Richard Thornhill*, p. 9; *An Account of the Life and Character of Sir Chomley Deering* (London, 1711), p. 5.

30. *The Trial of Captain Edward Clark*, p. 9.

31. *OBP*, June 1782, trial of Allen and Morris; *Advice to Seconds*, pp. 24–25; *Art of Duelling*, p. 49; *British Code of the Duel*, p. 47. Bosquett, however, argued that a pace was five feet: *Young Man of Honour's Vade-Mecum*, p. 101.

32. *OBP*, February 1796, trial of Richard England (t17960217–27).

33. LMA, MJ/SP/Feb/1696/16; *OBP* January 1721, trial of James Melton (t17210113–18).

34. *Times*, 11 June 1799, p. 3a.

35. *The Vauxhall Affray: or The Macaronies Defeated* (2nd edn, London, 1773), p. 7; Clare Brant, 'Duelling by Sword and Pen: The Vauxhall Affray of 1773', *Prose Studies*, 19 (1996), pp. 160–72. In the end, the duel actually took the form of a boxing match.

36. *British Code of the Duel*, p. 43.

37. *Times*, 28 May 1798, p. 2a.

38. *London Evening Post*, 22 October 1761; *General Evening Post*, 14 March 1771; *Times*, 23 August 1790, p. 2b.

39. Thomas Comber, *A Discourse of Duels: Shewing the Sinful Nature and Mischievous Effects of Them* (London, 1687), p. 51.

40. Raymond Postgate, *'That Devil Wilkes'* (London, 1930), p. 49; *Westminster Journal*, 25 May 1771. See also accounts of the 1779 duel between Charles James Fox and William Adam: *Gentleman's Magazine*, 49 (1779), p. 610; John A. Atkinson, *Duelling Pistols and Some of the Affairs They Settled* (London, 1964), pp. 115–16; *OBP*, February 1796, trial of England.

41. *Gentleman's Magazine*, 74 (1804), p. 285.

42. *Advice to Seconds*, p. 21.

43. *Gentleman's Magazine*, 61 (1791), p. 672.

44. Stater, *Duke Hamilton is Dead!*, pp. 218, 229–34.

45. *The Case of Captain John Laverick, Relating to the Killing of Captain John Lawson* (London, 1748), pp. 6–9; LMA, MJ/SP/1748/04/54–59.

46. *Times*, 24 August 1796, p. 3b; 25 August 1796, p. 3d.

47. *Times*, 24 March 1796, p. 3c.

48. *Horace Walpole's Correspondence*, ix, pp. 318–19.

49. Latham and Matthews, eds, *Diary of Samuel Pepys*, vii, p. 343; Historical Manuscripts Commission, *Twelfth Report, Appendix, Part VII: The Manuscripts of S. H. Le Fleming, Esq.* (London, 1890), pp. 100, 299; idem, *Seventh Report, Part I: Report and Appendix* (London, 1879), pp. 466, 469, 470, 494, 506; Narcissus Luttrell, *A Brief Historical Relation of State Affairs*, 6 vols (Oxford, 1857), ii, pp. 628–29; *Horace Walpole's Correspondence*, xxxviii, pp. 227n., 243, 313.

50. Markku Peltonen, *The Duel in Early Modern England: Civility, Politeness and Honour* (Cambridge, 2003); Donald F. Bond, ed., *The Tatler*, 3 vols (Oxford, 1987), i, pp. 192–5, 211–19; idem, ed., *The Spectator*, 5 vols (Oxford, 1965), i, pp. 359–60, 418–19; *Gentleman's Magazine*, 6 (1736), p. 272, 25 (1755), pp. 112–13, 31 (1761), pp. 57, 58 (1788), p. 1039; Cockburn, *History and Examination of Duels*, p. 156.

51. Donna Andrew, 'The Code of Honour and its Critics: The Opposition to Duelling in England, 1700–1850', *Social History*, 5 (1980), p. 420.

52. Donna Andrew, ed., *London Debating Societies, 1776–1799*, London Record Society, 30 (1994), passim.

53. *Horace Walpole's Correspondence*, xxxviii, p. 535.

54. *Cursory Reflections on the Single Combat, or Modern Duel* (London, 1773), p. 14.

55. BL, Add. MS, 41,354, fol. 82.

56. *OBP*, January 1698 [1697?], trial of Anthony Robinson and others.

57. Baldick, *The Duel*, p. 69; Latham and Matthews, eds, *Diary of Samuel Pepys*, iii, p. 170, viii, p. 363; *Weekly Journal: or Saturday's-Post*, 28 January 1721; Shoemaker, 'Taming of the Duel', p. 537.

58. Richard Hey, *A Dissertation on Duelling* (Cambridge, 1784), pp. 95–97.

59. For examples, see the indictments in TNA, KB 33/17/1–2.

60. Simpson, 'Dandelions on the Field of Honour', p. 138; V. G. Kiernan, *The Duel in European History: Honour and the Reign of the Aristocracy* (Oxford, 1988), pp. 102, 198–99, 204–22; *Daily Universal Register*, 28 July 1787, p. 4a; 5 December 1789, p. 2b; 8 December 1789, p. 2d; 16 December 1789, p. 3b; M. D'Archenholz, *A Picture of England: Containing a Description of the Laws, Customs and Manners of England* (Dublin, 1791), pp. 213–14; Shoemaker, 'Taming of the Duel', pp. 544–45.

61. César de Saussure, *A Foreign View of England in 1725–1729*, trans. and ed. M. van Muyden (1902; reprint edn London, 1995), pp. 112–13; [Coustard de Massi], *The History of Duelling … Containing the Origin, Progress, Revolutions and Present State of Duelling in France and England* (London, 1770), pp. 151–52.

62. LMA, MJ/SP/1749/09/133–134; *OBP*, September 1749, trial of Samuel Cross (t17490906–73).

63. [Béat-Louis de Muralt], *Letters Describing the Character and Customs of the English and French Nations … Translated from the French* (London, 1726), p. 42; *M. Misson's Memoirs and Observations in his Travels over England*, trans. J. Ozell (London, 1719), pp. 304–5; D'Archenholz, *Picture of England*, p. 212.

64. *OBP*, February 1725, trial of Simon Small (t17250224–66); June 1789, trial of William Ward (t17890603–17).

65. Ibid., July 1751, trial of Charles Troop (t17510703–39).

66. Ibid., January 1750, trial of William Hopton (t17500117–18).

67. Ibid., January 1754, trial of John Hudson (t17540116–40).

68. *Times*, 20 May 1789, p. 3a.

69. *OBP*, February 1725, trial of Simon Small (t17250224–66).

70. Ibid., April 1791, trial of Robert Smith (t17910413–42).

71. M. Grosley, *A Tour to London: or New Observations on England and its Inhabitants*, trans. T. Nugent (London, 1772), p. 57; *OBP*, July 1759, trial of John Price (t17590711–25); LMA, Accession 1268, deposition dated 10 July 1759.

72. LMA, OB/SP/1774/62, depositions concerning the death of Thomas Brown. See also *OBP*, September 1774, trial of Oliver Davis (t17740907–64).

73. *Public Advertiser*, 1 January 1771. See also *General Evening Post*, 9 November 1771 and 29 August 1780.

74. Saussure, *Foreign View of England*, pp. 112–13; BL, Add. MS 27828, fol. 119. See also Grosley, *Tour to London*, p. 59.

75. *OBP* December 1793, trial of David Davis (t17931204–64). See also *Weekly Journal: or British Gazetteer*, 12 February 1726.

76. Saussure, *Foreign View of England*, p. 112.

77. *OBP*, December 1768, trial of Thomas Knight (t17681207–37); *Weekly Journal: or British Gazetteer*, 12 February 1726.

78. *OBP*, July 1751, trial of Charles Troop (t17510703–39); May 1761, trial of William Smith (t17610506–8).

79. Latham and Matthews, eds, *Diary of Samuel Pepys*, ii, p. 127; iii, p. 93; v, p. 133; viii, p. 239; ix, pp. 516–17; quote from iv, p. 167.

80. Zacharias von Uffenbach, *London in 1710: From the Travels of Zacharias von Uffenbach*, trans. and ed. W. H. Quarrell and M. Mare (London, 1934), pp. 88–91.

81. H. D. Miles, *Pugilistica: Being One Hundred and Forty Years of the History of British Boxing*, 3 vols (London, [1880]), i, pp. 9–10; John Godfrey, *A Treatise upon the Useful Science of Defence, Connecting the Small and Back-Sword* (London, 1747), pp. 38–39. See also *M. Misson's Memoirs and Observations*, pp. 307–8.

82. Dennis Brailsford, *Bareknuckles: A Social History of Prize-Fighting* (Cambridge, 1988), p. 6.

83. *London Evening Post*, 28 February and 28 April 1761; *General Evening Post*, 4 April 1771; *Westminster Journal*, 2 February 1771.

84. *Daily Universal Register*, June 1785 to December 1787, passim; quote from 12 December 1787, p. 3d.

85. [Muralt], *Letters*, p. 42; *Daily Advertiser*, 4 May 1742, clipping in Daniel Lysons, *Collectanea: Publick Exhibitions and Places of Amusement*, 4 vols (British Library, shelfmark C103.k.11, n.d.), iv, pt 1, fol. 124.

86. *The Memoirs of the Life of Daniel Mendoza* (London, 1816; reprint, ed. Paul Magriel, London, 1951), pp. 14–25.

87. Brailsford, *Bareknuckles*, pp. 8–9; *OBP*, April 1791, trial of Smith.

88. Newspaper clipping in Lysons, *Collectanea*, iv, pt 2, fol. 159.

89. *Complete Art of Boxing*, p. 54.

90. *Daily Advertiser*, 4 May 1742 and 22 August 1747, both in Lysons, *Collectanea*, iv, pt 1, fols 124, 144; *Daily Advertiser*, 3 July 1745.

91. D'Archenholz, *Picture of England*, p. 213.

92. Brailsford, *Bareknuckles*, p. 10; Bob Mee, *Bare Fists* (Stratford-upon-Avon, 1998), pp. 7–8, 12–13.

93. *Complete Art of Boxing*, p. v; Tony Gee, *Up to Scratch: Bareknuckle Fighting and Heroes of the Prize Ring* (Harpendon, 1998), pp. 35–36;

*Daily Universal Register,* 19 April 1787, p. 2c; Brailsford, *Bareknuckles,* p. 25.

94. *Daily Universal Register,* 20 December 1787, p. 3a, 25 December 1787, p. 2c.

95. Brailsford, *Bareknuckles,* pp. 70–71; Miles, *Puglistica,* p. 85.

96. *Westminster Journal,* 25 May 1771.

97. Saussure, *Foreign View of England,* pp. 172–74.

98. *London Journal,* 23 June 1722, in Lysons, *Collectanea,* iv, pt 1, fol. 121; Mee, *Bare Fists,* p. 48.

99. J. Plumb, 'The Commercialization of Leisure', in N. McKendrick et al., *The Birth of a Consumer Society* (London, 1983), pp. 274, 280–82.

100. *Hint on Duelling,* pp. 32–36; Stanton, *Principles of Duelling,* p. 27.

101. 25 George II, c. 36.

102. *Daily Universal Register,* 29 March 1787, p. 3c; 19 April 1787, p. 2c. See also *General Evening Post,* 9 September 1780.

103. *Daily Universal Register,* 8 August 1786, p. 2d; Joanna Innes, 'Politics and Morals: The Reformation of Manners Movement in Later Eighteenth-Century England', in E. Hellmuth, ed., *The Transformation of Political Culture* (Oxford, 1990), p. 71.

104. *Daily Universal Register,* 5 September 1786, p. 2a; 21 April 1787, p. 3b; 7 July 1787, p. 4b; 21 December 1787, p. 3d; *Times,* 1 May 1788, p. 3b; 4 October 1790, p. 3b; and 16 May 1692, p. 3a.

105. Brailsford, *Bareknuckles,* pp. 16, 40, 49.

106. [Pierce Egan], *Boxiana: or Sketches of Ancient and Modern Pugilism* (London, 1812), p. 110; Gee, *Up to Scratch,* p. 40.

107. *Complete Art of Boxing,* pp. 48–49; [Egan], *Boxiana,* p. 3.

108. Brailsford, *Bareknuckles,* chapters 3–8.

109. Egan, *Boxiana,* p. 9.

110. *OBP,* December 1793, trial of Davis; Lincoln's Inn Library, transcript of Dudley Ryder's law notes by K. L. Perrin, document 12, fol 25, *Tipp* v. *Herbert.*

111. [Massi], *History of Duelling,* p. 152; D'Archenholz, *Picture of England,* pp. 211–12.

112. *Times,* 4 January 1791, p. 2c.

113. LMA, OB/SP/1774/62; *OBP,* February 1757, trial of Powel; CLRO, Sessions Papers, April 1777, depositions re death of Benjamin Fisher.

114. Kiernan, *Duel in European History,* p. 215.

115. [Muralt], *Letters,* p. 42.

116. *General Evening Post,* 4 July 1771; *Daily Universal Register,* 20 December 1787, p. 2b.

117. The number of recorded duels peaked in the 1790s and then declined

gradually, only falling sharply after 1842: Simpson, 'Dandelions on the Field of Honour', pp. 106–7.

118. According to Kiernan (*Duel in European History*, p. 218), the last recorded duel in England was fought in 1852.

119. [Louis Simond], *Journal of a Tour and Residence in Great Britain, during the Years 1810 and 1811* (2 vols, Edinburgh, 1815), i, p. 127.

120. Ibid., i, p. 126; *Complete Art of Boxing*, p. 71. According to Grosley, the reason fighters did not wear shirts was so that each combatant could demonstrate 'that he is not afraid of blows, and that he has nothing upon him that can either ward them off or deaden their effect': *Tour to London*, p. 58.

## Notes to Chapter 8: Going to Law

1. *Times*, 12 February 1800, p. 3d.

2. Charles Moore, *A Full Inquiry into the Subject of Suicide*, 2 vols (London, 1790), ii, p. 253; John Trusler, *A System of Etiquette* (Bath, 1804), p. 68.

3. See, for example, Lawrence Stone, *Road to Divorce: A History of the Making and Breaking of Marriage in England* (1990; reprint, Oxford, 1995), p. 238.

4. James Oldham, 'Truth-Telling in the Eighteenth-Century English Courtroom', *Law and History Review*, 12 (1994), pp. 113–16; idem, *The Mansfield Manuscripts and the Growth of English Law in the Eighteenth Century*, 2 vols (Chapel Hill, North Carolina, 1992), ii, pp. 851–53, 1022–23.

5. *The Trial Between William Fawkener, Esq. ... and the Hon. John Townshend* (London, 1786), pp. 18–20; TNA, KB 33/17/2, Hill. 15 George III, *Morgan v. Chapman*.

6. See above, Chapter 4.

7. *Universal Spectator*, 6 March 1731.

8. D. Hay, 'Property, Authority and the Criminal Law', in Hay et al., *Albion's Fatal Tree: Crime and Society in Eighteenth-Century England* (1975; reprint, Harmondsworth, 1977), pp. 17–63; E. P. Thompson, *Whigs and Hunters: The Origin of the Black Act* (1975; reprint, London, 1990), pp. 258–69.

9. M. D'Archenholz, *A Picture of England: Containing a Description of the Laws, Customs and Manners of England* (Dublin, 1791), p. 206.

10. N. Rogers, 'Impressment and the Law in Eighteenth-Century Britain', in N. Landau, ed., *Law, Crime and English Society, 1660–1830* (Cambridge, 2002), pp. 87–88; *General Evening Post*, 26–28 December 1771.

11. Lincoln's Inn Library, transcript of Dudley Ryder's law notes by K. L. Perrin, document 16, fol. 27, *Bricknell v. Wilkinson*.

12. J. A. Sharpe, '"Such Disagreement Betwyx Neighbours": Litigation and Human Relations in Early Modern England', in J. Bossy, ed., *Disputes and Settlements: Law and Human Relations in the West* (Cambridge, 1983), p. 175.

13. *Public Advertiser*, 2 August 1763.

14. Ruth Paley, ed., *Justice in Eighteenth-Century Hackney: The Justicing Notebook of Henry Norris and the Hackney Petty Sessions Book*, London Record Society, 28 (London, 1991), pp. xviii, xxxi, 6; R. B. Shoemaker, *Prosecution and Punishment: Petty Crime and the Law in London and Rural Middlesex, c. 1660–1725* (Cambridge, 1991), chap. 4.

15. Shoemaker, *Prosecution and Punishment*, chap. 5; Norma Landau, 'Appearance at the Quarter Sessions of Eighteenth-Century Middlesex', *London Journal*, 23 (1998), pp. 37–41.

16. CLRO, Sessions Papers, December 1704, informations concerning the wounding of Mary Faulkner. Although Walgrave initially agreed to go and 'make satisfaction', another man persuaded him not to do it.

17. Mary Thale, ed., *The Autobiography of Francis Place* (Cambridge, 1972), pp. 225–26.

18. Stone, *Road to Divorce*, p. 184; Oldham, *Mansfield Manuscripts*, i, pp. 151–55, citing *Nash* v. *Lindegreen*.

19. Shoemaker, *Prosecution and Punishment*, pp. 128–29, 135, 160–61, 164; N. Landau, 'Indictment for Fun and Profit: A Prosecutor's Reward at Eighteenth-Century Quarter Sessions', *Law and History Review*, 17 (1999), pp. 507–36.

20. CLRO, Sessions Papers, undated 1719/20 (Thorold Mayor), petition of Elizabeth Jacobs.

21. *Morning Chronicle, and London Advertiser*, 10 June 1779. For the trial, see *OBP*, July 1778, trial of Alexander Leith (t17780715-5).

22. Dudley Ryder's law notes, document 12, p. 23, *Johnson* v. *Horton*; p. 59, *Ambrose* v. *Skinner et al.*

23. Douglas Hay, 'Prosecution and Power: Malicious Prosecution in the English Courts, 1750–1850', in Hay and F. Snyder, eds, *Policing and Prosecution in Britain, 1750–1850* (Oxford, 1989), pp. 343–95.

24. Thomas DeVeil, *Observations on the Practice of a Justice of the Peace* (London, 1747), pp. 18–19; LMA, MJ/SR/2358, R.71; Norma Landau, 'The Trading Justice's Trade', in Landau, ed., *Law, Crime and English Society*, p. 68.

25. Dudley Ryder's law notes, document 16, p. 54, *Longslow* v. *Boxal*.

26. [John] Trusler, *The London Adviser and Guide: Containing Every Instruction and Information Useful and Necessary to Persons Living in London, and Coming to Reside There* (London, 1786), p. 130.

27. *A Trip Through London: Containing Observations on Men and Things* (8th edn, London, 1728), p. 36.

28. *London Evening Post*, 2 July 1751; LMA, MJ/SP/October 1760, bundle 6, petition of George Steed. For other evidence of vexatious defamation prosecutions, see Robert B. Shoemaker, 'The Decline of Public Insult in London, 1660–1800', *Past and Present*, 169 (2000), pp. 112–13.

29. [T. Baston], *Thoughts on Trade and a Public Spirit* (London, 1716), pp. 96–97; LMA, MJ/SP/February 1709, nos 23–24; Shoemaker, *Prosecution and Punishment*, pp. 145–46.

30. Netta Goldsmith, *Worst of Crimes: Homosexuality and the Law in Eighteenth-Century London* (Aldershot, 1998).

31. *OBP*, September 1736, trial of John Warwick (t17360908–37); October 1736, trial of Richard Curtis and Edward Joyce (t17361013–30); January 1737, trial of John Warwick et al. (t17370114–27); February 1737, trial of John Drinkwater (t17370216–57); October 1739, trial of John Drinkwater (t17391017–42); April 1741, trial of John Theobalds (t17410405–53).

32. Shoemaker, *Prosecution and Punishment*, pp. 315–18; Hay, 'Prosecution and Power', pp. 388–92.

33. LMA, MJ/SP/October 1708, no. 32; *Gentleman's Magazine*, 1 (1731), p. 264; *London Journal*, 3 July 1731.

34. J. H. Meister, *Letters Written during a Residence in England* (London, 1799), p. 39.

35. Christopher W. Brooks, *Lawyers, Litigation and English Society since 1450* (London, 1998), p. 92; R. Boote, *An Historical Treatise of an Action or Suit at Law* (London, 1766), pp. iii, x.

36. Brooks, *Lawyers, Litigation and English Society*, pp. 45–47, 93–94; W. A. Champion, 'Recourse to Law and the Meaning of the Great Litigation Decline, 1650–1750: Some Clues from the Shrewsbury Local Courts', in C. Brooks and M. Lobban, eds, *Communities and Courts in Britain, 1150–1900* (London, 1997), p. 186; Stone, *Road to Divorce*, pp. 188–89.

37. *London Chronicle*, 17 November 1785; *Trip Through London*, p. 35.

38. *Public Advertiser*, 18–19 April 1757; *OBP*, October 1757, trial of Terence Shortney and John Frip (t17571026–23).

39. Sollom Emlyn, ed., *A Complete Collection of State Trials*, 8 vols (2nd edn, London, 1730), i, p. iii; Henry Horwitz, *Chancery Equity Records and Proceedings, 1600–1800: A Guide to Documents in the Public Record Office*, Public Record Office Handbook, 27 (London, 1995), p. 26; Donna Andrew, ed., *London Debating Societies, 1776–1799*, London Record Society, 30 (London, 1994), passim.

40. *Old England*, 19 May 1750.

41. David Lemmings, *Professors of the Law: Barristers and English Legal Culture in the Eighteenth Century* (Oxford, 2000), p. 19.

42. Dudley Ryder's law notes, document 16, p. 54, *Longslow v. Boxal*.

43. Henry Fielding, *An Enquiry into the Causes of the Late Increase of Robbers* (1751; Oxford, 1988, ed. M. R. Zirker), section 7, pp. 157–58.

44. J. M. Beattie, *Crime and the Courts in England, 1660–1800* (Princeton, 1986), pp. 42–48; P. King, *Crime, Justice and Discretion in England, 1740–1820* (Oxford, 2000), pp. 48–51.

45. *Parliamentary Papers*, v (1816), p. 131; Shoemaker, *Prosecution and Punishment*, pp. 140, 276.

46. *Parliamentary History*, 29 (1817), 16 March 1792.

47. King, *Crime, Justice and Discretion*, p. 51.

48. Brooks, *Lawyers, Litigation and English Society*, pp. 50–52; Henry Horwitz and Patrick Polden, 'Continuity or Change in the Court of Chancery in the Seventeenth and Eighteenth Centuries?', *Journal of British Studies*, 35 (1996), pp. 43–49.

49. Meister, *Letters Written during a Residence in England*, pp. 39–40.

50. J. M. Maguire, 'Poverty and Civil Litigation', *Harvard Law Review*, 26 (1923), pp. 361–79.

51. Brooks, *Lawyers, Litigation and English Society*, pp. 39–40, 73–74, 98–100.

52. Rogers, 'Impressment and the Law', p. 94.

53. Shoemaker, *Prosecution and Punishment*, p. 211.

54. Brooks, *Lawyers, Litigation and English Society*, pp. 99–100, 111; Horwitz and Polden, 'Continuity or Change', p. 46; Margot Finn, 'Women, Consumption and Coverture in England, *c.* 1760–1860', *Historical Journal*, 39 (1996), pp. 714–15.

55. Tim Meldrum, 'A Women's Court in London: Defamation at the Bishop of London's Consistory Court, 1700–1745', *London Journal*, 19 (1994), p. 6; Randolph Trumbach, *Sex and the Gender Revolution*, i, *Homosexuality and the Third Gender in Enlightenment London* (Chicago and London, 1998), pp. 25–26, 327; Stone, *Road to Divorce*, p. 36.

56. Shoemaker, *Prosecution and Punishment*, pp. 207–12.

57. See above, Chapter 3.

58. Stone, *Road to Divorce*, pp. 34–38, quote from 190; Trumbach, *Sex and the Gender Revolution*, pp. 25, 326.

59. Brooks, *Lawyers, Litigation and English Society*, p. 55.

60. Ibid., p. 31; *A Trip from St James to the Royal Exchange* (London, 1744), p. 3.

61. Brooks, *Lawyers, Litigation and English Society*, pp. 31–35, 98; Lemmings, *Professors of the Law*, pp. 84–85, 93. The proportion of King's Bench

business identified as originating in London and Middlesex was 21 per cent in 1606 and between 48 per cent and 62 per cent in the 1820s, but many such cases actually came from other parts of the country.

62. Horwitz and Polden, 'Continuity or Change?', pp. 30–31, 40, 49; Horwitz, *Chancery Equity Records*, p. 27; Lemmings, *Professors of the Law*, p. 95.

63. Brooks, *Lawyers, Litigation and English Society*, p. 102; Lemmings, *Professors of the Law*, p. 294.

64. Shoemaker, *Prosecution and Punishment*, p. 63; Peter Linebaugh, 'Tyburn: A Study of Crime and the Labouring Poor in London during the First Half of the Eighteenth Century' (Ph.D. dissertation, Warwick University, 1975), p. 46; Ruth Paley, 'The Middlesex Justices Act of 1792: Its Origins and Effects' (Ph.D. dissertation, Reading University, 1983), p. 395; Hay, 'Prosecution and Power', pp. 386–88.

65. Shoemaker, *Prosecution and Punishment*, pp. 96–101.

66. Landau, 'Trading Justices' Trade', p. 59; BL, Add. MS 33053, fol. 223; Shoemaker, *Prosecution and Punishment*, p. 91.

67. Norma Landau, *The Justices of the Peace, 1679–1760* (Berkeley, 1984), p. 197; Shoemaker, *Prosecution and Punishment*, pp. 228–29; *Times*, 17 March 1792, p. 2.

68. Shoemaker, *Prosecution and Punishment*, pp. 117, 276.

69. [Baston], *Thoughts on Trade and a Public Spirit*, p. 129.

70. *Memoirs of the Life and Times of Sir Thomas DeVeil* (London, 1748), p. 18.

71. *A Trip Through the Town: Containing Observations on the Humours and Manners of the Age* (4th edn, London, 1735), p. 59.

72. Shoemaker, *Prosecution and Punishment*, pp. 228–30; LMA, MJ/SP/September 1696, no. 29; Landau, 'Trading Justices' Trade', p. 70.

73. *The Diary*, 3 July 1793.

74. Landau, 'Trading Justices' Trade', pp. 64, 68–69; Paley, 'Middlesex Justices Act', p. 394.

75. *Parliamentary Papers*, v (1816), pp. 61, 130–31.

76. Shoemaker, *Prosecution and Punishment*, pp. 89–90; DeVeil, *Observations*, p. 2.

77. Fielding, *Enquiry*, pp. 154–63.

78. Lemmings, *Professors of the Law*, pp. 208, 213; J. H. Langbein, *The Origins of the Adversary Criminal Trial* (Oxford, 2003), pp. 168–69; Allyson May, *The Bar and the Old Bailey, 1750–1850* (Chapel Hill, North Carolina, 2003), pp. 106–15.

79. *OBP*, January 1748, trial of John Smallwood (t17480115–13); Langbein, *Origins of the Adversary Criminal*, pp. 291–96.

80. John Hawkins, *The Life of Samuel Johnson* (Dublin, 1787), p. 522.

81. 58 George III, c. 73; Leon Radzinowicz, *A History of English Criminal Law*, 5 vols (London, 1948–90), ii, pp. 74–81.

82. Douglas Hay and Francis Snyder, 'Using the Criminal Law, 1750–1850', in Hay and Snyder, eds, *Policing and Prosecution*, pp. 37–40.

83. John Brewer, 'The Wilkites and the Law, 1763–74', in Brewer and John Styles, eds, *An Ungovernable People: The English and their Law in the Seventeenth and Eighteenth Centuries* (New Brunswick, New Jersey, 1980), pp. 128–71.

84. Lemmings, *Professors of the Law*, pp. 327–28; Christopher Brooks, 'Litigation, Participation and Agency in Seventeenth- and Eighteenth-Century England', in David Lemmings, ed., *The British and Their Laws in the Eighteenth Century* (forthcoming); David Punter, 'Fictional Representation of the Law in the Eighteenth Century', *Eighteenth-Century Studies*, 16 (1982), pp. 73–74.

85. Valerie Pearl, 'Change and Stability in Seventeenth-Century London', *London Journal*, 5 (1979), pp. 16–17, 25–26; Brooks, *Lawyers, Litigation and English Society*, pp. 126–27.

86. See above, Chapter 2.

87. Malcolm Gaskill, 'The Displacement of Providence: Policing and Prosecution in Seventeenth- and Eighteenth-Century England', *Continuity and Change*, 11 (1996), pp. 354, 361; Richard Burn, *The Justice of the Peace and Parish Officer*, 2 vols (London, 1755), ii, p. 448.

88. See above, Chapter 3.

89. Gaskill, 'Displacement of Providence', p. 357; J. P. Eigen, '"I Answer as a Physician": Opinion as Fact in Pre-McNaughton Insanity Trials', in M. Clark and C. Crawford, eds, *Legal Medicine in History* (Cambridge, 1994), pp. 171–72; Thomas R. Forbes, *Surgeons at the Old Bailey: English Forensic Medicine to 1878* (New Haven, 1985).

90. Cited by John Beattie, *Policing and Punishment in London, 1660–1750* (Oxford, 2001), pp. 108–13 (emphasis added).

91. Donna Andrew and Randall McGowen, *The Perreaus and Mrs Rudd: Forgery and Betrayal in Eighteenth-Century London* (Berkeley, 2001), pp. 26, 33–34, 219–20; Amanda Vickery, *The Gentleman's Daughter: Women's Lives in Georgian England* (New Haven, 1998), p. 238; *General Evening Post*, 8 February 1780.

92. *OBP*; [Béat-Louis de Muralt], *Letters Describing the Character and Customs of the English and French Nations … Translated from the French* (London, 1726), p. 72.

93. Stone, *Road to Divorce*, pp. 249–51.

94. For two trials which excited widespread public interest, see Andrew and McGowen, *The Perreaus and Mrs Rudd*.

95. Samuel Stanton, *The Principles of Duelling: With Rules to be Observed in Every Particular Respecting it* (London, 1790), p. 27.

96. Fielding, *Enquiry*, p. 154; Andrew, ed., *London Debating Societies*, p. 125, no. 717.

97. Stone, *Road to Divorce*, pp. 253–54; Brooks, *Lawyers, Litigation and English Society*, p. 51.

## Notes to Chapter 9: Print

1. CLRO, Sessions Papers, August 1695, information of Mainwearing Davis.

2. *A Short Treatise upon the Propriety and Necessity of Duelling* (Bath, 1779), p. 16.

3. [Charles Daubeny], *Some Considerations Relative to a Most Extraordinary Trial* (n.p., 1793) p. 1; T[homas] M[eade], *Considerations Reconsidered: Being a Reply to a Pamphlet Lately Circulated Relative to a Trial ... Brought by Thomas Meade Esq. against the Reverend Charles Daubeny* (Oxford, 1794).

4. Adrian Johns, *The Nature of the Book: Print and Knowledge in the Making* (Chicago and London, 1998), chap. 2.

5. Peter Earle, *A City Full of People: Men and Women of London, 1650–1750* (London, 1994), p. 37; Naomi Tadmor, ' "In the Even my Wife Read to me": Women, Reading and Household Life in the Eighteenth Century', in James Raven et al., *The Practice and Representation of Reading in England* (Cambridge, 1996), p. 165.

6. Paula McDowell, *The Women of Grub Street: Press, Politics and Gender in the London Literary Marketplace, 1678–1730* (Oxford, 1998); *The Just Complaint of the Poor Weavers Truly Represented* (London, 1719); *A Second Humble Address from the Poor Weavers and Manufacturers to the Ladies* (London?, 1720?).

7. William Holdsworth, *A History of English Law*, 17 vols (London, 1903–72), viii, pp. 347, 360–67; *English Reports*, 178 vols (London and Edinburgh, 1900–32), lxxxvii, p. 89, *R. v. Darby* (3 Mod. 139). See also *State Law: or The Doctrine of Libels Discussed and Examined* (2nd edn, London [1730?]), p. 75; *The Doctrine of Libels and the Duty of Juries Fairly Stated* (London, 1752), p. 7.

8. Edward Reyner, *Rules for the Government of the Tongue* (1656), dedication.

9. *Charges to the Grand Jury, 1689–1803*, ed. Georges Lamoine, Camden Society, fourth series, 43 (London, 1992), passim. The quotation, from p. 204, is from D. Dolins, *The Charge of Sir Daniel Dolins, Kt to the Grand Jury and Other Juries of the County of Middlesex* (London, 1725).

10. Robert Morris, *A Letter to Sir Richard Aston, Kt ... Containing a Reply to his Scandalous Abuse, and Some Thoughts on the Modern Doctrine of Libels* (London, 1770), p. 8.

11. *Freeholder*, 24 February 1716; Lamoine, ed., *Charges to the Grand Jury*, p. 220, from J. Gonson, *The Charge of Sir John Gonson to the Grand Jury of the City and Liberty of Westminster* (London, 1728).

12. John Tottie, *The Folly and Guilt of Satirical Slander* (Oxford, 1763), p. 13. See also C. D. Piguenit, *An Essay on the Art of News-Paper Defamation* (London, 1775), p. 2.

13. [T. Hayter], *An Essay on the Liberty of the Press, Chiefly as it Respects Personal Slander* (London, [1755]), p. 19.

14. Lisa Forman Cody, '"Every Lane Teems with Instruction, and Every Alley is Big with Erudition': Graffiti in Eighteenth-Century London', in Tim Hitchcock and Heather Shore, eds, *The Streets of London From the Great Fire to the Great Stink* (London, 2003), pp. 98–100.

15. Adam Fox, *Oral and Literate Culture in England, 1500–1700* (Oxford, 2000), chaps 6–7; Pauline Croft, 'Libels, Popular Literacy and Public Opinion in Early Modern England', *Historical Research*, 68 (1995), pp. 266–85; Thomas Cogswell, 'Underground Verse and the Transformation of Early Stuart Political Culture', in S. D. Amussen and M. A. Kishlansky, eds, *Political Culture and Cultural Politics in Early Modern England* (Manchester and New York, 1995), pp. 277–300.

16. Tim Hitchcock, *Down and Out in Eighteenth-Century London* (forthcoming); Barry Reay, *Popular Cultures in England, 1550–1750* (London, 1998), pp. 58–59; V. A. C. Gatrell, *The Hanging Tree: Execution and the English People, 1770–1868* (Oxford, 1994), p. 141.

17. *The Spittle-Fields Ballad: or The Weavers Complaint against the Callico Madams* [London, 1719]. For an earlier version, see GL, A.1.3, no. 64 (62), reprinted in Alfred Plummer, *The London Weavers' Company, 1600–1970* (London, 1972), p. 297.

18. CLRO, Sessions Papers, July 1719.

19. G. Parker, *A View of Society and Manners in High and Low Life*, 2 vols (London, 1781), ii, p. 58.

20. *OBP*, July 1779, trial of Robert Wright (t17790707–48).

21. Ibid., December 1781, trial of William Moore (t17811205–56); W. H. Pyne, *The Costume of Great Britain* (London, 1808), no. 43.

22. LMA, MJ/SR/1651, R.316 (September 1684); Isaac Broderick, *An Appeal to the Public: or The Case of Mr Isaac Broderick* ([London], 1731), p. 60; *Daily Advertiser*, 29 October 1772.

23. *Frauds and Abuses at St Paul's, in a Letter to Parliament* (London, 1712);

*An Answer to a Pamphlet Entitul'd, Frauds and Abuses at St Paul's* (London, 1713); *Facts against Scandal: or A Collection of Testimonials, and Other Authentick Proofs, in Vindication of Mr Richard Jennings, Carpenter* (London, 1713), p. 51; *A Continuation of Frauds and Abuses at St Paul's* (London, 1713). For a history and chronology of this dispute, see 'The "Frauds and Abuses" Controversy', *Wren Society*, 20 vols (Oxford, 1924–43), xvi, pp. 139–81. According to Lisa Jardine, this dispute centred around the issue of how much independence should be accorded to skilled craftsmen: *On a Grander Scale: The Outstanding Career of Christopher Wren* (London, 2002), pp. 466–68.

24. Richard Russell, *A Letter to Dr Addington of Reading* (London, 1749), pp. 7, 14; Richard Russel[l], *A Letter to Mr Thomas Bigg ... Occasioned by his Having Written a Defamatory Letter to Dr Addington* (London, 1751), advertisement and p. 1.

25. W[illiam] Woolley, *A Cure for Canting* (London, 1794), pp. 8–11.

26. Hannah Barker, *Newspapers, Politics and English Society, 1695–1855* (Harlow, 2000), pp. 29, 47, 49–50; Jeremy Black, *The English Press in the Eighteenth Century* (1987; reprint Aldershot, 1991), pp. 61, 104–5.

27. César de Saussure, *A Foreign View of England in 1725–1729*, trans. and ed. Madame van Muyden (London, 1995), p. 102; Norman G. Brett-James, *The Growth of Stuart London* (London, 1935), p. 510.

28. Black, *English Press*, pp. 95–97; Barker, *Newspapers, Politics and English Society*, p. 101.

29. *Weekly Journal, or Saturday's Post*, 11 October, 1718; *London Evening Post*, 3 December 1761; Donna Andrew and Randall McGowen, *The Perreaus and Mrs Rudd: Forgery and Betrayal in Eighteenth-Century London* (Berkeley, 2001), pp. 58–59.

30. *Weekly Journal, or Saturday's Post*, 4 October 1718.

31. *London Daily Advertiser*, 30 April, 9, 11, 12 and 30 May 1752; Henry Fielding, *Covent Garden Journal*, 38 (12 May 1752) and 60 (22 August 1752), reprint edn, ed. B. A. Goldgar (Oxford, 1998), pp. 325–27, 432–33.

32. *Morning Post and Daily Advertiser*, 29 June, 1 and 5 July, 1779; *OBP*, June 1782, trial of Bennet Allen and Robert Morris (t17820605-1).

33. R. B. Walker, 'Advertising in London Newspapers, 1650–1750', *Business History*, 15 (1973), pp. 129–30; Black, *English Press*, pp. 27–28; James Oldham, *The Mansfield Manuscripts and the Growth of English Law in the Eighteenth Century*, 2 vols (Chapel Hill and London, 1992), ii, 854, *R* v. *Bate*.

34. [John Hill], *Circumstances which Preceded the Letters to the Earl of M[exborough] and may tend to the Discovery of the Author* (London, 1775), p. 9

(emphasis in original); *Morning Post, and Daily Advertiser*, 28 February to 6 April 1775, passim.

35. *Morning Post*, 29 March 1775.

36. Oldham, *Mansfield Manuscripts*, ii, p. 858–61, *R.* v. *Bate; Morning Herald*, 8 August 1781.

37. LMA, MJ/SP/August 1721, no. 5; *London Evening Post*, 29 December 1741.

38. *OBP*, February 1796, trial of Michael Robinson (t17960217–71).

39. [Erasmus Jones], *The Man of Manners: or Plebeian Polish'd* (London, 1737), p. 28.

40. Walker, 'Advertising in London Newspapers', pp. 120–23; *Weekly Journal*, 22 May 1725, cited by Black, *English Press*, p. 52; [John] Trusler, *The London Adviser and Guide: Containing Every Instruction and Information Useful and Necessary to Persons Living in London, and Coming to Reside There* (London, 1786), p. 124.

41. See above, Chapter 2.

42. *Fog's Weekly Journal*, 14 February 1736, cited by Black, *English Press*, p. 59.

43. *True Domestic Intelligence*, no. 67, 20–24 February 1680.

44. CLRO, Misc. MS 115.9, 19 August and 21 October 1796.

45. Donna Andrew, 'The Press and Public Apologies in Eighteenth-Century London', in N. Landau, ed., *Law, Crime and English Society, 1660–1830* (Cambridge, 2002), pp. 208–29; Plummer, *London Weavers' Company*, p. 309; *Daily Advertiser*, 29 October 1772; *Times*, 9 September 1786, p. 4c.

46. Andrew, 'Press and Public Apologies', pp. 213–15, 218–27; see above, Chapter 3.

47. *This is Not the Thing: or Molly Exalted* (London, [1763?] (LMA, SC/PD/XX/4513A); R. Norton, *Mother Clap's Molly House: The Gay Subculture in England, 1700–1830* (London, 1992), p. 130.

48. *General Evening Post*, 18 July 1771; Robert B. Shoemaker, 'Streets of Shame? The Crowd and Public Punishments in London, 1700–1820', in S. Devereaux and P. Griffiths, eds, *Penal Practice and Culture, 1500–1900* (forthcoming).

49. Broderick, *Appeal to the Public*, p. 60.

50. Francis Place, 'Specimens of Songs and Fragments of Songs from Memory: Songs Sung about the Streets', no. 14, BL, Add. MS 27825, fol. 150v; Gatrell, *The Hanging Tree*, chaps. 4–5, especially pp. 140–42.

51. *Weekly Journal, or Saturday's Post*, 11 October, 1718; *Fog's Weekly Journal*, 16 August 1729; Black, *English Press*, p. 156.

52. Raymond Postgate, *'That Devil Wilkes'* (London, 1930), pp. 44–45; *OBP*, June 1782, trial of Bennet Allen and Robert Morris (t17820605–1).

53. Jan Bondeson, *The London Monster: A Sanguinary Tale* (London, 2000), pp. 67, 71. See also below, Chapter 10.

54. *The Life and Noble Character of Richard Thornhill, Esq., who had the Misfortune to Kill Sir Cholmley Deering, Bart* (London, 1711); *An Account of the Life and Character of Sir Chomley [sic] Deering, Bar.* (London, 1711); *The Case of Col. Richard Thornhill, Showing the True Occasion of his Fighting Sir Cholmley Deering Bar.* (London, 1711); *A True Account of What Past [sic] at the Old Bailey, May the 18th, 1711 Relating to the Tryal of Richard Thornhill, Esq.* (2nd edn, London, 1711); *A Full and True Account of a Horrid and Barbarous Murder Committed Last Night ... on the Body of Richard Thornhill, Esq.* (London, 1711).

55. [Daniel Defoe], *A Strick Enquiry into the Circumstance of a Late Duel* (London, 1713), p. 32; Victor Stater, *Duke Hamilton is Dead! A Story of Aristocratic Life and Death in Stuart Britain* (New York, 1999), pp. 251–52.

56. *The North Briton: To Which is Added, by Way of an Appendix, the Letters which Passed between the Rt. Hon. Earl Talbot, etc. and John Wilkes, Esq.*, 2 vols (Dublin, 1763); BL, Add. MS 30869, fol. 139 (3 July 1767); Postgate, 'That Devil Wilkes', p. 50.

57. Bondeson, *London Monster*, pp. 126–27; *Times*, 7 July 1789, p. 2c, 14 July 1789, p. 1c, 3 August 1789, p. 3a.

58. *The Vauxhall Affray: or The Macaronies Defeated* (2nd edn, London, 1773); Clare Brant, 'Duelling by Sword and Pen: The Vauxhall Affray of 1773', *Prose Studies*, 19 (1996), pp. 160–72.

59. *Times*, 14 September to 8 December 1790, passim, quote from 7 October (emphasis in the original).

60. W. S. Lewis, ed., *Horace Walpole's Correspondence*, 48 vols (London, New Haven and Oxford, 1937–83), xxiv, pp. 537–38, xxviii, pp. 481–82; *Gentleman's Magazine*, 49 (1779), p. 610; John A. Atkinson, *Duelling Pistols and Some of the Affairs They Settled* (London, 1964), pp. 115–16.

61. TNA, SP 35/21/56, 57.

62. *Spitalfields and Shoreditch in an Uproar* [London, 1736]; *London Evening Post*, 29 July 1736. On 4 August the printer of 'two scandalous and seditious ballads' was committed to Newgate, and informations were taken against several others for printing such papers: TNA, SP 44/130, p. 115.

63. TNA, SP 37/10, fos 63–124.

64. J. Paul de Castro, *The Gordon Riots* (London, 1926), pp. 17, 25, 57, 74–75, 190; *St James Chronicle*, 19–21, 21–23 August 1794; *Gentleman's Magazine*, 70 (1800), p. 894.

65. *OBP*, July 1768, trial of John Grainger et al. (t17680706–46). For the background to this riot, see John Stevenson, *Popular Disturbances in*

*England, 1700–1832* (2nd edn, London, 1992), pp. 85–87. For the poster in the King's Bench Prison riot, see BL, Add. MS 30884, fos 66–72.

66. *The Manufacturer*, 1, 30 October 1719, GL, A.1.3, no. 64 (3). This volume contains copies of most of the pamphlets and newspapers published during the dispute. The newspapers are reprinted in Robert N. Gosselink, ed., *The Manufacturer (1719–21) by Daniel Defoe, Together with Related Issues of the British Merchant and The Weaver* (Delmar, New York, 1978).

67. *London Journal*, 17 February 1733.

68. *St James Chronicle*, 19–23 August 1794; John Stevenson, 'The London "Crimp" Riots of 1794', *International Review of Social History*, 16 (1971), pp. 40–58.

69. *The Just Complaint of the Poor Weavers Truly Represented* (London, 1719), pp. 40–43.

70. GL, MS 4655/11, fos 292–93; Plummer, *London Weavers' Company*, pp. 303–4. Among the disturbances were two attacks on weavers' houses because they allegedly did not support the bill. The two published affidavits denying the charge: GL, A.1.3, no. 64 (57–60).

71. *St James Chronicle*, 21 August 1794.

72. *London Evening Post*, 31 July 1736.

73. Tim Hitchcock, '"You Bitches ... Die and be Damned": Gender, Authority and the Mob in St Martin's Round-House Disaster of 1742', in Hitchcock and Shore, eds, *The Streets of London*, pp. 78–79; *London Evening Post*, 17 July 1742.

74. *General Evening Post*, 15 June 1780; TNA, HO 42/44, fos 264, 270, 274, 280.

75. CLRO, Sessions Papers, February 1769, advertisement of Jacob James. See also the *Times*, 9 September 1786, p. 4c.

76. Andrew and McGowen, *The Perreaus and Mrs Rudd*, chap. 3.

77. *OBP*, October 1725, trial of Foster Snow (t17251013–25); December 1725, supplementary material re Foster Snow (o17251208–1); Broderick, *Appeal to the Public*, pp. 28–46, 60.

78. Lawrence Stone, *Road to Divorce: A History of the Making and Breaking of Marriage in England* (Oxford, 1990), p. 250. This case is discussed in the introduction to this chapter.

79. *The Trial of John Almon, Bookseller* (London, 1770); [G. Rous], *A Letter to the Jurors of Great Britain* (London, 1771); Robert Morris, *A Letter to Sir Richard Aston, Knt* (London, 1770), pp. 5, 8, 66. See also Oldham, *Mansfield Manuscripts*, ii, pp. 833–36.

80. Woolley, *A Cure for Canting*, pp. 8, 82; *The Trials of the Reverend William Woolley, Clerk, for Publishing a Libel on Sir Richard Hill, Bart, and the*

*Reverend Rowland Hill, Clerk, Intitled A Cure for Canting* (London, 1794); Russel[l], *A Letter to Mr Thomas Bigg*, p. 19.

81. *A Satisfactory Refutation of Sir Hypo Bardana's 'Circumstances' by 'Camlin'* (London, [1775]), p. vi.

82. Andrew, 'Press and Public Apologies', pp. 210 n. 5, 227.

83. *Poor Robins Intelligence: or News from City and Country*, no. 2, 17 July 1691.

84. [John Dunton], *The Nightwalker: or Evening Rambles in Search after Lewd Women* (London, 1696–97), September 1696, preface and p. 1; Ned Ward, *The London Spy* (4th edn, 1709; reprint ed. Paul Hyland, East Lansing, Michigan, 1993), pp. 9–11.

85. *Weekly Journal: or British Gazetteer*, 1 April 1721; *Daily Post*, 1 January 1741. See also *London Evening Post*, 10 January 1741.

86. *General Evening Post*, 17 December 1771.

87. Ibid., 1 April 1781.

88. *Daily Advertiser*, 9 October 1755, cited by Andrew, 'Press and Public Apologies', pp. 211–12.

89. Stone, *Road to Divorce*, p. 252; Nicholas Rogers, 'Pigott's Private Eye: Radicalism and Sexual Scandal in Eighteenth-Century England', *Journal of the Canadian Historical Association*, 4 (1993), pp. 247–63; Black, *English Press*, pp. 266–67.

90. *Daily Journal*, 13 April 1728; T. C. Duncan Eaves and Ben D. Kimpel, 'Two Notes on Samuel Richardson', *Library*, 5th series, 23 (1968), p. 245; TNA, KB 28/107, membrane xxviii; Oldham, *Mansfield Manuscripts*, ii, pp. 858–61; *Morning Herald*, 8 August 1781.

91. Black, *English Press*, pp. 157–59.

92. *London Evening Post*, 3 December 1761; *Weekly Journal, or Saturday's Post*, 11 October 1718; BL, Add. MS 20733, fol. 1v, 6 November 1779.

93. *Daily Universal Register*, 17 January 1785; Black, *English Press*, p. 40; *Public Advertiser*, 22 August 1767; *General Evening Post*, 30 March 1771.

94. Woolley, *Cure for Canting*, pp. 11–12; *Satisfactory Refutation*, p. 37 (emphasis in original); [Daubeny], *Some Considerations*, p. 135; M[eade], *Considerations Reconsidered*, p. 107.

95. Donna Andrew, '"To the Charitable and Humane": Appeals for Assistance in the Eighteenth-Century London Press', in H. Cunningham and J. Innes, eds, *Charity, Philanthropy and Reform: From the 1690s to 1850* (Houndmills, 1998), p. 101.

96. BL, Add. MS, 27825, fos 144–45; Gatrell, *The Hanging Tree*, pp. 125–26.

*Notes to Chapter 10: The Monster*

1. Georg Forster, *Werke*, xii, *Tagebücher* (Berlin, 1973), pp. 297–98, quoted in Jan Bondeson, *The London Monster* (London, 2000), p. 51.

2. The attacks are listed in Bondeson, *London Monster*, pp. 222–23. This book contains the most comprehensive secondary account of these events, though it does not draw conclusions about their wider historical significance.

3. *OBP*, July 1790, trial of Rhynwick Williams (t17900708–1).

4. Ibid. For the only other previous trial, see *OBP*, October 1785, trial of Charlotte Springmore and Mary Harrison (t17851019–57).

5. *Whipping Tom Brought to Light and Exposed to View* (London, 1681). The other attacks are discussed above, Chapter 6.

6. For an overview, see Bondeson, *London Monster*, chaps 12–13.

7. [John Julius Angerstein], *An Authentic Account of the Barbarities Lately Practised by the Monsters* (London, 1790), pp. 51–52, 65–68.

8. *Whipping Tom*, p. 1.

9. For violence, see above, Chapter 6; for the weavers' attacks, see Chapter 5.

10. Bondeson, *London Monster*, pp. 180–81, 199–201.

11. The *Proceedings* report that as he was speaking Coleman was 'peeping over his shoulder, and making a clapping with his hands'.

12. *OBP*, July 1790; *Diary*, 27 July 1790, clipping in Sarah Sophia Banks, 'A Collection of Broadsides' (British Library, L.R.301.h.3), fol. 49aa; Theophilus Swift, *The Monster at Large: or The Innocence of Rhynwick Williams Vindicated* (London [1791]), p. 167.

13. Bondeson, *London Monster*, pp. 73–77; Swift, *Monster at Large*, pp. 112–14.

14. *Whipping Tom*, p. 2.

15. [Angerstein], *Authentic Account*, p. 47; *OBP*, December 1790, trial of Renwick Williams, otherwise Rhynwick Williams (t17901208–54).

16. Swift, *Monster at Large*, pp. 65, 104–11; *World*, 19 June 1790, p. 3c; Bondeson, *London Monster*, p. 91. As the Porter sisters lived in a bagnio (bath house), albeit an allegedly respectable one, Williams might not have been unreasonable in expecting them to be sexually available.

17. See above, Chapter 2.

18. *Whipping Tom*, p. 2.

19. LMA, MJ/SP/April 1712/30; MJ/SBB/702 (April 1712). See also Neil Guthrie, '"No Truth or Very Little in the Whole Story?" A Reassessment of the Mohock Scare of 1712', *Eighteenth-Century Life*, 20 (1996), pp. 40–41.

20. *Public Advertiser*, 11 May 1790, p. 3d.

21. Bondeson, *London Monster*, p. 74.

22. *Public Advertiser*, 1 May 1790, p. 4b.

23. [Angerstein], *Authentic Account*, pp. 22–24.

24. *OBP*, July 1790; Bondeson, *London Monster*, p. 15; *Diary*, 27 July 1790, in Banks, 'Collection of Broadsides', fol. 49aa.

25. [Angerstein], *Authentic Account*, pp. 16, 30.

26. Ibid., p. 14; *OBP*, December 1790.

27. See above, Chapter 2.

28. [Angerstein], *Authentic Account*, pp. 19–21; *World*, 11 May 1790, in Banks, 'Collection of Broadsides', fol. 49aa; Bondeson, *London Monster*, pp. 23–24. For similar examples, see ibid., pp. 39, 53–54.

29. *World*, 15 June 1790, p. 3a-b; Swift, *Monster at Large*, p. 212; Bondeson, *London Monster*, pp. 60, 86–87, 90, 94.

30. *Court Chronicle*, 15 May 1790, in Banks, 'Collection of Broadsides', fol. 49aa.

31. [Angerstein], *Authentic Account*, p. 12; Bondeson, *Monster at Large*, pp. 15, 29.

32. For similar expectations in response to the Lascars in 1780, see *General Evening Post*, 5–8 February 1780.

33. *Morning Herald*, 8 April 1790, in Banks, 'Collection of Broadsides', fol. 49aa; [Angerstein], *Authentic Account*, p. 77.

34. *Morning Herald*, 9–10 April 1790, in Banks, 'Collection of Broadsides', fol. 49aa.

35. *World*, 20 April 1790, in Banks, ' Collection of Broadsides', fol. 49aa; [Angerstein], *Authentic Account*, p. 72.

36. LMA, MJ/SBB/702 (April 1712), p. 43 (order dated 11 March). A royal proclamation was issued on 17 March.

37. *Morning Herald*, 16 April 1790, in Banks, 'Collection of Broadsides', fol. 49aa; ibid., fol. 44aa (poster advertising award); [Angerstein], *Authentic Account*, p. 33.

38. Banks, ' Collection of Broadsides', fos 46aa (poster announcing the formation of the association), 47aa (manuscript agreement). There was a similar organisation in Westminster: Bondeson, *London Monster*, p. 52. For more on such voluntary associations, see above, Chapter 2.

39. Swift, *Monster at Large*, pp. 7, 210; TNA, HO 47/17, fol. 456; *OBP*, December 1790; *Times*, 15 June 1790, p. 3c. The paper failed to mention his name 'from a regard to the family'.

40. [Angerstein], *Authentic Account*, pp. 6–7; *Public Ledger*, 21 May 1790, cited by [Angerstein], *Authentic Account*, pp. 100–2; *Times*, 15 May 1790, p. 3a and 21 May 1790, p. 3d; Bondeson, *London Monster*, pp. 56–58.

41. Donna Andrew, ed., *London Debating Societies 1776–1799*, London Record Society, 30 (1994), p. 287. See also p. 283.

42. Rhynwick Williams, *An Appeal to the Public* (London, [1792]), pp. 13, 24, 46.

43. Jonathan Swift, *Journal to Stella*, ed. H. Williams, 2 vols (1948; reprint, Oxford, 1974), ii, p. 511; Guthrie, '"No Truth or Very Little in the Whole Story?"'; Daniel Statt, 'The Case of the Mohocks: Rake Violence in Augustan London', *Social History*, 20 (1995), pp. 179–99.

44. Bondeson, *London Monster*, pp. 195, 210.

45. Swift, *Monster at Large*, p. vii; *Times*, 15 May 1790, p. 3a.

46. Erich Goode and Nachman Ben-Yehuda, *Moral Panics: The Social Construction of Deviance* (Oxford, 1994).

47. Banks, 'Collection of Broadsides', fos 48aa (poster accusing Thicknesse of being the Monster), 57aa ('The Monstrous Assassin'); *World*, 15 June 1790, p. 2c; Bondeson, *London Monster*, pp. 65–72, 119–22; Philip Gosse, *Dr Viper: The Querulous Life of Philip Thicknesse* (London, 1952), pp. 273–79.

48. See above, Chapters 3 and 6.

49. Norbert Elias, *The Civilizing Process: The History of Manners and State Formation and Civilization* (1939; trans. E. Jephcott, Oxford, 1994). For an argument about the growing significance of bourgeois public opinion, see Jürgen Habermas, *The Structural Transformation of the Public Sphere* (Neuwied and Berlin, 1969; trans. T. Burger, Cambridge, 1989). The work of Michel Foucault sees changes in public life as cultural phenomena emanating from society as a whole, though crucial roles are assigned both to the state and enlightenment thought. See, for example, his *Discipline and Punish: The Birth of the Prison* (Paris, 1975; trans. A. Sheridan, London, 1977).

50. Jessica Warner, *Craze: Gin and Debauchery in an Age of Reason* (London, 2003); L. Davison, 'Experiments in the Social Regulation of Industry: Gin Legislation, 1729–1751', in idem et al., eds, *Stilling the Grumbling Hive: The Response to Social and Economic Problems in England, 1689–1750* (Stroud, 1992), pp. 25–48.

51. L. Davison et al., 'The Reactive State: English Governance and Society, 1689–1750', in idem, eds, *Stilling the Grumbling Hive*, pp. xi–liv. But see also Joanna Innes, 'Parliament and the Shaping of Eighteenth-Century English Social Policy', *Transactions of the Royal Historical Society*, 5th series, 40 (1990), pp. 63–92.

52. See above, Chapter 2.

53. Erik Gustaf Geijer, *Impressions of England, 1809–1810*, trans. E. Sprigge and C. Napier (London, 1932), p. 171.

54. Anna Bryson, *From Courtesy to Civility: Changing Codes of Conduct in Early Modern England* (Oxford, 1998); Lawrence Klein, 'Politeness and the

Interpretation of the British Eighteenth Century', *Historical Journal*, 45 (2002), pp. 869–98; Philip Carter, *Men and the Emergence of Polite Society: Britain, 1660–1800* (Harlow, 2001).

55. *OBP*, July 1722, trial of John Nichols (t17220704–68).

56. G. J. Barker-Benfield, *The Culture of Sensibility: Sex and Society in Eighteenth-Century Britain* (Chicago, 1992), chaps 5–6; Anthony Fletcher, *Gender, Sex and Subordination in England, 1500–1800* (New Haven, 1995), chaps 16, 19.

57. *World*, 10 May 1790, 3a.

58. W[illiam] W[instanley], *The New Help to Discourse* (London, 1684), pp. 280–81; Lawrence Klein, 'Politeness for Plebes: Consumption and Social Identity in Early Eighteenth-Century England', in A. Bermingham and J. Brewer, eds, *The Consumption of Culture, 1600–1800* (London, 1995), pp. 362–82.

59. Jeremy Gregory, '*Homo Religiosus*: Masculinity and Religion in the Long Eighteenth Century', in T. Hitchcock and M. Cohen, eds, *English Masculinities, 1660–1800* (London, 1999), pp. 85–110.

60. Leonard W. Cowie, *Henry Newman: An American in London, 1708–43* (London, 1956), pp. 55–59; *A Dissuasive from the Sin of Uncleanness* (London, 1701), pp. 2–3; Josiah Woodward, *The Baseness and Perniciousness of the Sin of Slandering and Back-Biting* (3rd edn, London, 1729), pp. 16–17.

61. Klein, 'Politeness for Plebes', pp. 374–75.

62. [Erasmus Jones], *The Man of Manners: or Plebeian Polish'd* (London, 1737), pp. 4, 5, 48.

63. *OBP*, July 1790.

64. Ibid., February 1774, trial of Jane Robinson, William Dickenson et al. (t17740216–69); December 1746, trial of Thomas Stephens (t17461205–9); July 1756, trial of John Girle (t17560714–26).

65. In contrast, Paul Langford argues that discourses of politeness contributed to growing plebeian conformity to the standards of polite behaviour from the 1780s: 'The Uses of Seventeenth-Century Politeness', *Transactions of the Royal Historical Society*, sixth series, 12 (2002), pp. 311–31. For the adoption of ideals of domesticity and respectability by the working class in the early nineteenth century, see Anna Clark, *The Struggle for the Breeches: Gender and the Making of the British Working Class* (Berkeley, 1995).

66. M. Grosley, *A Tour to London: or New Observations on England and its Inhabitants*, trans. T. Nugent (London, 1772), p. 62.

67. Karl Westhauser, 'The Power of Conversation: The Evolution of Modern Social Relations in Augustan London' (Brown University Ph.D. thesis, 1994), p. 380; Robert B. Shoemaker, 'The Decline of Public Insult in London, 1660–1800', *Past and Present*, 169 (2000), p. 126.

68. Bondeson, *London Monster*, pp. 76–77.

69. Paul Langford, 'British Politeness and the Progress of Western Manners: An Eighteenth-Century Enigma', *Transactions of the Royal Historical Society*, sixth series, 7 (1997), p. 62; Geijer, *Impressions of England*, pp. 91, 125–26

70. 'Rules of Behaviour, of General Use, Though Much Disregarded in this Populous City', *London Magazine*, May 1780, p. 187; [Jones], *Man of Manners*, p. 43; François La Rochefoucauld, *A Frenchman in England in 1784*, ed. J. Marchand and trans. S. C. Roberts (London, 1995), p. 9.

71. Clark, *Struggle for the Breeches*, pp. 27–30.

72. Peter Clark, *British Clubs and Societies, 1580–1800: The Origins of an Associational World* (Oxford, 2000); Craig Muldrew, 'From a "Light Cloak" to an "Iron Cage": Historical Changes in the Relation between Community and Individualism', in A. Shepherd and P. Withington, eds, *Communities in Early Modern England* (Manchester, 2000), p. 170; Richard Sennett, *The Fall of Public Man* (1977; reprint, London, 1993), p. 83.

73. *The Autobiography of Francis Place*, ed. Mary Thale (Cambridge, 1972), p. 189

74. *The Cheats of London Exposed: or The Tricks of the Town Laid Open to Both Sexes* (London, [1770]), pp. 62, 88; Stephen Greenblatt, 'Psychoanalysis and Renaissance Culture', in his *Learning to Curse: Essays in Early-Modern Culture* (London, 1990), pp. 131–45; Sennett, *Fall of Public Man*, chaps 4–6; Michael Mascuch, *Origins of the Individualist Self: Autobiography and Self-Identity in England, 1591–1791* (Cambridge, 1997).

75. Faramerz Dabhoiwala, 'Sex, Social Relations and the Law in Seventeenth- and Eighteenth-Century London', in M. Braddick and J. Walter, eds, *Negotiating Power in Early Modern Society* (Cambridge, 2001), p. 99; Randolph Trumbach, *Sex and the Gender Revolution*, i, *Heterosexuality and the Third Gender in Enlightenment London* (Chicago and London, 1998), p. 29; Miles Ogborn, *Spaces of Modernity: London's Geographies, 1680–1780* (New York and London, 1998), p. 79.

76. John Brewer, 'This, That and the Other: Public, Social and Private in the Seventeenth and Eighteenth Centuries', in Dario Castiglione and Lesley Sharpe, eds, *Shifting the Boundaries: Transformation of the Languages of Public and Private in the Eighteenth Century* (Exeter, 1995), p. 15.

## Notes to Appendix: Sources and Methods

1. Full references to the published sources referred to here are provided in the Select Bibliography.

2. The published *Autobiography of Francis Place*, ed. Mary Thale (Cambridge, 1972), only touches the surface of the large collection of Place manuscripts kept in the British Library. The most useful for this project were his 'Collections Relating to Manners and Morals' (Add. MSS 27825–27830).

3. *Weekly Journal, or British Gazetteer* (1721), *London Journal* (1731), *London Evening Post* (1741, 1751, 1761), *General Evening Post* (1771, 1780). (The end of the century was covered by the *Times*.)

4. Volumes of the *Gentleman's Magazine* for 1731–50 are also available from the Internet Library of Early Journals, where they can be searched using the index, along with a similar publication, the *Annual Register*, which can be browsed from 1758 to 1778.

5. Donna Andrew, ed., *London Debating Societies, 1776–1799*, London Record Society, 30 (1994).

6. Sarah Sophia Banks, 'A Collection of Broadsides, Cuttings from Newspapers, Engravings, etc., of Various Dates', 9 vols (1780?–1810?), BL, shelfmark L.R.301.h.3–11; Daniel Lysons 'Collectanea: or A Collection of Advertisements and Paragraphs from the Newspapers, Relating to Various Subjects', 6 vols, BL, shelfmarks C.191.c.16, C.103.k.11, C.103.k.12.

7. A significant number of the manuscript Old Bailey sessions papers in the LMA were uncatalogued at the time this research was conducted; new listings of these records will unearth many more informations relating to homicide cases for future investigation. Riot, assault and defamation were prosecuted less frequently at King's Bench. Although depositions relating to King's Bench cases were not fully catalogued, some were consulted: TNA, record series KB 1.

8. LMA, DL/C/240, 243, 247, 255, 262, 272–73, 276–78, 280–81, 283–84, 638.

9. TNA. For the correspondence, see record series, SP 34–37, 44; for prosecution briefs, see KB 8, T 1, TS 11.

10. LMA, DL/C/31, 33–34, 36–54, 79–81, 145–85.

11. For more on these records, see Robert B. Shoemaker, 'Using Quarter Sessions Records as Evidence for the Study of Crime and Criminal Justice', *Archives*, 20 (October 1993), pp. 145–57.

12. The years examined were 1660, 1663, even numbered years between 1664 and 1690, and odd numbered years between 1693 and 1781.

13. TNA, CP 60/3085 (1690), 40/3507–8 (1740), 60/949 (1740), 3633 (1760); KB 27/2078 (1690), 122/74 (1715), 122/179 and 181 (1740), 122/298 (1760), 122/443–44 (1780). The records of the London Mayor's Court were also investigated in sufficient detail to ascertain that defamation cases were rarely prosecuted there: CLRO, MC 1/217, 217a, 239b, 240; MCD box 1/50–51 (1716–25).

14. *Middlesex County Records: Calendar of Sessions Books*, 51 vols [London, 1911–23], available in the BL and LMA.

15. LMA, MJ/SPB/11–15 (1721, 1731, 1741, 1751); MJ/SBB/1167–76, 1254–1260, 1333–1340, 1420–1431 (1761, 1771, 1781, 1791).

16. TNA, record series E 197, SP 34–36, T 64, T 90.

17. GL, MSS, 9846 (1763–1805), 11168 (1720–24); BL, Add MS 38715, fols 1–24 (1670–1713).

18. For references to all these printed works, see the bibliography. For Ryder's notes, see Lincoln's Inn Library, transcript of Dudley Ryder's law notes by K. L. Perrin.

# Select Bibliography

This is a list of the most important modern published works on topics relevant to those covered in this book.

## WEBSITES

British Library: www.bl.uk

COLLAGE (prints from the Guildhall Library):
www.collage.cityoflondon.gov.uk

Corporation of London Record Office:
www.cityoflondon.gov. uk/leisure_heritage/libraries_archives_museums_galleries/clro

Eighteenth-Century Collections Online:
www.galegroup.com/EighteenthCentury/index.htm

Eighteenth-Century Resources: newark.rutgers.edu/%7Ejlynch/18th

Internet Library of Early Journals: www.bodley.ox.ac.uk/ilej

London Metropolitan Archives:
www.cityoflondon.gov.uk/leisure_heritage/libraries_archives_museums_galleries/lma

National Archives (Public Record Office): www.pro.gov.uk

Old Bailey Proceedings Online: www.oldbaileyonline.org

Tate Collection Online: www.tate.org.uk

## MODERN EDITIONS OF PRIMARY SOURCE MATERIALS

### Legal Records

*The English Reports*, 178 vols (London and Edinburgh, 1900–32). Available on cd-rom in the National Archives.

Lamoine, Georges, ed., *Charges to the Grand Jury, 1689–1803*, Camden Society, fourth series, 43 (London, 1992).

Oldham, James, *The Mansfield Manuscripts and the Growth of English Law in the Eighteenth Century*, 2 vols (Chapel Hill, North Carolina, 1992).

Paley, Ruth, ed., *Justice in Eighteenth-Century Hackney: The Justicing Notebook of Henry Norris and the Hackney Petty Sessions Book*, London Record Society, 28 (London, 1991).


## Travellers' Accounts of London

Lichtenberg, Georg Christoph, *Lichtenberg's Visits to England*, trans. and annotated by Margaret L. Mare and W. H. Quarrell (Oxford, 1938).

La Rochefoucauld, François de, *A Frenchman in England in 1784*, ed. J. Marchand and trans. S. C. Roberts (London, 1995).

de Saussure, César, *A Foreign View of England in 1725–1729*, trans. and ed. M. van Muyden (1902; reprint London, 1995).

von Uffenbach, Zacharias, *London in 1710: From the Travels of Zacharias von Uffenbach*, trans. and ed. W. H. Quarrell and M. Mare (London, 1934).


## Londoners' Diaries, Correspondence and Memoirs

Latham, R. and W. Matthews, eds, *The Diary of Samuel Pepys*, 11 vols (London, 1970–83).

Lewis, W. S., ed., *Horace Walpole's Correspondence*, 48 vols (London, New Haven, and Oxford, 1937–83).

Luttrell, Narcissus, *A Brief Historical Relation of State Affairs from September 1678 to April 1714*, 6 vols (Oxford, 1857).

Thale, Mary, ed., *The Autobiography of Francis Place* (Cambridge, 1972).

Reynolds, E. E., ed., *The Mawhood Diary*, Catholic Record Society (London, 1956).


## Prints

O'Connell, Sheila, *London 1753* (London, 2003).

O'Connell, Sheila, *The Popular Print in England, 1550–1850* (London, 1999).

Paulson, Ronald, *Hogarth*, 3 vols (Cambridge, 1991–93).

Sharpe, J. A., ed., *Crime and the Law in English Satirical Prints* (Cambridge, 1986).

Shesgreen, Sean, *Images of the Outcast: The Urban Poor in the Cries of London* (Manchester, 2002).

Uglow, Jenny, *Hogarth: A Life and a World* (London, 1997).

### Periodicals

Fielding, Henry, *The Covent Garden Journal and A Plan of the Universal Register Office*, ed. B. A. Goldgar (Oxford, 1988).

*The Spectator*, ed. Donald Bond, 5 vols (Oxford, 1965).

*The Tatler*, ed. Donald Bond, 3 vols (Oxford, 1987).

Ward, Ned, *The London Spy*, ed. Paul Hyland (4th edn, 1709; reprint East Lansing, Michigan, 1993).

## CHAPTER 1: STREET LIFE

Corfield, Penelope J., 'Walking the City Streets: The Urban Odyssey in Eighteenth-Century England', *Journal of Urban History*, 16 (1990), pp. 132–74.

Dillon, Parick, *The Much-Lamented Death of Madam Geneva: The Eighteenth-Century Gin Craze* (London, 2002).

Earle, Peter, *A City Full of People: Men and Women of London, 1650–1750* (London, 1994).

Earle, Peter, *The Making of the English Middle Class* (London, 1989).

George, M. Dorothy, *London Life in the Eighteenth Century* (1925; reprint Harmondsworth, 1979).

Henderson, Tony, *Disorderly Women in Eighteenth-Century London: Prostitution and Control in the Metropolis, 1730–1830* (London, 1999).

Hitchcock, Tim, *Down and Out in Eighteenth-Century London* (forthcoming).

Hitchcock, Tim, and Heather Shore, eds, *The Streets of London: From the Great Fire to the Great Stink* (London, 2003).

Hitchcock, Tim, and Robert Shoemaker, 'Historical Background', *Old Bailey Proceedings Online*, http://www.oldbaileyonline.org/history

McKellar, Elizabeth, *The Birth of Modern London: The Development and Design of the City, 1660–1720* (Manchester, 1999).

O'Connell, Sheila, *London 1753* (London, 2003).

Ogborn, Miles, *Spaces of Modernity: London's Geographies, 1680–1780* (London, 1998).

Rudé, George, *Hanoverian London, 1714–1808* (Berkeley, 1971).

Schwarz, L. D., *London in the Age of Industrialisation: Entrepreneurs, Labour Force and Living Conditions, 1700–1850* (Cambridge, 1992).

Shoemaker, Robert B., 'Reforming the City: The Reformation of Manners Campaign in London, 1690–1738', in L. Davison et al., eds, *Stilling the Grumbling Hive: The Response to Social and Economic Problems in England, 1689–1750* (Stroud, 1992), pp. 99–120.

Warner, Jessica, *Craze: Gin and Debauchery in an Age of Reason* (London, 2003).

## CHAPTER 2: STOP THIEF!

Babington, Anthony, *A House in Bow Street: Crime and the Magistracy in London, 1740–1881* (London, 1969).

Beattie, J. M., *Policing and Punishment in London, 1660–1750* (Oxford, 2001).

Howson, Gerald, *Thief-Taker General: The Rise and Fall of Jonathan Wild* (London, 1970).

Paley, Ruth, '"An Imperfect, Inadequate and Wretched System"? Policing London before Peel', *Criminal Justice History*, 10 (1989), pp. 95–130.

Paley, Ruth, 'Thief-Takers in London in the Age of the McDaniel Gang, c. 1745–1754', in Douglas Hay and Francis Snyder, eds, *Policing and Prosecution in Britain, 1750–1850* (Oxford, 1989), pp. 301–40.

Philips, David, 'Good Men to Associate and Bad Men to Conspire: Associations for the Prosecution of Felons in England, 1760–1800', in Douglas Hay and Francis Snyder, eds, *Policing and Prosecution in Britain, 1750–1850* (Oxford, 1989), pp. 113–70.

Reynolds, Elaine A., *Before the Bobbies: The Night Watch and Police Reform in Metropolitan London, 1720–1830* (Stanford, 1998).

Styles, John, 'Sir John Fielding and the Problem of Criminal Investigation in Eighteenth-Century England', *Transactions of the Royal Historical Society*, 33 (1983), pp. 127–49.

Wales, Tim, 'Thief-Takers and their Clients in Later Stuart London', in Paul Griffiths and Mark S. R. Jenner, eds, *Londinopolis; Essays in the Cultural and Social History of Early Modern London* (Manchester, 2000), pp. 67–84.

## CHAPTER 3: PUBLIC INSULTS

Clark, Anna, 'Whores and Gossips: Sexual Reputation in London, 1770–1825', in A. Angerman et al., *Current Issues in Women's History* (London and New York, 1989), pp. 231–48.

Dabhoiwala, Faramerz, 'The Pattern of Sexual Immorality in Seventeenth- and Eighteenth-Century London', in Paul Griffiths and Mark S. R. Jenner, eds, *Londinopolis: Essays in the Cultural and Social History of Early Modern London* (Manchester, 2000), pp. 86–106.

Gowing, Laura, *Domestic Dangers: Women, Words and Sex in Early Modern London* (Oxford, 1996).

Meldrum, Tim, 'A Women's Court in London: Defamation at the Bishop of London's Consistory Court, 1700–1745', *London Journal*, 19 (1994), pp. 1–20.

Shoemaker, Robert B., 'Reforming Male Manners: Public Insult and the Decline of Violence in London, 1660–1740', in T. Hitchcock and M. Cohen, eds, *English Masculinities, 1660–1800* (London, 1999), pp. 133–50.

Shoemaker, Robert B., 'The Decline of Public Insult in London, 1660–1800', *Past and Present*, 169 (2000), pp. 97–131.

Trumbach, Randolph, *Sex and the Gender Revolution*, i, *Homosexuality and the Third Gender in Enlightenment London* (Chicago and London, 1998), chap. 2.


## CHAPTER 4: SHAMING PUNISHMENTS

Beattie, J. M., *Crime and the Courts in England, 1660–1800* (Princeton, 1986).

Beattie, J. M., *Policing and Punishment in London, 1660–1750* (Oxford, 2001).

Cockburn, J. S., 'Punishment and Brutalization in the English Enlightenment', *Law and History Review*, 12 (1994), pp. 155–79.

Gatrell, V. A. C., *The Hanging Tree: Execution and the English People, 1770–1868* (Oxford, 1994).

Laqueur, Thomas, 'Crowds, Carnival and the State in English Executions, 1604–1868', in A. Beier et al., eds, *The First Modern Society* (Cambridge, 1989), pp. 305–55.

Linebaugh, Peter, 'The Tyburn Riot against the Surgeons', in D. Hay et al., *Albion's Fatal Tree: Crime and Society in Eighteenth-Century England* (Harmondsworth, 1977), pp. 65–117.

McGowen, Randall, 'The Body and Punishment in Eighteenth-Century England', *Journal of Modern History*, 59 (1987), pp. 651–79.

McGowen, Randall, 'Civilizing Punishment: The End of the Public Execution in England', *Journal of British Studies*, 33 (1994), pp. 257–82.

Sharpe, J. A., 'Civility, Civilizing Processes and the End of Public Punishment in England', in P. Burke et al., eds, *Civil Histories: Essays Presented to Sir Keith Thomas* (Oxford, 2000), pp. 215–30.

Sharpe, J. A., *Judicial Punishment in England* (London, 1990).

Shoemaker, Robert B., 'Streets of Shame? The Crowd and Public Punishments in London, 1700–1820', in P. Griffiths and S. Devereaux, eds, *Penal Practice and Culture, 1500–1900* (forthcoming).

Smith, G. T., 'Civilised People Don't Want to See That Kind of Thing: The Decline of Public Physical Punishment in London, 1760–1840', in C. Strange, ed., *Qualities of Mercy* (Vancouver, 1996), pp. 21–51.

Wilf, Steven, 'Imagining Justice: Aesthetics and Public Executions in Late Eighteenth-Century England', *Yale Journal of Law and the Humanities*, 5 (1993–94), pp. 51–78.

## CHAPTER 5: CROWDS AND RIOTS

de Castro, J. Paul, *The Gordon Riots* (London, 1926).

Fitts, James L., 'Newcastle's Mob', *Albion*, 5 (1973), pp. 41–49.

Gilmour, Ian, *Riot, Risings and Revolution: Governance and Violence in Eighteenth-Century England* (London, 1992).

Harris, Tim, 'Perceptions of the Crowd in Later Stuart London', in J. F. Merritt, ed., *Imagining Early Modern London: Perceptions and Portrayals of the City from Stow to Strype, 1598–1720* (Cambridge, 2001), pp. 250–72.

Hayter, Tony, *The Army and the Crowd in Mid-Georgian England* (London, 1978).

Holmes, Geoffrey, 'The Sacheverell Riots: The Crowd and the Church in Early Eighteenth-Century London', *Past and Present*, 72 (1976), pp. 55–85.

Rogers, Nicholas, 'Crowd and People in the Gordon Riots', in Eckhart Hellmuth, ed., *The Transformation of Political Culture: England and Germany in the Late Eighteenth Century* (Oxford, 1990), pp. 39–55.

Rogers, Nicholas, 'Crowds and Political Festival in Georgian England', in T. Harris, ed., *The Politics of the Excluded, c. 1500–1850* (Basingstoke, 2001), pp. 233–64.

Rogers, Nicholas, *Crowds, Culture and Politics in Georgian Britain* (Oxford, 1998).

Rogers, Nicholas, 'Popular Protest in Early Hanoverian London', *Past and Present*, 79 (1978), pp. 70–100.

Rogers, Nicholas, *Whigs and Cities: Popular Politics in the Age of Walpole and Pitt* (Oxford, 1989).

Rudé, George, *Paris and London in the Eighteenth Century: Studies in Popular Protest* (London, 1970; New York, 1973).

Rudé, George, *The Crowd in History* (New York, 1964).

Shoemaker, Robert B., 'The London "Mob" in the Early Eighteenth Century', *Journal of British Studies*, 26 (1987), pp. 273–304; reprinted in *The Eighteenth Century Town, 1688–1820* ed. Peter Borsay (London, 1990).

Stevenson, John, 'The London "Crimp" Riots of 1794', *International Review of Social History*, 16 (1971), pp. 40–58.

Stevenson, John, *Popular Disturbances in England, 1700–1832* (second edition, London, 1992).

Tilly, Charles, *Popular Contention in Great Britain, 1758–1834* (Cambridge, Massachusetts, 1995).

Warner, Jessica and Frank Ivis, '"Damn You, You Informing Bitch": *Vox Populi* and the Unmaking of the Gin Act of 1736', *Journal of Social History*, 33 (1999), pp. 299–330.

## CHAPTER 6: VIOLENCE

Bryson, Anna, *From Courtesy to Civility: Changing Codes of Conduct in Early Modern England* (Oxford, 1998).

Gurr, T. R., 'Historical Trends in Violent Crime: A Critical Review of the Evidence', *Crime and Justice: An Annual Review of Research*, 3 (1981), pp. 295–353.

Guthrie, Neil, '"No Truth or Very Little in the Whole Story?" A Reassessment of the Mohock Scare of 1712', *Eighteenth-Century Life*, 20 (1996), pp. 33–56.

Hunt, Margaret, 'Wife-Beating, Domesticity and Women's Independence in Early Eighteenth-Century London', *Gender and History*, 4 (1992), pp. 10–33.

Hurl, Jennine, '"She Being Bigg with Child is Likely to Miscarry": Pregnant Victims Prosecuting Assault in Westminster, 1685–1720', *London Journal*, 24 (1999), pp. 18–33.

Sharpe, J. A., 'The History of Violence in England: Some Observations'; and L. Stone, 'A Rejoinder', *Past and Present*, 108 (1985), pp. 206–24.

Shoemaker, Robert B., 'Male Honour and the Decline of Public Violence in Eighteenth-Century London', *Social History*, 26 (2001), pp. 190–208.

Statt, Daniel, 'The Case of the Mohocks: Rake Violence in Augustan London', *Social History*, 20 (1995), pp. 179–99.

Stone, Lawrence, 'Interpersonal Violence in English Society 1300–1980', *Past and Present*, 101 (1983), pp. 22–33.


## CHAPTER 7: DUELS AND BOXING MATCHES

Andrew, Donna T., 'The Code of Honour and its Critics: The Opposition to Duelling in England, 1700–1850', *Social History*, 5 (1980), pp. 409–34.

Atkinson, John A., *Duelling Pistols and Some of the Affairs They Settled* (London, 1964).

Baldick, Robert, *The Duel: A History of Duelling* (1965; reprint London, 1979).

Brailsford, Dennis, *Bareknuckles: A Social History of Prize-Fighting* (Cambridge, 1988).

Gee, Tony, *Up to Scratch: Bareknuckle Fighting and Heroes of the Prize-Ring* (Harpenden, 1998).

Kiernan, V. G., *The Duel in European History: Honour and the Reign of the Aristocracy* (Oxford, 1988).

Mee, Bob, *Bare Fists* (Stratford-upon-Avon, 1998).

Shoemaker, Robert B., 'The Taming of the Duel: Masculinity, Honour and Ritual Violence in London, 1660–1800', *Historical Journal*, 45 (2002), pp. 525–45.

Simpson, Antony, 'Dandelions on the Field of Honour: Dueling, the Middle Classes, and the Law in Nineteenth-Century England', *Criminal Justice History*, 9 (1988), pp. 99–155.

Stater, Victor, *Duke Hamilton is Dead! A Story of Aristocratic Life and Death in Stuart Britain* (New York, 1999).

Wise, Arthur, *The History and Art of Personal Combat* (London, 1971), chaps 7–8.


## CHAPTER 8: GOING TO LAW

Brooks, Christopher W., *Lawyers, Litigation and English Society since 1450* (London, 1998).

Gaskill, Malcolm, 'The Displacement of Providence: Policing and Prosecution in Seventeenth- and Eighteenth-Century England', *Continuity and Change*, 11 (1996), pp. 341–74.

Hay, Douglas, 'Prosecution and Power: Malicious Prosecution in the English Courts, 1750–1850', in idem and F. Snyder, eds, *Policing and Prosecution in Britain, 1750–1850* (Oxford, 1989), pp. 343–95.

Hay, Douglas and Francis Snyder, 'Using the Criminal Law, 1750–1850', in idem eds, *Policing and Prosecution in Britain, 1750–1850* (Oxford, 1989), pp. 3–52.

Horwitz, Henry and Patrick Polden, 'Continuity or Change in the Court of Chancery in the Seventeenth and Eighteenth Centuries?', *Journal of British Studies*, 35 (1996), pp. 24–57.

Landau, Norma, ed., *Law, Crime and English Society, 1660–1830* (Cambridge, 2002).

Oldham, James, *The Mansfield Manuscripts and the Growth of English Law in the Eighteenth Century*, 2 vols (Chapel Hill, 1992).

Lemmings, David, *Professors of the Law: Barristers and English Legal Culture in the Eighteenth Century* (Oxford, 2000).

Paley, Ruth ed., *Justice in Eighteenth-Century Hackney: The Justicing Notebook of Henry Norris and the Hackney Petty Sessions Book*, London Record Society, 28 (London, 1991).

Shoemaker, Robert B., *Prosecution and Punishment: Petty Crime and the Law in London and Rural Middlesex* (Cambridge, 1991).

Stone, Lawrence, *Road to Divorce: A History of the Making and Breaking of Marriage in England* (1990; reprint Oxford, 1995).

## CHAPTER 9: PRINT

Andrew, Donna T., 'The Press and Public Apologies in Eighteenth-Century London', in N. Landau, ed., *Law, Crime and English Society, 1660–1830* (Cambridge, 2002), pp. 208–29.

Andrew, Donna and Randall McGowen, *The Perreaus and Mrs Rudd: Forgery and Betrayal in Eighteenth-Century London* (Berkeley, California, 2001).

Barker, Hannah, *Newspapers, Politics and English Society, 1695–1855* (Harlow, 2000).

Black, Jeremy, *The English Press in the Eighteenth Century* (1987; reprint Aldershot, 1991).

Brant, Clare, 'Duelling by Sword and Pen: The Vauxhall Affray of 1773', *Prose Studies*, 19 (1996), pp. 160–72.

Fox, Adam, *Oral and Literate Culture in England, 1500–1700* (Oxford, 2000), chaps 6–7.

Gatrell, V. A. C., *The Hanging Tree: Execution and the English People, 1770–1868* (Oxford, 1994), chaps 4–5.

Rogers, Nicholas, 'Pigott's Private Eye: Radicalism and Sexual Scandal in Eighteenth-Century England', *Journal of the Canadian Historical Association*, 4 (1993), pp. 247–63.

Walker, R. B., 'Advertising in London Newspapers, 1650–1750', *Business History*, 15 (1973), pp. 112–30.

## CHAPTER 10: THE MONSTER

Barker-Benfield, G. J., *The Culture of Sensibility: Sex and Society in Eighteenth-Century Britain* (Chicago, 1992).

Bondeson, Jan, *The London Monster* (London, 2000).

Carter, Philip, *Men and the Emergence of Polite Society: Britain, 1660–1800* (Harlow, 2001).

Clark, Peter, *British Clubs and Societies, 1580–1800: The Origins of an Associational World* (Oxford, 2000).

Elias, Norbert, *The Civilizing Process: The History of Manners and State Formation and Civilization* (1939; trans. E. Jephcott, Oxford, 1994).

Fletcher, Anthony, *Gender, Sex and Subordination in England, 1500–1800* (New Haven, 1995).

Klein, Lawrence, 'Politeness and the Interpretation of the British Eighteenth Century', *Historical Journal*, 45 (2002), pp. 869–98.

Klein, Lawrence, 'Politeness for Plebes: Consumption and Social Identity in Early Eighteenth-Century England', in A. Bermingham and J. Brewer, eds, *The Consumption of Culture, 1600–1800* (London, 1995), pp. 362–82.

Mascuch, Michael, *Origins of the Individualist Self: Autobiography and Self-Identity in England, 1591–1791* (Cambridge, 1997).

# Index